The Management of Pakistan's Economy 1947-82

VIQAR AHMED
and
RASHID AMJAD

UGC Monograph Series in Economics

OXFORD UNIVERSITY PRESS
KARACHI

Oxford University Press, Walton Street, Oxford OX2 6DP
OXFORD NEW YORK TORONTO
DELHI BOMBAY CALCUTTA MADRAS KARACHI
KUALA LUMPUR SINGAPORE HONG KONG TOKYO
NAIROBI DAR ES SALAAM CAPE TOWN
MELBOURNE AUCKLAND MADRID
and associated companies in
BERLIN IBADAN

First Edition 1984

Fifth Impression 1993

ISBN 0 19 577316 0

The publishers are grateful to the Ford Foundation for their assistance in the production of this book.

Printed at
Industrial Graphics, Karachi.
Published by
Oxford University Press
5-Bangalore Town, Sharae Faisal
P.O. Box 13033, Karachi-75350, Pakistan.

Preface

National economic management is a new but growing science. The developing world's experience of the recent decades underlines the fact that economic and social progress is an induced process. Governments are not only called upon to initiate the development process but are also required to influence its composition, pace, tone, and direction through an appropriate policy-mix. A consistent framework encompassing various policies within the bounds of an overall national strategy needs to be worked out by the national policy-makers. But experience has also clearly shown that the formulation of economic policies and, even more important, the actual implementation of these policies is a formidable task. Policy formulation skills are scarce in the developing world. Capabilities in the fields of policy review, monitoring, and implementation are even harder to find. We are thus increasingly faced with ever-expanding responsibilities of the governments relating to national economic management on the one hand and greater scarcity of capabilities in this area on the other. Economic management has thus become a critical area for study as well as introspection.

This book is a modest attempt to look critically at the management of Pakistan's economy during the period 1947-82. While it has been written primarily for under-graduate and post-graduate students in economics, we feel that it should prove useful and interesting for policy-makers as well as for readers desirous of information and interested in an analysis of Pakistan's economic performance and development record since 1947. A deliberate attempt has been made, especially in the earlier chapters, to explain as simply as possible the features of Pakistan's economy, its historical development, and the process and evolution of economic decision-making. These are developed in more analytical detail in subsequent chapters especially those dealing with the major sectors.

Given the range of topics and issues that had to be covered, we have had to rely heavily on published material from a wide range of sources including government reports as well as those prepared by international financial institutions. In some cases particular sections of chapters are based on the authors' previously published work on the subject. Similarly, some sections draw very heavily from the published works of fellow economists. Wherever this has been done, the sources are clearly acknowledged.

Apart from the authors, two of their colleagues have provided direct inputs into the book. Mr. Omar Asghar Khan, Lecturer in Economics at the Punjab University, Lahore, authored Chapter 18, 'Impact of Foreign Aid on Economic Development'. The chapters on the agricultural sector have relied considerably on the work done by Dr. Akmal Hussain, Assistant Professor, Department of Public Administration who prepared an exhaustive survey of economic issues concerning this important sector as resource material for the book. Our special thanks are also due to Dr. Shahid Amjad Chaudhry, Dr. Meekal Ahmed, Dr. Naved Hamid, Dr. Ejaz Nabi, and Dr. M. Irfan, for their comments and suggestions on various sections of the book.

In any work of this kind there are a large number of people without whose assistance, co-operation, and indeed active support it is not possible to either undertake or complete the task. First and foremost, we must thank our respective institutions, the Pakistan Administrative Staff College, especially its Principal, Mr. Masrur Hasan Khan, and the Vice-Chancellor and Chairman, Economics Department, Punjab University, Lahore for giving us not only permission but considerable encouragement to undertake this task. Special thanks are also due to the University Grants Commission who conceived of this project in collaboration with the Ford Foundation. The Oxford University Press has played a major role not only in preparing the script for print but also in gently prodding us to complete the manuscript in time.

Finally, we would like to thank our wives for bearing with us especially through the many long evenings and weekends spent working on the book. It is to them that this book is dedicated.

Viqar Ahmed
Rashid Amjad

August 1984

Contents

PART I

MACRO FRAMEWORK

1 Pakistan's Economic Performance: 1947-82

Pakistan gained independence on 14 August 1947. Over the last thirty-five years different governments have pursued various economic policies to bring about an improvement in the country's overall economic condition. The task which this book sets for itself is to investigate and analyse the factors responsible for the formulation and implementation of the economic policies followed during this period which are responsible in many ways for creating the economic situation in which the country finds itself today.

A convenient starting point is to compare the basic parameters of our overall socio-economic condition as we inherited it in 1947 and the situation as we find it in 1982. Such an exercise has many advantages. It will give us a broad idea of the important economic changes which have taken place during this period and it will provide us with some basis to judge our economic performance. It will also give us a feel for the basic structural changes which have occurred during this period and which have fundamentally altered the country's socio-economic structure. Also, and perhaps most important of all, it will provide us with an insight into the important economic questions which are raised when we see the economic development and structural changes which have taken place during this period and to which we will attempt to find answers during the course of this book.

Let us start by raising a simple but most important question. In what ways are we economically better off today as compared to the time of Independence? Before we can attempt to answer this most pertinent question we must first select the yardstick by which we will judge this economic performance for there can be many different criteria by which people would evaluate a country's economic record. Some economists give the highest priority to the overall growth rate of the economy's total output (i.e., the Gross National Product or GNP) and that of per capita output (i.e., GNP divided by total population). Other economists would argue that growth of output in itself is not a sufficient criteria to judge economic development, which is a far more comprehensive phenomenon, and that we must see whether favourable structural changes (especially in terms of composition of output, sectoral distribution of labour force, composition of foreign trade, dependence on external funds) have occurred in the economy and which, over a period of time, will set into motion economic forces which will help transform the economy from its present under-developed state to one capable of sustained self-reliant growth and development. Still other economists view economic development in terms of the extent to which it has been able to eradicate poverty and its impact on the standard of living of the majority of the population, especially in terms of the availability of the basic necessities of life, i.e., food, clothing, shelter, education, and housing facilities. Finally, there are those who would compare a country's economic performance in relation to the performance of other developing countries which started with approximately the same resource endowment and which have been pursuing policies for the development of their economies over about the same period of time. They would, for example, compare Pakistan's economic performance with that of its immediate neighbour India, or with a country which has adopted a different economic system like China, or countries of roughly the same size like Brazil in Latin America and Egypt in North Africa.

In judging Pakistan's economic performance over these years we have analysed it in terms of the various criteria outlined above, i.e., growth performance, structural change, impact on poverty, and comparison with some selected countries. Unfortunately, in making the comparison, we cannot start from 1947 both because it was an abnormal year and because reliable statistics are not available. We, therefore, start from 1949-50, the first year for which official statistics are available. We have given separately data for All Pakistan, i.e., West and East together, and for West Pakistan in 1949-50. The end year selected is one for which data is most recently available, i.e., 1981-2. Here the figures refer to what is now Pakistan, i.e., the former West Pakistan, and comparisons are made mostly in terms of the West alone as are the growth rate figures.

Table 1.1: Basic Economic Indicators
(1959-60 prices)

	All Pakistan	Pakistan (West)	Pakistan (West)	Rate of growth (West)
	1949-50	1949-50	1981-2	per annum
GNP[1] (Rs billion)	19.9	12.38	59.64	5.0
Population (million)	78.8	35.31	85.0	2.9
Per capita income (Rs)	253	351	702	2.2
Per capita food grain (ounces per day consumption)	14.9	14.8	17.9[2]	0.7
General wholesale price index	100	100	498	5.0
Foreign debt (Percentage of GNP)			US$9.0 billion (40 per cent)	

1. At 1959-60 factor cost.
2. For 1979-80.

Source: (i) For GNP, population, per capita income, price index, and foreign debt, for Pakistan (West), Government of Pakistan, *Pakistan Economic Survey, 1981-2*, Islamabad. For 1949-50, all Pakistan, CSO, *Twenty-five Years of Pakistan in Statistics*, Karachi, 1972. (ii) Per capita food grain consumption for all Pakistan 1949-50, Government of Pakistan, *Fourth Five Year Plan*, Islamabad, p. 5. For Pakistan (West) calculated from Government of Pakistan, *Pakistan Economic Survey, 1979-80*, Islamabad.

1.1 Basic Economic Indicators

Some basic indicators showing Pakistan's economic performance over the last thirty-five years are given in Table 1.1. The Gross National Product, the sum of goods and services produced in Pakistan (West), an indicator of overall economic activity, has increased almost five-fold during this period which gives us a 5 per cent growth rate per annum. The GNP, which in terms of 1959-60 prices was Rs 12 billion[1] in 1949-50, had increased to Rs 60 billion in 1981-2. Over the same period the population also more than doubled which gives a population growth rate of 2.9 per cent per annum.

To take this population growth into account we divide the GNP by the total population to give us the per capita income. This, in terms of 1959-60 prices, almost doubled during this period, from Rs 351 in 1949-50 to Rs 702 in 1979-80, giving us a growth rate of 2.2 per cent per annum. The movement of the general level of prices during this period is indicated by the fact that Re 1 is worth only a fifth of its value in 1949-50, giving us an inflation rate of 5 per cent per annum. The growth rate of the GNP has also been accompanied by a massive amount of foreign debt incurred during this period. In 1981-2, Pakistan's total outstanding foreign debt amounted to US$ 9.0 billion which was 40 per cent of our total GNP.

It is now generally accepted by almost all economists that we cannot directly translate the GNP or per capita income into indicators of economic welfare of the people or interpret it as resources available to ordinary people for their consumption needs. This is for a number of reasons. Firstly, and most importantly, they do not take into account the uneven distribution of income. Secondly, a certain amount of the total output produced is set aside for savings and investment and hence is not available for consumption. Thirdly, there is government expenditure on defence and public administration. In an economy like Pakistan all these factors are extremely significant. The overall distribution of income is quite uneven. The amount of domestic savings, although not high by international standards, is on the average about 10 per cent. Resources spent on defence and public administration have averaged approximately 10 per cent of the GNP. After taking into account these resources set aside from consumption, and adding any foreign resource inflows into the country, about 85 per cent of the total GNP was available for consumption in 1979-80.

To what extent are the available resources able to meet the basic consumption needs of the vast majority of the population and to what extent has the situation improved during the last thirty-five years? One estimate (although a rather crude one as amongst others it does not take into account changes in the age structure of the population) is that of per capita food grain consumption. This has increased only marginally from 14.8 ounces in 1949-50 to 17.9 ounces in 1979-80, a growth rate of less than 0.7 per cent per annum. A better estimate of consumption-needs is to calculate the percentage of population with an income level *less* than the amount required to purchase an adequate diet which ensures a supply of basic nutrients to the human body. The incidence of poverty according to this methodology is therefore seen in terms of the percentage of the population living below the poverty line, i.e., have an income level less than the amount required to meet basic nutrient needs.

There are wide discrepancies in the results of the different studies carried out on consumption needs being met and the percentage of the population living below the poverty line. Working with *Consumer Expenditure Survey* data between 1963-4 and 1971-2 and using a 'poverty line' defined as meeting 90 per cent of the minimum calorie requirements of 2,100 calories, Professor Naseem[2] estimated that on the average about 52 per cent of the households in the rural areas lived below the 'poverty line' during these years. For the urban areas,[3] using a slightly different estimate of the 'poverty line' in terms of monthly income, he showed that over 40 per cent of the population lived below the 'poverty line' between 1963-4 and 1969-70. A more recent study[4] for 1979 has estimated that almost 40 per cent of the rural population lives below the 'poverty line' measured in terms of a minimum calorie requirement of 2,550 calories.

Given the wide divergence in the estimates of per capita consumption and dietary needs being met, it is not possible to come up with a very reliable estimate of the population living below the 'poverty line'. On the whole one can safely say that even after thirty-five years of economic development at least one third of the total population of this country still lives below the 'poverty line'.

1.2 Social Services

There is a close relationship between economic development and the provision of essential social services like education and health, for not only as an economy develops are we more able to provide these essential facilities but a better educated and healthier labour force also helps to accelerate the process of economic development. To what extent is Pakistan able to provide basic social welfare facilities like education and health and important basic needs like housing, water, and sanitation after thirty-five years of economic development?

Table 1.2 provides us with broad indicators of the provision of education and health services in the country. In percentage terms there is an improvement during this period in both the provision of education and of health facilities. But this is far more a reflection of the extremely low levels from which the country started rather than of what it has so far been able to achieve. In 1979-80 only 54 per cent of school-age children between five to nine years were enrolled in primary schools.

Table 1.2: Social Services—Basic Indicators

	Pakistan (West) 1949-50	Pakistan (West) 1979-80
1. Education		
a) Percentage of school-age children attending primary school (I-V) (5-9 years)		
All	15.8[1]	54.0[4]
Male	25.7[1]	73.04[4]
Female	4.4[1]	33.00[4]
Secondary school (VI-X) (9-14 years)		
All	9.4[1]	23.04[4]
Male	14.4[1]	33.00[4]
Female	2.7[1]	10.00[4]
b) Total Enrolment Arts and Science colleges (000s)		
All	21[2]	241[2]
Female	2[2]	78[2]
Professional colleges (000s)		
All	4.9[2]	72.5[2]
Female	0.4[2]	13.2[2]
University (000s)		
All	0.74[2]	57.0[2]
Female	0.07[2]	14.9[2]
2. Health (population per)		
Registered Doctor	15,365[3]	5,334[5]
Nurse and LHV	70,620[3]	15,736[5]
Hospital bed	2,431[3]	1,600[5]
Maternity and Child Welfare Centre (Numbers)	107[3]	772[3]

1. CSO, *Twenty-five Years of Pakistan in Statistics*, Karachi, 1972, p. 218 (compilation).
2. Government of Pakistan, *Pakistan Economic Survey, 1980-1*, Islamabad, p. 236.
3. Government of Pakistan, *Pakistan Basic Facts, 1979-80*, Islamabad, p. 107 (compilation).
4. Dr. Siraj-ul-Haq Mahmud, Fida Hussain, and Viqar-un-Nisa, 'Social Sector Programmes: Allocations, Priorities, and Prospects', in *Pakistan Administration*, PASC, Lahore, Vol. XVIII, No. 2, July-December 1981, p. 6.
5. Ibid., p. 16.

The figure for male enrolment was 73 per cent and for females 33 per cent. These figures especially for females are abysmally low. In absolute terms this means that out of 13 million children, in the age group between five to nine years, nearly 6 million will have received no primary education. These dismally low figures in primary education mean that we continue to add each year to the already high level of illiteracy in the country which, in 1979-80, was at a level of 76 per cent of which the figure for males was 64 per cent and for females 88 per cent.[5] The figures for secondary school attendance are again extremely low, at 20 per cent of all school-age children between ten to fourteen years, with the female level being only about 10 per cent and that the males being 30 per cent. The absolute numbers enrolled in Arts, Science, and Professional Colleges and Universities have increased but in terms of the proportion of the total population the figures are still extremely low.

The provision of health facilities also shows some improvement when compared to the extremely poor situation which existed in 1949-50 but the situation is still extremely unsatisfactory. Because of the large-scale emigration of doctors, there was in 1979-80 only one doctor available for 5,334 people, one nurse, or lady health visitor, for about 16,000 people, and one hospital bed for 1,600 people. It is estimated that minimal health facilities are available at the moment to roughly half of the population and that the nature and quality of the services offered are in general very unsatisfactory.

Exact estimates as regards the availability of clean drinking water and housing facilities are not available. But rough estimates indicate that people with no access to clean drinking water represent about 70 per cent of the total population and those with inadequate shelter represent about 65 per cent of the total population.[6]

The available evidence, although scanty, indicates that in the provision of basic necessities, and social services, Pakistan's record has been quite disappointing.

1.3 Structural Changes

Pakistan's economy at the time of partition was predominantly agricultural in that both the major share of the Gross Domestic Product and the bulk of the labour force was employed in this sector and that over 99 per cent of its exports consisted of primary commodities. With manufacturing consisting mainly of small-scale units and contributing only 7 to 8 per cent of the Gross Domestic Product, over 60 per cent of the total imports consisted of consumer goods and the rest were made up of industrial raw materials and capital goods imports.

Pakistan, at the time of Independence, therefore, fitted into the classical text book definition of an under-developed economy. It was predominantly agrarian, exporting primary commodities (with heavy dependence on a few commodities, i.e., raw jute and cotton), and dependent on imports for manufactured commodities, mainly consumer goods.

Figures 1.1 and 1.2 provide us with details of the sectoral breakdown of Gross Domestic

Figure 1.1: Sectoral Breakdown of Gross Domestic Product
(at constant factor cost of 1959-60)

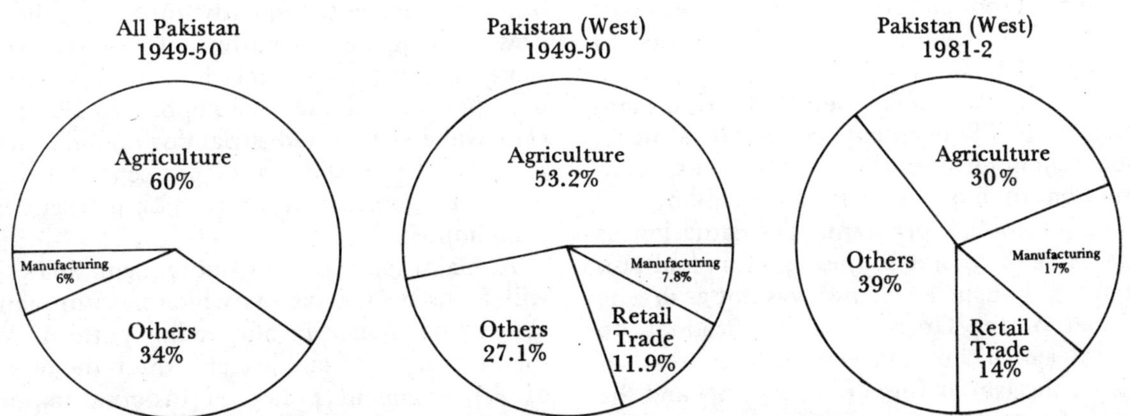

Source: (i) Government of Pakistan, *Third Five Year Plan,* Planning Commission, 1965, p. 2, for All Pakistan 1949-50. (ii) Government of Pakistan, *Pakistan Economic Survey, 1981-2,* Islamabad, 1982, for Pakistan (West).

Figure 1.2: Sectoral Breakdown of Labour Force

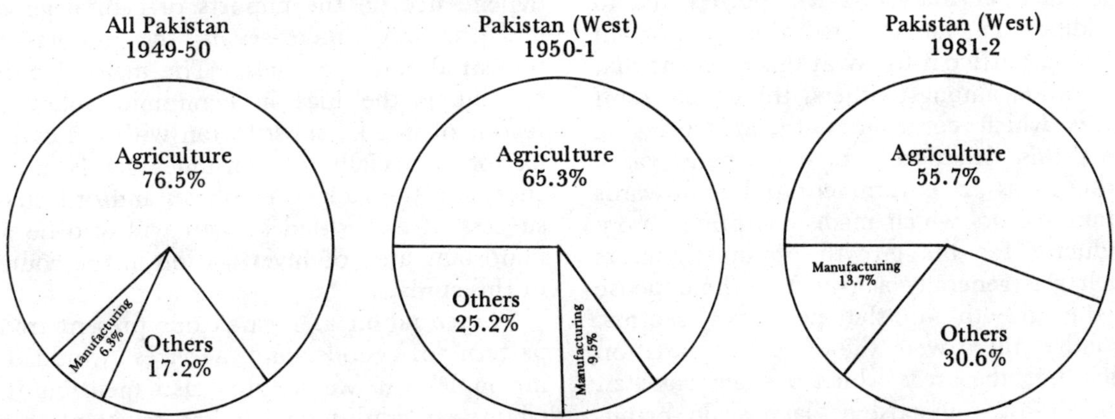

Source: (i) CSO, *Twenty-five Years of Pakistan in Statistics,* Karachi, 1972 p. 13, for All Pakistan 1949-50. (ii) J. Hamid, *Choice of Technology, Employment, and Industrial Development,* PIDE, Monograph, 1978, p. 4, for Pakistan (West) 1950-1. (iii) Government of Pakistan, *Pakistan Economic Survey, 1981-2,* Islamabad, 1982, for Pakistan (West) 1981-2.

Product and employment of the labour force. In 1950 for Pakistan (West) agriculture was the major sector contributing more than half of the Gross Domestic Product. The other sectors contributing to Gross Domestic Product were wholesale and retail trade (11.9 per cent), manufacturing (7.8 per cent), public administration and defence (7.2 per cent), and transport (5 per cent). In terms of employment, 65 per cent of the labour force was in the agricultural sector, 9.5 per cent in manufacturing, and the rest, i.e., about 25 per cent, was shared amongst the other sectors.

By 1981-2 the situation had changed drastically. Agriculture no longer dominated the economy and its contribution to the Gross Domestic Product had fallen to 30 per cent. The share of manufacturing had increased to 17 per cent, wholesale and retail trade to 14 per cent, public administration and defence to 9.9 per cent, transport, storage, and communication to 7 per cent, construction to 5.5 per cent, and banking and insurance to 2.4 per cent. The situation as regards employment in these sectors had also altered although the change was not as drastic as that of the Gross Domestic Product. In 1981-2 agriculture still employed more than half of the labour force (55 per cent) and the share of manufacturing was 13.7 per cent.

What are the factors responsible for bringing about these major structural changes in the economy? A major part of the analyses undertaken in this book will be devoted to providing an answer to this important question. Suffice it to say at this moment that there were, amongst others, three important factors which contributed towards bringing about this situation. Firstly, there was a marked bias in government policy towards certain sectors which made conditions more conducive for the growth of these sectors which was generally achieved at the expense of the growth of the neglected sectors. Secondly, there were the effects of partition which left the areas which became Pakistan with almost non-existent large-scale manufacturing, banking and insurance, public administration, and defence sectors. Thirdly, there was the adoption of capital-intensive technology by fast growing sectors. This meant that these sectors were not able to generate sufficient employment so that the change in the sectoral composition of employment was not of the same magnitude as the change in the composition of output.

Figures 1.3 and 1.4 show the major changes in Pakistan's trade pattern over these thirty-five years. Starting with a situation when primary commodity exports accounted for 99.2 per cent of the total exports, the situation in 1980 was that their share had fallen drastically to 38.2 per cent. Manufactured goods now provide 43.8 per cent of total exports and semi-manufactured goods contribute 18 per cent. Similarly there have been drastic changes in the pattern of imports. The share of consumer goods has declined from 60.2 per cent of the total imports to 19.8 per cent while that of industrial raw materials has increased from 16.8 to 47 per cent and that of capital goods from 23 to 33.2 per cent of total imports.

A major part of our subsequent analysis will focus on the factors which have brought about this change in our trading pattern. We shall see that, to a large extent, this is the result of a government policy of fostering import substitution with industrialization in consumer goods throughout the period. This is reflected in a decline in consumer goods imports but it is responsible for the still heavy dependence on the imports of capital goods and the large increases in the imports of industrial raw materials. The major factors explaining the bias in economic policy in favour of import substitution with industrialization, especially in consumer goods industries, and the lack of emphasis and/or lack of success at export-led growth will also be an important area of investigation in the course of this study.

The situation as regards our present trade pattern of goods and services would be incomplete if we do not also mention the labour emigration which has taken place in the last twenty years. This export of manpower started in the sixties (mainly to the

UK) and increased enormously in the seventies (mainly to the Middle East). The exact number of overseas migrants is difficult to estimate but according to some sources it could be as high as 2 million in 1982 (see Section 2.1). These workers also provide almost US$ 2,000 million in the form of remittances, a figure only slightly lower than our total exports of goods and services of US$ 2,200 million in 1979-80. Also, while studying our balance of payments situation, we must take into account the debt repayment bill on the foreign loans incurred over the last thirty-five years and which, at about US$ 728 million in 1981-2, were 26.6 per cent of our total exports earnings, excluding remittances, and 12.2 per cent of total foreign exchange earnings.[7]

1.4 Changes in the Distribution of Ownership and Control of Economic Assets

The important and far reaching structural changes which have occurred in the economy during the last thirty-five years have also significantly altered the pattern and distribution of the ownership and control of economic assets. Since important economic decisions and overall directions in development policy are clearly influenced by the more powerful of the existing economic interest groups, it is important to analyse the changes which occurred in the distribution of both the ownership and the control of economic assets during this period.

1.4.1 The Shares of the Private and the Public Sectors

We start by dividing the economy between the private and the public sectors. In the earlier stages, especially in the fifties and sixties, there was a deep commitment to the role of the private sector in economic development and the control of the public sector was limited either to the provision of essential public utility services (transport, electricity, water, etc.) or in the industrial sector to those considered essential for defence purposes. The situation in 1982 was drastically different. As a result of the government's policy of nationalization in the early seventies and with the diminished role of the private sector in undertaking major new investment, especially in manufacturing, the public sector had begun to play a far more important part in the country's overall development effort. In 1979-80 it accounted for about 11 per cent of the total industrial output[8] and about 70 per cent of the total investment.[9] It had complete control over domestic banking and insurance and a monopoly in the export of raw cotton and rice.

Figure 1.3: Foreign Trade: Economic Classification of Exports

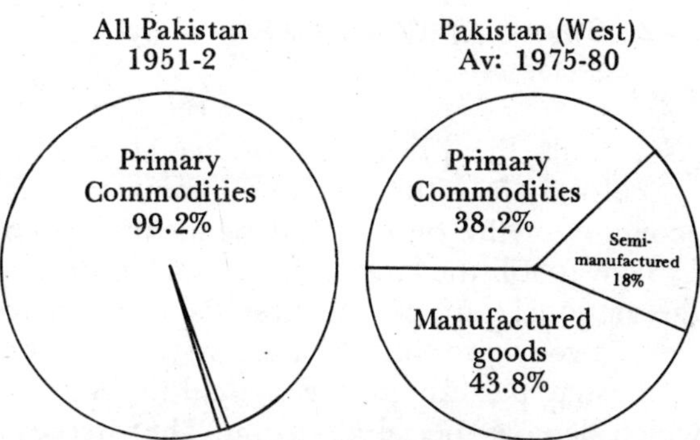

Source: (i) CSO, *Twenty-five Years of Pakistan in Statistics*, Karachi, 1972, for All Pakistan 1951-2. (ii) Government of Pakistan, *Pakistan Economic Survey, 1979-80*, Islamabad, 1980, for Pakistan (West) average, 1975-80.

Figure 1.4: Foreign Trade: Economic Classification of Imports

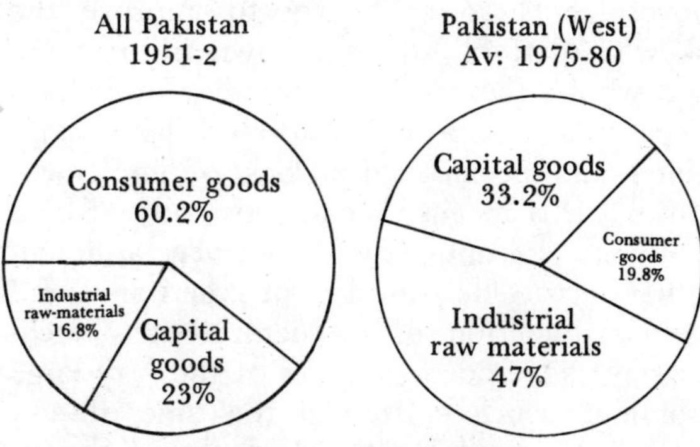

Source: Same as for Fig. 1.3.

The changing role of the private and public sector in the country's economic development is one of the interesting aspects of Pakistan's growth experience. The earlier commitment to the private sector, its success, especially in the development of large-scale manufacturing, and then its rejection at the end of the sixties are an important part of the story. Why did the public sector begin to play a major role in the seventies and what were the factors which led to a decline of the private sector during this period? To what extent was this a result of the political and economic changes which occurred during this period? These are some of the more important questions to which we will try to provide answers in the course of this study.

1.4.2 Ownership Pattern in the Agricultural Sector

As regards the private sector, we start with agriculture for this sector dominated the economy at the time of Independence and in 1982 was still the largest single contributor to the national output. In West Pakistan there were two important characteristics of the ownership pattern in the agricultural sector which deserve special attention. The first was the uneven distribution of land ownership. The second was the widespread existence of tenancy in all sizes of categories of land holdings. Over the years a number of measures, both land and tenancy reforms, have been introduced by different governments so as to try to improve the skewed pattern of land ownership. On the whole, the results of these reforms have been marginal both because of the ceilings fixed and because of a lack of implementation. This means that the structure of land holdings continue to be uneven although other factors like the law of inheritance and the introduction of mechanized new technology has eroded the sizes of the very large holdings which existed at the time of partition. According to the Agricultural Census of Pakistan, in 1960 over 77 per cent of the farms comprising less than 12.5 acres controlled only about 30 per cent of the area whereas between 8 to 10 per cent of the farms comprising more than 25 acres accounted for about 45 per cent of the total area. Similarly there was widespread existence of tenancy, especially in size classes of farms between 5 to 25 acres. The results of the 1972 Agricultural Census also revealed a similar inequality in the distribution of holdings.

There are a number of important questions regarding ownership patterns in the agricultural sector. Perhaps most important and controversial is regarding the extent to which the uneven size distribution of land holdings and the existence of tenancy relations hindered or expedited agricultural growth and overall labour absorption and resource allocation, especially after the introduction of new agricultural technology.

1.4.3 Ownership Pattern: Large-Scale Manufacturing

The other important structural change which occurred in Pakistan's economy during this period was the emergence from an almost non-existent base of a significant large-scale manufacturing sector. The very high growth rate of the large-scale manufacturing sector was mainly the result of favourable government economic policies and the void created at the time of partition when most of the industries dependent on raw materials produced in Pakistan were located in geographical areas which became India. Industrialization in Pakistan during the fifties and sixties was carried out mainly by the private sector and by a class of industrial entrepreneurs who were originally traders and had settled in Karachi after partition. One of the important features of industrial growth up to the end of the sixties was that it resulted in an extreme concentration of the ownership of industrial and financial assets. In 1970, forty-four industrial groups controlled 35 per cent of the total industrial assets and a handful of industrial groups controlled over 65 per cent of the total banking and insurance sector of the economy.[10]

In the seventies, the new government reversed the pro-industrial policies which had been followed earlier and for the first time the private sector in industry felt itself faced by a more hostile economic and political environment. Nationalization, which was introduced mainly in the intermediate and capital goods industries, only marginally influenced the concentration of ownership of industrial assets, but the takeover of the banking and insurance sector by the government did help break the link between the industrial and financial capital. With the private sector not investing in industry, the public sector stepped in with major investments in the heavy and intermediate goods industry and, by the end of the seventies, it emerged as the major shareholder of industrial assets.

There are a number of important questions regarding the emergence of this small group of industrial families which dominated earlier industrialization in Pakistan. How were they able to get into a position of such economic eminence in the fifties and sixties? In an economy dominated by large agricultural interest groups, how were they able to create conditions so conducive to their economic growth, and policies which, at least in the fifties, clearly discriminated against the agricultural sector? What factors and institutional arrangements led to the emergence of such an extreme concentration in the ownership of industrial and financial assets? Why did the government in the seventies reverse the pro-industrial policies and why were these industrial families not able to come to some understanding with it so that they could have shared in the industrialization process in the seventies?

1.4.4 Ownership Patterns in other Sectors

As regards the service sector in transport and communications, railways and air travel have traditionally been in the public sector. Road transport, which had been at the time of Independence solely in the hands of the private sector, is now also significantly controlled by the public sector. With the expansion of the public sector transport operations, and the setting up of the National Logistic Cell in the late seventies, public sector control in terms of passenger transport is approximately one-third and for haulage of goods it is about 30 per cent. Utilities like water, gas, and electricity have traditionally been and continue to be controlled by the public sector whereas the retail trade has been almost completely controlled by the private sector except for a very small number of government controlled 'Co-operatives' and Utility Stores.

Finally, we must mention the extent of the control of foreign private investment over the economy. Whereas in a number of developing countries like Taiwan, South Korea, and Singapore, foreign private investment has been very high, this has not been the case in Pakistan. In the manufacturing sector, for example, only about 10 to 15 per cent of the total industrial assets in 1979-80 were controlled by foreign firms, mainly in the pharmaceutical and fertilizer industries. In banking and insurance there have been traditional British-based banks but more recently foreign banks from the Middle East have also begun operating in the country.

1.5 Foreign Loans and Debt Repayment

Any attempt to interpret the economic changes in Pakistan without taking into account the role of foreign loans and the external environment would amount to ignoring one of the most important factors which have influenced economic decision-making and economic policies.

Foreign loans, which were 1.1 per cent of the GNP in 1954-5, showed a sharp increase during the sixties when they jumped to 8.7 per cent in 1964-5 but then declined to 3 per cent in 1969-70. In the seventies they increased from 2.8 per cent of the GNP in 1972-3 to 9.9 per cent of the GNP in 1976-7.

With foreign loans accounting for a substantial amount of the total investment, and financing a major part of the total imports, the country's economic policies have been very closely influenced by the terms and conditions attached to the loans by the donor countries. With the passage of time debt repayments have also increased substantially until they became, in 1981-2, over 26 per cent of the country's total export earnings of goods and services.

1.6 Regional Inequalities

Almost all countries of the world find themselves faced with problems of regional inequalities as either the gains or momentum of growth tend to get concentrated in certain areas, and regions or areas with poorer natural resources tend to be left behind.

Pakistan has been inflicted with more than its share of this sensitive problem. A major factor in the break-up of the country in 1971, and the severance of the eastern wing, was a growing feeling among the people of that region that resources had been transferred from it and that economically it was lagging behind. Although the extent to which this happened and the factors which caused it became a source of disagreement between economists of the two regions,[11] there was little disagreement that the economic policies followed over this earlier period had paid little heed to this important problem.

Over the years this problem had also begun to be felt in the provinces of West Pakistan. However, a detailed district-wise study would show that to divide areas in terms of provinces can be quite misleading as there are considerable disparities between divisions and districts of the same province.[12]

We must learn from the former East Pakistan experience so that we can make a positive effort to ensure that this problem is not repeated in what is left of our country. In tracing the country's thirty-five years history we will see what actually accentuated regional disparities, where the government's role should have been more positive in taking corrective measures, and why it failed to do so.

1.7 Inter-Country Comparison

Inter-country comparisons of key economic variables must be viewed with extreme caution especially when interpreting a country's growth performance over a period of time. This is not only because of differences

Table 1.3: Inter-Country Comparison

	GNP per capita (US$)	Growth rate of GNP per capita	Adult literacy rate	Life expectancy rate at birth	Daily per capita calorie supply	Primary education: Male per cent	Primary education: Female per cent	Population per physician	Percentage of population with access to safe drinking water
	1978	1960-78	1975	1978	1977	1977	1977	1977	1975
India	180	1.4	36	51	2,021	95	64	3,620	33
China	230	3.7	NA	70	2,467	127 (AV)[2]		NA	NA
Egypt	390	3.3	44	54	2,760	87	56	1,070	66
Indonesia	360	4.1	62	47	2,272	91	81	14,580	12
Brazil	1,570	4.9	76	62	2,562	89	90	1,700	77
Pakistan	230	2.8	21	52	2,281	69	32	3,780[1]	29

1. World Bank estimates are different from the estimates given in Table 1.2 based on Planning Commission figures of 5,942. The discrepancy is possibly due to the fact that World Bank estimates are based on registered doctors while Planning Commission's are based on those actually in the country, i.e, excluding those who have migrated.

2. Some students are above the official primary school age.

Source: (i) IBRD, *World Development Report*, 1979, Washington. (ii) 'China for Primary Education', Kaplan *et al.*, *Encyclopedia of China Today*, 1979.

in resource endowments, and peculiar economic and historical conditions which are specific to each country, but also because different countries may set for themselves completely different objectives. By judging their performance in terms of any particular objective we would bias our result in favour of the country which had set that particular objective as a goal as against the other country which gave it a low priority. Then of course there are differences in economic systems, a reflection of a country's political ideology which in many cases determine the country's economic objectives as well as provide the means and power to implement them.

Given these obvious limitations, inter-country comparisons can at best provide only a rough idea of a country's economic record. We have selected a few of these indicators for five countries, namely India, China, Egypt, Indonesia, and Brazil, so as to compare them with that of Pakistan.

Let us start with a comparison of our economic performance with India, both because it is our immediate neighbour and because it gained independence at the same time. As far as the growth of per capita income is concerned, India has fared poorly, as compared to us, with an achievement of almost less than half of ours. As regards the social services, its position is marginally better except in the case of education where for primary education it seems far ahead. As regards nutrition, in terms of daily per capita calorie supply, it is slightly behind. We could conclude that on the growth front and food supplies we have done better and are behind as regards the provision of social services. But India's poor growth performance could also be due to the fact that by emphasizing heavy industries, in the fifties and sixties, it ignored agriculture which slowed down the overall growth of its GNP (as agriculture and consumer goods industries have lower capital output rates and can generate higher growth of output with less investment) but that it has built an industrial base for growth in the future. As we have said earlier, some of these important factors may get ignored and give us a biased result. But the indicators we have shown do give us some feel for economic performance.

A comparison with the Peoples Republic of China is both interesting and informative although the fact that China, after 1949, has followed a completely different economic system and political ideology must be taken into account. In terms of the criteria we have listed, China's performance is more impressive than Pakistan's especially when we take into account the fact that China has made these achievements mainly through its own resources and our achievements have been mainly financed through foreign borrowings.

NOTES

1. That is Rs 12,380 million.
2. See S.M. Naseem, 'Poverty and Landlessness in Pakistan', in *Poverty and Landlessness in Rural Asia,* ILO Geneva, 1977.
3. S.M. Naseem, 'Mass Poverty in Pakistan: Some Preliminary Findings', in *Pakistan Economic and Social Review*, Vol. XIV, Special Issues, 1976, Numbers 1-4.
4. R. Amjad and M. Irfan, *Poverty in Rural Pakistan*, ILO/ARTEP, 1983 (Mimeograph).
5. Government of Pakistan, *Pakistan Economic Survey, 1979-80,* Islamabad, p. 196.
6. S.J. Burki, *et al.*, *Pakistan: Operational Implications of Adopting Basic Needs Targets*, Policy Planning Programme Review Department, IBRD Mimeograph.
7. Government of Pakistan, *Pakistan Economic Survey, 1981-2*, Islamabad, 1982.
8. A.G.N. Kazi, *Keynote address at International Symposium on the Economic Performance of Public Enterprises in Pakistan,* held in Islamabad in November 1981 (Mimeograph).
9. Government of Pakistan, *Pakistan Basic Facts, 1979-80*, Islamabad, p. 49.
10. R. Amjad, *Private Industrial Investment in Pakistan, 1960-70*, Cambridge University Press, 1982.
11. Planning Commission, *Report of the Advisory Panels for the Fourth Five Year Plan, 1970-1*, Vol. I, Islamabad, 1970.
12. N. Hamid and A. Hussain, 'Regional Inequalities and Capitalist Development', *Pakistan Economic and Social Review*, Vol. XIV, Special Issues, 1976.

2 Growth and Structural Change: 1947-82

In order to interpret meaningfully the important economic decisions which helped shape the development strategy pursued in the last thirty-five years, we must first establish the overall movements of the economic indicators during this period. Such an analysis will help us to understand the economic situation as it prevailed during different time periods. It will also provide us with a background against which we can try to analyse the impact of economic policies which were in operation at that time as well as the response of the planners to important economic changes. Our task at this stage will, however, be limited mainly to establishing the economic situation as it existed in different phases of the country's history. A detailed analysis of the factors responsible for bringing about these situations will be done in the later chapters.

It is possible to divide Pakistan's economic history until 1982 into four distinct phases which also coincide closely with particular forms of political governments which existed during those periods. These are: the period of the fifties, when the newly independent country was run according to a parliamentary form of government, when growth rates of the industrial sector were very high but the agricultural sector stagnated because of which there was little growth in per capita income; the period of the sixties, when the country was ruled by a military dictatorship which converted itself into a Presidential system of government based on limited franchise. During this period growth rates in both the manufacturing and industrial sector were high, resulting in the growth of per capita income. However, this was accompanied by large increases in foreign borrowing which put the country heavily in foreign debt. Also, there is some evidence, though not accepted by all, that inequalities in inter-regional and intra-personal income worsened. Then there is the period (which followed the dismemberment of Pakistan) from December 1972 to 1977 when there was a return to a Parliamentary system of government. This period saw important structural changes in the economy but, because of adverse external conditions and inconsistent domestic policies, both industry and agriculture showed little growth and only the large increases in foreign remittances led to some positive increase in the Gross National Product and per capita income. Finally, we come to the early eighties when there has been a return to martial law and a military government. This period has seen a strong revival of growth in both industry and agriculture, mainly because of better economic management as well as more favourable weather conditions, but because of the continuing uncertain political climate there has been little increase in private sector investment.

It must, however, be pointed out that this particular division with emphasis on growth rates of important sectors alone has at times been mistakenly interpreted as a reflection of how well or how badly the economy was doing during these periods. Although growth rates are an important indicator of economic performance it must be kept in mind that there are also a number of other equally important economic and social indicators. In fact one of the major lessons which we shall learn from Pakistan's economic experience is that high growth rates can both result in as well as hide a number of important weaknesses of the economy (for example, unequal distribution of income) which in turn can lead to disastrous political, economic, and social consequences.

Growth rates and political systems which existed during different time periods must only be taken as a convenient way of dividing the overall period and nothing more should at least up till now be read into them.

Macro Indicators

There are a number of key macro economic indicators whose movements we shall establish during the different periods. First are the growth rates of population and labour force and the migration of labour which in recent years has become exceedingly important. Second are the growth rates of total output, per capita income as well as those of the important sectors like agriculture and manufacturing. Third are the levels of investment, savings, and foreign resource inflows (including foreign aid) the latter reflecting the balance of payments situation and the trade gap. Fourth is the importance of the foreign trade sector in the economy of Pakistan. The behaviour of these important variables will help us to establish what happened to the economy during these different time periods. As to why it happened and to what extent it can be attributed to the economic policies pursued by the existing governments, or to external factors, or to other causes, are factors we will analyse in our more detailed study of these important sub periods.

2.1 Population, Labour Force, Employment, and Overseas Migration

Our first task is to establish, within the limitations of existing data and the peculiar problems associated with measuring employment in a developing economy, the growth of the labour force in Pakistan and the important structural changes in the distribution of employment amongst sectors over the last thirty-five years.

It is important, before we proceed, to draw attention to some of the major problems and shortcomings in carrying out such an exercise. First and foremost are the problems of measuring employment in economies where the bulk of the population is employed in the agriculture and service sectors, where productivity is generally low, because there are wide seasonal fluctuations in employment which result in the well known phenomena of 'underemployment' and 'disguised' unemployment which are exceedingly difficult to quantify. Second are problems associated with the quality of the data on the labour force and employment in Pakistan. As compared to other developing countries, Pakistan has carried out, at fairly regular intervals, population censuses and labour force surveys (the former being carried out as recently as in 1981 and the latter is last available for 1979-80). However, estimates based on earlier censuses have been subsequently revised and Labour Force Survey data is of poor quality. This makes it exceedingly difficult to make reliable estimates of the overall growth of the labour force as well as sectoral breakdowns. In the analysis that follows these data limitations should be borne in mind.

2.1.1 Size and Growth of the Labour Force

Of the factors which influence the size and growth of the labour force, the growth rate of population and its demographic composition are the most important. However, while these two factors help primarily to determine the 'potential' labour force (defined as those above ten years of age) the 'actual' size of the labour force is a result both of demand factors as well as a range of socio-economic influences from the supply side. Amongst the latter the most important are those bearing upon female labour force participation rates. Also, the spread of education at the secondary and higher levels, decreasing social acceptability of child labour, rural-urban migration, improvement in health facilities, growth of real income—all have an important bearing both on female as well as male participation rates.

An attempt is made to see how these factors have influenced the size and growth of the labour force in Pakistan over time but this again must be qualified by 'statistical anamolies' in the available data which make reliable estimates difficult to establish.

Population and Age Structure

According to the last 1982 census, the population of Pakistan, as of 1 March 1981, was nearly 84 million and is estimated to have gone up to almost 86 million as of January 1982.[1] Estimates of population for different years based both on population censuses as well as data supplied by the Planning Commission are given in Table 2.1. The important correction to the census is that made by the Planning Commission to the 1961 census figures when on the charge of under-enumeration the estimates were revised upwards by 7.5 per cent.

Based on these revised 1961 Planning Commission estimates, and census figures for later years, the growth rate of population for the sixties and seventies works out at nearly 3 per cent per annum. For the fifties, depending on the use of census or Planning Commission estimates, the growth rates of population range from 2.4 to 3.35 per cent. However, for national income accounting purposes, to estimate increases in per capita income for the fifties, the census estimate of growth is the officially accepted one although both the 1951 and 1961 census estimates have been revised in light of the Planning Commission figures.

Pakistan's population growth rate during the sixties and seventies, at 3 per cent, is amongst the highest in developing countries and much higher than its other South Asian neighbours. During the seventies, amongst the group of thirty-eight low-income countries, only Kenya had a higher population growth rate (3.3 per cent) while the corresponding

Table 2.1: Population Trends

Year	Population census	Planning Commission estimates (mid-year)	Average annual population growth rate: Census	Average annual population growth rate: Planning Commission
1951	33,740[1]			
1961	42,880	46,921[2]	2.4	3.35
1972	65,309	64,298		3.0
1981	83,782 1 March)		3.0	
1982	85,650 (1 Jan)	86,481[3]		3.0

1. The 1951 census figures have been adjusted for 5 per cent under-enumeration of urban population of Pakistan and an estimated population of 1,755,152 of the North West Frontier region not covered by the census has been added to it. Also population of Gwadar (13,000), not part of Pakistan in 1951, has been added as well as that of Mohmand Agency (Frontier region) which was not included in the earlier estimate of the Frontier region.

2. The Planning Commission has estimated that there was under-enumeration in the 1961 census to the tune of 7.5 per cent. As such the 1961 population figure used for various economic indicators is taken to be 46,200. The estimate of 46,921 is the mid-year estimate.

3. Projection based on 1972 Planning Commission estimates.

Source: (i) Government of Pakistan, *Pakistan Economic Survey, 1981-2*, Islamabad, Statistical Annexure, p. 1, for census estimates. (ii) World Bank, *Pakistan Economic Development and Prospects*, Report No. 382-Pak., April 1982, for Planning Commission estimates.

Table 2.2: Average Annual Vital Rates 1962-80

Years	Births per 1,000	Deaths per 1,000	National growth rate
1962-5[1]	50.0	20.0	3.00
1962-5[2]	42.0	15.0	2.70
1975[3]	40.5	—	—
1979-80[4]	41.0	12.0	2.90

1. Ministry of Health, Government of Pakistan, the Family Planning Scheme for Pakistan during *Third Five Year Plan, 1965-70*, 1965 (based on Population Growth Estimate, Chandra Deming Formula, 1962-5).

2. M. Naseem, Iqbal Farooqui, and Ghazi Mumtaz Farooq (eds.), *Final Report of the Population Growth Estimate Experiment, 1962-5*, PIDE, Dacca, 1971.

3. Population Planning Council of Pakistan, *World Fertility Survey: Pakistan Fertility Survey*, First Report, 1976.

4. Planning and Development Division, Population Division, *Plan 1980-3*.

Source: World Bank, *Pakistan Economic Development and Prospects*, Report No. 3328-Pak., April 1981.

figures for other South Asian countries were India (2.23),[2] Bangladesh (2.7), and Sri Lanka (1.7).

The main factor responsible for the high rate of population growth has been the fall in the death rates (mainly as a result of improved medical facilities) as compared to little decline in the birth rates (Table 2.2). The latter reflects a massive failure of past and present governments' population planning programmes.

Estimates of population below ten years of age are given in Table 2.3. It is now generally agreed that estimates based on the 1961 Census are inaccurate and reflect age misreporting. The Planning Commission estimates for 1975 which have formed the benchmark for 1978 estimates (and projections for 1983) have essentially extrapolated the results of the 1972 Census. The available estimates show that 26.9 per cent of the population in 1951 was below ten years of age as compared to 1975 when it was estimated at 32.3 per cent. According to the latest Labour Force Survey data available for 1978-9 this had increased to 32.86 per cent. In relation to these figures the 1982-3 estimates used for the Fifth Plan projections are on the low side and difficult to justify.

Labour Force Participation Rates

Labour force participation rates in Pakistan have been traditionally low resulting mainly from a high dependency ratio (i.e., proportion of population below ten years of age) as well as very low participation rates of females especially in the rural areas. Table 2.4 shows trends in labour force participation for selected years based on population censuses for 1951 and 1961, Labour Force Surveys for

Table 2.3: Percentage of Population Below Ten Years of Age

	1951[1]	1961[2]	1972	1975	1978-9	1982-3 (Plan projections)
All	26.9	32.8	31.53	32.3	32.86	31.85
Male	26.0	31.9	30.37	32.4	32.49	31.85
Female	28.0	33.8	32.85	32.1	33.25	31.85

1. Based on estimates of population excluding Frontier region, Gwader, and those living in Pakistan claiming nationalities other than Pakistani.

2. Excluding population of the Frontier region (census estimates).

Source: (i) Population Census, CSO, *Twenty-five Years of Pakistan in Statistics*, Karachi, 1972, for 1951 and 1961. (ii) Population Census, Government of Pakistan, *Pakistan Statistical Yearbook 1980*, Karachi, p. 10, for 1972. (iii) ILO, *Employment Strategy for Pakistan—Project Findings and Recommendations*, Geneva, 1977 (Restricted), p. 155, for Planning Commission estimates for 1975. (iv) *Pakistan Labour Force Survey, 1978-9*, Karachi, 1982, for 1978-9. (v) Q.F. Wilson, *Manpower Projections and Planning for Fifth Five Year Plan*, ILO (Mimeograph), Islamabad, 1978, for Fifth Plan estimates for 1982-3.

Table 2.4: Trends in Labour Force Participation Rates

	1951[1]	1961	1971-2	1974-5	1977-8	1978-9	1982-3 (Projections)
Total	30.7	32.4	29.43	29.05	29.38	31.0	29.9
Male	55.1	55.0	51.79	52.01	52.28	51.94	52.67
Female	2.1	6.1	5.34	4.21	6.47	8.09	5.55
Unemployment		0.56	0.61	0.50	0.50	—	0.50

1. Estimates for 1951 and 1961 are based on population estimates excluding Frontier and Gwader. For 1951 labour force estimates based on population more than twelve years of age. For other years more than ten years of age.

Source: ILO/ARTEP, *Employment and Structural Change in Pakistan—Issues for the Eighties*, Bangkok, 1983.

1970-1 and 1974-5 corrected for age and sex distribution, and Fifth Five Year Plan estimates for 1977-8 and 1982-3. The results of the recent 1978-9 Labour Force Survey are also included.

Based on population estimates (Table 2.1) and labour force participation rates (Table 2.4) we present alternative estimates of the labour force during the sixties and seventies. Based on Planning Commission estimates (excluding Frontier region) the growth rate of the labour force during the sixties was slightly higher than 2.8 per cent but this has accelerated to over 3 per cent during the seventies and early eighties.

The important shift in the sectoral distribution of employment (Table 2.6) has been the declining share of the agricultural sector especially during the fifties and sixties. However, more than half of the population is still engaged in the agricultural sector. The share of manufacturing increased rapidly in the

Table 2.5: Estimates of the Labour Force

	1961					
	Census (excluding Frontier region)	Planning Commission[1] (excluding Frontier region)	Planning Commission (including Frontier region)	1971-2	1977-8	1982-3
Total	12,763	13,720	14,921	18,650	22,220	26,060
Male	11,641	12,514	13,603	17,020	20,510	23,740
Female	1,122	1,206	1,318	1,630	1,710	2,320

1. Based on blowing up census estimates by 7.5 per cent.

Source: (i) Government of Pakistan, *Pakistan Economic Survey, 1981-2*, Islamabad, Statistical Annexure, p. 1. (ii) World Bank, *Pakistan Economic Development and Prospects*, Report No. 382-Pak., April 1982. (iii) ILO, ARTEP, *Employment and Structural Change in Pakistan—Issues for the Eighties*, Bangkok, 1983.

Table 2.6: Sectoral Distribution of Employed Labour Force
(Percentages)

Sector	1951[1]	1961[2]	1971-2	1977-8	1982-3
Agriculture	66.4	60.8	58	56.6	55.4
Manufacturing	9.9	13.6	13.50	13.37	13.78
Mining	0.1	0.2			
Transport, storage, and communication	1.7	2.9	5	4.7	4.8
Electricity, gas, and water	1.8	0.2	0.75	0.50	0.52
Construction		2.1	4.25	4.1	4.2
Commerce	7.0	7.1	10	10.5	11.0
Services	11.3	12.4	8.50	10.2	10.3
Others	1.8	0.7	—	—	—
Total	100.0	100.0	100.0	100.0	100.0

1. Excludes children between ten to twelve years. Based on 1951 census estimates and excludes population of the Frontier region. The original figures do not distinguish between unemployed and 'other activities'. We have assumed the level of unemployment at 1.5 per cent (same as that for 1961) and got a figure of 1.8 per cent for other activities.

2. Excludes population of the Frontier region.

Source: ILO/ARTEP, *Employment and Structural Change in Pakistan—Issues for the Eighties*, Bangkok, 1983.

fifties. Despite a very high growth rate of output in large-scale manufacturing its overall share in employment declined. This was both because of capital-intensive techniques of production adopted by the large-scale sector and the slow growth of the small-scale sector. The other important shift has been the increase in the share of transport, communication, and storage sectors mainly during the fifties and sixties.

2.1.2 Overseas Migration—Estimates of the Total Number of Pakistani Workers Overseas

Perhaps the most significant economic event during the second half of the seventies and early eighties has been the dramatic increase in the migration of Pakistani workers mainly towards the Middle East. This exodus of workers has been of a number large enough to have had a direct impact on the domestic employment situation and the functioning of the labour market in Pakistan.

The *Pakistan Economic Survey, 1981-2* reports that 'according to the recent estimates there are about 1.4 million Pakistanis living/working abroad'. Unfortunately, there is no explanation provided as to how this figure is arrived at. Also, the official estimates of labour migration provided in the same Survey show total labour emigration from 1971 to 1981 as being 788,474 (Table 2.7).

More reliable estimates on overseas migration are provided by a recent study[3] based on a survey of households carried out by the Pakistan Institute of Development Economics (PIDE) in 1979. According to the survey, 9.3 per cent of the rural households and 15.9 per cent of the urban households in Pakistan have at least one migrant member. The average number of migrants in the two categories of households are 1.60 and 1.49 respectively. Given that rural and urban population of Pakistan in 1978-80 was 58 million and 23 million respectively, the number of households in Pakistan can be calculated by taking the average size of rural and urban household

Table 2.7: Official Estimates of Overseas Migration (Numbers)

Year	Private (overseas employment promotors)	Public	Direct	Total
1971	3,340	194	–	3,534
1972	3,359	1,171	–	4,530
1973	7,654	4,646	–	12,300
1974	14,652	1,676	–	16,328
1975	21,766	1,311	–	23,077
1976	38,516	3,174	–	41,690
1977	77,664	2,606	60,175	140,445
1978	78,685	3,246	47,602	129,533
1979	80,615	3,058	34,586	118,259
1980	91,482	17,114	24,801	133,397
1981	119,711	821	32,549	153,081

Source: Government of Pakistan, *Pakistan Economic Survey, 1981-2*, Islamabad, 1982.

Table 2.8: The Distribution of Migrants by Rural and Urban Areas in 1979

	Rural area migrants		Urban area migrants		Total migrants	
Province	Number of migrants (million)	As per cent of total rural migrants	Number of migrants (million)	As per cent of total urban migrants	Number of migrants (million)	As per cent of total migrants
Punjab	0.83	73.6	0.43	64.7	1.26	70.4
Sind	0.10	9.2	0.15	22.9	0.25	14.0
NWFP	0.16	14.1	0.05	7.8	0.21	11.7
Baluchistan	0.04	3.1	0.03	4.6	0.07	3.9
Total	1.13	100.0	0.66	100.0	1.79	100.0

Source: Gilani, *et al.*, *Labour Migration: Pakistan to Middle East and its Impact on the Domestic Economy*, PIDE, Islamabad, 1981.

to be 7.6 and 8.1. This gives the total number of rural and urban households to be, respectively, 6 million and 3 million. These numbers multiplied by the average number of migrants in the household then give the estimated number of migrants from the country to be 1.79 million in 1979. If we add to this figure the annual flows of 1980 and 1981, i.e., 286,478, we arrive at a figure of 2 million which is substantially higher than the government estimates.

Of the 2 million migrant workers in 1979, according to the PIDE study, over 1 million came from rural areas and 660,000 from urban areas. A province-wise rural-urban distribution of the migrants is given in Table 2.8.

2.2 Growth Rates and Sectoral Composition of Output

In terms of growth rates of the GNP, and the important sectors, the economy falls into distinct time periods as shown in Tables 2.9 and 2.10. During the fifties, the industrial sector grew at a very fast pace, although this high growth rate must be interpreted with caution taking into consideration the fact that we started from a very small industrial base. The agricultural sector, however, stagnated throughout the period, growing at less than the rate of population growth. Given the dominance of this sector, in that it contributed over 60 per cent to total output, there was little growth of GNP and no growth in per capita income. During the sixties, both industry and agriculture grew at a fast pace and this led to a substantial growth in per capita income. During 1972-7, both the agricultural and industrial sectors stagnated and the growth in GNP was mainly the result of increases in foreign remittances from Pakistani workers in the Middle East. Finally, since 1976-7, both industry and agriculture have prospered due to better export performance, new projects, better weather conditions, and better availability of inputs.

As we can see from Table 2.9 the growth rates of the GNP and per capita income for the fifties as well as for the sixties were higher for West Pakistan, compared to that for All Pakistan, showing that the growth rates were lower in East Pakistan during both these periods. There is very little difference between the growth rates of Gross Domestic

Table 2.10: Annual Growth Rates for Major Sectors, Pakistan (West)
(Per cent per annum)

Years	Agriculture	Large-scale manufacturing	Other sectors
1949-50 to 1959-60	1.6	15.4	3.7
1959-60 to 1969-70	5.0	13.3	7.1
1969-70 to 1976-7	1.5	1.2	4.1
1976-7 to 1981-2	4.1	10.0	7.1
1949-50 to 1981-2	3.0	10.1	5.6

Source: Government of Pakistan, *Pakistan Economic Survey, 1981-2*, Islamabad, 1982.

Table 2.9: Annual Growth Rates of the Gross National Product
(Per cent per annum)

Years	GNP		GDP		Per capita GNP	
	All Pakistan	Pakistan (West)	All Pakistan	Pakistan (West)	All Pakistan	Pakistan (West)
1949-50 to 1959-60	2.6	3.1	2.5	3.1	0.2	0.6
1959-60 to 1969-70	5.4	6.8	5.3	6.7	2.7	3.8
1969-70 to 1976-7	—	4.2	—	3.7	—	0.8
1976-7 to 1981-2	—	6.8	—	6.5	—	3.7
1949-50 to 1981-2	—	5.2	—	5.1	—	2.2

Source: (i) CSO, *Twenty-five Years of Pakistan in Statistics*, Karachi, 1972, for all Pakistan. (ii) Government of Pakistan, *Pakistan Economic Survey, 1981-2*, Islamabad, 1982, for Pakistan (West).

Product and Gross National Product till the end of the sixties as there was little income being transferred, either from or to Pakistan. During the seventies the differences in growth rate between the GNP and the GDP is due to the inflow of foreign remittances from workers abroad.

The rates of growth for the two main sectors, agriculture and industry, are shown in Table 2.10. Figures for the industrial sector are only for the growth of the large-scale manufacturing sector which was defined by the CSO until 1976 as units that employ more than twenty people and use power in their manufacturing operation and, after 1976, as all units employing more than ten people. Estimates for the rest of the industrial sector, i.e., small-scale manufacturing and household enterprises, are extremely unreliable as very little information has been collected for this very important sector and they are, therefore, not shown separately. Till 1969-70 an indirect estimation technique was used for the growth of the small-scale sector. An estimate of a benchmark year, 1959-60, was computed on the basis of the number of persons engaged in small industries and a computed value added per worker and subsequently a growth rate equal to the growth rate of population was assumed. From 1969-70 onwards it is based on a Statistics Division's Survey of Small and Household Manufacturing Industries (SHMI) 1969-70 and Punjab SHMI Survey 1975-6. According to these estimates the small-scale sector grew at a rate of 7.3 per cent between 1971-2 and 1981-2.[4]

It is with regard to the large-scale manufacturing sector, whose data are quite reliable, that Pakistan's achievement is quite impressive in terms of its growth rate for most periods. This is especially true for the sixties when the very high growth rates, achieved this time from a significantly large base, were among the highest in the world. These high growth rates stand in marked contrast to the extremely low growth rates in manufacturing which followed in the seventies. A number of economic and non-economic factors contributed towards this situation but one must also keep in mind a significant difference between industries which were established in the seventies as compared to those in the sixties. Earlier industrialization had been mainly restricted to consumer goods industries, with traditionally low capital output ratios, whereas industrialization in the seventies was mainly in the more capital-intensive long gestation projects, i.e., with high capital output ratios such as the steel mill. An important factor responsible for the spurt of industrial growth in the late seventies was that some of these major projects had been completed and were now coming into production.

The high growth rate of agricultural output in the sixties also stands in marked contrast to the extremely low growth rates of this important sector during the fifties and seventies. The spurt in agricultural growth in the sixties (namely the so-called 'green revolution') was the result of the increased use of inputs, especially water and fertilizers, and the introduction of high yielding varieties of seed in the case of crops like wheat and rice. The increase in agricultural production in the late seventies was mainly the result of good weather conditions as well as the increased availability of key inputs.

The growth rates of these two major sectors, therefore, clearly show that there have been wide fluctuations in their performance during the different sub-periods and their movements have determined the course of national and per capita output. What caused these fluctuations in output and to what extent the government played a contributory part is the subject of considerable debate and criticism as we shall see both in our review of these two important sectors as well as in the chapter dealing in detail with the different sub-periods.

2.3 Sectoral Composition of Output

The differences in the growth rates of the major sectors have resulted in a transformation of the sectoral shares in the Gross Domestic Product. These changes are reflected in

Table 2.11 where the most important shift till the end of the sixties is the increasing share of the large-scale manufacturing sector which in West Pakistan, starting from a very small base of 2.2 per cent, had contributed 12.5 per cent of the Gross Domestic Product by 1969-70. Because of the slowing down of growth in the manufacturing sector in the seventies its share during this period in fact registered a small decline and by 1981-2 it was 12.3 per cent of the Gross Domestic Product. The share of the agricultural sector fell from 53.2 per cent in 1949-50 to 30 per cent in 1981-2. The growth and increasing share of the construction sector has been due to the large immigration at Independence, rapid urbanization, and the implementation of the Indus Basin Replacement Works. The growth of the service sectors is mainly due to the replacement after partition of some of the essential services like banking and insurance whose owners had migrated at the time of Independence.

2.4 Investment, Savings, and Foreign Resource Inflows

Of the large number of factors which influence the growth rate of an economy, the level of investment, which is normally shown as a percentage of the Gross National Product, is amongst the most important. The amount of investment undertaken is financed from either domestic savings or foreign resource inflows. The movement of these three important variables, i.e., gross fixed investment, gross domestic savings, and foreign resource inflows, together with the breakdown of investment and savings between the private and public sectors, tell us a great deal about the pace and the process by which the economy is trying to develop itself.

Table 2.11: Composition of the GDP in Pakistan (West) at 1959-60 Factor Cost
(Percentages)

Sector	1949-50	1959-60	1969-70	1981-2
Agriculture	53.2	45.8	38.9	30.3
Large-scale manufacturing	2.2	6.9	12.5	12.3
Construction	1.4	2.5	4.2	5.4
Others	43.2	44.8	44.4	52.0
Total	100	100	100	100

Source: Government of Pakistan, *Pakistan Economic Survey, 1981-2*, Islamabad, 1982.

2.4.1 Definitions and Data Sources

Given the importance of these variables, we must first establish the macro-economic identities used in defining them and then briefly discuss the methodology used in estimating their values.

Gross Fixed Investment	= Gross Domestic Savings plus External Resource Balance. *(i)*
External Resource Balance	= Imports of goods and Non-Factor Services minus exports of goods and Non-Factor Services. *(ii)*
Gross Domestic Savings (as per cent of GDP)	= Gross Fixed Investment minus External Resource Balance. *(iii)*
Gross National Savings (as per cent of GNP)	= Gross Domestic Savings plus Net Factor Income from abroad. *(iv)*
Gross Fixed Investment	= Gross National Savings plus External Resource Balance minus Net Factor Income from abroad. *(v)*

Gross fixed investment is financed either by savings generated in the domestic economy, i.e., gross domestic savings, or through foreign resources made available which help supplement domestic savings. The amount of foreign resource inflows is represented by the external resource balance, i.e., the gap between the country's import of goods and non-factor services and the export of goods and non factor services. The reason why this measure is used is because the trade gap represents the physical resources made available by foreign loans and grants and other financial transactions, including the use of reserves and the net factor income from abroad. Gross domestic savings is then derived as a residual and calculated as the difference between gross fixed investment and the external resource balance *(Eqn. iii)*.

During a time period when the net factor income from abroad is not significant, the external resource balance can be taken as a fairly good indicator of the foreign loans and grants flowing into the economy and which, together with domestic savings, make up the total investment being undertaken. However, during a time period when the net factor income from abroad is making a significant contribution then the external resource balance could reflect not only foreign loans but also income which is available to the economy in foreign exchange. To take into account these foreign exchange resources which are made available to the domestic economy the identity used is that of gross national savings. In this case, we add to gross savings the net factor income from abroad. In terms of our identities *(Eqn. v)* this basically means that in the external resource balance, to the extent that it is now being met by the net factor income from abroad, the reliance on sources like foreign loans and grants to finance gross fixed investment is decreased and there is a corresponding increase in gross domestic savings by this amount.

Two important points, therefore, must be kept in mind when we are estimating the inflows of external resources into the economy. The first, that the external resource balance represents a resource gap being met from outside the domestic economy, i.e., the extra savings added to the country's own resources to finance total gross fixed investment undertaken. Secondly, to the extent that net factor income from abroad is positive the reliance on foreign loans and grants is diminished.

Using this methodology, savings are indirectly computed and foreign resource inflows calculated from the balance of payments accounts. This leaves us with estimating the level of gross fixed investment. The CSO defines gross investment as expenditure incurred on the replacement, additions, and major improvements of fixed capital, viz., land improvement, building, civil and engineering works, machinery, transport equipment, and furniture and fixtures, in the private and public sectors. This is estimated in the following way. Fixed investments in the government sector are obtained from an analysis of the budget and those of autonomous bodies through a detailed questionnaire. As regards the private sector, in the case of agriculture, transport, and construction, it is worked out through a commodity flow method. Non-monetized investment in the agricultural sector is based on special studies. As regards industry and other sectors, it is based on annual surveys and special studies carried out for this purpose.

How reliable are the statistics on which investment estimates are made during the time period covered? The answer is a mixed one. For the fifties, the data on gross fixed investment for all sectors were mainly based on a commodity flow method and may, therefore, be considered as not being all that reliable. For the sixties and seventies, the CSO used the methodology explained earlier and the estimates are fairly good although obviously some sector estimates like non-monetized investments in agriculture can still be considered as rough estimates rather than representative of exact magnitude.

2.4.2 Movements of Investment, Savings, and Foreign Resource Inflows

How have these key variables behaved during the different time periods in which we have divided the thirty-five years of the country's economic history? They tell an extremely interesting story.

During the fifties, the All Pakistan figures, which are the only ones available, show that the level of investment was low and, at its peak in 1954-5, was estimated at 8 per cent of the GDP. It had, however, increased considerably over the earlier years of the fifties when it had started at a very low level of 4.6 per cent. Investment was mainly undertaken by the private sector and the public sector contributed only about 30 per cent to the total fixed investment in 1954-5. In the earlier years of the fifties almost all of the investment was financed by domestic savings and, in 1954-5, foreign resource inflows were still only 1 per cent of the GNP.

In the sixties the situation changed drastically and the figures for West Pakistan show an almost doubling of the investment level between 1959-60 and 1964-5. There is also at the same time a large increase in the level of foreign resource inflows which appreciated from 5.4 per cent of the Gross National Product in 1959-60 to 8.9 per cent in 1964-5. Gross domestic savings also witnessed a substantial increase from 6.0 to 12.2 per cent of the Gross National Product. After 1964-5 the level of investment began to decline and it was 15.6 per cent in 1969-70 as compared to 21.1 per cent in 1964-5. This was also associated with a substantial decline in foreign resource inflows which, by the end of the sixties, were only 3.1 per cent of the Gross National Product. Gross domestic savings stagnated at the same level as in 1964-5. The division between public and private investment increased substantially in favour of the private sector whose share in the total investment increased from 38.8 per cent in 1959-60 to over 50 per cent in the sixties (Table 2.13).

The decline in the level of gross fixed investment, which had started in the late sixties, continued in the early seventies till about 1972-3 after which it began to improve. By 1976-7 it had reached a figure of 17.7 per cent of the GDP. The increase in investment also coincided as it had done in the sixties

Table 2.13: Share of Private and Public Investment in Total Investment
(Current prices: Rs million)

	Pakistan (West)				
	1959-60	1964-5	1960-70	1974-5	1981-2
Total Gross Domestic Fixed Capital Formation	2,014	6,010	6,746	16,218	48,573
Private (percentage)	38.8	53.7	51.7	52.1	33.6
Public	61.2	46.3	48.3	67.9	66.4

Source: (i) Government of Pakistan, *Third Five Year Plan, 1965-70*, Planning Commission, Islamabad, pp. 5-9. (ii) Rashid Amjad, *Private Industrial Investment in Pakistan 1960-70*, Cambridge, 1982. (iii) Government of Pakistan, *Pakistan Economic Survey, 1981-2*, Islamabad, 1982.

Table 2.12: Investment, Savings, and Foreign Resource Inflows
(Percentages of GDP/GNP)

	All Pakistan		Pakistan (West)			Pakistan (West) at current market prices			
	1949-50	1954-5	1959-60	1964-5	1969-70	1972-3	1974-5	1976-7	1981-2
Gross Fixed Investment	4.6	7.9	11.1	21.1	15.6	11.4	14.5	17.7	14.9
Private	3.3	5.7	4.3	11.3	8.1	5.6	4.6	5.2	5.0
Public	1.3	2.2	6.8	9.8	7.5	5.8	9.9	12.5	9.9
Foreign resource inflows	–	1.1	5.4	8.9	3.1	– 0.5	8.9	8.5	9.1
Gross Domestic Savings	4.6	6.8	6.0	12.2	12.5	11.9	5.6	9.2	5.8
Gross National Savings	4.6	6.8	6.0	12.2	12.5	12.5	6.6	12.4	12.1

Note: Estimates till end-sixties are percentages of GNP after which they are GDP except for Gross National Savings which is a percentage of GNP in all cases.

Source: (i) Government of Pakistan, *Third Five Year Plan, 1965-70*, Planning Commission, Islamabad, pp. 5-9, for 1949-50 and 1954-5. (ii) Rashid Amjad, *Private Industrial Investment in Pakistan 1960-70*, Cambridge, 1982, for 1959-60, 1964-5, and 1969-70. (iii) Government of Pakistan, *Pakistan Economic Survey, 1981-2*, Islamabad, 1982, for 1972-3, 1974-5, 1976-7, and 1981-2.

with large increases in foreign resource inflows into the country, which were now at a higher level than they had been in the sixties, averaging about 10 per cent of GNP. But there was one important difference between the sixties and the seventies: the share of private investment in total investment declined drastically and in the seventies public investment contributed about 70 per cent of the total. The situation was now almost the reverse of what it had been in the fifties.

Since 1977 the new military government which took over has tried to restore the business confidence of the private sector, but, given the overall unsettled political situation and a changing international environment, it has met with little success. In fact the level of investment as a percentage of the Gross Domestic Product declined marginally during these years and the bulk of the share continued to be undertaken by the public sector.

There are a number of important questions which are raised after studying the movements of these key variables.

The first question relates to the fluctuations in the level of investment which, at least in the sixties and seventies, are closely associated with changes in the levels of foreign resource inflows. What factors caused these fluctuations and to what extent can they be explained by changes in foreign loans inflows?

The second important question relates to the levels of the domestic savings. Why have they been so low and why, except for the first half of the sixties when they showed some increase, have they failed to grow, especially during the seventies?

The third question relates to the mix between private and public investment. Whereas in the fifties the private sector dominated investment and contributed almost 70 per cent of the total, the situation in the seventies changed drastically when large public investments were undertaken. What factors were responsible for the changes in the private-public mix of the total investment undertaken during the period?

2.5 The Foreign Trade Sector

In looking at the foreign trade sector we must separate from the rest of the fifties the period of the Korean boom from 1950 to 1952 when the level of exports and imports increased considerably. After the collapse of the Korean boom, however, the level of exports declined drastically and then it stagnated at the lower level for the rest of the fifties. Despite the fact that the government devalued the currency in 1955, because of the adverse balance of trade situation, the level of exports failed to rise. The share of exports in the Gross National Product, which was at its peak in 1950-1 at 17.2 per cent, had declined to 5.6 per cent by 1959-60 (Table 2.14).

During the fifties and sixties, as the All Pakistan figures clearly show, exports were never a significant proportion of the Gross National Product and during most of the sixties they were less than 5 per cent. Although during the first half of the sixties the marginal share of exports in the Gross National Product increased this was not sustained during the second half of the period. Imports have always been a more significant portion of the Gross National Product and were subject to considerable growth during the first half of the sixties, mainly because of the increase in foreign aid inflows. However, they slowed down significantly during the second half because of cutbacks in foreign resource inflows.

With the break up of Pakistan, the share of exports in West Pakistan's economy increased mainly because goods which had earlier been sent to East Pakistan were successfully diverted into foreign markets. In 1972-3, after the massive currency devaluation in 1972 when the Rupee was depreciated from Rs 4.76 to Rs 11 per dollar, exports increased significantly, and after more than seventeen years (i.e., since 1955) the economy once again had a balance of trade surplus. In that year the share of exports in the Gross Domestic Product rose to 14.9 per cent. However, in subsequent years, till 1976-7, there was little growth in exports and their share of the GDP declined to 9.4 per cent. During the same period, because of the increase in oil prices and world inflation, the import bill increased by more than three times and the share of imports in the Gross Domestic Product rose to almost 18 per cent in 1976-7. During the last three years of the seventies there had been some revival of growth in the export sector and exports increased substantially especially during 1979-80 but have subsequently slowed down.

An important change which occurred in the seventies was the migration of Pakistani workers, mainly to the Middle East, and the share of foreign remittances to the Gross National Product in 1979-80 was nearly 10 per cent (Table 2.15). These remittances, as we have emphasized in an earlier section, played a major part in cushioning the adverse balance of trade situation which would otherwise have spelt complete disaster for the economy.

As regards the foreign trade sector, we can conclude that the export sector has never played a dominant role in the growth of the national economy. Its overall share in the GNP has never been of great significance and Pakistan, except for a very few brief periods, has not had great success in the export market. Considering the fact that the growth of exports has always been a major goal of the country's economic policy and a number of measures including export subsidies have been provided, the limited success of export policies needs to be investigated. At the same time the country's import bill has always

Table 2.15: Annual Official Remittances
(US$ million)

Year	Annual official remittances
1975-6	339
1976-7	578
1977-8	1,156
1978-9	1,395
1979-80	1,743
1980-1[1]	2,128

1. Estimates.
Source: State Bank of Pakistan.

Table 2.14: Trade Ratios
(Current prices : Rs million)

	All Pakistan					Pakistan (West)		
	1950-1*	1954-5*	1959-60	1964-5	1969-70	1972-3	1976-7	1981-2
Imports of goods and nfs[1] (M)	2,288	1,558	2,461	5,374	5,098	9,598	26,741	60,160
Exports of goods nfs (X)	3,703	1,773	1,843	2,408	3,337	9,961	13,991	30,318
M/GNP[2] (market prices)	10.6	7.1	7.5	11.1	6.6	14.4	17.9	18.4
X/GNP[2]	17.2	8.0	5.6	4.9	4.3	14.9	9.4	9.3
Marginal rate								
ΔM/Δ GNP[2]	—	8.4	—	18.3	−1.0	—	20.8	18.8
ΔX/Δ GNP	—	0.8	—	3.5	3.2	—	4.9	9.2

1. Non-factor services.
2. As ratio of GDP in the seventies.

Source: (i) J.J. Stern and W.P. Falcon, *Growth and Development in Pakistan 1955-68*, Occasional Paper No. 23, Harvard University Centre for International Affairs, for all years (fifties and sixties) except 1950-1 and 1969-70. (ii) CSO, *Twenty-five Years of Pakistan in Statistics*, Karachi, 1972, for 1950-1 and 1969-70 figures for imports and exports, and 1969-70 figure for GNP. (iii) Government of Pakistan, *Pakistan Economic Survey, 1981-2*, Islamabad, 1982, for the seventies.

* The figures for 1950-1 and 1954-5 have been corrected for devaluation so as to give an accurate idea of the share of imports and exports in GNP. Otherwise because of devaluation the rupee value of exports as well as its share of GNP would increase by the amount of devaluation, whereas GNP itself would not be influenced to the same extent.

been significantly larger than our exports and this has steadily increased. Especially during the seventies, with the increase in oil prices, imports increased manifold and put considerable pressure on the balance of payments situation. The capacity of the economy to import because of the lack of exports has been significantly linked with foreign resource inflows either in the form of aids and grants or, more recently, in the form of the foreign remittances.

2.6 Foreign Economic Assistance

The role of foreign aid as a key determinant in financing the investment programmes of both the government and the private sector and in paying for the country's import bill has clearly emerged from our study of the economic variables whose behaviour we have investigated. We now concern ourselves with three other important aspects of foreign economic assistance. What is the total amount of foreign economic assistance committed during the different periods? What have been the major sources of this foreign economic assistance? Finally, what is the present level of debt service ratio on the loans that we have incurred?

Estimates of the total foreign economic assistance to Pakistan during the different time periods are given in Table 2.16. A major increase took place during the sixties although after the September 1965 war with India foreign economic assistance slowed down and during the second half was far below the expectations of the planners. During the seventies too the economy was relying heavily on foreign assistance although, because of the high level of inflation, the data on foreign assistance do not give a correct picture of the real increase which took place in this period. A better indicator is the level of foreign assistance as a percentage of Gross Domestic Product which was given in Section 2.3.

An important point as regards foreign assistance is the decline in the grant element in the overall period. This was well over 50 per cent in the fifties but had reduced itself to 26 per cent in the second half of the sixties and was 15 per cent in the seventies.

In terms of foreign aid commitment from different sources there is a major difference between the sixties and the seventies. During the sixties the bulk of foreign assistance came from Consortium sources comprising countries like the USA, UK, West Germany, Japan, Canada, and international financial institutions like the International Bank for Reconstruction and Development (IBRD/World Bank) and its affiliates like the International Finance Corporation. During the Second Plan period the total of Consortium countries and Agencies came to over 95 per cent of all foreign aid commitment to Pakistan with the United States providing 45.6 per cent, followed by the World Bank Group, i.e., IBRD, IDA, and IFC, at 17.1 per cent, and West Germany with 10.9 per cent. During the Third Plan period the share of the Consortium countries declined to about 80 per cent, with the United States' share coming down to 25 per cent, and there was an increase to about 15 per cent from the Socialist bloc comprising the USSR, Yugoslavia, China, Czechoslovakia, and Poland.

During the seventies, especially after 1974-5, there was a substantial increase in the share of foreign assistance from non-Consortium countries which began to make up almost 50 per cent of the total. A major portion of this came from the oil producing

Table 2.16: Commitments of External Assistance

Years	Total assistance (US$ million)	Grant (per cent)	Loans (per cent)
1950-1 to 1954-5	337	64	36
1955-6 to 1959-60	1,073	54	46
1960-1 to 1964-5	2,757	40	60
1965-6 to 1969-70	2,746	26	74
1970-1 to 1981-2*	11,982	15	85
Total	18,895	23	77

* Till December 1981

Source: Government of Pakistan, *Pakistan Economic Survey, 1981-2*, Islamabad, 1982.

Table 2.17: Debt Service Ratio: Selected Years
(Net of Debt Relief)

	1960-1	1964-5	1969-70	1972-3	1976-7	1981-2
Percentage of export earnings (goods and services)	3.4	8.8	22.5	–	–	38.0
Percentage of foreign exchange earnings (i.e., including remittances)	3.4	8.8	22.5	18.1	15.8	18.8

Source: (i) Stern and Falcon, *Growth and Development in Pakistan 1955-68*, Occasional Paper No. 23, Harvard University Centre for International Affairs, 1970, for export earnings in 1960-1, 1964-5, and 1969-70. (ii) Government of Pakistan, *Pakistan Economic Survey, 1981-2*, Islamabad, 1982, for 1972-3, 1976-7, and 1981-2.

countries who began to divert a small portion of their oil revenues to developing countries to meet the increasingly high prices of oil imports. During the period 1972-3 to 1979-80 OPEC sources contributed about 20 per cent of the total foreign economic assistance.

It is the repayment of these large foreign loans which we have incurred during the last thirty-five years that now pose some of the most difficult problems with which the country is faced. The debt service ratio is steadily increasing in terms of our export earnings. In the mid-sixties it was 10 per cent but by the end of the sixties it had increased to over 20 per cent and in 1981-2 the ratio had further increased to 38 per cent of our export earnings. If we take into account the inflow of remittances from Pakistanis working abroad and see the debt service ratio in terms of total foreign exchange earnings it is about 19 per cent of the total (Table 2.17).

To conclude, foreign economic assistance, which started in 1950, by December 1981 had led to US$ 19 billion worth of assistance being contracted. Of this US$ 4 billion was in the form of grants, US$ 0.4 billion in the form of loans repayable in non-convertible Rupees, and US$ 14 billion in the form of loans and credits repayable in foreign exchange. Disbursements of loans and credit up to the end of December 1981 amounted to US$ 12 billion of which Pakistan has repaid over US$ 2 billion leaving a net debt (disbursed and outstanding) of US$ 9 billion on 31 December 1981.

However, it would be a grave over-simplification to interpret the foreign assistance to Pakistan just in terms of sums of money to pay for the investment and import bills of the country. Foreign loans have played an extremely important part in the formulation of the overall economic policy which we have pursued in the last thirty-five years. It is this controversial area of the influence on domestic policy which the loan-giving countries exert on the recipient country which we shall also try to investigate during this study. For the moment at least we can see clearly that, given the extremely heavy dependence on loans, the country's economic policy-makers were certainly sufficiently indebted to be responsive to the loan-givers. To what extent they were able to resist the pressures they were subject to, to what extent the policy recommendations coincided with their aims, and to what extent they were able to pursue independent policies are important areas of investigation which we will try to cover in our study.

NOTES

1. Government of Pakistan, *Pakistan Economic Survey, 1981-2*, Islamabad, 1982, Statistical Annexure, Table 2.1.
2. According to the 1981 census the growth rate of population in India was 2.23 per cent in the seventies compared to 2.2 per cent during the sixties (*Economic and Political Weekly*, Vol. XVI, Special Number, 1981, p. 1728). For Bangladesh and Sri Lanka see World Bank, *World Development Report 1980*, Washington D.C., p. 142. The figures are for 1970-8.
3. Ijaz Gilani, *et al*, *Labour Migration from Pakistan to Middle East and its Impact on the Domestic Economy*, Vols. 1, 2 and 3, Islamabad, Pakistan Institute of Development Economics, Research Report Series No. 126, 127, and 128, 1981.

3 The Social Services

Growth and structural change, discussed in the previous chapter, present only a partial view of the development process in Pakistan. A discussion of the macro framework must also take into account the efforts made to achieve a more fundamental goal, i.e., an improvement in the people's quality of life through the provision of such social services as education, health, housing, water supply, and nutrition. A brief reference has already been made to social services earlier (Section 1.2). This chapter attempts to cover the range of social policies and programmes pursued so far and the results attained.

A look at government expenditures on Physical Planning and Housing, Education, Health, Social Welfare, and Manpower Development (Table 3.1) indicates the low priority assigned to the social sector as a whole, with the exception of housing in the fifties when public sector housing effort was needed for the resettlement of refugees and for relieving the acute housing shortage. In fact social sector expenditure has usually been considered a residual item and the first to be cut in case of a crisis. The decline in actual expenditures on various social amenities, sometimes in terms of both the absolute amounts and the percentage of total expenditures during the Third Plan as a result of the 1965 war, in 1972-4 due to the 1971 war, and in 1976-7 and 1977-8 due to the stringent financial conditions and the low resource mobilization, as shown in Table 3.1, amply bears this out.

The extent to which social policy can succeed in transferring essential social services to the relatively under-privileged depends to some extent upon the role played by the public sector and the bureaucracy which manages them, the private sector having only a limited role in the provision of social services particularly after nationalization of educational institutions in 1972. Irrespective of the increases in development and non-development expenditures in the social sector, the biases of those who are responsible for dis-

Table 3.1: Public Sector (Federal + Provincial) Development Expenditure on Social Sectors
(Percentage of total development expenditure)

	First Plan 1955-6		Second Plan 1960-5		Third Plan 1965-70		1970-5	1975-6	1976-7	1977-8	1978-9	1979-80
	Target	Actual	Target	Actual	Target	Total	Actual	Actual	Actual	Actual	Actual	RE
Physical Planning and Housing	20.0	9.9	15.0	11.9	8.9	7.5	7.0	8.9	7.8	7.4	7.4	6.4
Education	6.0	5.5	4.0	6.5	6.8	6.1	4.9	5.2	3.4	3.7	3.7	3.7
Health	2.0	2.0	1.0	2.7	2.6	2.9	2.5	4.6	3.3	2.9	3.1	3.1
Social Welfare	–	0.1	–	0.3	0.1	0.2	0.1	0.1	0.1	neg.	neg.	0.1
Manpower Development	–	–	–	0.2	–	0.2	0.3	0.2	0.1	neg.	0.1	0.2

Source : (i) Government of Pakistan, *Twenty-five Years of Statistics in Pakistan, 1947-72*, Islamabad, 1972, p. 310, for targets of First, Second, and Third Plans. (ii) Government of Pakistan, *Pakistan Economic Survey, 1980-1*, Islamabad, p. 241 (Statistical Annexure) for actual expenditure in First, Second, and Third Plans and for data relating to the seventies (compilation).

pensing these facilities become critical in the distribution of housing plots, seats in prestigious schools, access to medical care, and overseas employment opportunities.

3.1 Education

As an area of human activity, education has much to contribute to the cultivation of the mind and the spirit, curiosity, contemplation, and reasoning.[1] This serves to underline the role of education in fulfilling certain developmental goals like overcoming poverty by improving the quality of manpower, inculcating the needed know-how, and improving productivity besides functioning as an instrument for reducing economic and social disparities. The general role of education, i.e., providing enlightenment and improving the reasoning power of the human being, is thus quite compatible with its specific functions like imparting certain types of knowledge, skills, and techniques.

3.1.1 The Structure of Education

Pakistan has a four-tiered educational structure: Primary (grades I to V for ages five to nine); Secondary (grades VI to X for ages ten to fourteen); College: Intermediate and Degree (grades XI to XIV for ages fifteen to eighteen); and University (grades XV to XVI and above for ages nineteen plus). Education up to primary level in national and regional-languages-medium schools has always been free. In 1972 secondary education (grade VI to X) was also made free. All privately managed schools and colleges were nationalized but English-medium schools were exempted.

Education is a provincial subject and, therefore, the management of almost all types of educational institutions is under the provincial governments. However, the federal government provides much of the development finance, policy formulation, and coordination in education.

3.1.2 Expansion in Education

Substantial expansion has taken place in education in Pakistan in the last three decades in terms of the total number and the range of educational institutions, enrolment, and expenditure by the federal and the provincial governments. Table 3.2 shows the expansion in educational institutions and enrolment at different levels. The total enrolment in the education sector was 9 million in 1979-80 compared to only 1 million in 1949-50. Table 3.3 compares the percentage increase in enrolment and the number of educational institutions.

Government expenditure on education has also increased sharply in the last three decades (Table 3.4). Starting from a very low level of less than 1 per cent of the GNP, the outlay on education increased slowly except in the early seventies when it failed to keep pace with the rise in the GNP in the aftermath of the Bangladesh crisis. As can be seen from the Table, non-development expenditure increased

Table 3.2: Expansion in Education

	Primary schools		Middle schools		High schools		Secondary vocational schools		Arts and Science colleges		Professional colleges		Universities	
	No.	Enrolment (thousand)	No.	Enrolment (thousand)	No.	Enrolment (thousand)	No.	Enrolment (thousand)	No.	Enrolment (thousand)	No.	Enrolment (thousand)	No.	Enrolment (thousand)
1949-50	9,411	920	2,134	250	469	67	59	5	46	21	19	4,925	2	737
1959-60	17,901	1,890	1,974	422	1,069	149	100	13	126	76	40	12,434	4	4,092
1969-70	41,290	3,910	3,560	899	1,995	337	190	29	290	175	59	33,633	7	15,475
1972-3	49,580	4,460	4,406	1,045	2,498	391	391	59	334	186	76	37,596	8	18,678
1975-6	52,800	5,240	4,783	1,237	3,047	491	290	31	404	211	91	56,140	12	22,772
1977-8	53,964	5,455	5,026	1,290	3,258	526	242	33	435	229	95	62,113	14	49,942
1979-80	56,920	5,931	5,290	1,395	3,464	552	248	35	439	241	99	72,479	15	57,019
1981-2	62,579	6,451	6,075	1,492	3,872	588	254	39	442	245	102	82,496	20	

Source: Government of Pakistan, *Pakistan Economic Survey, 1980-1,* Islamabad, p. 235 (Statistical Annexure) for number of educational institutions and p. 236 (Statistical Annexure) for enrolment.

slightly faster than development expenditure.

We should also take a look at the distribution of development and non-development expenditure between various educational levels. Primary education is the cornerstone of the entire system and, for a country with a very high number of illiterates, basic education for a majority of the population should command top priority. As Table 3.5 indicates, primary education has received the highest percentage of expenditure on education but this has not been enough to expand the grass-roots-level education as fast as one would wish. Indeed, in order to achieve universal primary education, for boys by 1982 and girls by 1987, drastic adjustments in the existing educational priorities will be needed. This will reduce the availability of funds for post-primary education the demand for which is rapidly increasing particularly by the urban middle and upper income groups.

The literacy rate, only 3 per cent in 1951,[2] rose to 16.3 per cent (West Pakistan only) for five years of age and above in 1961.[3] According to the 1972 census, literacy had risen to 21.7 per cent and the projection for 1979-80 was 24 per cent.[4]

Efforts have been made to widen the coverage of the educational system in terms of subjects and the medium of communication. Great stress has been laid, particularly during 1977-80, on religious education and the entire structure of education relating to Islam and the *Shariah* has been revitalized and given due recognition and status. Similarly the professional education field has been widened to cover a number of neglected areas like Business Administration, Commerce, Agriculture, and Applied Sciences and Technology. Education through the medium of correspondence, radio, and television has also been given attention. Much greater financial help to students is now available in the form of scholarships and *Qarz-e-Hasna.*

The rapid enlargement of the educational edifice and the commitment of large outlays to this sector has created a number of issues and problems. A certain sense of inadequacy in both efforts and financing still persists. Pakistan's expenditure on education as a percentage of the GNP (Table 3.4) is still below the 1975 ratio of educational outlays to GNP of a number of other developing countries like Indonesia (2.17 per cent), Thailand

Table 3.3: Number of Institutions and Enrolment
Percentage increase (1949-50 to 1979-80)

Level of education	Enrolment	Number of institutions
Primary	614	504
Secondary	472	147
High schools	671	638
Vocational	600	320
Arts and Science colleges	1,047	854
Professional colleges	1,371	421
Universities	3,767	650

Source: Government of Pakistan, *Pakistan Economic Survey, 1980-1,* Islamabad, pp. 235-6.

Table 3.4: Government Expenditure on Education in Relation to GNP

Year	Development expenditure	Non-development expenditure	To	Percentage of GNP
1949-50	NA	NA	43.9	0.2
1959-60	48.0	115.8	163.8	0.97
1964-5	450.9	160.4	290.5	1.11
1969-70	170.1	408.6	578.7	1.33
1972-3	201.3	595.5	1,000.7	1.63
1973-4	340.6	828.7	1,169.3	1.44
1974-5	523.4	1,221.1	1,744.5	1.65
1975-6	751.1	1,731.1	2,488.2	1.99
1976-7	782.3	2,020.3	2,802.6	1.98
1977-8	855.0	2,445.0	3,300.0	1.96
1978-9	1,067.0	2,808.9	3,875.9	2.02
1979-80	1,060.2	3,093.3	4,153.5	1.82

Source: (i) Government of Pakistan, *Pakistan Economic Survey, 1976-7,* Islamabad, p. 179 (Statistical Annexure) for development and non-development expenditure from 1949-50 to 1976-7 and pp. 12-13 (Statistical Annexure), for GNP for the same years. (ii) Government of Pakistan, *Pakistan Basic Facts, 1979-80,* Islamabad, p. 103 for expenditure in 1977-8, 1978-9, and 1979-80. (iii) Government of Pakistan, *Pakistan Economic Survey, 1979-80,* Islamabad, p. 13 (Statistical Annexure), for GNP for 1977-8, 1978-9, and 1979-80.

(2.97 per cent), Burma (3.11 per cent), Sri Lanka (4.90 per cent), and Malaysia (4.99 per cent).[5]

The adult literacy rate in Pakistan (24 per cent) is also much lower than that of the average for low-income countries which is 38 per cent. It also compares unfavourably with Indonesia (62 per cent), Thailand (84 per cent), Burma (67 per cent), Sri Lanka (78 per cent), and Malaysia (60 per cent).[6]

There are disparities in the distribution of educational facilities. The literacy rate for the male population (1972 census) is 30.2 per cent as against only 11.6 per cent for females. (However, the rate of increase in female enrolment in both primary and secondary levels between 1972-3 and 1979-80 is higher than in males-plus-females enrolment.[7] The rate of increase in the output of educated persons between the same years is also higher for females than males-plus-females in matriculation and intermediate).[8] Urban areas have a much higher literacy rate (41.5 per cent) than rural areas (14.3 per cent).[9] About 60 per cent of all primary schools have accomodation which is below minimum requirements and a large number of schools have no accomodation and function in the 'open air'.[10]

3.1.3 Participation Rate

The enormity of the task of achieving universal education, even at the primary level alone, can be judged by the low participation rate in spite of the rapid expansion in the educational structure. Only 53 per cent of the primary-age-group children (five to nine years) were in schools in 1978[11] compared to 46 per cent in 1970 (West Pakistan)[12] and 36 per cent in 1960.[13] At the secondary level only 15 per cent of the age-group ten to fourteen years are in schools[14] which is almost the same as in 1960 in West Pakistan.[15] Enrolment at the college and the university levels in 1978 was only 8 per cent and 2 per cent of the fifteen to nineteen and twenty to twenty-four years age-group respectively.[16]

3.1.4 Drop-outs

The drop-out rate is also very high as shown by the number of school-leavers at each stage of education and also the high percentages of failures in various public examinations. A study in the early sixties of the retention and wastage ratios in classes I to V between 1962-3 and 1966-7 in West Pakistan by comparing enrolment in class I in 1962-3 and class V in 1966-7 showed a drop-out percentage of 50.62 for all students (49.88 per cent for males and 53.32 per cent for females).[17] The drop-out rate in 1977-8 for class I only was about 50 per cent.[18] More than 6 per cent of the students fail at the secondary and other levels of education.[19]

A number of reasons have been advanced

Table 3.5 Government Development and non-Development Expenditure on Education by Levels (Percentage)

Year	Primary	Secondary	College	University	Technical	Teacher	Miscellaneous
1949-50	47.3	21.8	1	14.8	2	2.9	13.2
1959-60	36.7	21.0	13.0	9.2	negligible	4.3	15.8
1964-5	30.3	14.0	7.3	10.6	10.3	2.3	25.2
1969-70	34.0	15.8	8.5	7.7	8.0	2.8	23.2
1972-3	31.5	11.3	8.5	8.0	7.9	1.5	31.3
1975-6	30.8	17.3	10.0	7.0	13.1	1.5	20.3
1976-7	30.4	20.6	9.8	7.5	12.4	1.5	17.6
1979-80	38.6	19.7	9.3	10.2	12.4	1.7	8.1

1. Included under University.
2. Included under Teacher Education.
Source: Government of Pakistan, *Pakistan Basic Facts, 1979-80*, Islamabad, p. 103 for 1979-80 and *Pakistan Economic Survey, 1976-7*, Islamabad, p. 179 (Statistical Annexure) for the rest.

for this high drop-out rate. An ILO-UNDP report cites 'the opportunity cost of child labour, negative attitude towards female education, and a general lack of demand for education' as reasons for the high drop-out rates in schools.[20] This can also be partly explained by the perceived quality of education and its relevance to future employment possibilities.

At higher levels, low pass-percentages for various examinations indicate the number of discards at each stage of education. In 1974-5 the pass percentage for all universities was 48.29 for B.A., and 67.3 for M.A.,[21] compared to 31.6 per cent in 1949, 42.8 per cent in 1959-60, and 47.3 per cent in 1966-7.[22]

According to the Planning Commission, the total intake of students during 1963-77 for the different departments of M.Sc., Engineering in Pakistan was 924 of whom only 64 (7 per cent) completed the courses.[23] Out of 142,100 students, who matriculated in 1977, only 72,000 (50 per cent) could get through the intermediate examination in 1979.[24] The low participation rate and high drop-out rates are both indications of the unfavourable social environment on one hand and the internal inefficiency of the education system on the other.

3.1.5 Education, Employment, and Equity

Before Independence, the main objectives of the education system as designed by the British were to train sufficient numbers of lower level government employees and to shape the mores and attitudes of the future elite by westernizing their cultural pattern. These objectives were well served by separating local-language-medium schools for the masses from exclusive English-medium educational institutions for the elite and by a disproportionate emphasis on a liberal arts education. After Independence, compulsions of economic and social development have changed the pattern of employment opportunities available in the country. The economy's requirements for a large variety of skills and knowledge at various levels are continuously rising. At the same time, attainment of greater equity in income and access to income-earning opportunities are now major social goals. How does our education system fare on the counts of employment and equity?

There is a 'mis-match' between the output of the education sector and the demand pattern in the labour market. This is indicated by the shortages of certain essential skills, particularly at the intermediate level, and the high rates of educated unemployed.

Table 3.6: Percentages of Enrolment in different Streams at Intermediate, Degree, and Post-graduate levels in General Colleges and Universities

		Streams							
Level	Sex	Arts	Science	Commerce	Agriculture*	Home Ecos.	Education	Law and others	Total
Intermediate	M	46	43	9	1	—	1	—	100
	F	72	24	—	—	3	1	—	100
	T	53	38	6	1	1	1	—	100
Degree	M	51	27	22	—	—	—	—	100
	F	80	16	—	—	4	—	—	100
	T	60	24	15	—	1	—	—	100
Post-graduate	M	22	20	2	—	—	16	40	100
	F	43	21	—	—	—	29	7	100
	T	27	20	1	—	—	19	33	100

*Agriculture is taught in general colleges, up to Intermediate level.
Source: Government of Pakistan, *Fifth Five Year Plan*, Islamabad, p. 326.

According to the *Labour Force Survey 1974-5,* unemployment among matriculates and above was 5.05 per cent as against 3.01 per cent among 'primary but less than matriculate', 1.07 per cent among 'incomplete primary', and 1.13 per cent among the uneducated.[25] The domination of the liberal arts still continues. The share of arts students in the total enrolment at the post-graduate level actually increased from 66.1 per cent in 1960 to 71.7 per cent in 1973.[26] Table 3.5 shows enrolment in different streams of education in 1977-8 (this data is not comparable to that given above due to the differences in classification).

Attempts have been made to correct these imbalances by shifting enrolments from arts to science and job-related subjects at higher levels and by introducing agro-technical courses at the secondary level. However, the imbalance is likely to persist in the foreseeable future. Even if the Fifth Plan targets are fully achieved, the enrolment pattern in the eighties will be : Arts : 45 per cent; Science : 41 per cent; job-related subjects : 14 per cent.[27] Moreover, in science and job-related subjects like commerce, medicine, engineering, and technology, as well as in certain specialized arts subjects, the courses are not always tailored to job needs. This can be ensured by associating major potential employers with curriculum development.

It should also be realized that a vast majority of the students seek education for the sake of career-building. If education is unrelated to this aim it is likely to command neither their attention nor respect for the process of learning. In the long run, education needs to be closely tied to manpower planning so that the demand for and the supply of various skills and specializations at various levels can be balanced. If this happens and the education sector begins to produce skills in proportion to job opportunities, this can also settle the old debate of 'quality' vs., 'quantity' in education; the market demands both and the trade-off between them can be determined by the market's capabilities to absorb them.

The question of equity is also linked with that of employment. Since facilities for education in job-related subject areas are limited relative to demand, such jobs command high scarcity rents and the competition for access to such opportunities is likely to be stiff. This puts the lower income groups at a disadvantage forcing them to move to subjects whose employment potential is lower. High rates of failures, repeaters, and drop-outs also have a regressive-income-distribution effect since their incidence is higher among lower income groups.[28]

The existence of elite English-medium schools side by side with national and regional-languages-medium schools also creates equity problems. Since command over the English language is still an asset in getting prized government and non-government jobs,[29] entry to such jobs becomes restricted to those lucky enough to have access to the limited seats in English-medium schools. It is interesting to note that these schools were not nationalized in 1972.

Education is highly subsidized. Government-borne cost per student is much higher at higher levels of education. Although a subsidy exists at all levels, greater benefit accrues to income groups who have greater access to higher education. Table 3.7 shows

Table 3.7: Unit Cost at Different levels of Education (Fifth Plan estimates) (Rs)

Level of Education	Developmental	Recurring	Annual total
Primary			
Squatting	110	150	260
Children using furniture	160	150	310
Secondary	650	400	1,050
College			
Intermediate level	1,275	1,000	2,275
Degree level	1,700	1,200	2,900
Technical			
Diploma level	5,000	2,000	7,000
Degree level	12,000	5,000	17,000
University	10,200	5,000	15,200

Source: Government of Pakistan, *Fifth Five Year Plan*, Islamabad, p. 301.

estimates of unit cost at different levels of education made for the Fifth Plan.

Even the scholarship programme which provided over Rs 60 million in 1979-80 may not have a net progressive effect on income distribution since most of these scholarships are awarded on the basis of merit and not parental income.

3.1.6 Conclusion

Education represents the hopes and aspirations of individuals but it is also a powerful instrument for the resuscitation of the religious and cultural heritage as a binding force for the nation. The task of revitalizing education, therefore, is not limited to financial allocations and a linear expansion of the system, important as these are. Beyond these relatively easier tasks lie such challenges as improving the educational standards, management and administrative efficiency, greater research efforts and the ensuring of a healthy environment around educational campuses and compounds by offering attractive service conditions to the teaching community, strengthening the examination system, streamlining the administrative structure and making educational curricula meaningful and worthwhile to pursue. Success in this sector will also be measured in terms of the ability of the system to ensure access to education, especially higher education, to lower income groups, the rural population, and women. Education is a critical equalizing force but it can also act as a disequalizer if not handled with sound judgement. The inequities created by one generation through the mal-distribution of educational opportunities may last for many generations to come.

3.2 Health

The health status of the people depends upon a number of factors which include, besides the nature and the quality of the available health services, income level, nutrition, sanitation, housing, drinking water, and other environmental variables. Thus it is not surprising to find that the existing health conditions in Pakistan are generally unsatisfactory and that the health services are quite inadequate and unevenly distributed. At the same time organizational efforts and a consistent increase in expenditure on the health sector continue and the improvement shown in various health indicators like the death rate, infant mortality rate, and control of certain diseases is quite notable.

The development of health services in Pakistan dates back to very early times as evidenced by the still popular indigenous medical system. Western medicine introduced by the British did not entirely replace the traditional system since it was confined to urban centres and principally to caring for government servants and their dependents. Gradually the western (Allopathic) system was expanded to provide some cover to the general population by means of hospitals and dispensaries established by the provincial governments and local bodies.

3.2.1 Expansion in Health Facilities

There has been considerable expansion in both the physical infrastructure of health facilities and the output of health personnel (Table 3.8). Government development and non-development expenditure on health has also increased steadily although the total expenditure of the federal and the provincial governments has remained below 1 per cent of the GNP and has moved within a range of 0.35 to 0.79 per cent (Table 3.9).

The impact of such efforts is evident through changes in certain health variables. The average life expectancy at birth, which was forty-seven years for males and forty-five years for females in 1962-5, had gone up to fifty-three for males and fifty-two for females in 1978.[30] This compares favourably with the average in thirty-eight low-income countries which is fifty (average age for both males and females).[31] The average life expectancy for certain individual countries in 1976 was fifty-one years in India, fifty-two in Iran, sixty-one in Turkey, sixty-nine in Sri Lanka, and seventy-two in People's Republic of China.[32] The infant mortality rate had declined substantially from 235 per thousand in 1947[33] to 105 in 1978.[34] The crude death rate had also fallen from thirty per thousand in 1950 to fourteen in 1978.[35]

3.2.2 Some Issues in the Health Sector

The most common complaint regarding our health system is that the availability of its services is erratic particularly in the more remote areas because of the unreliable delivery of medicines and a shortage of equipment and personnel. This causes frustration among the population and lowers their estimation of the overall quality of the health cover. As the Fifth Five Year Plan points out, funds for meeting recurring expenditures are insufficient. In many cases the infrastructure is available but it cannot be utilized in full due to the shortage of funds for personnel, drugs, and maintenance.[36]

The reason is that while infrastructure, in the form of buildings and durable equipment, is regarded as development expenditure for which funds are more easily available and not subjected to much public scrutiny, maintenance and other recurring items are classified as non-development expenditures. Because of the general criticism of non-development expenditures, departments are under pressure to reduce them. The squeeze on non-development expenditures can be judged from the fact that the ratio between development and non-development expenditures declined

Table 3.9: Federal and Provincial Government Expenditures on Health
(Rs million)

Year	Development expenditure	Non-Development expenditure	Total	Total expenditure/GNP
1960-1	8.70	57.00	65.70	0.35
1964-5	75.22	78.00	153.22	0.58
1969-70	67.99	128.00	195.99	0.45
1972-3	95.55	171.90	267.45	0.43
1973-4	157.67	210.10	367.77	0.45
1974-5	309.00	278.00	587.00	0.55
1975-6	629.09	360.64	989.73	0.79
1976-7	590.80	439.20	1,030.00	0.69
1977-8	684.34	558.60	1,242.94	0.73
1978-9	647.50	641.59	1,289.09	0.67
1979-80	683.45	661.89	1,345.34	0.59

Source: Government of Pakistan, *Pakistan Basic Facts, 1979-80*, Islamabad, p. 111 for expenditures and pp.19-20 for GNP.

Table 3.8: Expansion in Health Facilities

Year	Hospitals	Dispensaries	Mother and child health centres	Beds in hospitals/ dispensaries	Registered doctors[2]	Registered nurses	Registered lady health visitors
1949	301	769	102	14,180	1,912	214	7
1950	304	807	107	14,524	2,298	418	76
1955	333	964	198	19,197	3,923	963	142
1960	343	1,195	358	22,100	6,458	1,929	230
1965	383	1,695	554	25,603	10,082	2,945	627
1970	495	2,136	668	34,001	14,109	4,543	1,169
1975	525	3,061	715	37,776	17,887	6,144	1,636
1976	525	3,063	715	38,775	18,757	6,685	1,688
1977	528	3,220	726	40,518	19,863	7,186	1,738
1978	536	3,306	748	42,469	20,931	7,768	1,823
1979	550	3,367[1]	772	44,367	21,938	8,382	1,921

1. Does not include 211 rural health centres and 645 sub-health centres.
2. Does not include dentists (829).
Source: Government of Pakistan, *Pakistan Basic Facts, 1979-80*, Islamabad, 1980, p.107.

from 1:6.5 in 1960-1 to 1:1.8 in 1969-70 and 1 0.9 in 1979-80.[37]

The rural population has traditionally received far fewer health facilities than their urban brethren because of the problems of transportation, logistics, and personnel support mainly due to the reluctance of doctors, nurses, and other medical workers to work in the villages and also the low percentage of funds allocated to the rural sector.

The result is that the health facilities, already inadequate for the country as a whole, are also unequally distributed. Only 19 per cent of the total number of hospital beds are in the rural areas.[38] Only 32 per cent of the rural population lives within a two-mile radius of health facilities and 78 per cent within a five-mile radius as against almost 100 per cent in the case of the urban population.[39]

There is a similar imbalance between preventive and curative health measures. In developing countries in general there has been an over-emphasis on sophisticated hospital-based care while neglecting preventive public health programmes and simple primary care at conveniently located facilities. This can be attributed to (a) the professional bias of physicians; (b) the mystique and popular appeal of hospital-based medical care; and (c) the influence of urban-based policy-makers who have already achieved adequate nutrition and sanitation and whose needs now are for sophisticated curative care.[40]

There is, of course, a tendency among the people to neglect preventive measures like hygiene and sanitation and to seek medical care only in cases of illness. But the health authorities have only ratified this practice by giving low priority to preventive measures. During 1970-8 preventive programmes were allocated 40 per cent of the total health outlay but during the Fifth Five Year Plan period this percentage will decline quite rapidly to 8.4.[41] Part of the preventive work will be transferred to the Rural Health Programmes. But even this programme will be receiving only 39 per cent of the total outlay.

In the *Population Growth Survey (1971)* it was found that the major causes of deaths in Pakistan are infective and parasitic diseases, which accounted for about 64 per cent of deaths, followed by malaria which was responsible for over 10 per cent of the deaths. These two causes of death can be effectively tackled by preventive programmes but, in spite of this, such programmes have not been pursued with much vigour. The result is that our entire health policy is dependent upon the availability of doctors instead of the team work of doctors, para medical staff, and community health workers.[42] Our present medical education is also heavily biased in favour of the curative approach and the doctors trained at great expense are capable of practicing only in hospital settings. It is time to take stock of the entire health effort and the curative and preventive programmes in relation to their cost-effectiveness.

Another serious problem in Pakistan is the imbalance between the number of doctors and the size of the para-medical staff. Ideally the doctors/para-medical staff ratio should be 5:1 but in Pakistan the ratio is 1:2 (1977-8).[43] It is noteworthy that even in industrialized countries there is a strong tendency towards a greater emphasis on para-medical workers in order to improve the spread and effectiveness of basic health care and to help keep costs down. The proposal to expand the role of para medics in providing primary care under the Rural Health Programmes is a step in the right direction. However, greater effort is needed to train more ancillary staff so that in the urban areas also the para-medical workers are able to supplement the overall health effort in a more effective way. The indigenous medical system can also be encouraged in order to provide greater medical cover without much extra expenditure.

3.3 Housing

Housing in Pakistan presents a fairly grim picture in both the urban and rural sectors. The urban population in Pakistan is growing at an average annual rate of 4.4 per cent[44] including the annual inflow of about 300,000 people from the villages. Consequently slums, shanty towns, and *katchi abadies* are mushrooming in all big cities. By the year 2,000 about 50 per cent of the total population, i.e., about 60 million, will be living in the cities.[45]

It is estimated that there is at present a shortage of 1 million houses in urban areas.[46] In addition 116,000 houses will be needed to accomodate the additional number of households created every year. In the rural areas, where the housing problem is more of a qualitative nature, 173,000 new housing units will be needed for the additional population.[47] However, the actual construction of houses lags behind. During 1970-8 the rate of house construction was slightly over 3,300 per year.[48] Most of this effort has taken place in the private sector through individual house owners and, for the last few years, private construction companies. The government has restricted itself to the survey, planning, and design of sites and services. The funds for house construction come mainly from private savings and are supplemented by institutional finance which is available in the form of loans from the House Building Finance Corporation. Commercial banks too provided loans for the construction of houses but the State Bank of Pakistan banned these advances in 1980.

The public and semi-public sectors developed 16,500 urban residential plots during 1970-8 whereas the private sector developed 35,000 plots. In the construction of houses, the private sector's share was 243,500 as against the public sector's share of only 21,500.[49] Since there were no restrictions on the size of the plots or on construction standards, most of the construction was in the form of luxury houses.

The fifties and the sixties were marked by generally ineffective planning: there was hardly any institutional structure to formulate effective programmes and to ensure their implementation. The First Plan, for example, stressed the 'undesirability of committing resource to non-essential public buildings or costly high-income projects'.[50]

But the policies contained in the First Plan were not adhered to and the programmes were not completed. Large amounts of public funds were invested in self-paying schemes of industrial, commercial, and high-income residential areas where private capital should have been encouraged. While targets in government buildings and other sub-sectors were surpassed, there was a shortfall in low-cost housing. The planning effort itself was lacking in a well defined co-ordinated approach and was mostly project-oriented.[51]

The growth in housing and related facilities could not keep pace with economic growth and the enlargement of urban centres. The lack of resources, ineffective control, overcrowding, and incapability to provide essential services resulted in a deterioration in the living conditions. This found its ugly manifestation in the emergence of slums and *katchi abadies* in the form of unauthorized occupation of vacant government or private lands. The magnitude of the problem of *katchi abadies* can be judged from the fact that, according to the Dutch Advisory Mission on slum improvement in Karachi, about one-third of the total population of Karachi lived in slums. There were 312 *katchi abadies* whose areas were constantly expanding.[52]

Some of the main trends in the housing sector during the seventies were renewed government efforts to improve the institutional structure for policy formulation and implementation, incentives for the private sector in house construction, the regulation of *katchi abadies*, the construction boom, and rise in land prices.

During the seventies the Federal Ministry of Works, Housing, Environment, and Urban Affairs was established for formulating policies at the national level. In the provinces, Housing and Physical Planning Departments were established. Development Authorities were also established in almost all major cities in the country and arrangements were made for research and experimentation in housing.[53]

A number of tax concessions, including income-tax rebates, were given on low-income housing. Loans for the construction of houses from the House Building Finance Corporation increased fifty times between 1970-1 and 1977-8.[54] Commercial Banks also participated in financing construction in the seventies but this practice was stopped in 1980.

An attempt has been made to regularize the *katchi abadies* by conferring ownership rights on the occupation of state land on payment of concessional prices. But *katchi abadies* continue to grow in spite of government efforts to discourage this trend.

Throughout the seventies, rising activities in construction and a continuous increase in land prices in urban areas were witnessed. After nationalization of many industries in the early seventies, when private investment declined sharply, private capital was spent mostly on the purchase of residential and commercial plots partly as a hedge against inflation. Even the local development authorities at times tended to follow this trend. There were complaints about the exorbitant prices charged by some development authorities for land and also about the practice of developing/auctioning plots in small lots which tended to raise their prices which in turn became the floor prices for land.[55]

The trend towards higher prices of land was further encouraged by large remittances from abroad a substantial part of which was spent on the purchase of land and on construction. High profits in trading also led to the construction of shopping plazas in big cities. A number of private construction companies have entered the field and are in fact encouraged by the government. The local development authorities are expected to regularize the private construction industry. However, the large number of unapproved residential colonies in Lahore and Karachi show that there are problems in performing these functions.

Thus housing in Pakistan is deficient in terms of both quantity and quality and for the time being at least the government is banking upon the private sector to improve the situation as far as possible within the available resources.

3.4 Drinking Water, Sanitation, and Sewerage

The quality of life also depends upon access to safe drinking water, waste disposal, and general sanitation. In Pakistan, in both urban and rural areas, there are serious deficiencies in such facilities. Access to safe drinking water is available to only 26.8 per cent of the total population. But most of these facilities are concentrated in urban areas where 61.1 per cent of the population is covered while in the rural areas safe water supply is available to only 13.9 per cent of the population.[56] Very few villages have a good water supply system. In most of the villages drinking water is drawn from wells which are far from sanitary. In others the ground water is brackish, or saline, and the villagers drink polluted canal water. In many other villages rain water is collected in earthen pots which is shared by animals and human beings. It was expected that by 1982-3, 49.2 per cent of the total population will have safe drinking water. The targets for the urban and rural areas were 81.4 and 35.7 per cent of the population respectively.[57]

As for sanitation and sewerage, only 9.7 per cent of the total population have these facilities but these are concentrated almost entirely in the urban sector where the coverage is 34.7 per cent of the population as against only 0.2 per cent for the rural areas. The Fifth Five Year Plan expected that by 1983 sewerage and drainage will be available to 17.4 per cent of the total population. The target for the urban population was 50.8 per cent but for the rural areas only 3.49 per cent.[58]

In the Fifth Five Year Plan allocations have been made for various sub-sectors within physical planning and housing. However, it is probably the fulfilment of the targets which will reflect reality better. In 1979-80 target-fulfilment was higher for such sub-sectors as urban water supply (109.6 per cent), government offices (80.9 per cent), government servants' housing (82.7 per cent), private sector housing (90 per cent), and urban residential plots (85.1 per cent). But achievements were low in rural sanitation (43.8 per cent), rural water supply (36.6 per cent), and urban sewerage and drainage (34.8 per cent).[59]

3.5 Nutrition

Nutrition is an important development concern. It is closely related to the improvement of health standards and it can in fact be regarded as a major preventive measure since a high nutrition level enables people to resist diseases. Nutritional deficiencies are usually caused by under-nourishment which in turn is caused by low family-income, ignorance of good nutrition practices, and unequal distribution of food within the family. Such deficiencies are also the result of imbalances between the intake of calories and proteins. According to the Fifth Five Year Plan, in 1977-8 consumption on the average was 2,381 calorie per capita in Pakistan which is a little higher than the daily energy requirements of 2,354 calories per capita. Similarly the protein intake in 1977-8 was 63.2 grams per head per day whereas the required intake is 42.3 grams.

The main problem, however, is one of distribution between various income levels and within households. According to the *National Micro-Nutrient Survey (1976-7)*, 56.7 per cent of children below five years had low weight in relation to their age due to nutrition deficiencies. The haemoglobin test indicated that 59.3 per cent of the total population had an adequate level while 24.5 per cent were marginal cases and 16.2 per cent were deficient.[60] As Burki[61] points out, the poorest sections of the population—who spend the highest proportions of their income on food—are the worst sufferers. Active nutrition intervention will require, besides raising the incomes of the very poor, measures like the development of low-cost nutrient food, strengthening the nutrition component in the health services network, and adding micro-nutrients to food at the processing stage.

3.6 Conclusion

The level and quality of social services in a poor society is limited by the state of its underdevelopment. Inadequacy in the social sector is only an index of poverty and a reflection of existing realities. However, as economic growth takes place and production and resources grow, social services also need to be enlarged in scope and size. With industrialization, urbanization, and expansion in the range of economic activities, the society's need for education, health, housing, etc., undergoes both qualitative and quantitative changes. But development does not automatically convert itself into the felt needs in the social sphere. Herein lies the role of social policy and the challenge to policy-makers in its different segments.

It is, therefore, unfair to evaluate social policy in a developing society in terms of the adequacy of social services. The intrinsic worth of social policy lies in : (a) ensuring due share for the social sector in resource allocations in accordance with the growth in available resources; (b) maintaining the quality of service in education, health, housing, and other sub-sectors while these services are fast expanding; and (c) imparting sufficient flexibility in social programmes so that adjustments can be made in response to changes in the requirements and demands of the society.

NOTES

1. World Bank, *World Development Report, 1980*, p. 46.
2. Hafiz Pasha, Kathryn Hyer, and Rabia Arshad, 'Education and Employment in Pakistan', in *Em-*

ployment Planning and Basic Needs in Pakistan*, ILO and Pakistan Manpower Institute, Islamabad, 1978, p. 241.
3. Institute of Education and Research, Punjab University, *Statistical Profile of Education in West Pakistan*, National Commission on Manpower and Education Research Study No. 14, 1971, p. 257.
4. Government of Pakistan, *Pakistan Economic Survey, 1980-1*, Islamabad, p. 197.
5. Zymelman, *Patterns of Education Expenditures*, World Bank Staff Working Paper No. 246, 1976.
6. World Bank, *World Development Report, 1980*, pp. 154-5.
7. Government of Pakistan, *Pakistan Economic Survey, 1980-1*, Islamabad, Table 13.2, p. 236.
8. Ibid., Table 13.3, p. 237.
9. Ibid., p. 197.
10. Government of Pakistan, *Fifth Five Year Plan*, Islamabad, p. 299.
11. Government of Pakistan, *National Education Policy*, 1978, Islamabad, p. ii.
12. Government of Pakistan, *Fourth Five Year Plan*, Islamabad, p. 145.
13. Government of Pakistan, *Second Five Year Plan*, Islamabad, p. 341.
14. Government of Pakistan, *National Education Policy*, 1978, Islamabad, p. iii.
15. Government of Pakistan, *Second Five Year Plan*, Islamabad, p. 343.
16. Government of Pakistan, *National Education Policy*, Islamabad, 1978, p. iii.
17. Institute of Education and Research, Punjab University, *Statistical Profile of Education in West Pakistan*, p. 16.
18. Government of Pakistan, *Fifth Five Year Plan*, Islamabad, p. 299.
19. Government of Pakistan, *National Education Policy*, Islamabad, 1978, p. iii.
20. Hafiz Pasha, *et al.*, 'Education and Employment in Pakistan', in *Employment Planning and Basic Needs in Pakistan*, ILO and Pakistan Manpower Institute, Islamabad, 1978, p. 242.
21. Government of Pakistan, University Grants Commission, *Statistics on Higher Education in Pakistan*, Islamabad, 1978, p. 189.
22. Government of Pakistan, *Twenty-five Years of Pakistan in Statistics, 1947-72*, Islamabad, 1972, p. 242.
23. Government of Pakistan, *Fifth Five Year Plan*, Islamabad, p. 321.
24. Government of Pakistan, *Pakistan Economic Survey, 1979-80*, Islamabad, p. 225, Statistical Annexure, (calculated).
25. Hafiz Pasha, *et al*, 'Education and Employment in Pakistan', in *Employment Planning and Basic Needs in Pakistan*, ILO and Pakistan Manpower Institute, Islamabad, 1978, p. 262.
26. Ibid., p. 257.
27. Government of Pakistan, *Fifth Five Year Plan*, Islamabad, p. 329.
28. World Bank, *Education Sector Policy Paper*, 1980, p. 31.
29. For example, the Central Superior Services examination and interviews are still conducted in English.
30. Government of Pakistan, *Fifth Five Year Plan*, Islamabad, p. 346.
31. World Bank, *World Development Report, 1980*, p. 150.
32. World Bank, *Sector Policy Paper on Health*, 1980, pp. 67-9.
33. Government of Pakistan, *Pakistan Economic Survey, 1976-7*, Islamabad, p. 212.
34. Government of Pakistan, *Fifth Five Year Plan*, Islamabad, p. 363.
35. Ibid., p. 346.
36. Ibid., p. 363.
37. Government of Pakistan, *Pakistan Basic Facts, 1979-80*, Islamabad, p. 111.
38. Government of Pakistan, *Fifth Five Year Plan*, Islamabad, p. 361.
39. Ibid., p. 359.
40. World Bank, *Sector Policy on Health*, 1980, p. 40.
41. Government of Pakistan, *Fifth Five Year Plan*, Islamabad, p. 368.
42. Ibid., p. 365.
43. Ibid., p. 364.
44. Ibid., p. 275.
45. Ibid., p. 272.
46. Ibid., p. 271.
47. Ibid., p. 275.
48. Ibid., p. 270.
49. Ibid., pp. 269-70.
50. Planning Commission, Government of Pakistan, *Physical Planning and Housing—Fifteen Years of Planned Development*, Islamabad, 1965, p. 40.
51. Ibid., p. 43.
52. *Editorial* in daily *Dawn*, Karachi, dated 1 February 1979.
53. Government of Pakistan, *Fifth Five Year Plan*, Islamabad, p. 270.
54. Ibid., p. 271.
55. Mian Anwer Ali, article in *Pakistan Times*, Lahore, dated 1 December 1978.
56. Government of Pakistan, *Fifth Five Year Plan*, Islamabad, p. 693.
57. Ibid., p. 693.
58. Ibid., p. 693.
59. Government of Pakistan, *Pakistan Basic Facts, 1979-80*, Islamabad, p. 123.
60. Government of Pakistan, *Fifth Five Year Plan*, Part I, Islamabad, p. 23.
61. Burki, 'Meeting Basic Needs in Mixed Economies', in Qureshi and Arif, (eds.): *Strategies of Planning and Development*, Planning and Development Board, Punjab, 1980, p. 323.

PART II

ECONOMIC DECISION-MAKING IN A HISTORICAL PERSPECTIVE

4 | Economic Decision-Making

There remains an important gap between what actually happened to Pakistan's economy over the last thirty-five years and possible explanations of why it happened. This is to identify the process of economic decision-making in a country like Pakistan. By this we mean not simply the formal decision-making machinery of the government (although this in itself is important and will be discussed in detail) but starting from a description of the kinds of economic decisions that have to be taken, mainly by the state authorities, we must look at the different forces, domestic and foreign, which can influence the decision-making process. If we can identify, to the extent possible, the various forces which play an important role in the country's decision-making process then at least we have a basis on which to interpret the possible reasons why these decisions were taken.

Therefore this chapter on economic decision-making in Pakistan is not just a formal description of the planning machinery's evolution over time or a discussion of the different ways and means by which the government tries to influence resource allocation in the economy. It takes a much broader frame for the simple reason that to assume that all economic decisions taken by the government just flow out of the country's planning machinery, based on some 'rational' economic criteria, is not only untrue but naive and misleading. To take but a simple example: foreign loans play a very vital role in determining the size of the country's investment programme and those who supply the loans attach certain conditions before they agree to sanction them. The extent of the interference or influence the foreign loan-giving agency or government will exert will depend on a host of factors including the political and economic strength of the government at that moment in time and the size of the loan. There could be hard bargaining as regards the use of the loan and economic and administrative pre-conditions which must be met before it is sanctioned. But the fact remains that the decision finally taken is influenced in this case by those who are not part of the country's formal planning machinery.

Our aim in this chapter is three-fold. The first is to see what are the different kinds of economic decisions that have to be taken in a mixed economy like Pakistan's and to analyse their characteristics, their time frame, their objectives, and the available means used to achieve them. The second is to attempt to identify the different forces, both domestic and foreign, which can influence the decision-making process. The third is a formal resume of the planning machinery in Pakistan, its evolution over time, its administrative structure, its varying power and influence during different periods, and its biases and leanings as regards the use of market forces over administrative controls in influencing the direction of the economy.

4.1 Economic Decision-Making by the State Authorities

We have divided the different types of decisions which are taken by the state authorities into four main categories, mainly on the basis of the duration or time period of the economic problem or choice with which the decision is concerned. The nature of the decision, the level of state authority which takes it, the objective to be achieved, the nature of the problem to be solved, and the economic means available to solve it are shown in Table 4.1. Below we give a detailed description.

4.1.1 Very Short-Run or Day-to-Day Management of the Economy

Adverse economic conditions, which may prevail in a country at any particular moment of time, can be the result of either any immediate happening (say a physical calamity, for example, floods) or the result of short-term developments (for example, bad weather conditions leading to poor harvests) or the result of long-term developments (for example, no growth in the agricultural sector over a large number of years). Economists have a tendency to ignore day-to-day management as they see it as falling more under the pur-

Table 4.1: Economic Decision-Making by the State Authority
(An illustration of key decisions)

Type of decision	Level of decision-making	Objectives	Means available/ measures taken
1. Very short-run (day-to-day running of the economy)	Local administration Provincial government Central government	i. Provision of essential goods and utilities according to the accepted 'norm' ii. Ensuring immediate relief in physical calamities (for example, floods, rains)	a. Movement of goods from surplus areas b. Emergency imports c. Strong action against black marketing and hoarding
2. Short-run (normally one year)	Provincial government Central government Planning Commission	i. Raising revenues for the functioning of the state machinery ii. Financing of the annual development programme and its implementation iii. Achievements of output targets in major sectors, especially agriculture and industry iv. Price stability v. Foreign trade balance	a. Direct and indirect taxes b. Foreign and domestic borrowing c. Provision of key inputs d. Price incentives e. Commercial policy measures, for example, protection and import controls f. Controlling money-supply and interest rates
3. Medium-term development planning (five year period)	Central government Planning Commission	i. Formulation of Five Year Plan with objectives, strategy, and production targets ii. Overall goal of sustained growth in per capita income, creation of employment opportunities, and self-reliance	a. Fiscal policy b. Monetary policy c. Commercial policy d. Foreign borrowing
4. Structural changes	Central government	i. Equitable distribution of economic assets ii. Strengthening the economic and bargaining conditions of the weaker economic classes and groups iii. Restrictions on monopoly practices interfering with the free functioning of the market economy	a. Land Reform and Tenancy Regulation b. Nationalization c. Trade Union activity and minimum wages

view of 'administrative' action but, in a developing country like Pakistan, it is the day-to-day management of the economy that government agencies give great importance to and, in many instances, it takes priority over almost any other form of planning in the country.

The following reasons are why the state authorities give such a high priority to the day-to-day management of the economy:

a. The per capita consumption level in 'normal' conditions of the most essential commodities for the bulk of the population is at a very low level. Any circumstance which affects this 'norm' adversely can result in a situation in which the bulk of the population finds itself facing severe hardships and in extreme cases near-famine conditions.
b. The people in most cases identify economic hardship as a result of government incompetence even in cases where this might not be so. If essential commodities and the availability of public utilities fall below the accepted 'norm' for any sustained time period it can lead to public disturbances which threaten the credibility of the government in power and, in extreme circumstances, it can lead to a situation where the government finds its very existence threatened.

The government of the day, therefore, closely monitors the availability and prices of essential commodities and services especially in the urban centres where the chances of public disturbances are most likely. These cover the following items:

i) The provision of essential consumptions–items like *atta*, *daals*, meat, cooking oil, sugar, etc. Not only must the government ensure that there is no shortage or disappearance from the market of these commodities but also that there are no sharp increases in prices.
ii) The provision of public utilities like water, electricity, and transport. The lack of public transport facilities, especially in urban areas, has been a major source of public disturbances in Pakistan. Also frequent electricity failures and shortages of drinking water can create serious problems for the administration.

The government's capacity to respond to such situations depends on a number of factors and its capability in meeting the situation will depend on the extent of the shortage, the extent of its awareness of the arising situation, the overall domestic economic conditions, and the external environment for borrowing on an emergency basis.

The measures which the government may take when faced with such a situation can be illustrated by seeing its likely response to a severe shortage of an essential food item like sugar in the market. The steps taken will normally be:

i) If the deficit is limited to a particular region, or province, it will try to rush food supplies from other areas where a surplus exists.
ii) It will take strong measures against those who are hoarding the commodity and accentuating the crisis.
iii) If the shortage is widespread it will undertake imports on an emergency basis.

4.1.2 Short-Run Management

The short-run period, from the viewpoint of economic decision-making by the state authorities, is taken to cover the period of one year. The broad economic objectives are set out in the Annual Budget and the Annual Development Plan. When an overall Five Year Plan is in operation the Annual Plan becomes the instrument for achieving the targets of the Plan and it includes those projects which are within the framework of the Five Year Plan. If, however, the economic conditions have changed drastically, as compared to what was envisaged when the Five Year Plan was formulated, the Annual Plan will take into account these new circumstances and to this extent deviate from the original targets. During periods of considerable uncertainty the Annual Plan becomes the main instrument of development planning in the country.

The short-run management of the economy has the following important objectives:

i) Raising revenues for running the state machinery. The government must generate funds for maintaining the administrative machinery of the state as well as the police and the armed forces. These funds are generated through direct and indirect taxes and revenues from government agencies.
ii) Raising resources to finance the development programmes to be undertaken by the public sector.

After meeting the demands of (i) the government has to see to what extent the surplus from its revenue-raising activities can finance its development programme, to what extent it must borrow from domestic sources and abroad to make up the gap, and to what extent must it go in for deficit financing.

iii) Achieving output levels and growth targets of the major sectors especially in agriculture and industry.

iv) Maintaining stable prices.

v) Keeping the foreign trade balance within manageable levels so that the deficit does not go beyond what is covered from foreign borrowing.

Conflicts in Short-Term Management

The broad objectives of short-term management being given, what is important to understand is that the government can be faced with situations where there is a fundamental conflict between the objectives and that there may be important trade-offs in terms of what course it should opt for. Let us look at these different situations.

i) *The Ideal Situation*

The ideal situation is one when production in the major sectors is growing at a satisfactory pace, there is overall price stability, revenues are sufficient to meet both non-developmental and a large portion of the development expenditure, the environment for foreign borrowing is favourable, both for financing development expenditure and the balance of payments support, and exports are doing well in the world market.

ii) *The Problem Situation*

For a country like Pakistan the state of affairs as presented in the ideal situation are, however, quite rare and far between. In most cases there will be problems in terms of each of the objectives outlined earlier and important decisions will have to be taken as regards the course of action to be followed.

Situation 1: Large increases in non-development expenditure

Suppose that there is a sharp increase in non-development expenditure (say defence) as in the case of the 1965 war or after 1971. The government has a choice between the following measures:

i) To increase revenues mainly through higher indirect taxes. This will mean higher prices especially for essential items.

ii) To cut down development expenditure. This will adversely influence the growth of important sectors directly dependent on development expenditure and also the long-term prospects for economic growth and development.

iii) To go in for deficit financing. This, if the amounts involved are large, would lead to inflationary pressures building upon the economy and could lead to a significant increase in prices after a time lag of between six months to a year.

iv) To increase foreign borrowing. This would further increase the debt burden and the amounts needed for debt repayment.

The government's decision will depend on a number of factors. If it is politically in a strong position it could opt for (i). In most cases the easier option is (iii) or (iv) or a combination of the two. In this case the government avoids taking an unpopular step and allows the adverse reaction of its action to be postponed till the future. In certain cases the government may opt for (ii) but governments tend to avoid this course of action not only as the capacity to spend is a power which they enjoy and they would be hard pressed to give it up but also for its adverse impact on future growth and development.

Situation 2: An increase in import prices

Let us consider the case where the government finds a sharp increase in the prices of certain essential imported commodities (for example, petroleum related products). The government has the following options:

i) To pass on these prices directly to the consumer This could lead to a sharp rise in the cost of living index.

ii) To absorb the increase in prices through subsidies and bear the cost of the difference between the market price and the import price. This would increase its non-development expenditure and further pose the problems discussed in Situation 1.

iii) To increase foreign borrowing to pay for the higher import bill if there has been no corresponding increase in exports or foreign remittances.

iv) To opt for (i) but to increase the wages of low paid employees so as to protect them from the effects of inflation.

If the government finds that the situation it faces is one in which there is already considerable inflation it would opt for (ii). However, it could compound the situation by not cutting down its non-development expenditure and resorting to deficit financing, thus in fact increasing the inflationary pressures on the economy. However, if the amount required to pay for the subsidy continues to increase, the government will have little option but to pass on the higher prices, i.e., alternative (i), and then try to make the situation bearable for the lower income groups by also increasing wages, i.e., (iv). However, to the extent that the increase in wages will mainly affect government employees and those working in the organized sector and that higher wages would lead to a further increase in prices, those employed in the non-organized sector could find themselves being subject to an even greater fall in their standard of living.

Situation 3: The pricing of agricultural commodities

One of the most important decisions which the government has to take is in regard to the prices of agricultural commodities which are to be paid to the farmers especially in a situation where the prices of inputs have been rising substantially thereby increasing the costs of agricultural production.

i) If agricultural output is increasing because of an increase in the productivity of certain crops then the government may allow the higher prices of inputs to be borne by the farmers, since the increases in output will lead to an increase in incomes, and therefore the government might not substantially alter the purchase price of the agricultural commodity.
ii) If production is not increasing then the government will be under considerable pressure to increase prices to compensate the farmers for the increases in input costs. The extent to which the government will do this will depend on the impact of the increase on the general price level and the cost of living index. It will then be faced with alternatives regarding subsidies as discussed in Situation 2.
iii) When agricultural production is stagnating, or even declining, the government in some cases may be compelled to increase the prices of the affected agricultural commodities so as to stimulate production.

Situation 4: The balance of payments problems

In certain situations the government can find itself in a severe adverse balance of payments situation with the import bill increasing drastically and exports either stagnating or increasing at a very slow pace. The government can then take the following measures:

i) Introduce stringent import controls. This could mean banning the import of certain luxury items and cutting down drastically on the import of other items. This could adversely influence domestic production, especially for those sectors heavily dependent on imported raw materials for inputs. The effect could be a decline in production and an increase in prices.
ii) Borrow from foreign donors or international agencies (for example IMF) on an emergency basis. This could mean enforcing policies such as devaluation, stringent monetary policies, and cutting down on non-development expenditures which are put as preconditions for the grant of the loan.
iii) Try to increase export earnings even if it means at times subsidizing the cost of the exports so as to increase foreign exchange earnings. This, in certain cases, could lead to domestic shortages if the output of these goods is inelastic and goods are increasingly being diverted from the domestic to the foreign market.

Since the effect of alternative (iii), even if successful, would take time to materialize, the choice falls between (i) and (ii). The extent to which the government will follow option (i) or (ii) or a combination of the two will depend on it being able to find short-term donors (for example, OPEC countries) and the pre-conditions for the grant of the loan, otherwise an extreme form of (i) would have to be introduced.

Situation 5: A crisis situation

The government can at times find itself in a crisis situation when a combination of factors can threaten the basic structure of the economy. One particular form of this crisis could be that prices are rising because of domestic and external factors, production in key sectors is stagnating, there is a severe balance of payments crisis, there are large increases in non-development expenditures, and the external environment is not conducive to foreign borrowing. Such a crisis situation, for example, existed in the country during the period of the civil war, in what was then known as East Pakistan, in 1971. To try to resolve such a crisis situation the government normally gives first priority to reviving production in key sectors even if it means higher prices and soaring inflation; the second priority is the balance of payments situation and in some extreme cases the government can find itself with no other alternative except to devalue its currency, again putting further pressure on prices. The situation and measures taken by the People's Party government during 1972 could be taken as an example of trying to resolve a crisis situation confronting the economy at that time.[1]

'Economic' Bases for Decision-Making

While the above discussion of different situations which a government can be faced with, and its possible set of responses to them in short-term management, is meant mainly to illustrate the forces and pressures which influence decision-making, the question must also be asked as to what in the circumstances would be 'correct' decisions from the point of view of 'efficient' economic management. Or, to pose the question differently, how can an economist help the government in deciding what course of action it should take even though the final decision that is taken may well turn out to reflect not the viewpoint of the economist but other forces and pressures which the government is subjected to and must follow.

The answers in many cases are not as simple and straightforward as economic textbooks may make one believe. In most cases there are both economic merits and demerits regardless of which step one takes. The main task of the economist in such circumstances is to present these alternatives to the decision-making bodies who must then weigh the alternatives before coming to a final decision. Of course this is not to suggest that there are not cases, while in fact there are many, when the choice from the 'economic viewpoint' is clear and straightforward and the government is fully aware that if it decides otherwise it is taking what may be termed as a 'bad' economic decision'.

While in this chapter we are not going into this important question of what we may term as some form of the basis for 'correct' economic decision-making, these issues are taken up at the sectoral level as well as when we evaluate the decisions taken by the government in our review of the different phases of the country's economic history.

4.1.3 Medium-Term Development Planning

Medium-term development planning and economic decision-making covers a period of five years and normally takes the form of a Five Year Development Plan. It generally consists of the following:

Broad Economic Objectives

The broad economic objectives which are normally set out are the same in most plans and very similar for most developing countries. These would, amongst others, consist of:

i) A target growth of per capita income over the Plan period.
ii) Reduction of unemployment and underemployment by creating new employment opportunities.
iii) Self-reliance and reduction in foreign loans and resources to finance the development effort.
iv) The provision of basic needs especially better health, education, housing, and drinking water.
v) A reduction in inter-regional and intra-regional income disparities.

Strategy

The strategy to achieve broad objectives can be divided into three main parts, details of which are illustrated in Figs. 4.1 to 4.3.

The major sectors covered by the investment strategy are shown in Fig. 4.1 and there are important decisions to be made as regards sectoral emphasis. You could have a *balanced-growth* strategy with equal emphasis on all sectors; or you could have an *industrial-led* or *agricultural-led* growth strategy. The other very important decision is as regards the emphasis you give to the social sectors, including education, the impact of which might not be translated into immediate production gains. Again, within an *industrial-led* growth strategy, there are important differences between *heavy or basic industry* versus *consumer-goods industry*. Similarly, within the agricultural sector there might be considerable debate on whether to invest more in providing better irrigation, or in the provision of inputs, or investment in rural development, or in research and extension services programmes. An important question within the agricultural and industrial sector is whether the investment strategy should focus on the *large or small farmers* or on *large-scale* or *small-scale enterprises.*

How are basic decisions taken as regards the sectoral priorities in investment strategy? In simple economic terms, the different choices involved have advantages and disadvantages which have to be weighed against each other. Naturally, the course followed is greatly influenced by non-economic factors especially the relative position and strength of different groups as well as foreign loan-disbursing agencies.

Fundamental questions regarding the investment strategy can be reduced to the following economic choices:

i) To what extent is the society prepared to sacrifice its immediate consumption gains for greater increases at a later period in time?

ii) To what extent is the goal of self-reliance and self-sufficiency to be followed?

iii) To what extent is the society prepared to make the eradication of poverty and the provision of basic essential needs an immediate goal which it must try to achieve in the shortest period of time?

Cases of (i) and (ii) are normally identified with a strategy which emphasizes the growth of industry and, within industry, the basic or heavy industry sector. A case of (iii) would mean greater emphasis on the agricultural sector and labour-intensive small-scale industry with resources being set aside for the provision of education, health, and housing facilities.

Investment has to be financed and the different sources from which it can be raised are shown in Fig. 4.2. The three major sources are domestic, foreign trade and foreign loans, and foreign private investment. To the extent that, for most developing countries exporting mainly raw materials, opportunities to profit

Fig. 4.1: Investment Strategy

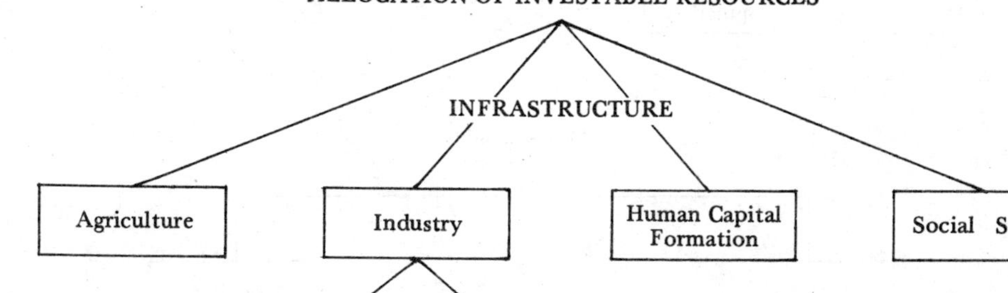

from foreign trade are limited, the choice is between how much you can raise from the domestic economy (which in most cases means the agricultural sector or the urban population) or by resorting to foreign borrowing or allowing foreign private investment into the economy.

In a private enterprise market-oriented economy, investment will only be forthcoming if there is a demand for the goods which any sector is going to produce. The main sources of demand for the two major sectors are shown in Fig. 4.3. In the case of the industrial sector, industrial growth can take place through (i) import substitution by imposing higher tariffs or import controls on previously imported commodities, (ii) the expansion of the domestic market which, in the case of Pakistan, at least during the first two decades, would have meant a heavy dependence on the growth of the agricultural sector, and (iii) the growth of exports especially after opportunities for import substitution are exhausted. In the case of the agricultural sector, the major sources of demand are the growth of population especially in the urban centres, the growth and expansion of the agro-based industry, and the growth of the export market.

The Translation of an Economic Strategy into Operational Planning and the Setting of Sectoral Production Targets[2]

Once a set of overall objectives have been agreed upon and the strategy to be followed for the achievement of these objectives has been marked out then the next stage is to translate this strategy into some form of operational planning.

This process normally begins with the projection of a specific rate of increase in income

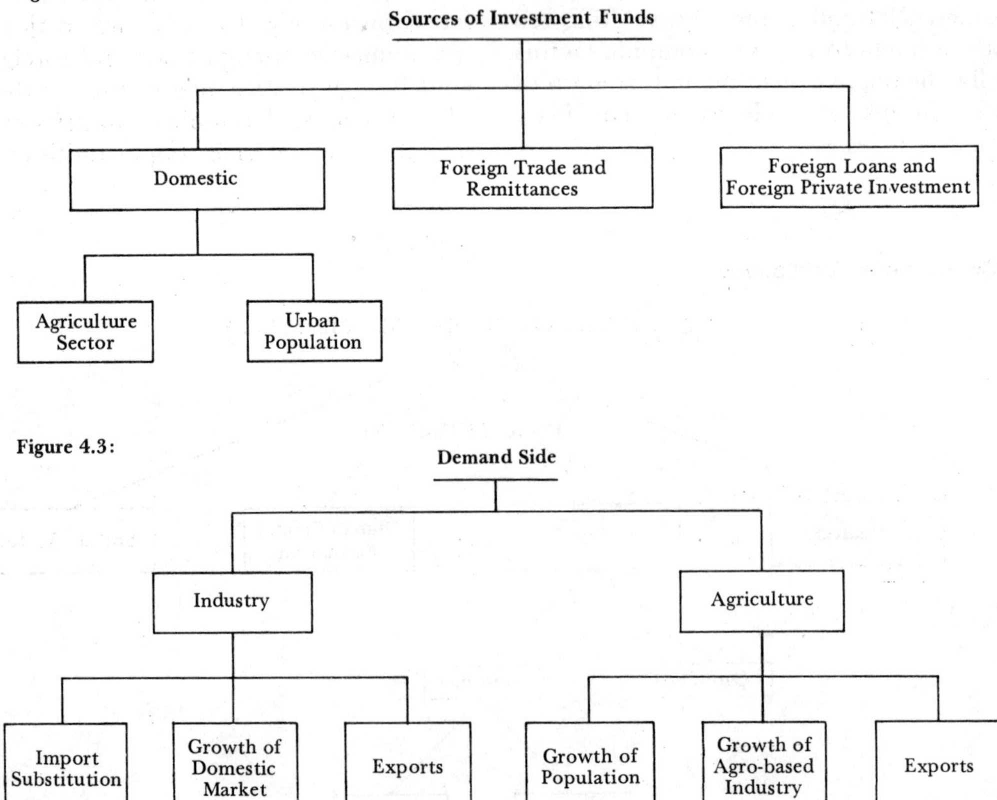

or production over the planning period as the prime target. This rate is usually determined by relating the amount of savings or investment to the proposed increase in income or output by a capital-output ratio which gives the units of capital outlay required to increase income or output by one unit. The formulation of a comprehensive plan then involves the construction of a growth model for the period of the plan which estimates the effect of the assumed rate of growth on such aggregates as public and private consumption, savings, investments, imports and exports, employment, and the demand and supply implications involved in producing the national product by economic sectors and, sometimes, by regions. A variety of economic, statistical, and mathematical calculations are made to relate inputs of labour, raw materials, land and capital equipment, and the resulting output. Similar calculations show the relationship between income generated and expended for consumption, investment, government services, exports, etc. The results are tested to determine their compatibility with the targets, their consistency with each other, and whether they are within reach of available resources.

Comprehensive planning includes both the formulation of an integrated public investment plan and a plan for the private sector.

The Phasing of the Five Year Plan

As discussed in Section 4.1.2 on short-term management, the Five Year Plan is broken down into Annual Plans which act as the recurrent instruments for detailing exactly what must be done to convert the former into programmes for action. Thus an Annual Plan deals with current development activities without losing sight of longer-term goals. The size and composition of each Annual Plan is determined, on the one hand, by the financial and other resources available at the time and, on the other, by the readiness to proceed with new projects and the progress made with projects started previously.

In contrast with the Five Year Plan, the Annual Plans are more detailed. A typical Annual-Operational-Plan starts with an account of the progress of the medium-term Plan in the previous year. The more important projects and programmes to be carried out during the current year, along with estimates of costs and available resources, are described. The most important sector of an Annual Plan describes the specific monetary, credit, fiscal, and other measures to be adopted during the year to achieve the annual targets.

4.1.4 Basic Structural Changes

The broad economic justification for bringing about basic structural changes, especially in the existing pattern of property ownership, rests on the following main grounds:

i) To reduce existing inequalities in the distribution of assets.
ii) To prevent economic exploitation of those groups who are at a considerable disadvantage due to the existing distribution of economic assets.
iii) To try to reduce to the extent possible, if not radically alter, the existing unequal distribution of ownership of assets which act as a major impediment to economic growth and development.

The most important structural changes within the agricultural sector are regarding the question of inequality in the land ownership pattern, the need for land reforms, and the ceilings which should be fixed for the size of the holdings. It also covers the rights of tenants and the extent to which the law guarantees them certain basic rights against discriminatory ejectment as well as the extent to which they remain at the will of the landlord.

In the industrial sector the most important questions are regarding the ownership of the public sector and in what circumstances and to what extent is this justified. Should only the heavy and the intermediate goods industry be under the control of the public sector, and should this also be the case only if the private sector is not willing or capable to manage these industries? Should the state extend its control over the industrial sector when there is extreme concentration in the ownership of industrial assets which leads to cartels and monopoly-pricing behaviour? Another important question in this sector is the fixing of minimum wages to protect the interest of the workers and the extent to which trade union activity should be allowed to protect the workers against excesses by the management, especially against unfair termination of services.

The banking sector is extremely important with regard to inter-sectoral flow of funds. Also, in a situation where there are links between the ownership of industrial and banking assets, those industrialists are in a far more advantageous position because of the easy availability of financial resources. Should banking therefore be in the public sector?

In other sectors, especially transport, there are again questions of public versus private ownership, not so much with regard to the railways and air transport where the public sector normally has control, but with regard to road transport and the extent to which it should be left to the public or the private sector.

It is these structural changes which are most dependent on the different classes and groups which exercise state control and, in a democratic framework, they are determined by the economic philosophy of the political party which is in power. Who these important groups are and the manner in which they can influence decision-making is the question to which we now turn in the next section.

4.2 Forces which Influence Economic Decision-Making

Economic decisions are not taken in a vacuum. They are influenced by individuals, vested interest groups, and various economic classes for the simple reason that the decisions themselves can have an important impact on and greatly influence the economic condition and well-being of these different groups. In some cases an economic decision might be taken purely in response to a set of economic conditions and the groups favourably affected might not have made a conscious effort to obtain the decision in their favour. But if, as a result of the decision, certain groups are adversely affected they will exert pressure to have the decision changed or an alternative path followed which does not affect them so unfavourably.

In Table 4.2 we have listed some of the groups which can play an important role in influencing the economic decision-making of the state authorities. The list is made mainly on the basis of the sectors to which they belong but it also takes into consideration other characteristics which give certain sections of the population an important weight either because they belong to a politically sensitive group (like the urban population) or to a powerful group (like the military and the bureaucracy) or they represent foreign interests which have an important economic and political stake in the country.

The most important criteria which determines a domestic group's power and influence is its ownership and control over economic assets as, for example, in the case of large landowners (with holdings greater than 150 acres). But other groups become important because of their sheer size and number as in the case of small farmers (less than 7.5 acres) and the landless labour force which constitutes almost 70 per cent of the rural population. Similarly, because of weak political institutions, other groups like the bureaucracy become extremely important in influencing economic decision-making and, because of the country's dependence on foreign loans to finance development plans, the foreign interests also become critically important.

Conflicts and Contradictions among different Groups in Economic Decision-Making

The process of economic development generates conflicts and contradictions between different groups and classes and it is important to see how this happens when different economic decisions are taken.

i) *Import Substitution: Industrial Strategy behind Import Controls and high Tariffs*

In a predominantly agricultural economy, the decision to foster industrialization through import substitution, supported by import controls or high tariffs, favours the industrial and discriminates against the agricultural sector. This is because as a result of this decision the prices of industrial goods increase disproportionately in the domestic market while those of agricultural raw materials fall as compared to what they would fetch in the world market. The change in the ratio of prices between the agricultural and industrial sector, i.e., the terms of trade, adversely affects the different classes within the agricultural sector.

ii) *Price Controls on Agricultural Commodities*

A similar situation also arises when price controls are introduced on agricultural goods while the prices of industrial goods are not subject to any such controls. This would mean a transfer of income from the agricultural to the industrial sector.

iii) *Mechanization of Agriculture*

Availability of tractors at prices which are less than the opportunity cost of capital or foreign exchange can lead to a far greater number of tractors than is economically justifiable being introduced for agricultural practices thus causing the ejectment of tenants. In this case there can be a direct conflict of interests between the large landlords who can afford the tractors and find them profitable and the tenant farmers who are ejected from the land and who are not able to find gainful employment in other sectors of the economy.

iv) *Devaluation as a Means to Solving an Adverse Balance of Payments Situation*

In many cases when a country is faced with a persistent deficit in its balance of payments, it is put under considerable pressure especially from loan-giving agencies like the IMF and the IBRD (World Bank) to devalue its currency. Such a measure can be resisted strongly by the government both because of the inflationary effects of devaluation as well as because of the much higher rupee cost of debt repayment. There might also be a strong clash of interests between the industrialists and the agriculturists. The former would resist devaluation for it would increase the cost of importing machinery and reduce the profits on capital invested (especially of those not selling in the export market) whereas the

Table 4.2: Some of the Important Forces which Influence Economic Decision-Making in Pakistan

Sector	Classes/Groups	Sources of power
1. Agricultural sector	i. Large landlords	Land holdings ($>$150 acres)
	ii. Medium size farmers	
	iii. Small size farmers, tenants, landless labourers	A very significant portion of the rural population.
2. Manufacturing sector	i. Big industrialists/monopoly houses	Ownership of industrial assets
	ii. Medium/small size industrialists	
	iii. Industrial labour	Numbers/Trade Unions
3. Trading sector (services)	i. Big trading firms (both foreign and domestic trade)	Control trade and influence prices
	ii. Medium/small trading firms	
4. Foreign sectors	i. Western aid-giving countries (Consortium, i.e., USA, UK, France, W. Germany, Italy)	Play a major role in financing development plans and giving balance of payments support
	ii. Loan-giving agencies (World Bank, IMF, Asian Development Bank)	
	iii. Other loan-giving countries (USSR, Japan)	
5. Other important groups	i. Bureaucracy	Central state power
	ii. Urban groups, e.g., students	Create disturbances

latter could be in favour of it since it would raise the domestic prices of agricultural goods.

4.3 The Planning Machinery in Pakistan

4.3.1 The Changing Role of the Planning Commission

A description of the formal planning machinery of Pakistan must take into account its evolution over time and its changing role as regards the influence which it has exerted in economic decision-making over different time periods in the last three decades. During the fifties and seventies the formal planning machinery of the government, the Planning Board (during the fifties) and the Planning Commission (as it was called after the late fifties), was relegated to a position of little importance. It was only during the sixties that the Planning Commission enjoyed considerable power in the country's decision-making and this was reflected in the formulation and implementation of the Second and Third Five Year Plans.

It is important to remind ourselves, however, that the planning machinery should not be confused with the decision-making authority of the government especially since the day-to-day and the short-run period economic management is exercised mainly by the concerned ministries of the central and provincial governments or their executive heads. (For further details, see Section 4.3.2)

The role of the formal planning machinery in Pakistan, especially in the formulation of the Annual Plans and the Five Year Plans, has a chequered history and can be divided into five distinct phases:

The Period of Economic Co-ordination[3] *(1947-53)*

The first phase dates back to 1947-53 when some attempts were made at economic coordination and planning in the immediate post-Independence period. The effort began in 1950 with the Colombo Plan when the Development Board compiled, within a period of three months, a Six-Year Development Plan (1951-7) which envisaged a modest public expenditure of the national income of that time. The Six-Year Development Plan was a plan more in name than in content and represented merely a loose aggregation of a number of individual projects in various fields. No aggregate targets were mentioned for the economy as a whole nor was there any attempt to relate particular projects to overall targets. During this period, despite a multiplicity of planning committees and other organizational units, the planning machinery was hardly equipped to do its job effectively. The focus of all activities was the approval of isolated development projects and even this function could not be discharged properly as suitable machinery for project appraisal or operational techniques for economic analysis had not yet evolved.

The Period of the Planning Board (1953-8)

The creation of a Planning Board (later renamed the Planning Commission) in 1953 marked the beginning of the second phase of economic planning which lasted till 1958. The Planning Board had serious problems of a shortage of staff, the absence of statistical data, an uncertain status in the government, and resentment from other strongly entrenched Ministries and Departments particularly the Ministry of Finance and the State Bank which regarded it as a rival institution. It was for these reasons that the First Five Year Plan could not be published till April 1957, nearly two years after the First Plan period (1955-60) began. The First Plan was never really approved by the government. Its implementation suffered due to rapid changes in the government and a lack of political support. During 1953-8 the advice of the Planning Board was in most cases disregarded by the implementing agencies. The institutional liaison between the Planning Board and the other Ministries and Departments remained fairly weak and the Annual Development Programmes were never seriously followed. According to one description, 'priorities were ignored; budget decisions made in June distorted the planning decision made in May'.[4]

The Period of a Powerful Planning Commission (1958-68)

The third phase in the evolution of the planning process began in October 1958 with the assumption of power by the military government of Ayub Khan. The new regime chose to make economic development through a market economy and reliance on the private sector as its primary objective. The status of the Planning Commission was raised to a Division in the President's Secretariat. The President himself assumed the Chairmanship of the Planning Commission and a Deputy Chairman, with the *ex officio* status of a Minister, was made the operational head of the Commission.

An important development during 1958-64 was the institutionalization of the planning process. Provincial Planning Departments were organized, planning cells were created in various Ministries and Departments, and the Planning Commission was represented on practically all the decision-making committees in the government. Thus the Deputy Chairman of the Planning Commission was a member of the National Economic Council which was the highest decision-making body in the economic field. The Central Development Working Party, which scrutinized all development projects in the public sector above a certain minimum financial limit and accorded its approval at a technical level, was chaired by the Secretary to the Planning Division. The Industrial Investment Schedule for the private sector was formulated within the framework of the Five Year Plan in consultation with the Planning Commission which was also represented on the Permissions Committee constituted for the final sanction of private investment proposals. The Planning Commission also provided the Secretariat for the Executive Committee of the National Economic Council which looked after the day-to-day work of the National Economic Council and was responsible for the final approval of development projects. The Annual Development Programme was formulated entirely in the Planning Commission, in consultation with the sponsoring agencies, and this development programme was translated substantially into the annual budgets. The Planning Commission was also represented on the Foreign Exchange Control Committee which made decisions regarding the allocation of foreign exchange and thereby exercised a decisive influence on the pattern of allocation particularly in the private sector.

The Period of Decline of the Planning Commission (1968-77)

The decline of the Planning Commission as an important decision-making body coincided with the fall of Ayub Khan's government. The Planning Commission had become very closely identified with Ayub's government during the sixties and the rejection of the growth strategy followed during that period was also taken to reflect adversely on the Planning Commission. One reason for this was that some of the key economists who controlled the Planning Commission during the sixties were very closely identified with the growth philosophy and growth strategy followed and many people blamed them directly for having played a key role in the evolution and implementation of Ayub's growth strategy.

The first major blow to the power and authority of the Planning Commission came during the government of Yahya Khan (1969-71) when serious planning was almost completely given up by the government. After March 1969 the Third Five Year Plan was virtually abandoned. The publication of the Fourth Five Year Plan in 1970, to cover the period 1970-5, was given very little credibility because of the political conditions prevailing in the country at that time.

The government of the People's Party, which followed the collapse of the military government, continued to be extremely suspicious of the Planning Commission, again because of its very close proximity to Ayub Khan's government, and, in the earlier years, it was almost totally ignored. One reason for this was that the government decided to run the economy through Annual Plans, rather than through a comprehensive Five Year Plan, mainly because of the considerable economic uncertainties with which it was faced because of domestic and external factors. Furthermore, the economists in the Planning Commission, finding that it was no longer an important decision-making body, began to leave its rank so that there were very few competent economists left to run it. This further weakened its authority. In 1972 it also lost the autonomy that it had enjoyed during the sixties and was placed directly under the control of the Finance Ministry as a Division.

During the period from 1972 to 1977, therefore, the Planning Commission exercised little overall control over the management of the economy in the sense that it had little say in the important economic decisions that were taken. Of course it continued to help formulate the Annual Plans but now its function was to put together the projects 'approved' by the Finance Ministry and concerned Ministries rather than to guide and direct the overall investment programme in a particular direction, as it had done during the sixties.

The most important factor which contributed towards this situation was that there was no Five Year Plan in operation. The government had asked the Planning Commission to prepare a Five Year Plan and the one to cover the period 1977-82 was actually published but, after the change in government, the Plan was abandoned.

The new government which took over in July 1977 emphasized the need for a Five Year Plan and, within a year and a half of taking over, the Fifth Five Year Plan to cover the period 1978-83 was published. But the government never seriously pursued the Plan mainly because of the difficulty in implementing it during uncertain overall economic conditions. Little reference was therefore made to the Fifth Plan in the Annual Plans and the overall review of the economic performance.

The Planning Commission, during the period 1977-80, therefore exercised little real power as it had done in the earlier years of the seventies.

Recent Attempts at Revival of the Planning Commission (1980 to present)

More recently, however, the government has taken steps to revive the Planning Commission as an effective and authoritative economic decision-making body. A Deputy Chairman of the Planning Commission (with the rank of a Cabinet Minister) has been recently appointed and given the task of formulating the country's Sixth Five Year Plan to cover the period between 1982-3 to 1987-8. Similarly the government has appointed members to the Planning Commission (from different regions) to ensure both more technical competence as well as better regional representation.

Before we conclude, it is important to state that the above discussion has been restricted to the evolution of a planning body as well as its changing role and importance in economic decision-making in the country. We have not described the kind of decisions taken by the planning authority, what information it used, what forces came to play on it, and to what extent it was influenced by models either of the market or some controlled economies. This is not only because it is exceedingly difficult to trace these developments in any detail but also because this subject is taken up in the chapters relating to the country's economic management over different time periods as well as in the sectoral chapters.

4.3.2 The Structure of Economic Decision-Making in Pakistan

The role of the Planning Commission in the formulation of economic plans and in influencing economic decisions has, as we have seen, changed considerably over the years. However, the administrative machinery for the approval of plans (both Five Year and Annual Plans) and for different development projects has remained the same since the early sixties. This hierarchy is shown in Fig. 4.4.

The planning machinery is headed by the National Economic Council (NEC) as the supreme policy-making body in the economic sphere. It has the President as the Chairman and all Federal Ministers in charge of Development ministries and provincial Governors as members. In addition, a number of other persons are invited to attend the meetings of the NEC as and when the agenda relates to matters concerning them.

The functions of the NEC are: (i) to review the overall economic situation in Pakistan; (ii) to formulate plans with respect to financial, commercial, and economic policies and economic development; (iii) to approve the Five Year Plans, the Annual Development Plan, provincial development schemes in the public sector above a certain financial limit, and all non-Plan projects. It may appoint committees or bodies of experts as may be necessary to assist the Council in the performance of its functions.

In all cases to be submitted to the NEC, the Secretary of the Ministry concerned transmits to the Cabinet Secretary a concise memorandum of the case (generally referred to as the Summary). When a case has been decided by the NEC, the Minister in charge is expected to take prompt action to give effect to the decisions. To ensure implementation of the Council decisions, the Secretary of each Ministry is expected to keep a record of all the decisions conveyed to him and to watch the progress of action until it is completed. The Cabinet Secretary is also expected to watch the implementation of the Council decisions.

The body directly below the NEC is the Executive Committee of the National Economic Council (ECNEC). It is headed by the Federal Minister for Finance, Planning, and Development. Its members include all Federal Ministers in charge of Development Ministries, provincial Governors or their nominees, and provincial Ministers in charge of Planning and Development Departments.

The functions of the ECNEC are: (a) to sanction development schemes (both in the public and private sectors) pending their submission to the NEC; (b) to allow moderate changes in the plan and sectoral adjustments within the overall plan allocation; (c) to supervise the implementation of economic policies laid down by the Cabinet and the NEC.

Another body concerned with economic policy is the Annual Plan Co-ordination Committee which is a purely advisory body responsible for advising the Cabinet and the NEC regarding the co-ordination of policies. It is headed by the Secretary-General, Finance, Planning, and Economic Co-ordination. All Federal Secretaries of development ministries, heads of provincial Planning and Development Departments, and heads of the State Bank of Pakistan, the Board of Industrial Management, and PIDC are its members.

Below ECNEC is the Central Development Working Party (CDWP) which is responsible for the scrutiny and sanction of development projects. The Secretary, Planning Division, is the Convener of the CDWP with Federal Secretaries of the concerned departments, Federal Finance Secretary, and Chairmen of the Provincial Planning and Development Departments as Members. It reviews all projects which are presented for the approval of the federal government costing Rs 10 million and more. Thus, by providing for representation of various Ministries and Agencies, the process of approval of projects is now a joint exercise.

The responsibility for the overall economic evaluation of Annual Plans remains with the Planning Division which places a report each year before the NEC evaluating economic achievements and failures. Mid-Plan reviews outlining the progress of the Five Year Plan are also published by the Planning Commission.

4.3.3 The Planning Machinery in Pakistan—A Critical Appraisal

Throughout Pakistan's thirty-five years' history there have been constant attempts and experimentation at evolving a sound planning

Figure 4.4: Economic Decision-Making Structure

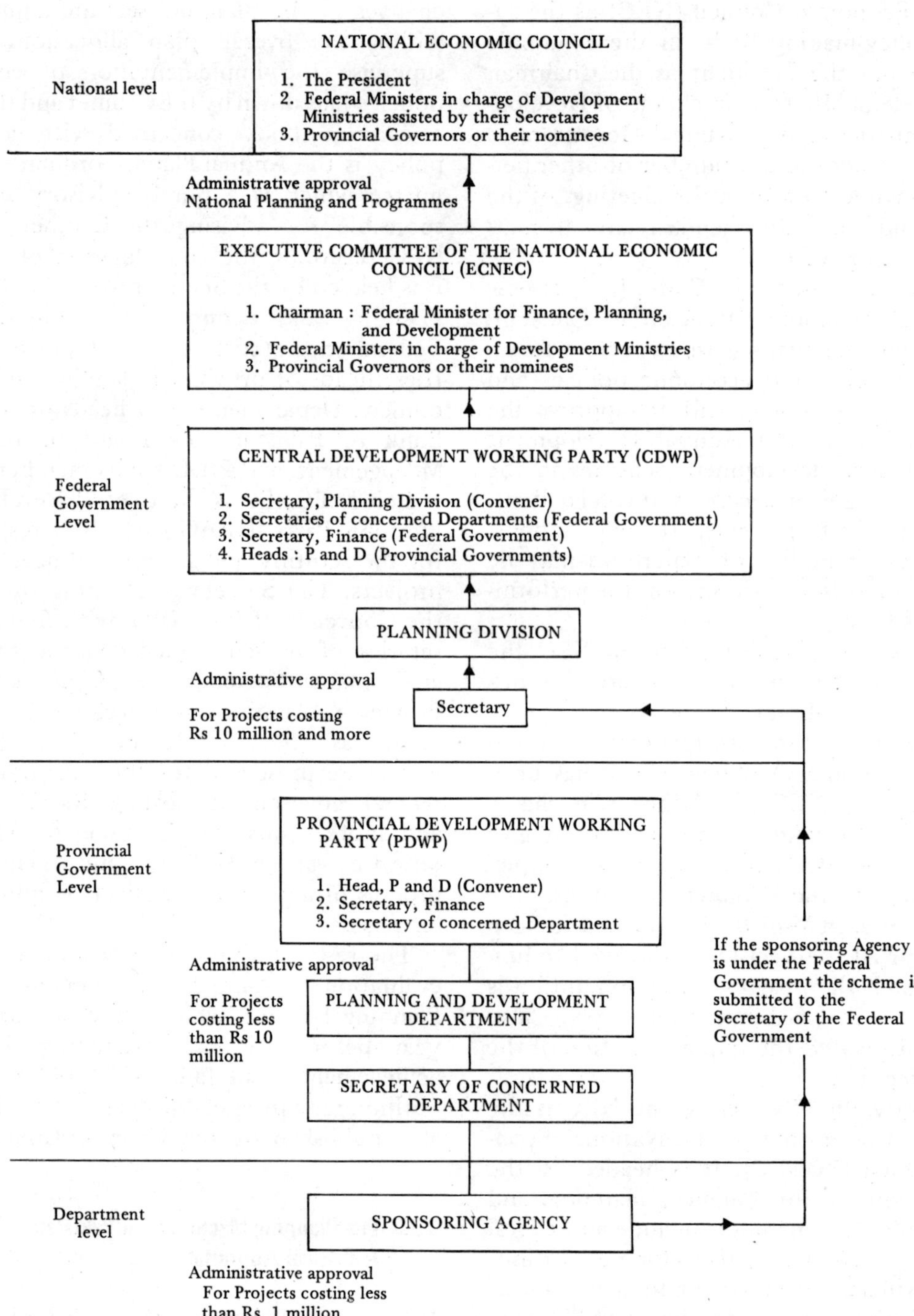

machinery and planning authority to guide the overall economic development effort. What have been the major problems in the past and what are the major problems with which it is faced at present? Let us look at these in turn:

i) *The Administrative Obstacles of Planning*[5]

Before Independence the colonial administration was mainly geared to looking after the tasks of maintenance of internal order, the collection of taxes, and the administration of justice. It has been only after Independence that growth and economic development became important objectives and a primary task which the country faced was to re-orient the government machinery to meet the demands of accelerated development.

One major obstacle which has stood in the way of establishing a sound, efficient, and independent planning authority is the lack of an effective administrative machinery and this has greatly limited the tasks of development policy and planning. Some of the factors which still continue to be major hinderances and act as administrative obstacles and bottlenecks to planning are discussed below:

Lack of Competent Personnel

An important reason why competent persons are not attracted to joining the planning bodies in the country are low salaries, poor placement and promotional policies, and frequent and irrational transfer of personnel. Also there is no doubt that the civil service system with an elite cadre of 'generalists' or general administrators whose influence far exceeds its size are placed in positions to pass judgement on technical matters about which they know little. The technicians' lower salaries, promotional opportunities and status, as well as their frequent exclusion from the formulation of policy, have also kept many technically competent economists from seeking government employment.

Dilatory Procedures

In Pakistan, documents and files must follow a prescribed series of steps through administrative layers. Papers received in a government office are first routed to subordinated clerical personnel for recording and checking against preceding action. They are then routed to all interested officials, sometimes at the same level, sometimes upwards through multiple layers in the administrative hierarchy. Each officer adds his comments, often in considerable detail, in this 'noting process'. Decisions are made only at or near the top. Too much of the time of high officials is taken up merely with the review of papers and files received from subordinates and in passing them on to still higher officers. In decrying the wastefulness of this process it has been pointed out that 'often there seems to be a disposition to shift the file from one office to another, or from one Ministry to another. The resultant delays are sometimes unbelievably long'.[6]

While many attempts have been made to shorten these delays, either by reducing the number of administrative layers or by setting deadlines, so far only peripheral improvements have been achieved.

Lack of Co-ordination

In many cases the co-ordination of development activities has become extremely difficult because responsibility for different aspects of a project or programme are divided among many Ministries and Agencies. This excessive fragmentation may make it exceedingly difficult to carry out projects and programmes in accordance to a coherent policy.

ii) *Inadequate Preparatory Work on Projects*

When a potentially desirable project has been identified, a feasibility study has to be made to determine whether it is practicable and justified. A feasibility study involves a detailed examination of the economic, technical, financial, commercial, and organizational aspects of a project. By far the greatest number of failures to carry out public sector projects and programmes at reasonable cost and in reasonable periods of time are traceable to inadequate project selection and preparation.

According to the Planning Commission of Pakistan, preparatory work on public sector projects in the country was frequently lacking and 'impatience and enthusiasm frequently took the place of prudence and engineering judgement'.[7]

It is only when inadequately prepared projects have been approved and begin to run into difficulties, which greatly increases costs and delays execution, that the value of careful pre-investment and engineering studies become apparent.

iii) *The Lack of Implementation of Plans*

A major reason for the lack of implementation of the country's various five year plans has been the widespread failure of the governments of the day to maintain the discipline implicit in their plan. What is planned and what is done in many cases bears little relationship to each other. At times it almost appears that plans are prepared by a planning agency in one corner of a government and policy is made by various bodies in other corners.

Figure 4.5: Organization of the National Planning Commission

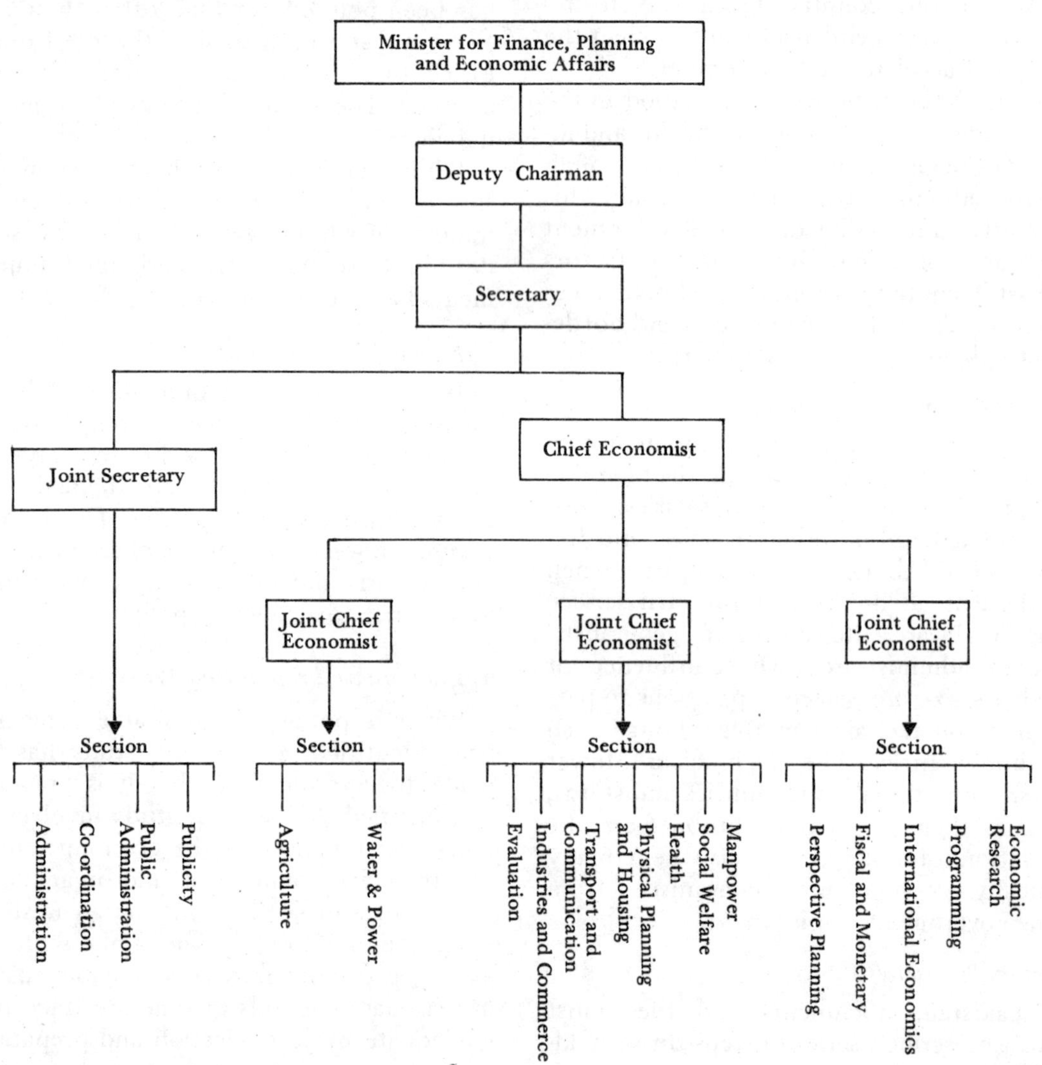

In Pakistan's planning history, except for the Second Five Year Plan which was to some extent vigorously implemented, almost all the other Five Year Plans were either never implemented from the start (this being the case for the First, Fourth, and Fifth Plans) or were subject to considerable change (Third Five Year Plan). In some cases, it is true, that economic conditions changed drastically so that the original Plan could not be rigidly followed but, rather than trying to adapt the Plan to the changed environment, in many cases the government went in for *ad hoc* decision-making, responding more at times to the 'whims and fancy' of the executive authority than to the economic realities as they existed on the ground.

iv) *Lack of Evaluation of Plan Progress and Project Implementation*

As pointed out above, flexibility is an essential element of development planning because in many cases changes in economic conditions make deviations from the original Plan unavoidable. A central planning agency must therefore constantly review and assess progress in relation to events. It must identify potential bottlenecks as early as possible, determine their causes, evaluate the extent to which deviations threaten the attainment of Plan objectives, and suggest measures for dealing with problems.

Unfortunately, whenever evaluations have been prepared by the country's planning authorities they have been issued long after the end of the period to which they refer. In many cases the mid-term reviews of the Five Year Plans have been published almost near the end of the Plan period and the final reviews of the Plan have come long after the new Plans have been launched and therefore been of little use in formulating targets and policies for the new Plan. The fault in many cases lies not only with the central planning agency, i.e., the Planning Commission, since implementation of a plan is decentralized in many operating organizations and evaluation of a plan's progress depends on complete, accurate, and timely reports on the progress of sector programmes and projects. Unfortunately these are in most cases made available after very long delays and the planning agency becomes aware of shortfalls when it is too late to rectify them.

The need for a good reporting system on plan and project implementation is therefore an essential pre-requisite for a good evaluation system. It is essential for the purpose of progress reporting that a project be divided into a series of discrete segments (for example, selection of a site, acquisition of land, issuance of tenders, erection of a plant, purchase and installation of machinery, construction of an access highway, training personnel for the plant, etc.,) for which specific time schedules and cost estimates be set for each reporting period.

NOTES

1. See Section 7.1 for details.
2. This section is based on Albert Waterston, *Development Planning–Lesson of Experience*, World Bank Publication, 1974.
3. The description of the first three phases is mainly taken from Mahbub-ul-Haq, *Planning Machinery in Pakistan*, Pakistan Administrative Staff College, Reading Paper No. 268, Lahore (Mimeo).
4. Clair Wilcox, 'Development Planning and Programming in Pakistan', quoted in Albert Waterston, *Planning in Pakistan*, Baltimore, 1963.
5. This section relies heavily on Albert Waterston, 'Administrative Obstacles to Planning,' in *Development Planning–Lessons of Experience*, World Bank Publication, 1974, pp. 249-92.
6. National Planning Board, *First Five Year Plan, 1955-60*, p. 118, in Albert Waterston, 'Administrative Obstacles to Planning', in *Development Planning–Lessons of Experience*, World Bank publication, 1974, p. 264.
7. Planning Commission, *Second Five Year Plan, 1960-5*, p. 201, in Albert Waterston, 'Administrative Obstacles to Planning', in *Development Planning–Lessons of Experience*, World Bank Publication, 1974, p. 326.

5 The Initial Phase: 1947-58

For those who wish to understand the main characteristics of Pakistan's economic progress in the last thirty-five years must follow closely the developments in the early years of its economic history for the economic decisions taken then played an extremely important role in determining the direction of the economy at least over the next two decades.

In terms of the economic events which were to play a critical role in the first phase, i.e., for the period from August 1947 till October 1958, the following were perhaps the most important. The initial years after Independence in 1947 and the flow of refugees into the country; the decision not to devalue the currency in September 1949 following the devaluation of the Pound Sterling when India and a number of other countries followed suit; the years from mid-1950 to early 1952 when, as a result of the war in Korea, there was a boom in the world prices of raw materials; the decision in 1952 to impose import controls after the collapse of the Korean boom and the balance of payments crisis that followed; the joining of military pacts with the Western countries, i.e., SEATO and CENTO[1] in 1954 and the beginning of significant aid flows into the country; the decision to devalue the currency in 1955 and, finally, the military *coup* of October 1958 which marked the end of the first phase of the country's economic history.

This chapter is divided into two main parts. The first presents a broad overview of the major economic developments during this period. Part two extracts from the broad overview the key economic decisions that were taken and analyses them in terms of the framework we have developed in the last chapter.

5.1 A Broad Overview

Let us identify some of the key economic developments which took place during this period (Table 5.1).

i) The fifties saw the establishment and rapid expansion of the large-scale manufacturing sector. Although the high growth rates must be interpreted with caution, because of the very small base from which the economy started, the achievements in the manufacturing sector during this period were impressive and laid the foundations of a consumer goods industry in Pakistan. However, there was a distinct slowing down in growth during the last three years, i.e., 1955-6 to 1957-8.
ii) Throughout the period the dominant sector of the economy, i.e., agriculture, stagnated and its growth rate was in fact even less than the growth in population so that the per capita consumption of food grain declined and in many cases had to be supplemented through food imports.
iii) Because of little growth in the agricultural sector, the small share of manufacturing, and the high growth rate of the population, the overall per capita income saw *no* increase during this period.
iv) There were, however, other important achievements which tend to be discounted in relation to the economy's overall poor record. The settlement of the large exodus of refugees, about 7 million in number, the setting up of the administrative machinery of government, the establishment of vital economic institutions like the State Bank, and other financial institutions, were all achieved with considerable success during this period.

Sub-Periods

Both for the sake of convenience and because of the industrial bias in government policy during this period, we have divided the overall period into the following major sub-periods, mainly in regard to the establishment and growth of industry in the country.

a. *The Establishment of Merchant Capital*

At the time of Independence there were two important features of the economy. The first was that the areas which became Pakistan were predominantly agricultural with almost no industry. The second was that most of the trade, especially in the foreign sector, was in the hands of non-Muslims most of whom migrated to India. The vacuum which was created by this exodus was filled by Muslim trading communities who had earlier been spread all over the sub-continent and who now migrated to Pakistan settling mainly in Karachi, the capital and the main port of the country.

In the early years, the devaluation of the Indian currency was an important economic event. Because of the very close trading links between the two countries India expected that Pakistan would follow suit. Pakistan, however, did not. This meant that imports from India into Pakistan became cheaper and exports into India more expensive.

The main motivation behind the non-devaluation decision was to be able to sell raw jute to Indian industry at a higher price. India responded by suspending trade between the two countries and hence blocking the major source of manufacturing imports into the country. As a result of the non-devaluation of the Pakistani currency the government had to impose quantitative controls of a rather loose

Table 5.1: Growth Rates of Key Sectors and Movements of Important Economic Variable Pakistan (West) 1949-50 to 1957-8

	1949-50 to 1950-1	1950-1 to 1951-2	1951-2 to 1952-3	1952-3 to 1953-4	1953-4 to 1954-5	1954-5 to 1955-6	1955-6 to 1956-7	1956-7 to 1957-8	1949-50 to 1957-8
Growth Rate									
(i) Agriculture	2.6	–9.1	0.18	13.6	–0.8	2.1	2.3	1.9	1.43
(ii) Large-scale manufacturing	23.5	18.7	23.6	28.7	24.1	17.5	8.1	4.9	19.1
(iii) Per capita income	1.4	4.4	–0.9	6.8	0.6	0.8	0.5	0.3	6.97
	1949-50	1950-1	1951-2	1952-3	1953-4	1954-5	1955-6	1956-7	1957-8
Balance of Payments of Trade[1] (Rs million)									
(i) Exports	535	1343	922	867	641	491	742	698	434
	(1218)	(2554)	(2009)	(1510)	(1286)	(1223)	(1784)	(1608)	1422)
(ii) Imports	912	1167	1473	1017	824	783	965	1516	1314
	(1284)	(1620)	(2237)	(1384)	(1118)	(1103)	(1325)	(2335)	(2050)
Balance	–117	174	–552	–150	–183	–292	–223	–818	–881
	(–66)	(934)	(–228)	(126)	(168)	(120)	(–459)	(–727)	(–628)
Price Index[2]									
Karachi	96.8	95.5	99.9	107	111	108	107	113	123
Lahore	90.1	82.5	92.7	99.3	101	96	94	102	111

1. Figures in parentheses refer to All Pakistan, i.e., including East Pakistan.
2. General cost of living index for industrial workers (April 1948 to March 1949 = 100).

Source: (i) For Balance of Trade, All Pakistan, and Price Index *Twenty-Five Years of Pakistan in Statistics.* (ii) Government of Pakistan, *Pakistan Economic Survey, 1979-80*, Islamabad.

nature on imports and exports so as to be able to deal with the situation *vis-a-vis* trade with other countries whose imports were now much cheaper in cost.

This situation changed drastically with the advent of the Korean war which led to large increases in the prices of raw materials in foreign markets, especially raw jute and raw cotton, thereby improving the country's balance of payments situation. It also meant that the non-devaluation decision in 1949 had paid off. India had to finally accept the par value of Pakistan's currency by the end of 1950 leading to a restoration of trade and the quantitative controls introduced earlier were relaxed leading to a more liberal import policy.

The newly established trading classes benefitted greatly from the Korean boom. They bought raw materials from the agricultural sector at cheap prices and sold them in the foreign markets at very high prices making large profits. Merchant capital thrived and accumulated during the period of the Korean boom.

b. *The Transformation of Merchant Capital into Industrial Capital*

In the earlier years the government had tried to move capital into industry but had failed to do so largely because trading during the Korean boom was far more profitable than investing in industry. The favourable conditions for the conversion of merchant capital into industrial capital was the result of another important economic event again related to the Korean war: the collapsed prices of raw materials after the end of the war. During the boom years, which lasted from mid-1950 to early 1952, the increase in foreign exchange earnings had, as mentioned earlier, allowed the government to practice a more liberal import policy and the control system which had been set up after the non-devaluation of 1949 had been mainly dismantled. But with the collapse of the Korean boom, the government, fearing a foreign exchange crisis as export prices fell, re-imposed controls. These controls on both imports and exports were then maintained throughout the fifties.

As a result of the imposition of these controls, mainly on the import of consumer goods, the prices of these goods increased sharply in the domestic market which changed the terms of trade in favour of industry and against the agricultural sector. This led to a sharp increase in the profitability of the industrial sector and, in comparison with the other sectors including trading, industry now became the most attractive sector. Traders, who had earlier made high profits and amassed surpluses during the Korean boom, now converted merchant capital into industrial capital by importing industrial machinery (which was made all the more easier because of the foreign exchange reserves built up) and went into the production of consumer goods especially cotton textiles.

c. *The Period of High Industrial Growth*

A number of factors contributed to the very high rate of industrial growth in the early years. A large market for domestic production was created by imposing import controls and for the early entrants, who could charge monopoly prices, profits were very high. According to Papanek,[2] the rate of return on industrial investment was so high that industrialists were able to recover their initial investments in a period of one to two years. The incentive to re-invest was therefore considerable and the large profits made were saved and re-invested into industry. The foreign exchange reserves built up during the Korean boom continued to make it possible to import industrial machinery (there being no domestic capital goods sector all machinery had to be imported).

The industrial sector, mostly agro-based, continued to obtain supplies of agricultural raw material at prices far below the world prices, i.e., the prices the agricultural sector would have received if it had been allowed to export its commodities. The government ensured that the prices of agricultural commodities continued to remain low through a combination of price controls and export duties on agricultural products.

The government also played an important direct role in the country's industrialization programme. In some cases private industrialists were not very keen to invest in the then East Pakistan as well as in some industries in West Pakistan. The government set up the Pakistan Industrial Development Corporation (PIDC) whose major objective was to help establish industries which were handed over to the private sector when they were completed. In fact in a large number of projects set up by the PIDC, especially in the then East Pakistan, the private sector was very closely associated from the beginning in raising capital for the proposed projects. During the early fifties the PIDC set up a number of industrial projects which were then handed over to the private sector. This was especially true for the jute mills which were set up in the then East Pakistan.

High profits, high savings, high investment, and high rates of growth were the main features of the industrial development in the earlier years but the very forces which had made these conditions possible were now signalling a slowing down.

d. *Slow-downs and Contradictions*

The initial accumulation of industrial capital had taken place as a result of the large tribute paid by the agricultural sector to the industrial sector and by the urban consumers. The former had supplied agricultural raw materials at cheap prices and had paid high prices for manufactured consumer goods in return. The urban consumer had similarly paid high prices and those who received employment (of which little was generated in the capital-intensive large-scale industries which were being set up) received relatively very poor wages.[3]

The neglect of the agricultural sector during this period took its toll. The central government took little interest in its direct development leaving it to the provincial governments with their meagre resources to do what they could for this important sector. Some investments were made in large irrigation projects (for example Thal Development, Lower Sind Barrage, Taunsa Barrage, Kurian Garahi Project) but these took long periods to realise and although they brought new land under cultivation they did little to increase productivity in existing areas. Ravaged by floods, the agricultural situation worsened and for many years the country was dependent on imported food grain leading to a drain of the country's foreign exchange reserves although foreign donors (the USA, Canada, Australia) also helped to bail the country out.

The lack of agricultural growth, together with the important fact that per capita food consumption declined during this period, also meant that the market for the manufacturing sector was stagnant. Import substitution industrialization with regard to consumer goods was now drawing to an end as the market created from the stoppage of imports was now almost exhausted. With a stagnant agricultural sector, the manufacturing sector found itself faced with a severe problem in finding a market. The government had hoped that the devaluation of the currency in 1955 would help create an export market. Although it did lead to an increase in some exports of manufactured goods, the increase was not sufficient to boost the sagging market for industrial goods.

e. *The Shift towards Agriculture—too little too late?*

It was principally as a reaction towards this situation that, by the beginning of 1956, government emphasis began to shift from the industrial to the agricultural sector, at least as far as its official pronouncements were concerned. In his Budget Speech on 15 March 1956, the then Finance Minister declared: 'the first phase of industrial development is over and it is now necessary to pay greater attention to agricultural development'.[4] The devaluation at the end of 1955 was also explained in the same light. The old rate of exchange, which had been essential for the cheap imports of capital goods and the cheap supply of raw materials from the agricultural sector, was said to have served its purpose. The time had come to move towards the export market and also to shift priority towards the agricultural sector.[5]

The government's proposed strategy for agricultural development was to be two-fold. In the short-term there was to be an increase in the distribution of fertilizers at a heavy subsidy, the procurement of better seed, pest control schemes, the control of soil erosion, salinity and water logging, and the introduction of mechanized agriculture in selected areas.[6] In the long-term emphasis was to be laid in the expansion of irrigation facilities. Overall rural development was to be co-ordinated and implemented through the Village Aid Programme.[7]

The realization that agriculture should now provide the basis for the expansion of the economy had of course not come about on its own. As we have seen it was motivated in many ways by the fact that for the further growth of the industrial sector the growth of the agricultural sector was a prerequisite. But the then government had little time to see the shift of its overall policy put into practice. In October 1958 a military *coup d' etat* abolished the parliamentary form of government. abrogated the 1956 Constitution, proclaimed martial law, and ushered in a new phase in Pakistan's economic history.

5.2 Economic Management during the Fifties —An Analysis of the Key Decisions

There can be little doubt that for almost the entire period of the fifties the most important aspect of the government's economic policies was the marked pro-industrial bias in its development strategy. What the principal reasons were for this strategy being followed must form the core of any analysis on economic management and decision-making during the fifties. However, there were a number of other problems with which the new government was faced and it is the short-term implications of these problems and the government's response to them with which we shall begin and then discuss in more detail the reasons put forward for the pro-industrial policy which dominated the economic scene during this period.

5.2.1 Day-to-Day Decision-Making/Very Short-Run Economic Management

a. *The Non-Devaluation Decision of September 1949*

One of the most important decisions with which the government was faced was the devaluation, in September 1949, of the Pound Sterling which was followed by the devaluation of a number of other currencies including India's. The reason why the Pakistani government did not devalue its own currency at that moment is one of the most controversial questions of the period and the genesis of the pro-industrial bias in government policy in many ways can be traced back to this decision.

On the surface it would have seemed natural that the Pakistani government should devalue especially since its major trading partner, India, had already devalued. The reason not to devalue therefore had to be justified on strong grounds especially since some observers felt that the decision was motivated principally by the desire to assert the country's independence *vis-a-vis* India, i.e., to show that Indian economic policy did not determine the country's economic decision-making.

The government of the day, however, strongly maintained that the reason for non-devaluation was principally motivated 'entirely by economic considerations'.[8] The argument advanced by the Finance Minister in his Budget Speech of 13 March 1950 against devaluation was two-fold.[9] Firstly, the country did not face a severe adverse balance of payments situation and the country's exports, consisting mainly of raw materials, were not price-elastic. Secondly, and more importantly, the country was on the threshold of industrial development necessitating the import of a large volume of machinery and capital goods.

The government felt that 'conditions favourable to industrialization should be created and maintained'.[10]

However, the most important factor behind the non-devaluation was the desire to protect the interests of the producers of exportable raw materials,[11] and this primarily meant getting a better price for raw jute exports to India. Some observers have therefore termed this decision as an 'East Pakistani decision' in principle strongly supported by the politicians of that wing of the country. As a result of this decision India suspended trade by not accepting the value of the Pakistani currency and a trade deadlock ensued. But the Korean boom changed the situation when, as a result of it, Pakistan had a strong balance of payments surplus. Its exports of raw materials came under heavy demand and India had to rescind its earlier decision and trade was once again opened between the two countries.

b. *Food Grain Shortages and Floods*

The government's economic efforts, during the fifties, centred on responding to the situations created by harvest failures mainly as a result of floods and other natural disasters. As early as 1948 there were severe floods in the Sind and Punjab and these had the effect of converting the expected surplus into a deficit and necessitating import of considerable quantities of food grain. Again, in 1951, the failure of the Monsoon, continued drought conditions, and locust attacks led to a disastrous wheat crop harvest of 2.99 million tons in 1952 as compared to 3.93 million tons in the previous year. This meant importing almost 804,000 tons of wheat during 1952-3 and the deficit in 1953-4 was expected to be almost 1.5 million tons. In order to meet the shortage, the government approached the USA, Canada, and Australia, as well as other countries, to provide long-term credits as well as outright gifts to help in the import of food grain. Again, during 1954, floods in the Punjab and East Pakistan adversely affected the food grain situation. This situation was repeated the following year. During 1956-7 the country again faced shortfalls in food production and had to resort to importing food grain though it had to pay much higher prices for these imports as they were bought from the world market at a very short notice.

As expected the government's major objective in response to the food grain shortage was to ensure its essential supply especially in the urban centres. Its capacity to do so depended on both its foreign exchange reserve position and emergency borrowing from foreign donors. In order to resolve the crisis it became increasingly dependent on Western aid-giving countries, especially the USA, which provided it with loans to help finance imports as well as grants and gifts of food grain.

c. *Prices, Black marketing, Hoarding, and Smuggling*

The immediate impact of an adverse food grain situation was on the price level. Throughout this period the government gave very high priority to keeping prices in check especially of essential food-stuff and consumer goods. A system of price controls and rationing was enforced although it was put under considerable pressure when extreme shortages developed. The higher prices of food grain in India also led to considerable smuggling and this further increased domestic shortages. The adverse supply situation led to black marketing (i.e., selling at prices much higher than the controlled prices) and the hoarding of commodities which further aggravated the pressure on prices.

The government tried to relieve the pressure on the prices of essential goods in two ways. The first was to take measures to increase production. As regards the supply of agricultural commodities it met with little success but, in the case of manufactured goods, the large increases in domestic production, especially cotton textiles, helped to improve the situation. The second was through imports. In the case of food grain this was done by emergency buying in the world market or by borrowing or obtaining grants from foreign donors. In the case of manufactured goods (besides price controls) the government tried to regulate prices by allowing a more liberal import policy where domestic shortages would occur, but this situation was very much dependent on the overall balance of payments situation.

d. *The Devaluation Decision in July 1955*

Ever since the collapse of the Korean boom, in early 1952, the balance of payments position had deteriorated and pressure to devalue the currency had been rising. The government, as we have seen, resisted devaluation mainly to provide capital goods (which had to be imported) at cheap prices to the industrial sector and tried to relieve the pressure on the balance of payments situation by imposing import controls. The foreign exchange reserves, which had been built up during the Korean boom, were being exhausted and by 1955 the government was beginning to feel the strain. In the Budget Speech for the year 1955-6, delivered on 31 March 1955, the Finance Minister had stated that 'the core of our problem in the development effort was the shortage of foreign exchange. We needed foreign exchange to import capital machinery and equipment from abroad in order to develop the productive capacity of our economy. Our foreign exchange earnings, which were always small in relation to our requirements, became still smaller when prices of jute and cotton, our main exchange-earning commodities, fell to nearly half in 1952. This was a serious challenge to our plans but we decided to take up the challenge. We decided to use the bulk of our resources for the import of capital goods and curtail import of consumer goods . . . this called for severe sacrifices on the part of the nation . . . it caused widespread suffering and deprivation'. He went on to say, however, that 'the confidence that our people reposed in their future through difficult days of consumer shortages and high prices has not been belied'.[12] The achievements in the industrial sector, especially in the production of textiles and jute, were then cited as the success that had been achieved.

The devaluation of the Pakistan rupee, in July 1956, by 30 per cent in relation to the Pound Sterling was mainly justified by stating that the first phase of industrialization was over and, with the exhaustion of the home market, there was a need to move into the export market. The old rate of exchange had served its purpose and was now an impediment in the exports of manufacturers and was causing progressive reduction in the incomes of the producers of raw materials. An important factor was the need to place the jute industry on a sound footing in the world market.

The impact of devaluation on the balance of payments situation was mixed. There was some improvement in exports but imports, which were earlier also being curtailed by government control, saw no fall. In 1955-6 the balance of trade showed a surplus and the government took this to mean the success of the devaluation decision. However, because of the increased rupee prices of exports and imports, and increases in money incomes of those producing for the export sector, domestic prices rose, especially for food items, (again made worse by bad harvests), and this reflected itself in a rising cost-of-living index.

Another adverse affect of devaluation was that the government had to pay more for the import of food grain and, though the government tried to reduce the effect on retail prices by providing subsidies, there were increases in retail prices. However, the improvement in the balance of payments situation lasted only for the year of the devaluation and in subsequent years the economy went into heavy imbalance again (Table 5.1). This was mainly because, though exports increased in volume, the increase in foreign exchange earnings was very low due to a fall in the world prices of Pakistani exports and an adverse movement in the terms of trade.

5.2.2 Short-Term Management and Development Strategy

Throughout the fifties there was a marked absence of any real commitment to a well worked out long-term development framework in the form of a five year plan. The Colombo Plan, which was published in 1951 as a Six Year Development Plan (1951-7), was a collection of projects, rather than a serious planning exercise, without any sectoral growth rates or production targets or a macro framework. Similarly the First Five Year Plan, which was to cover the period from 1955 to 1960, although a very impressive document, was never seriously implemented. It was officially published as late as March 1957 and was never given formal approval by the legislature.

In the early Budget speeches there is some reference to the Colombo Plan but it does not appear at any stage to have formed the basis of the development expenditure during those years. Similarly, although the Budgets and Annual Plans during 1956-7 and 1957-8 were said to follow the broad priorities given in the First Plan document, in reality, after the first two years had passed, it was exceedingly difficult to follow the strategy as outlined in the Plan document. One major factor which contributed towards this was the frequent changes of political governments during this period.

The broad objectives and strategy of the governments' short-term economic management and development strategy are therefore mainly contained in the Annual Budget Speeches and Development Plans put forward by the government of the day. A careful analysis of these documents reveals the following important priorities:

a. The rehabilitation of refugees
b. The commitment to strengthening defence capability through increases in defence expenditure
c. Priority to industrialization
d. Price stability

a. *The Refugee Problem*[13]

The most pressing immediate economic problem with which the newly independent country was faced was the large-scale migration of Muslim refugees who arrived in Pakistan from different parts of India at the time of partition. Till the end of 1955 it is estimated that about 7 million refugees entered West Pakistan (in East Pakistan it was 1.25 million) as compared to about 5.6 million Hindus and Sikh refugees who had left Pakistan for India. Rehabilitation therefore presented a problem of collosal magnitude. The Punjab, according to the 1951 census, received about 5.3 million refugees while the remainder went to Karachi and the interior of Sind. The extent of the impact of the refugee influx on the local population can be gauged by the fact that (again according to the 1951 census) the migrants, as a percentage of the total population of Karachi, were 55 per cent and, in the case of the Punjab, 25.6 per cent.

The immediate problem was that of providing relief to the migrants through the provision of food, clothing, shelter, and medical attention. This was done in the main group camps which were set up in the border areas. Relief was, however, only a temporary measure and the process of rehabilitation had to be undertaken almost immediately. A rough distinction was made between agriculturists and non-agriculturists and rehabilitation was accordingly made in rural or urban areas.

The bulk of the refugees were settled in rural areas mainly on the land left behind by the Hindus and Sikhs. The Punjab government, by March 1949, succeeded in settling 2.3 million refugees on 2.5 million acres of evacuee property land and, by 1950, almost all agricultural refugees had been provided with land from a pool of 3.9 million acres of evacuee property and 500,000 acres of government land. Each refugee family (estimated at five members) was allotted from 5 to 12 acres, and a pair of bullocks and plough were provided for five families settled on up to 60 acres of land.

At this initial stage, the refugees in rural areas were settled temporarily and steps were taken to verify the rights enjoyed by the refugees while in India. The claims made by the refugees were then compared with records obtained from the Government of India and after verification they were issued with 'quasi-permanent' allotments. Those who had earlier been tenants and tenants-at-will were allowed to remain on the lands allotted to them but a landlord-tenant agreement had to be executed between them and those provided with 'quasi-permanent' allotments.

Urban rehabilitation for the non-agricultural refugees posed even greater problems with the most urgent being that of housing. Earlier makeshift arrangements were provided but then a number of townships were established in the major urban centres to accommodate the refugees. In order to help the artisans and craftsmen among the refugees, the government established a Refugee Rehabilitation Finance Corporation to provide credit facilities which, by December 1956, had advanced nearly Rs 17 million in loans, invested Rs 3 million in industrial colonies, distributed sewing machines worth Rs 4 million on instalment credit, and supplied raw materials worth Rs 12 million to refugees at cheap rates.

A vast amount of resources had to be made available by the central government to help the provincial governments in meeting the large expenditure undertaken by them both during the relief phase and in the rehabilitation of the refugees. The central government offered both loans and grants-in-aid. The latter totalled Rs 257 million during 1947-8 to 1957-8. The Centre also imposed special taxes to raise funds which yielded Rs 119 million till March 1957. This, together with a special contribution of Rs 50 million, was distributed amongst the provinces. In addition the central government gave loans to provincial governments amounting to nearly Rs 37 million and re-imbursed them to the extent of Rs 67 million for expenditures incurred by them in the past.

Karachi was provided with special grants of Rs 47 million mainly for housing. The Centre also allocated Rs 158 million for Kashmir refugees by the end of March 1957 and finally the central government invested about Rs 15 million in the capital of the Refugee Rehabilitation Finance Corporation so that the total central government expenditure on refugees by 1958 was almost Rs 491 million.

b. *Commitment towards Improving Defence Capability through Increases in Defence Expenditure*

Immediately after Independence, the tension with neighbouring India and the aftermath of the Kashmir conflict led to a firm commitment on the part of the government to give very high priority to strengthening the country's defence capability. This was done mainly by setting aside a major portion of the country's revenue and capital expenditure for building up the defence forces. After the joining of the military pacts principally with the USA, i.e., CENTO and SEATO, a part of the defence expenditure was borne by the USA in the form of direct military aid but, even after taking this into account, a

Table 5.2: Defence Expenditure as a Proportion of Revenue Receipts, Development Expenditure, and GNP
All Pakistan (selected years) (Rs million)

	1949-50	1954-5	1957-8
Defence expenditure	625.4	635.1	854.2
(i) Per cent of revenue receipts			
a. Central government	63.7	46.6	48.0
b. Centre and provinces	47.0	33.6	34.9
(ii) Percentage of total development expenditure	193.0	114.8	60.7
(iii) Percentage of GNP	3.0	—	2.0

Source: Ministry of Finance, Government of Pakistan, *Budget in Brief, 1969-70*, Islamabad.

large portion of the country's revenues were directed towards defence. In Table 5.2 we have shown defence expenditure as a proportion of the total revenue receipts of the central government as well as defence expenditure in relation to the total development expenditure undertaken by both the central and provincial governments. The first ratio gives us an idea of the amount that defence expenditure took out of the total revenue which the government raised and in most years it was more than half of the total. Similarly, defence expenditure, in relation to total development expenditure, shows that in the earlier years defence was given a much higher priority than the development expenditure of the government and although in later years the figure was reduced it was still extremely significant.

In relation to the economic potential and capability, defence received far more than what should be its share in a developing economy. But the threat of its neighbours and the joining of the military pacts (i.e., CENTO and SEATO) played the most important role in determining its size in the national budgets.

c. *Priority to Industrialization*

Development strategy during the fifties was very heavily biased towards promoting industrial growth in Pakistan. In the very first Budget Speech the government's pro-industrial stance was clearly spelled out when the Finance Minister declared that 'it is of the utmost importance that encouragement should be given to new industries. Pakistan is at present mainly an agricultural country and in rapid industrial development lies our chief hope of increasing prosperity and a high standard of living for people . . . new industries will be warmly welcomed and that so far as our resources permit, they will be given every possible financial consideration.'[14] Also, as we have seen earlier, one of the important considerations behind the non-devaluation decision was the desire to obtain capital goods to establish industries at cheaper prices so that conditions favourable towards industrialization should be created and maintained.

A large number of fiscal incentives, especially in the form of accelerated depreciation allowances and tax concessions on industrial profits, were given and capital goods were made exempt from custom duties.[15]

However, in the earlier years, despite governments' pronouncements and incentives, the private sector moved into industry in only a small way. Trading was still much more profitable and the business community was still hesitant to invest in industry. The collapse of the Korean boom and the import controls on consumer goods changed this situation drastically and considerably increased profitability in the industrial sector. Also, as mentioned earlier, the government helped the private sector by setting up industrial units through the PIDC, mainly in collaboration with the private sector, and then transferring complete control to them.

One way of analysing the effect of the government's pro-industrial policy is to see the terms of trade between the agricultural and industrial sector at 'world prices'. What this means basically is that we see what a basket of agricultural goods would fetch in the world market and what a basket of industrial goods, with the same value as the agricultural basket in the domestic market, would fetch in the world market. For example, if the bundle of agricultural goods and industrial goods were both sold in the domestic market for Rs 100 but the agricultural goods fetched US$ 30 in the world market and the industrial goods US$ 15 then, relative to 'world prices', industrial goods would be receiving twice as much more in the domestic market.

These estimates of the terms of trade between industry and agriculture at world prices are shown in Table 5.3. However, over time there is some improvement as industrial prices declined relatively with improved efficiency and more competition in the domestic market although the marked bias in favour of the industrial sector emerges very clearly.

d. *Import Controls*

The decision not to devalue the currency in 1949 necessitated the imposition of selective import controls on the economy. These controls, which were relaxed only during the period of the Korean boom when the balance of payments situation was extremely favourable, were to be an important feature of the economy throughout the fifties.

These import controls became a very powerful lever in the hands of the government to affect and influence resource allocation in the domestic economy. Firstly, the import control system after 1952 favoured mainly the establishment of consumer goods industries by restricting the import of consumer goods and hindered the establishment of capital goods and intermediate goods industries since imports were freely allowed. Secondly, the government gave import licence privileges mainly to those importers who had imported during the 1950-2 period. These importers were called 'category holders' and this policy was referred to as the 'category system'. It obviously bestowed considerable economic gain on those who were in this category as they had almost a virtual monopoly in the trade of the imported items.

Table 5.3: Agricultural Domestic Terms of Trade Relative to World Price Standards[1]
(Three-year averages)

1951-2 to 1953-4	39.8	1957-8 to 1959-60	54.1
1952-3 to 1954-5	36.7	1958-9 to 1960-1	57.6
1953-4 to 1955-6	36.2	1959-60 to 1961-2	59.1
1954-5 to 1956-7	43.0	1960-1 to 1962-3	62.0
1955-6 to 1957-8	48.8	1961-2 to 1963-4	61.9
1956-7 to 1958-9	53.9		

1. This is the ratio of the implicit exchange rate of agricultural goods (weighted by marketings) to manufactured goods (weighted by agricultural purchases). The implicit exchange rate being the ratio between the domestic wholesale price of a commodity in local currency and the foreign price of the same item.

Source: S.R. Lewis, *Industrialization and Trade Policies*, Oxford University Press, London, 1970.

e. *Price Controls*

Apart from controlling imports, the government, during this period, also controlled prices with the major objective of bringing down the prices of consumer goods so as to lower the cost-of-living index. According to the government, the need for such controls arose whenever demand exceeded supplies.[16] Controls were exercised during different periods on the prices of cloth and yarn, together with other essential articles like drugs and medicines, paper, chemical dyes, cigarettes, vehicles, and construction materials. In the case of petrol, oil, and lubricants, prices were regulated by the oil companies in consultation with the government.

Price controls on manufactured goods were not only vehemently opposed by the private industrialists but they have also been subject to considerable criticism by economists[17] as one of the major faults of the economic policy-makers during this period. In many cases they resulted in the hoarding or black marketing of products and at times the controls became a means of using government power to bestow gains on certain sections of the community which benefitted from these controls.

5.2.3 Overall Development Priorities: Long-Term

We have repeatedly pointed out that during the fifties there was no overall long-term development plan being seriously implemented by the government and the concerned development departments and agencies. It could therefore be argued that since a long-term development strategy did not exist it would not be very useful to analyse the period in a long-term perspective.

However, an analysis of the pattern of private and public investments which actually took place during the period is still important for ex-post it shows the emphasis in development expenditure. From this a picture can emerge which, if not one of long-term strategy that was planned to be followed, still shows the long-term impact of the priorities which were implemented.

There are serious data problems in undertaking the exercise for the private sector and investment estimates available for selected years should be considered as rough approximations. Estimates of the public sector are, however, reliable since they are based on actual government expenditures.

In Table 5.4 we have shown the breakdowns of investment both for the public and private sector for two years, i.e., 1949-50 and 1954-5, to give an idea of the sectoral distribution of both private sector investments and public sector development expenditures during this period. Table 5.5 gives estimates of public sector expenditures only for the period 1955-60. The data clearly shows the following important features:-

(i) Investment in the industrial sector dominated the private sector investment in all these years and this situation remains unchanged even if we add together both public and private investment in the other sectors.

ii) Investment in the agricultural sector was minimal compared to industry as well as some of the other sectors. Only when we add investments in irrigation and a percentage share of the power sector (which we can attribute to agricultural development) is the total investment in the agricultural sector increased, but it still remains lower as compared to the industrial sector.

iii) Significant investments were made in infrastructural development especially in the transport and communication sector. There was also substantial private sector investment in housing which was undertaken mainly by the higher income groups.

iv) Investments in the social sectors, i.e., education and health, were minimal and these sectors had a very low priority in the total development expenditure.

Table 5.4: Gross Monetary Investment by Economic Sectors
All Pakistan (selected years) (Current price: Rs million)

	1949-50		1954-5	
	Public	Private	Public	Private
Agriculture	18	15	29	25
Irrigation	72	5	151	10
Power	23	—	50	—
Industry, Fuel, and Mining	10	200	105	665
Transport and Communications	73	40	144	25
Housing and Urban Development	55	145	87	205
Education, Health and others	7	—	33	—
Traders' Stocks	—	110	—	100
Total	258	515	599	1,030

Source: G. Papanek, *Pakistan's Development: Social Goals and Private Incentives*, Harvard, 1967, p. 286.

Table 5.5: Sector-wise Development Expenditure of Federal and Provincial Governments.
All Pakistan (Rs million)

	1955-60	
Agriculture	806	(11.7)
Water	1,461	(21.2)
Power	634	(9.2)
Industry	1,018	(14.7)
Fuels and Minerals	166	(2.4)
Transport and Communication	1,599	(23.1)
Physical Planning and Housing	690	(10.0)
Education, Health,and Social Welfare	533	(7.7)
Total	6,907	(100)

Note: Figures in Parenthesis are percentages of the total.
Source: Government of Pakistan, *Pakistan Economic Survey, 1979-80*, Islamabad.

NOTES

1. SEATO stood for the South East Asian Treaty Organization consisting of the following countries : Pakistan, Thailand, France, Philippines, Australia, New Zealand, USA, and UK, and CENTO for Central Treaty Organization whose initial membership consisted of Pakistan, Iraq, Turkey, and UK, but Iraq left the Organization in 1958.
2. See G.F. Papanek, *Pakistan's Development : Social Goals and Private Incentives*, Harvard University Press, Cambridge, 1967, p. 33.

3. See A.R. Khan, 'What has been happening to real wages in Pakistan?', *'Pakistan Development Review*, Autumn 1967, and N. Hamid, 'The Burden of Capitalist Growth—A Study of Real Wages and Consumption in Pakistan'. *Pakistan Economic and Social Review*, Spring 1974. According to both these studies real wages declined during 1954-8. The decline for all industries in West Pakistan was 3.7 per cent while in the cotton textile industry it was about 8 per cent. Hamid, op. cit.
4. Ministry of Finance, Government of Pakistan, *Fiscal Policy in Pakistan—A Historical Perspective*, Volume One, Islamabad, 1972, p. 241.
5. Ibid., p. 241.
6. Ibid., p. 241.
7. Ibid., p. 241.
8. Ibid., p. 71.
9. Ibid., p. 71.
10. Ibid., p. 71.
11. Ibid., p. 71.
12. Ibid., p. 221-2.
13. This Section is based on the statistics quoted in J.R. Andrus and A.F. Mohammed, *The Economy of Pakistan*, Stanford University Press, Stanford 1958, pp. 463-77.
14. Government of Pakistan, *Fiscal Policy in Pakistan*, p. 31.
15. These measures are given in detail in the different Budgets of these years. See Government of Pakistan, *Fiscal Policy in Pakistan*, op. cit., for details.
16. For details of the government's justification of price controls see *Budget Speech* for 1954-5, p. 190 in *Fiscal Policy in Pakistan*, op. cit.
17. See particularly M. Haq, *The Strategy of Economic Planning*, Oxford University Press, Karachi, 1963, pp. 49-55.

6 The Controversial Sixties

The sixties saw the economy achieving rapid growth in both the industrial and agricultural sectors and, distinct from the fifties, there were significant increases in per capita income. However, this period of rapid economic growth, achieved mainly as a result of the policies pursued, generated a great deal of economic tensions. These finally exploded in social and political unrest in the winter of 1968 and led to the downfall of Ayub's government. Increasing disparities in regional income between the provinces, a concentration of industrial economic power, the failure of real wages to increase significantly, and a general belief of increasing income-inequality, all contributed to the rejection of the Ayubian growth philosophy and strategy.

There is considerable controversy regarding overall economic performance during this period. For some, the sixties was one of considerable economic success and they relied on the economy's performance in terms of growth indicators to prove their case and argued that the resulting economic problems and tensions were either exaggerated or were a 'cost' one had to bear for rapid economic development. For others, the growth performance was exaggerated, especially if judged by the fact that it had led to very little improvement in the living standards of the majority of the people. Furthermore, the 'cost' of economic growth had been too high as the economic policies pursued during this period had played a significant part in accentuating inter-regional income disparities which finally led to the break up of the country. Given these extremely different interpretations of the economic performance of the sixties, it is not unfair to refer to this period as the 'controversial sixties'.

It must, however, be pointed out that regardless of the controversy on the overall economic policies pursued, there is agreement on the fact that the sixties was a period of 'sound' economic management especially as regards the short-run management of the country. In contrast to the fifties and seventies, the economy was subject to some kind of overall economic discipline within the frameworks provided by the Second and Third Five Year Plans. There was considerable monetary discipline and budget deficits were kept at a minimum. There was overall price stability although there were years of high inflation. Significant steps were taken to increase exports and in the case of manufactured goods there were substantial gains. The government machinery of economic controls over prices, imports, and industrial investment were steadily dismantled and greater recourse was made to 'market' forces which was considered to be a far more 'efficient' mechanism for the allocation of economic resources.

There is therefore much to recommend in a careful study of the sixties as regards the important economic decisions which led to these conditions during this period. But first we present a broad overall review of the period so as to familiarize ourselves with the significant economic developments and happenings which took place during this time.

6.1 A Broad Overview

The years between the military *coup d'etat* of October 1958 and the downfall of Ayub Khan in March 1969 can be divided into the following three distinct economic periods.

The *first phase* from October 1958 to the beginning of 1960 is one in which the government tried to impose 'strict' discipline on the economy by enforcing price and other economic controls, harsh punishments for black marketing, smuggling and hoarding, and measures against tax evasion. The *second period* is from June 1960 to June 1965 and it coincides with the period of the Second Five Year Plan. This period starts with the government reversing its earlier measures of strict controls over the economy towards a significant de-control over prices, investments, and foreign trade, a reiteration that private enterprise would be the main engine of economic development, and large increases in foreign loan inflows into the country. The September 1965 war with India, although of very short duration, is an important milestone in the sixties. The *third period*, which covers the years between 1965 and 1969, is marked by a decrease in foreign loan inflows, years of food grain shortages between 1965-7, a slowing down in industrial growth, a re-imposition of certain controls as foreign exchange constraint was felt, and increases in defence expenditure. The end of this period saw a spurt of very high agricultural growth in 1968 and 1969 because of the introduction of high yielding varieties of seed and, finally, the outbreak of severe social and economic unrest which signalled the downfall of Ayub's government.

The country's economic performance in terms of the growth rates of the important sectors, i.e., agriculture and manufacturing, the balance of payments situation, and the price index are given in Tables 6.1 and 6.2

Table 6.1: Growth Rates of Key Sectors and Movement of Important Economic Variables
Pakistan (West) 1957-8 to 1964-5

	1957-8 to 1958-9	1958-9 to 1959-60	1959-60 to 1960-1	1960-1 to 1961-2	1961-2 to 1962-3	1962-3 to 1963-4	1963-4 to 1964-5	1959-60 to 1964-5
Growth Rates								
(i) Agriculture	4.0	0.3	–0.2	6.2	5.2	2.5	5.3	3.7
(ii) Large-scale manufacturing	5.6	2.8	20.3	19.9	19.9	15.5	13.0	16.9
(iii) Per capita income	2.7	–1.6	2.1	3.2	4.1	3.7	6.1	3.5
	1957-8	1958-9	1959-60	1960-1	1961-2	1962-3	1963-4	1964-5
Balance of Trade[1] (Rs million)								
(i) Exports	434 (1,422)	444 (1,325)	763 (1,843)	540 (1,799)	543 (1,843)	998 (2,247)	1,075 (2,299)	1,140 (2,408)
(ii) Imports	1,314 (2,050)	1,024 (1,578)	1,805 (2,461)	2,173 (3,188)	2,236 (3,109)	2,800 (3,819)	2,982 (4,430)	3,672 (5,374)
Balance	–880 (–628)	–580 (–253)	–1,043 (–618)	–1,633 (–1,389)	–1,693 (–1,266)	–1,802 (–1,572)	–1,907 (–2,131)	–2,532 (–2,966)
Price Index[2] (1948-9 = 100)								
Karachi	123.1	118.3	125.0	127.3	130.0	128.0	131.9	139.0
Lahore	110.6	103.4	110.7	118.4	124.4	120.3	127.1	135.9

1. Figures in parentheses refer to All Pakistan, i.e., including East Pakistan.
2. General cost of living index for industrial workers.
Source: For Balance of Trade (All Pakistan) and Price Index, *Twenty-five Years of Pakistan in Statistics*. For others, Government of Pakistan, *Pakistan Economic Survey, 1979-80,* Islamabad.

and the trends in the levels of public and private investment and savings are shown in Table 6.3. The following important movements and trends clearly emerge:

i) Growth rates in the agricultural sector were significantly high in both the first and second half of the sixties. During the first half, the years of high agricultural growth were between 1960-1 and 1962-3 and then between 1963-4 and 1964-5. There was a marked slowing down during 1965-6 and in 1966-7. There was a very slow recovery in food crops in 1966-7 although overall agricultural growth was positive from a very low base of the previous year. The first significant year of the so-called 'green revolution' is between 1966-7 and 1967-8 when agricultural growth increased by 11.7 per cent after which there were significant increases in the next two years especially between 1968-9 and 1969-70.

ii) Both the first and the second half of the sixties witnessed impressive growth rates in the large-scale manufacturing sector. There was, however, a marked slowing down in the second half as compared to the first half and the overall growth rate of industry fell from 16.9 per cent to 9.9 per cent.

iii) During both periods there were significant increases in the per capita income which grew by 3.5 per cent per annum in the first half and by 3.7 per cent in the second. It is also interesting to see that in the first three years, i.e., between 1957-8 and 1960-1, the earlier phase of martial law and strict controls over the economy, there was no significant growth in the agricultural sector or per capita income although during 1959-60 and 1960-1 there was a very sharp increase in the growth rate of output in the large-scale manufacturing sector.

iv) Throughout the period there was a large deficit in the balance of trade which was financed by increasing the flow of foreign loans into the economy. During the first half of the sixties there was a sharp increase in exports in 1959-60, the year the exports bonus scheme was introduced, but then exports fell in the next two years, increasing very rapidly again only in 1962-3, and then increasing at a very slow rate. In the second half exports show a big jump only in 1967-8 but then again stagnate till the end of the period.

v) There was a general fall in prices in 1958-9 as the government employed strong measures against black marketing, hoarding, and smuggling. Throughout the first half there was only a very

Table 6.2: Growth Rates of Key Sectors and Movement of Important Economic Variables
Pakistan (West) 1965-6 to 1969-70

	1964-5 to 1965-6	1965-6 to 1966-7	1966-7 to 1967-8	1967-8 to 1968-9	1968-9 to 1969-70	1964-5 to 1969-70
Growth Rates						
(i) Agriculture	0.5	5.5	11.7	4.5	9.6	6.3
(ii) Large-scale manufacturing	10.8	6.7	7.6	10.6	13.9	9.9
(iii) Per capita income	4.7	0.2	3.8	3.5	6.9	3.7
	1965-6	1966-7	1967-8	1968-9	1969-70	
Balance of Trade[1] (Rs million)						
(i) Exports	1,204	1,297	1,645	1,600	1,609	
	(2,718)	(2,913)	(3,348)	(3,305)	(3,337)	
(ii) Imports	2,880	3,626	3,321	3,047	3,285	
	(4,208)	(5,192)	(4,655)	(4,897)	(5,098)	
Balance	–1,677	–2,329	–1,682	–1,347	1,677	
	(–1,490)	(–2,279)	(–1,307)	(–1,592)	(–1,761)	
Price Index[2] (1948-9 = 100)						
Karachi	147.0	162.1	162.2	165.0	173.4	
Lahore	134.6	143.8	146.2	147.9	152.8	

1. Figures in parentheses refer to All Pakistan, i.e., including East Pakistan.
2. General cost of living index for industrial workers.
Source: For Balance of Trade (All Pakistan) and Price Index, *Twenty-five Years of Pakistan in Statistics.* For others, Government of Pakistan. *Pakistan Economic Survey, 1979-80,* Islamabad.

small increase in prices except during 1964-5 when prices increased significantly. In the second half there was a sharp increase in prices in 1965-6 and 1966-7 as a result of the 1965 war and bad or poor agricultural harvests in these years. Prices then remained steady until there was a significant increase in 1969-70, mainly because of the political and social unrest in the country.

As regards the level of investment, domestic savings, and foreign aid inflows, the following movements clearly emerge as shown in Table 6.3.

i) The level of investment increased in the first half of the sixties after which there was a sharp break and it declined during the second half of the period.
ii) The increases in the level and movements of overall investment are closely related to the level of foreign loan inflows into the country (measured as the deficit on the balance of trade).
iii) The level of private savings, which increased in the earlier years of the sixties, slowed down after reaching a peak and stagnated for the rest of the period.

6.2 Very Short-Run Economic Management in the Ayub Period

Our analysis of economic management in the Ayub Period, after briefly reviewing a few important short-run decisions, will focus on some more general aspects of economic management which formed the broad premise on which the economy was run during this time. The reason for doing so is that, as distinct from the fifties when there was no overall clear long-term policy framework under which decisions took place, this was not true for the sixties when the Second and Third Five Year Plans were in operation.

Table 6.3: Behaviour of Key Macro Variables
Pakistan (West)

	1959-60	1964-5	1969-70
Gross fixed investment	11.1	19.7	14.1
Foreign resource inflows	5.3	8.7	3.0
Gross domestic savings	5.8	11.0	11.1

Source: R. Amjad, *Private Industrial Investment in Pakistan, 1960-70*, Cambridge University Press, 1982.

Unlike the fifties, when the newly independent state found itself faced with a number of pressing economic problems which put considerable strain on its economic resources and administrative capability, the sixties was a time of fewer day-to-day problems as regards the management of the economy. This was mainly because of good agricultural production in most years and less damage to crops by natural calamities like floods as had happened in the fifties. Also because of the high growth of output in the agricultural and industrial sectors during most years and little inflation from abroad there was general price stability, at least in the first half of the sixties.

a. *Initial Phase—Period of Controls and Harsh Punishments (Oct. 1958 to Jan. 1960)*

The military government, on taking over control, blamed the generally adverse economic conditions on mismanagement by the previous government and corrupt and unfair practices by the private sector especially in industry and retail trade. Besides adopting a very stringent monetary policy and cutting down on deficit financing, it also introduced strict price and profit controls in the form of administered prices and profit margins. And it prescribed heavy punishment for hoarding, black marketing, and smuggling. The initial impact of these controls was favourable and the general price index registered a fall in the early months after martial law. But the government soon found that it was an impossible task to administer prices and profit margins for the wide range of goods sold and produced in the economy. Within just over a year of taking over, the government began to dismantle the control system and moved towards a general policy of de-controls which we shall discuss in more detail at a later stage.

b. *Crisis Management (1965-7)*

The major crises which the government faced occurred between the years 1965 and

1967 when there was a burst of inflationary pressure, poor agricultural harvests during 1966-7, large increases in non-development expenditure (especially defence after the September '65 war with India), and cutbacks in foreign loan inflows which put a great strain on domestic resources and the balance of payments situation.

The immediate concern of the government during the years of poor harvests was to meet the food grain shortage and it resorted to large imports of food grain which, during 1966-7, were of the magnitude of 829,000 tons of wheat and 197,000 tons of rice. This was paid for from the country's own cash resources.[1]

Total food imports for 1966-7 were estimated at 2 million tons of wheat, rice, maize, and *sourgham,* valued at about Rs100 crores,[2] the bulk of which were provided as food assistance from the governments of the USA, Canada, and the FAO.

As a result of the difficult food situation and excessive monetary expansion, in order to meet the large increases in non-development expenditure (mainly defence), the price level came under considerable strain. The wholesale price index increased by almost 15 per cent during 1965-6 and by almost 10 per cent during 1966-7. However, both because of very good agricultural harvests in 1967-8 and a stringent monetary policy, the government was able to bring prices under control and there was a large decline in the general level of prices.

In the autumn of 1968 there was a general outbreak of discontent against the government which finally led to martial law being imposed in March 1969 and the abrogation of the Constitution. Of course a very large number of factors contributed towards this situation. We shall be looking into the major economic factors in some detail but there is little doubt that the economic crisis during 1965-6 and 1966-7 contributed towards the situation for it jolted the economy and the government was badly shaken even though it was able to bring the economic crisis under control.

c. *The Non-Devaluation Decision in 1967*[3]

As a result of the cutback in foreign aid after the September '65 war with India, the government began to feel a severe shortage of foreign exchange, a situation made worse by the increase in defence expenditure and the need to import food because of poor harvests.

Pressure therefore began to rise for a replacement of the multiple exchange-rate system and for outright devaluation mainly to boost export earnings (through cheaper exports) and to cut back on imports (as they would become more expensive). Furthermore, throughout the period the whole package of multiple exchange-rates had faced considerable criticism (especially from the IMF and the World Bank) because it undervalued the price of imported capital machinery and subsidized the industrial sector at the expense of the agricultural sector and the urban working classes.

In the 'working group', which was formed to look into this question, of its three members, the Planning Commission and the State Bank favoured devaluation but the Finance Ministry opposed it. The President, given these conflicting views, appointed a Committee consisting of the Finance Minister, Foreign Minister, Minister of Industries, Governor of the State Bank, and the Deputy Chairman of the Planning Commission. In the discussions which took place both the Foreign and Industry Ministers opposed devaluation, the former on the grounds that it would adversely affect Pakistan's 'image' in the outside world and the latter on the grounds that it would adversely influence industrial interests. The Deputy Chairman of the Planning Commission, whose organization had earlier built up a strong case for devaluation, did not now assert himself strongly and left the decision to the Finance Minister. The Finance Minister sought the World Bank's advice and the World Bank, which had earlier supported devaluation, now took a neutral stance. One reason why the World Bank which, in normal circumstances, would have favoured devaluation did not do so now was because of the recent UK devaluation. It did not want a spurt of devaluations to follow because the UK would then lose the advantage that it had hoped to gain through devaluation.

The Finance Minister finally opted for non-devaluation and the State Bank, which had earlier decided to favour devaluation, did not want to oppose the wishes of the Finance Ministry. The Foreign and Industry Ministers also said 'no' and the decision to devalue was dropped. Of course a number of steps had to be taken to control imports and these included reducing items on the free list and placing a number of items on a Cash-cum-Bonus scheme (i.e., at a higher import price) but the overall system of multiple exchange-rates continued to function.

d. *The Sugar Shortage (1967-8)*

The importance of very short-run management of the economy is perhaps best illustrated by the sugar shortages with which the country was faced during 1967-8. Because of the poor sugar-cane crop, sugar production was low and the government decided to import sugar to meet the shortage. However, in this case, the major importers also turned out to be the major domestic producers of processed sugar. It is alleged that a sugar shortage was now 'artificially' manoeuvred and sugar prices in the open market increased considerably so that most consumers found it impossible to purchase sugar in the market.

Although the crisis was resolved and prices were brought under control, the sugar shortage, brought the government in for considerable criticism and this is considered by many people as one of the important events which helped trigger the social and economic unrest against the Ayub government in the autumn of 1968.[4]

6.3 Pakistan's 'Model' of Economic Development in the Sixties

After the initial phase, lasting from October 1958 to the beginning of 1960 when strict controls were in operation, the government launched the Second Five Year Plan to cover the period from June 1960 to June 1965. The Plan embodied the basic objectives which the new government set itself and, more importantly, it laid out the framework under which economic development was to proceed during this period.

However, it is important to emphasize that the development strategy pursued during this period, which formed the basis of the Plan was a part of a 'model' of economic development and it is essential, before we analyse the short and long-term strategies, to state the basic premises, assumptions, and strategy of the 'model' itself.

The main features of this 'model' of economic development were outlined in the works of Mahboob-ul-Haq[5] and G. Papanek[6] and rested on the following propositions.

The first was that in the early stages of capitalist development a high degree of inequality is necessary to promote savings and create entrepreneurial dynamism. This has also been labelled the 'Doctrine of Functional Inequality'.[7] According to this strategy, resources are to be channelled to those groups in the community whose average and marginal rates of savings are thought to be high and this was the justification for the pro-industrial policies pursued and the concentration of industrial economic power amongst a few groups during this period.

The second proposition was that since domestic savings were low and export earnings not sufficient to achieve a high growth of output, foreign loans play an important role in bridging this gap. This formed the economic justification of the country receiving large amounts of foreign loans and getting into foreign debt. The 'model', however, visualized a decline in the amounts of foreign loans that would be required as development proceeds and the economy becomes more capable of generating domestic savings and foreign exchange earnings. However, according to the 'model', in order to achieve this stage the economy must obtain large amounts of foreign loans in the initial stages.

The important components of the strategy which were put forward in the 'model' were:

i) *A Policy of Economic De-Controls*

One of the major criticisms of the growth strategy pursued in the fifties was the existence of 'direct' controls, especially on imports (which were mainly on licence), and the undertaking of new investments in the industrial sectors. Also, from time to time, the government had imposed strict controls on the prices of domestically produced manufactured goods. These controls were considered to be both economically inefficient as well as a source of corruption.

Ayub's government, after launching the Second Plan, introduced a policy of de-controls over the economy. It dismantled controls on prices and profit margins, it 'liberalized' imports and made it much easier for those wishing to undertake new investments in the industrial sector. The main form of import liberalization was the shifting of a number of items from licence to selective importers to more easy accessibility to licences for imports as well as direct imports on bonus. In fact in 1964 a number of selected items were placed on the free-list, i.e., could be imported without permission. Similarly the government published the Industrial Investment Schedule and anyone wishing to invest in industries and projects listed on it needed no official sanction.

ii) *The Pro-Industrial Bias in Growth Strategy*

Despite the fact that this was a period of significant agricultural growth, both in the first and second half of the sixties, the overall pro-industrial bias in the growth strategy continued. This was to be implemented mainly by making available to the industrial sector machinery and imported inputs at the cheap overvalued exchange rate (which was about half of its 'true' market price). Also by keeping prices of agricultural inputs at below 'world' prices, it made domestic raw materials available to the industrial sector at very cheap prices. This, together with the policy of import controls and tariffs, tax concessions such as tax holidays, accelerated depreciation allowances, and loans at very low interest rates, added to a marked pro-industrial bias in the growth strategy.

It should, however, be pointed out that those who gained from these concessions were the large-scale manufacturers whereas the small-scale industrial sector participated to a much lesser extent in the overall industrial strategy that was followed.

iii) *The Neglect of the Social Sectors*

The strategy outlined in the 'model', by emphasizing economic growth as the major aim of economic development, also advocated a concentration of investment on those sectors which would lead to immediate gains in output. The 'strategy' therefore gave low priority to the social sectors especially for the provision of education, health, and housing facilities.

iv) *Low Priority to Equity and Social Justice Considerations*

As part of the 'model', not only measures to reduce increased inequalities were to be dispensed with but income inequalities were to be in some sense encouraged. The argument in support of this strategy was that it would lead to increases in domestic savings.

Other measures which followed from this strategy were that the wages of industrial labour were to be kept low (through restrictions on trade-union activity and banning the right to strike) so that the share of profits in value added in manufacturing were larger so as to lead to greater investment.

To summarize, Pakistan's 'model' of economic development for the sixties emphasized the maximization of the growth of output based on a strong support for the private sector and a postponement of equity and social justice for the future.

To evaluate the 'success' or failure of the 'model' in terms of its own pronouncements and assumptions and to identify the major factors which contributed to its rejection, we divide the overall period of the sixties into the two sub-periods of the first and second half of the sixties.

6.3.1 The Boom Years (1959-60 to 1964-5)

Short-Term Management

The short-term management of the economy (through the Annual Plans and Budgets) took place within the broad overall framework of the Second Five Year Plan and its major objectives, which were spelled out in the Budget Speech for the year 1960-1, were as follows:[8]

i) To stop the inflationary financing of government expenditure which in the past had put into circulation a volume of money out of all proportion to the increase in the availability of goods and services and thus had brought about a rise in prices.

ii) To increase foreign exchange earnings partly in order to rebuild the depleted reserves and partly to facilitate greater imports essential for domestic production and consumption.

iii) To create conditions favourable for an expansion of production and investment, involving the provision of incentives and the restoration of confidence on the part of both domestic and foreign investors. Besides these three measures, i.e., price stability, increase in exports, provision of incentives to stimulate production and investment, the short-term management during these years was also concerned with:

a. Refixing of targeted allocations in the Second Five Year Plan as regards development expenditures, both for the public and private sector, as the original allocations were exceeded in some cases (like the private industrial investment) in the first few years of the implementation of the Five Year Plan.

b. Regulating the policy of de-controls both to achieve price stability as well as to ensure that the economy adhered broadly to the direction fixed in the Five Year Plan.

Let us examine some of these objectives in more detail to see to what extent the government was successful in achieving them.

i) *Price Stability*

The government gave very high priority to price stability and followed a very conservative fiscal and monetary policy especially in the first few years of the sixties. For these conservative policies the government was subject to criticism by some quarters, especially by the trading community, who felt that this policy was adversely affecting the growth of the economy. Some went on to suggest that as a result of these policies economic activity would slacken and a deflationary situation would develop.

The government defended the policies it was pursuing strongly and the Finance Minister, in the Budget Speech for 1962-3, pointed out that the slower rate of monetary expansion during the past two years, as compared to the preceding period, was the result of deliberate government policy designed to reduce excess demand in the economy. He asserted that this policy had succeeded and had already paid dividends by way of stable prices.[9] He went on to say that 'unnecessary and impudent stimulation of the economy, through the injection of more money, cannot fail to aggravate our external difficulties. Our balance of payments and reserve position sets strict limits to our freedom of manoeuvre. A rapid increase in money supply, by increasing the demand for imported goods and diverting potential exports into the home market, would quickly exhaust our meagre margin of external resources and force us to impose import restrictions, rationing, and price controls'.[10]

The policies pursued by the government did result in considerable price stability during this period and, in the Budget Speech of 1964-5, the Finance Minister could boast that one of the most satisfying achievements had been success in restoring and maintaining price stability during the Second Plan when the actual increases had not exceeded 1.5 per cent a year.[11]

Only in the last year of the Second Plan, i.e., during 1964-5, did the price situation come under strain and the wholesale price index increased by about 6 per cent that year. The government felt that a major factor which had contributed towards this situation was the rapid rate of monetary expansion during the first six months and the government took measures through the State Bank to curb the expansion. This included an imposition of a 25 per cent margin requirement against opening letters of credit for imports, a tightening of the quota system in respect of scheduled banks' borrowing from the State Bank, and an increase in the cash reserve requirements of the banks from 5 per cent to 7.5 per cent.[12]

ii) *Increase in Export Earnings*

The government had emphasized from the beginning that foreign exchange resources were vital for the full utilization and development of the *economy's* productive resources. The large increases in foreign loans helped ease the balance of payments situation to a great extent but the government realized the need to increase export earnings. The major measure introduced to achieve this was the introduction of the *export bonus scheme* in January 1959 which provided price incentives for exporters of selected manufactured goods. To compensate for the overvaluation of the rupee, exporters of manufactured goods and some raw materials received import permits equivalent to 10 to 40 per cent of the value of their exports. These bonus vouchers could be sold and with the tight import restrictions, especially on luxury goods, the demand for these permits was strong enough to command a premium of 120 to 150 per cent. The overall effect of the scheme was that it gave exporters additional rupees equal to 30 to 40 per cent of the value of exports.

The export bonus scheme proved effective and, in the first three years of its operation, net exports of the commodities covered by the bonus vouchers increased by an estimated 40 per cent mainly in cotton and jute products. A number of other measures like the 'Export Guarantee Scheme', 'Pay as You Earn Scheme', and the establishment of an Export Promotion Bureau in addition to an Export Promotion Council were introduced to stimulate exports.

The major short-term policy decisions which the government had to take were with regard to the percentage amount of bonus different commodities could earn, the list of items which could be imported through bonus, and the ensuring of a balance between domestic consumption and the diversion of goods to the export market. In June 1967 the government decided to remove the multiplicity of bonus rates from 7 to 2 by making it 20 per cent for all commodities entitled to 20 per cent or less and 30 per cent in all other cases. The aim was to stop giving preferential treatment to certain commodities as well as to give further incentives to exports of manufactured goods.

iii) *Policy of De-Controls*

Closely related to the policy of price incentives in the export sector was the policy of import liberalization which was gradually introduced over the years and which, to a large extent, was made possible by the increase in foreign loans and commodity aid inflows into the country. In the initial years a number of items were placed on the Open General Licence and under automatic licencing. In the beginning of 1964 import items of iron and steel, valuing Rs 45 crore, were placed on the free import list. In June 1964 a number of other items valued at about Rs 54 crore were also added to this list which now included industrial raw materials like non-ferrous metals, dyes and chemicals, rubber, machinery, spares and, for East Pakistan, cement and coal.

The effect of the policy of de-controls was that besides acting as a damper on the prices of imported goods by reducing the profit margins of importers it also favourably affected the utilization of industrial capacity which then increased significantly.

Besides imports, the other significant aspect of de-controls was with regard to private industrial investment. As the Second Plan got under way the government had published an Industrial Investment Schedule and all industries and projects listed on it needed no further government approval. The investor could directly approach PICIC or IDBP for foreign exchange loans to cover investment costs of imported machinery.

There is no denying that the policy of decontrols contributed significantly to the upsurge of industrial production and private sector industrial investment. However, it also created problems in that it became difficult for the government to keep track of industrial investment sanctioned and in many cases greater investment took place in certain industries than was originally planned.

Long-Term Management

The long-term development strategy pursued during the first five years of the sixties was outlined in the Second Five Year Plan the main objectives of which were:

i) To increase national income by 24 per cent and per capita income by 12 per cent.
ii) To increase food production by 21 per cent.
iii) To increase large-scale industrial output by 60 per cent.
iv) To increase export earnings by 15 per cent.
v) To increase the marginal rate of savings to 20 per cent.
vi) To create 3 million new job opportunities.
vii) To accelerate economic growth in less developed areas.

The total development expenditure contemplated under the Plan was Rs 1,900 crore out of which Rs 1,150 crore was in the public sector and Rs 750 crore in the private sector. The total amount of foreign loans and foreign investment needed for the Plan was estimated at Rs 800 crore apart from Rs 170 crore in surplus agricultural commodities under PL 480. The Plan envisaged a gradual increase in foreign assistance so that the amount received in the final year of the plan would be about 60 per cent greater than in 1959-60.

In the beginning of 1961 the size of the Plan was raised from Rs 1,900 crore to Rs 2,300 crore with Rs 1,462 crore in the public and Rs 838 crore in the private sector. The revision was brought about by a number of factors including the rise in prices since the original project studies were made, a more accurate assessment of requirements in certain sectors for which the Plan had previously made only approximate block allocations, and an expansion of the original physical targets in a few vital areas.

The pattern of actual public sector development expenditure during the Second Five Year Plan is shown in Table 6.4. A breakdown of the private sector investment is available for only the last two years of the Plan but it does provide a broad indication of the nature of the private sector investment during the Plan period. These breakdowns clearly bring out the following sectoral biases in private and public investment:

i) The pattern of public sector expenditure was heavily concentrated in the agricultural sector mainly because of the large expenditures on the development of water resources which were over 20 per cent of the total expenditure and the benefits of which were almost solely reaped by the agricultural sector. If we include half of the expenditure in the power sector as accruing to the agricultural sector then the expenditure on agriculture was about 40 per cent of the total.
ii) As in the First Plan, the social sectors received low priority and only 9.2 per cent of the total development expenditure was made in the education, health, population planning, social welfare, and manpower development sectors.
iii) The situation regarding private sector investment shows a completely different emphasis with the manufacturing sector dominating the total investment undertaken by the private sector. The percentage breakdowns for the last two years are fairly indicative of what happened in the overall period. It shows that the manufacturing sector accounted for over 40 per cent of the total private sector investment and that this was almost entirely undertaken by the large-scale sector.

6.3.2 Slow-down, Contradictions, and Collapse (1965-70)

The second half of the sixties was considerably different from the first half. The problems with which the economy was faced, especially between 1965-7—a combination of bad harvests, increases in defence expenditure, and a slowing-down of foreign loan inflows into the economy—have already been discussed by us earlier. The impact of these factors was a slowing down in the growth rate especially of the manufacturing sector, a rise in prices, and the re-imposition of controls as the foreign exchange constraint was felt once again. Although the economy recovered in the last few years, mainly because of the dramatic increases in agricultural production with the introduction of the high yielding varieties of seed in wheat and rice, the overall growth strategy resulted in social and economic tensions which led to the downfall of Ayub's government and a reimposition of martial law in the spring of 1969.

Table 6.4: Sector-wise Development Expenditure of Federal and Provincial Governments—Second Five Year Plan (Actual) All Pakistan

Sector	Amount (Rs million)	Percentage
Agriculture	1,856	13.3
Water	2,821	20.3
Power	1,520	10.9
Industry and Fuels	1,305	9.4
Minerals	322	2.3
Transport and Communication	3,072	22.0
Physical Planning and Housing	1,666	11.9
Education	913	6.5
Health	381	2.7
Population Planning, Social Welfare, and Manpower	94	0.7
Total	13,950	100.0

Source: Government of Pakistan, *Pakistan Economic Survey, 1979-80*, Islamabad, p. 229.

Table 6.5: Pattern of Private Sector Investment
Selected Years (Rs million)

Sector	1963-4 Amount	1963-4 Percentage	1964-5 Amount	1964-5 Percentage
Agriculture	517.8	14.1	548.2	13.0
Mining and Quarrying	9.6	0.3	17.3	0.4
Manufacturing				
Large-scale	1,329.4	36.3	1,550.9	36.9
Small-scale	177.7	4.9	192.4	4.6
Construction	103.6	2.8	44.5	1.1
Electricity and Gas	154.5	4.2	206.4	4.9
Transportation and Communication	463.5	12.7	626.1	14.9
Banking, Insurance, etc.	38.1	1.0	46.0	1.1
Ownership of dwellings	533.5	14.6	611.4	14.6
Services	334.1	9.1	354.4	8.5
Total	3,661.8	100.0	4,197.6	100.0

Source: Data obtained from the CSO, Karachi.

During the years between 1965 and 1970 the economy was supposed to operate within the framework of the Third Five Year Plan which was to start from July 1965. The major change in strategy envisaged in the Third Plan as compared to the Second Plan was in the direction of industrial growth from consumer goods to intermediate and capital goods. However, because of uncertain economic conditions, especially foreign loan inflows after the September 1965 war with India, the launching of the Plan was delayed. When it was felt that a planning framework could be reintroduced by the middle of 1967 the changes in the expected foreign loan inflows and bad agricultural crops led to a change in the strategy as outlined in the Plan. The sector most affected by this change was the industrial sector where, because of the shortages in foreign exchange, the emphasis was placed on those industries which either earned or saved foreign exchange and this mainly meant a development of consumer goods industries. The other major change in the strategy was that far greater emphasis was now placed on the agricultural sector. In the Budget Speech for the year 1967-8 the Finance Minister explained this change in strategy as follows:

'The most important step in a series of measures which the government took was the revision of the Third Plan strategy. While the operational size, objectives, and the principal targets of the Plan have been maintained, the sectoral allocations and priorities have been rearranged in a manner as would achieve the projected acceleration in the growth rate with a lower level of total investment. The main elements of the revised strategy consist of greater concentration on agriculture, fuller utilization of the installed industrial capacity and indigenous resources, a shift in favour of less capital and less foreign exchange, intensive projects, and postponement or rephasing of long gestation schemes'.[13]

The key element in the revised strategy was agriculture which was now accorded the highest priority after the disastrous years of crop failures. The main elements of this strategy were:

i) the speedier flow of adequate quantities of such agricultural inputs as fertilizers pesticides, better seeds, irrigation water, and improved implements to the farmer;
ii) adequate and timely credit facilities;
iii) price incentives to cultivators through the fixation of higher floor prices;
iv) in the industrial sector emphasis was shifted towards a fuller utilization of the existing capacity together with a selective expansion of industries geared to agriculture and exports. The industrial investment schedule, which was the chief instrument for implementing the private sector programme, was twice revised since the beginning of the Third Plan in order to reflect the new schemes of priorities and objectives, mainly by linking industrial investment with import liability and export performance.

The change in government economic policies seemed to bear fruit in that the economy registered a marked increase in the growth rate of the GNP during 1966-7 and, in his Budget Speech of 1968-9, the Finance Minister declared that 'the year has turned out to be a landmark in the economic history of Pakistan'.[14] He went on to say that 'despite the set backs to the economy, during the first two years of the Third Plan, the overall growth rate has already forged ahead of the 5.5 per cent growth per annum achieved in the Second Plan and for the first time the 'fruit' that we are 'striving' for in the form of the Plan target of 6.5 per cent average growth now appears to be 'in sight' provided we pursue our objectives with the same devotion and determination as we have done during the current year.[15]

The government also claimed that its success was not limited only to the growth front but that it had also been successful in holding the price line and that, as a result of the concerted measures initiated to check monetary expansion on the one hand and to improve the supply position on the other, the trend of rising prices which characterized the first two years of the Plan had been revised during the current year.

Unfortunately, however, the so-called change in the government's economic 'fortunes' turned out to be short-lived. Despite the fact that the economy was showing rapid signs of recovery, and the achievements in the agricultural sector were truly formidable, in the autumn of 1968 widespread disturbances started throughout the country and although a combination of regional, political, economic, and social factors were responsible for these disturbances, there was little doubt that the economic factors were perhaps the most important.

What were these economic factors which led to the fall of Ayub Khan's government and with it a rejection of the 'model' of economic development which he had tried to implement? Let us try to examine briefly some of the major factors which have been given considerable prominence.

i) *Inter-Regional Disparity*

A major contention of the economists of the former East Pakistan[16] was that the gains of economic development during the fifties and sixties were restricted to West Pakistan and that not only had there been little development in East Pakistan but that there had also been a transfer of real economic resources from the eastern to the western province. The growth of economic disparity between East and West Pakistan over the period was blamed on both a disproportionate government expenditure in the two regions as well as government policies relating to planning and development strategy especially the pro-industrial overall strategy.

It was argued that as a result of these policies the disparity of per capita income between East and West Pakistan rose from 32 per cent in 1959-60 to 45 per cent in 1964-5 and then to 61 per cent in 1969-70 (Table 6.6).

Table 6.6: Per Capita GDP in East and West Pakistan at 1959-60 Constant Prices.
Report of the East Pakistan Economists

Year	Per capita GDP East	Per capita GDP West	West-East disparity ratio	Index of disparity
1959-60	269	355	1.32	100
1964-5	293	426	1.45	141
1969-70	314	504	1.61	191

Note: Index of Disparity: (Disparity ratio-I) X 100 expressed as index with base 1959-60

Source: Mazharul Haq, *The Strategy of Economic Planning*, Oxford University Press, 1967, p.266.

There was considerable dispute between economists in East and West Pakistan over the extent of the disparity in incomes, of the breakdown in total development expenditure between East and West Pakistan, and whether there had been a net flow of resources from the East to the West. The West Pakistan economists,[17] although not disputing the fact that disparity had widened, gave alternative estimates to show that the difference was far less than that claimed by the East Pakistan economists (Table 6.7). They also argued that the amount of disparity in development expenditure was not as great as made out by them if the expenditure on the Indus Basin Project (which was a replacement work) was excluded and, finally, that since both regions were deficit areas in terms of inflows of resources from the outside world there was little question of resource transfer from the Eastern to the Western Province. They further argued that a major cause of the widening economic disparity was the high rate of agricultural growth which the West had experienced in the sixties rather than a lower level of investment in the East.

Table 6.7: Index of Disparity in Per Capita Income (West minus East, divided by West)
Report of the West Pakistan Economists

Year	Index of disparity
1949-50	17.9
1954-5	19.5
1959-60	24.5
1964-5	31.1
1969-70	37.9

Source: M. Baqai, *et al.*, 'Disparity in Per Capita Incomes', in *Income Inequalities in Pakistan, Pakistan Economic and Social Review*, Special Issue, 1976, p. 291.

Despite the differences and controversies regarding the extent of the widening disparity, and the factors responsible for it, there was little dispute that disparity had in fact worsened and that the economic policies pursued during the sixties had also significantly contributed towards this situation.

ii) *Little or No Increase in the Level of Real Wages*

One of the important factors that led to the fall of Ayub Khan's government was the massive labour unrest in the winter of 1968-9 and the widespread strikes throughout the period. During the sixties, the period of high growth rate in the industrial sector with very high profits for the industrialists, the level of real wages failed to show any significant increase. Also the sharp increase in prices in the second half of the sixties nullified the slight increase in wages that had taken place in the first half of the sixties. This situation is clearly shown in Table 6.8 where, in comparison with 1954, the level of real wages was lower in 1967-8 and only 2 per cent higher as compared to 1959-60.

Table 6.8: Index of Real Wages in Large-Scale Manufacturing

Year	Index of real wages 1959-60 = 100
1954	103
1959-60	100
1964-5	108
1967-8	102

Source: S.E. Guisinger and M. Irfan, 'Real Wages of Industrial Workers in Pakistan', *Pakistan Development Review*, Vol. XIII, No. 4, 1974.

iii) *The Increase in Income-Inequalities in the Sixties*

There was widespread feeling that income-inequalities had increased during the sixties and the statement,[18] by Mahbubul Haq, then Chief Economist of the Planning Commission, made in April 1968, that twenty-two families owned 66 per cent of the industrial wealth and controlled 87 per cent of the banking and insurance in the country, certainly played an important role in stirring up public resentment against the economic policies of the Ayub government. Although subsequent studies[19] have shown that this claim was exaggerated they still confirm a very high degree of concentration in the ownership of the industrial and financial wealth of the country.

There is some dispute as to whether income distribution actually worsened in the sixties. Nulty's study based on consumer expenditure surveys showed that during 1962-3, 1963-4, and 1966-7 there was a clear trend of increasing income inequalities.[20] Khandker's[21] study for West Pakistan, also based on consumer expenditure surveys, showed a rise in inequality in the urban areas between 1963-4 and 1966-7 but a fall between 1966-7 and 1968-9, with the inequality in 1968-9 being less than in 1963-4. Azfar's study on the other hand reported a decline in income inequalities for both urban and rural areas in West and East Pakistan between 1963-4 and 1966-7.[22]

Despite these seemingly contradictory results there is little doubt that the *popular* feeling in the late sixties was that inequality had increased during this period. A major factor responsible for this feeling was the considerable increase in the level of conspicuous consumption and wasteful expenditure on extravagant and lavish housing and other consumer durables by the richer classes in the country. Also, even if the actual level of income distribution had not worsened, the number of people living in abject poverty was still very significant and the display of conspicuous consumption in the face of this extreme poverty stirred considerable tension and finally led to an outbreak of unrest in the country.

6.4 Conclusion

With the fall of Ayub Khan's government in March 1969 martial law was once again imposed and the Constitution was abrogated. In March 1971 civil war broke out and in December 1971, with the intervention of the Indian forces, the country was divided with East Pakistan becoming the State of Bangladesh.

In West Pakistan the Pakistan People's Party came to power on 20 December 1971 and continued to govern the country for almost five and a half years and it is its economic performance in this period to which we now turn.

NOTES

1. Budget Speech 1967-8, in *Fiscal Policy in Pakistan*, p. 558.
2. Ibid., p. 558.
3. The account presented here is based on discussions by the authors with those who were involved in the decision-making.
4. For details of the sugar shortage and crisis, see R Amjad, *Private Industrial Investment in Pakistan 1960-70*, Cambridge University Press, 1982.
5. Mahbubul Haq, *The Strategy of Economic Planning*, Oxford University Press, 1967.
6. G. Papanek, *Pakistan's Development: Social Goals and Private Incentives*, Harvard University Press, 1967.
7. Angus Maddison, *Class Structure and Economic Growth: India and Pakistan since the Moghuls*, Allen and Unwin, London, 1971.
8. *Fiscal Policy in Pakistan*, Volume I, pp. 345-6.
9. Ibid., p. 417.
10. Ibid., p. 417.
11. *Fiscal Policy in Pakistan*, Volume II, p. 471.
12. Ibid., p. 505.
13. Ibid., pp. 558-9.
14. Ibid., p. 587.
15. Ibid., p. 587.
16. For a detailed account of the case of the East Pakistani economists, see Mazharul Haq, *et al.*, 'Growth and Causes of Regional Disparity in Pakistan', in 'Income Inequalities in Pakistan', *Pakistan Economic and Social Review*, Special Issue, 1976.

17. For the arguments put forward by the West Pakistan-based economists, see M. Baqai, *et al.*, 'Disparity in Per Capita Incomes', in 'Income Inequalities in Pakistan', *Pakistan Economic and Social Review*, Special Issue, 1976.
18. *Dawn*, Karachi, 25 April 1968.
19. L. White, *Industrial Concentration and Economic Power in Pakistan*, Princeton University Press, 1975, and R. Amjad, *Private Industrial Investment in Pakistan 1960-70*, Cambridge University Press, 1982.
20. T.E. Nulty, *Income Distributions and Savings in Pakistan: An Appraisal of Developments Strategy*, Ph.D. Thesis (unpublished), Cambridge University, UK.
21. Both Khandker and Azfar Studies are published in 'Income Inequalities in Pakistan', *Pakistan Economic and Social Review*, Special Issue, 1976.
22. Jawaid Azfar, op. cit.

7 The Seventies

The seventies can be divided into two distinct sub-periods on grounds of overall growth performance, the approach towards economic development, and the form of political government. After the disastrous civil war in the then East Pakistan and the break up of the country, the People's Party government came into power on 20 December 1971 and remained in power till 4 July 1977. From that day till the present time the country has been controlled by a military government. In Section 1 of this chapter we review the overall management of the economy by the People's Party government with its emphasis on structural change and redistribution of income and, in Section 2, we review the performance of the military government till 1982 with its emphasis on growth and some steps towards Islamization of the economy.

7.1 The People's Party's Economic Performance (1972-7)

7.1.1 Structural Reforms

The structural reforms which the government carried out, some immediately after it came into power and others spread over its term of five years, showed that no basic or far reaching transformation of the economic structure was envisaged. The land reforms in agriculture introduced in March 1972, although reducing the ceiling on irrigated land from 500 to 150 acres and unirrigated from 1,000 to 300 acres, still left very large family holdings partly due to pre-emptive transfers to other members of the family. No compensation was payable for the resumed land which the government promised was to be handed over free of charge to the landless peasants or to holders of below subsistence holdings. The actual land which was resumed and distributed turned out to be fairly insubstantial.[1] In 1977, the ceiling on land ownership was further reduced to 100 acres of irrigated land and 200 acres of unirrigated land. This time the resumed land was acquired on payment of compensation but was to be given free to tenants and small cultivators. Again, as we see in Section 9.2, the land resumed was very little.

The nationalization in the industrial sector was initially limited to the capital and intermediate goods industry which, in a country where a consumer goods-led industrial growth had taken place, meant that less than 20 per cent of value-added of the large-scale manufacturing sector was taken over.[2] Here, too, most of the industries taken over were amongst the most inefficient in the industrial sector. Later, nationalization was extended to the vegetable *ghee* industry and, in August 1976, to ginning factories, rice husking, and flour mills. The nationalization of banks and insurance companies, however, was important and it had a far-reaching affect in that it did serve to break the link between the industrial and financial capital which had built up over the last twenty years and which had helped foster the concentration of economic power in the hands of a few families. The government also reserved the export of cotton and rice for the public sector.

Although the structural changes introduced by the government were marginal, there were two reforms which did have far-reaching influence. The labour policy provided immediate gains to organized labour and also basically strengthened their collective bargaining position. Labour also acquired benefits in the form of compulsory bonus, cash receipts for profit participation, and old age pensions. The workers' representatives were to be associated with the management to the extent of 20 per cent at the factory level. Workers were given a share in the capital of the company by setting aside a sum equal to 4 per cent of net profits. Greater medical coverage was also provided and compulsory group insurance was introduced. Employers were also to provide free education up to matriculation standard for one child of each worker. Most important of all, no employer could terminate the service of any worker without giving him the reason for his action in writing.

The second important measure was the reforms initiated to improve the conditions of the peasantry. The most important of these reforms was the more effective enforcement of the law preventing the ejectment of tenants from their holdings by the landlord, except under a decision of the court. The other was a significant change in the share of the produce between the tenant and the landlord and now the landlord had to bear the cost of the inputs and taxes. However, the extent to which this was implemented is disputable.

Of all the reforms introduced by the last government the most significant of all was the devaluation of the rupee in May 1972. The substantial net devaluation of the rupee (to US$ 1 = Rs 11) removed at one stroke the subsidy the industrialists had received in the earlier period because of the over-valued exchange rate. This reform, together with the increase in procurement prices of agricultural goods (which went up by almost 100 per cent in this period), made a deliberate attempt to alter the pro-industry anti-agriculture bias of the previous growth strategy.

7.1.2 Management of the Economy

From the structural reforms which were introduced and which had considerable impact on the performance of the economy, both favourable and unfavourable, we turn to the actual management of the economy during this period.

In carrying out this review, the approach we have adopted is slightly different from that adopted for the fifties and sixties. This has mainly been necessitated by the almost extraordinary conditions with which the economy was faced during this period especially the very large increases in the prices of imported petroleum and related goods which led to a very high level of inflation and a balance of payments pressure. To make matters worse, there were floods and pest attacks which damaged the crops severely in at least three of the five years.

The short-term management of the economy is covered in our review of the economic performance of the important sectors during this period and the long-term appraisal is made in terms of the overall objectives and strategy which the government seemed to be following for the period as a whole.

7.1.3 Short-Term Management

The short-term management of the economy during this period can be conveniently divided into two sub-periods (Table 7.1): (a) the initial two and a half years, when the economy showed a good recovery, and (b) the last three years when the economy was caught in a terrible depression-cum-balance-of-payments squeeze and a high level of inflation.

a. *The Recovery (December 1971 to 1973-4)*

The initial rehabilitation of the economy—the revival of the war shattered economy—with agriculture and industry stagnating, a high level of inflation, and the search for export markets for goods formerly sent to the then East Pakistan, was achieved with reasonable success. This was made possible by the good performance of both the agricultural and the industrial sectors—the high growth of the latter being greatly helped by the export boom which was to some extent a result of devaluation.

The government felt that the improved economic conditions were the result of both the structural changes which it had introduced and the measures which it had taken to boost output in the important sectors.[3] Improvements in the agricultural sector were seen to be the result of the higher support prices for wheat, rice, and sugar and the timely and adequate supply of essential inputs. The high growth rate achieved in industry was the result of better capacity utilization due both to a more liberal import policy and to an increase in exports. The substantial increase in exports was taken as proof that the devaluation measure had been successful. During 1972-3 foreign exchange reserves improved from US$ 171 million to US$ 342 million.

The government also felt that the economic reforms which it had introduced in the winter and spring of 1972 had prepared the economy to channel the gains in production towards meeting the essential requirements of the people. There was growing confidence about the prospects for future growth and the government, by the middle of 1973, could boast that 'the institutional changes together with remoulding of economic policies to satisfy basic needs of the common man, rather than greed of the privileged few, are designed to blaze a new trail of economic progress'.[4]

In the initial two years, although growth rates were high, the government was fully aware that the economy would take time to go back to the peak levels of 1969-70. What still caused considerable concern in the initial years was that *inflation* was still not under control and the price level had continued to rise. During 1972-3, the government had blamed inflation on three factors: the mishandling of the economy by the previous government, the devaluation of the currency, and, lastly, the monetary expansion caused especially by the increase in exports.[5] For the very large price increases in 1973-4, the government blamed external factors. It claimed that it was not to be blamed for inflation because, as a result of its internal policy, fiscal and monetary balance had been regained. There had been no significant deficit financing despite the pre-emption of resources for flood relief and rehabilitation. The growth in monetary assets was equal to the growth of the Gross National Product and monetary expansion had been almost entirely limited to the private sector. There had in fact been an overall contractionary effect in the government and foreign sector. The government therefore blamed the very high rate of inflation (more than 30 per cent during 1973-4) to the increase in oil prices, an unfavourable shift in the terms of trade, and the devasta-

Table 7.1: GDP By Major Sectors—Targets and Achievements
(Per cent growth)

	1972-3		1973-4		1974-5		1975-6		1976-7		1972-3[1] to 1976-7
Sector	T	A	T	(R)A	T	A	T	A	T	A	
Agriculture	5.1	3.1	2.9	5.4	6.0	2.0	9.9	3.9	8.0	2.0	2.3
Industry	12.6	5.6	6.7	6.1	8.5	3.0	11.3	1.5	7.6	0.8	2.9
Large-scale	15.6	6.3	—	—	10.0	3.0	13.6	1.0	9.0	2.0	—
Small-scale	2.6	2.7	—	—	2.9	3.0	3.0	3.0	3.0	3.0	—
Construction	10.0	13.5	12.9	10.8	12.0	15.0	10.0	15.2	15.2	2.3	12.0
Trade and transport	5.2	8.7	5.0	5.8	10.0	1.8	12.0	3.6	10.0	—	4.5
Rest	5.4	9.7	—	—	5.1	6.5	4.8	7.2	5.0	—	—
GDP	6.6	6.5	5.0	6.1	7.2	2.6	9.4	4.8	8.1	0.5	4.0

1. Sectoral Growth Rate for the period is at constant 1959-60 factor cost.
Note: T = Annual Plan Target; (R) = Revised; A = Actual Achievement.
Source: Government of Pakistan, *Annual Plans*, (various issues), Islamabad.

tion caused by floods which adversely affected the supply of most of the vegetables and other agricultural commodities.[6]

The increase in oil prices also threw off balance the advantages gained as a result of the increase in exports. There was considerable pressure on the balance of payments as the oil bill increased four times from US$ 60 million in 1972-3 to US$ 225 million in 1973-4 and the cost of fertilizer increased from US$ 40 million to US$ 150 million in the same period. The import bill almost doubled without any significant increases in the quantities imported.

b. *Stagnation, Inflation, and Structural Change (1973-4 to 1976-7)*

The next three years, starting in 1973-4, coincide with the 'big push' in public sector investments in long gestation projects and show a dismal performance in both the agricultural and manufacturing sector especially in relation to the high targets set in the Annual Plan. The reasons[7] given for these poor growth rates in agriculture were the abnormal weather conditions (a combination of floods and droughts) and the non-availability of water from Tarbela. The weak performance in the industrial sector was attributed by the government to the international recession and its weak recovery as well as to the failures of the cotton crop which directly influenced the textile industry. However, an important factor, which must also have had a direct bearing on industrial output, was the fact that private industrial investment had continued to stagnate from the second half of the sixties and, in a number of industries, increased output could only have been achieved if capacity was increased.

A review of government policy during this period shows that the government had in fact believed that the factors which had adversely affected the economy during 1974-5 were rooted in the international economic situation and it began the fiscal year 1975-6 in 'a climate of hope and optimism'.[8] However, these turned out to be premature and the economic crisis continued to deepen. Perhaps no factor influenced the economy's performance during 1974-5 more adversely than the disastrous cotton crop of that year when production was only 3 million bales against a target amount of 4 million. This was the result of heavy rains, floods, and massive pest attacks. The fall in cotton production had serious and widespread implications. It not only adversely affected cotton exports but it also denied the benefits of a surge in international cotton prices and the difficulties faced by the cotton textile industry were further aggravated.

During 1976-7 the economy was once again very seriously jolted at the beginning of the fiscal year. Widespread floods occurred, even severer in intensity than those of 1973, which devastated large areas of cultivated land. Heavy rains and pest attacks badly damaged the cotton crop. Finally, sluggish international demand further intensified the recession in the cotton textile industry. This situation was made worse by the mass movement launched by the opposition parties against the government. This started in the spring of 1977 and adversely affected output in the industrial sector. Although the country had a bumper wheat crop the overall situation, as shown in the growth rates for 1976-7, revealed a dismal economic situation.

7.1.4 Long-Term Strategy

Although it has been argued that during the period 1972-3 to 1976-7 the government did not have any clear cut statement of economic objectives and policies regarding where it wanted to steer the country's economy, a close study of the Annual Plans shows that a broad strategy definitely did exist. What is true is that it did not go in for medium-term planning and it was therefore not bound down by the discipline of a five year plan. However, there is considerable weight in the argument that given the extremely unsettled conditions, both international and domestic, a five year plan would have been impossible to implement at least till 1976.

An ex-post review of the economic policies followed by the last government indicates these broad objectives and the strategy to be pursued for the achievement of these objectives, mainly:

i) In the initial phase, covering the first two years, the major emphasis was on the introduction of structural reforms, a revival of economic activity, and a restructuring of the economy after its virtual collapse because of the civil war in East Pakistan and the loss of the East Pakistan market.

ii) After the initial rehabilitation of the economy, the main objectives of the long-term strategy were:

a. To transform the industrial sector from its consumer goods bias towards the setting up of basic industries mainly through an expansion of the public sector.

b. To invest substantially in infrastructure—especially in the development of water, power, gas, and communications.

c. To improve the conditions of the agricultural sector especially in relation to the industrial sector and, within agriculture, to improve the condition of the smaller farmers.

d. To redistribute consumption in favour of the poor through higher expenditures on social investment mainly education, health, and drinking water.

e. To increase employment opportunities especially in the rural areas.

The broad strategy which was followed for the achievement of these objectives, as far as can be discerned from the Annual Plans and the policies actually pursued, seems to be based on the following elements:

i) Since the increase in public investment and social services could not be met through public sector savings, they were to be financed through large amounts of foreign aid and deficit financing (Table 7.2).

ii) The pro-agricultural bias was to be achieved partly as a result of devaluation and partly through an increase in the support prices of agricultural commodities, the combined effect of which was to shift the terms of trade in favour of the agricultural sector.

iii) To counteract the large investments being made in long gestation projects, the strategy critically depended on an increase in industrial output through the better utilization of capacity and the high growth rate in the agricultural sector mainly through the increased supply of water from Tarbela.

iv) Since investment in capital intensive projects would generate little employment this was to be done through the People's Works Programme and for the educated unemployed through the National Development Volunteer Programme.

v) In the agricultural sector the smaller farmers were to be helped through the provision of inputs and other facilities by the Integrated Rural Development Programme.

vi) Since both international factors and domestic policies would fuel inflation, certain groups were to be protected against it in the urban areas. These were mainly the wage earners in the industrial sector and the lower grade employees in the government sector.

The most important and controversial aspect of the long-term development strategy was why the government decided to launch an ambitious investment programme at a time when the economy was already being squeezed. Although price inflation had slowed down

Table 7.2: Consolidated Revenues and Expenditure of Federal and Provincial Governments
(Rs million)

	1972-3	1973-4	1974-5	1975-6	1976-7
Capital expenditure	5,086	7,024	11,308	14,134	16,508
Financed by:					
Domestic resources	222	2,660	487	556	2,069
Foreign assistance	3,357	3,865	8,768	8,620	12,713
Expansionary financing[1]	1,507	499	2,035	3,858	1,726

1. Borrowings from the State Bank which add to the growth of money supply.
Source: IBRD, *Current Developments and Issues*, March 1977, Report No. 1423-Pak., (Washington).

from the peak of over 30 per cent in 1973-4 and 1974-5, it was still, even by government estimates, between 10 to 15 per cent. In the last three years, i.e., after 1973-4 (Table 7.3) there was a considerable acceleration of public investment especially in heavy industry and the level of overall investment was almost as high as the peak in the mid-sixties. This was financed through a combination of foreign loans and deficit financing.

Since the government did not have a medium-term planning framework in which these structural changes could be justified, the explanation given is difficult to evaluate in an overall perspective. The major reason seems to be that the government felt itself committed to bringing about structural changes so as to make the economy self reliant and that, rather than shy away from this commitment once the economic squeeze was being felt, its resolve to make the change became even stronger. To quote from the Annual Plan 1975-6, 'the only way out for the economy from the terrible squeeze experienced during the year was to move towards self reliance in food, fertilizer, energy, and basic industries'.[9] The government therefore took considerable pride in the fact that it was going through with its heavy public investment programme despite the fact that it had to resort to deficit financing to be able to generate funds to finance it's public investment.

There are two other reasons which can also help to provide an explanation. The first was that in the case of a major project, the steel mill, the previous military government had already made a commitment with the Soviet Union and even if on economic grounds a case could be made that in the short-run the economic costs would be very high, the decision to go ahead with the project was based on foreign policy imperatives rather than on narrow economic considerations. The second was that these projects also provided a convenient way in which to bring in as loans or as direct foreign investments the oil surpluses which were available with the oil producing countries of the Middle East. These countries had an interest in Pakistan's economy developing into a strong base for both heavy and intermediate goods industry and nuclear technology. But the real problem was that although the government itself had stated that 'the period during which a major programme of import substitution is being undertaken would require considerable external discipline in economic management',[10] it did not follow its own advice. The government seemed to display an attitude of 'waste' in its economic spending and this was clearly the case in the large increases in non-development expenditure as well as in the case of certain development projects like the Islamabad Sports Complex. But these few cases

Table 7.3: Share of Investment, Foreign Resource Inflow, and Domestic Savings in GDP

	1972-3	1973-4	1974-5	1975-6	1976-7 (E)
Investment	13.0	13.4	15.6	17.4	19.0
Fixed investment	11.5	12.3	13.7	17.4	17.6
Public	5.9	7.8	9.3	13.0	14.0
Private	5.6	4.5	4.4	4.4	3.6
Gross domestic saving	9.9	6.2	3.8	8.5	9.3
Gross national saving[1]	10.6	6.9	4.8	9.8	11.2
Public	–0.5	–0.2	–0.6	0.7	2.0
Private	11.0	7.0	50.4	9.1	9.2
Foreign resource inflow[2]	3.1	7.2	11.6	8.9	9.7

1. As per cent of GNP.
2. Balance of imports of goods and NFS, and exports of goods and NFS.
Source: IBRD, *Current Development and Issues,* March 1977, Report No. 1423-Pak., (Washington).

were exaggerated far out of proportion to the actual amount of funds which were set aside for them. Projects such as the Indus Highway which have been attacked as cases of economic waste can be very clearly defended both for their strategic importance as well as for the considerable benefits they would have brought to the people of the backward regions of the Sind and the Punjab.

7.1.5 A Critical Appraisal of the People's Party's Economic Strategy

The major failures and successes of the previous government's, economic strategy can be summarized below:

a. In the circumstances the economic and social development programmes were over-ambitious and their cost far exceeded the availability of domestic and foreign resources. By relying on deficit financing to meet the gap and by furthering inflation it squeezed the middle classes and they finally revolted against the regime.
b. Critical to the success of the strategy were high growth rates of agriculture and industry to cushion the long gestation of public sector programmes. The failures of these sectors meant that there was little growth of output from 1974-5 to 1976-7.
c. The strategy failed to generate additional employment mainly because the bulk of the investment was in capital-intensive projects. The People's Work Programme, which was to provide additional employment, was severely curtailed because its inflationary impact was considered to be too high. However, the employment situation was considerably improved by the large-scale emigration of the industrial labour force to the Middle East.
d. Although the government policies tried to shift the terms of trade in favour of the agricultural sector through higher procurement prices, it was only partially successful in its endeavours and, by the end of the period, agriculture's terms of trade were lower than what they had been at the beginning of the period (Table 7.4).
e. The government failed to establish the ideology of 'state capitalism' which it had initiated through the process of nationalization. It failed to establish a working relationship with the big monopoly houses which refused to invest throughout the period and preferred to invest abroad. Also, over time, the government exceeded its original policy of nationalization and began to nationalize industries other than those which had originally motivated the reform. This was especially true of the smaller units in the agro-based industries which hit the middle classes. The result of the lack of private investment during this period was that the economy was caught in a double squeeze. Higher oil prices and increases in remittances from workers abroad led to inflationary pressures and, with the private sector not investing, more funds were diverted towards consumption which further increased the demand pressures on the economy.

However, even after taking into account the above factors, credit must go to the government for a number of economic achievements:

a. First and foremost, by setting up basic industries, it rectified the imbalance in the growth of the industrial sector and laid the foundations on which a capital goods industry base could be built and whose favourable impact was felt after 1977.
b. It was able to protect the incomes of the industrial labour force and low income earners in the public sector during a period of high inflation although whether its policies brought about a significant

Table 7.4: Agricultural Terms of Trade
1959-60 = 100

	1965-6	1969-70	1972-3	1973-4	1974-5	1975-6
Agriculture Price Index	117	125	164	217	257	283
Manufacturing Price Index	102	119	146	180	238	271
Terms of Trade Index	115	106	112	121	108	104

Source: IBRD, 1977, p.43.

redistribution of income in favour of the poorer classes is disputable (Table 7.5).

c. It was instrumental in sending a very large number of people abroad, especially to the Middle East by making it simpler for people to go abroad. Although the remittances of these workers helped cushion the balance of payments squeeze, the very large increases were to come after 1976.

d. It brought about a fundamental change in the attitudes of the working class which became far more conscious of its economic rights.

7.2 The 1977-80 Phase

This study covers only the first three years of General Zia's governments and this is obviously too short a period to discern broad policy orientations and any long-term goals and strategies. But in many ways this short period marks a departure from the policies followed in the earlier phase. The private sector came back in favour and a fairly attractive structure of fiscal and non-fiscal incentives was gradually assembled in order to promote private investment in industry. However, the private sector's response, happy as it is with the change, is at best lethargic.

General Zia's regime also found the public sector rather unwieldy and overloaded with too many losing concerns. It had, therefore, to opt for a policy of slow denationalization. Attempts were also made to improve resource mobilization efforts, to control non-development expenditure, to restrain non-development imports and to promote exports, and thus to initiate the process of creating equilibrium conditions in the economy. Medium-term planning was restored. In general, this phase marks the economy's return to calm waters and to more predictable policies.

The economy responded by achieving higher growth rates (Table 7.6) and good performance in such critical areas as exports and food production. Some favourable factors such as higher remittances from Pakistanis working abroad and good weather for crops also helped. But inflationary pressures persist with no effective remedy in sight anywhere in the developing world. The level of deficit financing remains high. The widening trade gap needs to be covered with aid inflows. Domestic savings remain very low (Table 7.7).

Pakistan is, in short, experiencing definite changes in its economic policy framework but at a slow pace so as not to disturb the fragile equilibrium which is being established on the basis of a combination of incentives for private investment and effort, liberal imports

Table 7.5: Index of Real Wages in Large-scale Manufacturing
1959-60 = 100

1954	103
1959-60	100
1964-5	108
1967-8	102
1969-70	124
1972-3	143
1973-4	163
1974-5	159

Source: (i) 1954 to 1969-70, S. Guisinger and M. Irfan, 'Rural Wages of Industrial Workers in Pakistan', *Pakistan Development Review,* Vol XIII, No. 4, Winter 1974. (ii) 1972-3 to 1974-5, S. Guisinger, 'Wages and Relative Factor Prices in Pakistan', Mimeograph Draft, 1977.

Table 7.6: Sectoral Growth Rates percentage
Constant Prices of 1959-60

	1977-8		1978-9		1979-80	
	T	A	T	A	T	A
Agriculture	NA	2.4	6.0	4.2	6.6	6.0
Manufacturing	NA	8.5	7.4	4.8	8.1	8.1
Large-scale	NA	10.0	8.7	3.7	8.5	8.5
Small-scale	NA	3.0	3.0	7.3	7.3	7.3
Construction	NA	8.3	6.4	9.1	7.6	10.4
Trade and transport	NA	8.3	6.2	7.2	6.5	4.2
Others	NA	8.8	5.3	7.0	5.0	5.2
GDP	NA	6.4	6.1	5.9	6.5	6.2

Source: (i) Government of Pakistan, *Annual Plan, 1979-80,* Islamabad, for (a) targets and actual for 1978-9, p. 8. (b) targets for 1979-80, p. 8. (c) actuals for 1977-8, p. 3. (ii) Government of Pakistan, *Pakistan Economic Survey, 1979-80,* Islamabad, for actuals for 1979-80, p. 11.

of development needs, easier credit availability for priority sectors, relaxation of economic controls, and incentives for higher agricultural production.

But the major hallmark of the current phase is the initiation of the process of Islamization of the country's economic structure. The cautious steps taken so far are few and the overall framework is yet to acquire an Islamic look. But this is a task of historic magnitude. Starting with a lag of many centuries during which little effort could be made to apply Islamic principles to the changing socio-economic conditions and institutional structure in Muslim countries, considerable homework needs to be done and this underlines the need for a slow but firm start. But, given the people's commitment to Islam and the Islamic principles of faith in God, social justice, and fair play, the process which has been started is not likely to be reversed.

Short-term economic management at present seems to focus on a restoration of business confidence and a promotion of private investment and initiative while long-term management revolves round efforts to correct existing disequilibria in the economy and the process of Islamization.

Table 7.7: Saving, Foreign Resources Inflow, and Investment (Current Prices)
(Percentage of GNP)

	1977-8	1978-9	1979-80
Gross total investment	16.19	16.53	16.68
Gross fixed investment	15.65	15.69	15.87
Public sector	10.91	11.04	10.97
Private sector	4.73	4.65	4.89
Net external resource inflow	3.22	5.03	4.82
National savings	12.97	11.51	11.86
Public savings	1.72	1.00	2.82
Private savings	11.25	10.50	9.04
National savings as percentage of gross total investment	80.12	69.59	71.11
Net external resource inflow as percentage of gross total investment	19.88	30.41	28.89

Source: State Bank of Pakistan, *Annual Report, 1979-80*, p. 10.

7.2.1 Short-Term Management

The major element in short-term management is the restoration of private sector confidence and motivation in order to revive investment in industry and agriculture. This is being done by (a) denationalization of certain public sector projects; (b) protection of the rights of investors and the demarcation of spheres of activity between the public and private sectors; (c) offering a package of fiscal and other incentives; (d) relaxation of economic controls.

A number of agro-based industries which were run inefficiently and were heavily in the red[11] were denationalized in September 1977. Some small engineering units were also denationalized. In addition, some projects run by the Punjab Industrial Development Board are being handed over to the private sector.

In December 1977, the government also devised a formula for the demarcation of spheres of industrial activity for the public and private sectors. Only those industries were to be placed in the public sector 'which are basic, in which the private sector shows no interest or whose nationalization is in the national interest'.[12] Under this formula certain important industries like heavy and basic chemicals and cement were opened to the private sector.

A number of incentives have also been offered to the private sector, the most important of which is the tax holiday introduced in March 1978 aimed at encouraging industrial activity in some of the relatively backward regions. A number of concessions in import duties and income tax have also been given. Another major incentive is the grant of compensatory rebates ranging between 7.5 to 2.5 per cent on the export of a number of industrial goods. Incentives have also been offered to Pakistanis working abroad and for private foreign investors through the setting up of export processing zones. Since June 1978, the interest rate on fixed investment in agriculture and industry has also been reduced.[13]

An effort has also been made to relax economic controls and to simplify bureaucratic procedures, including the procedure for sanctioning private sector investments.

But the response from the private sector has been slow. Factors responsible for this slow reaction include high investment costs, high interest rates, high taxes, low profits, labour indiscipline, etc.[14] It is also said that streamlining the sanctioning procedure is not enough. A number of other approvals are also needed, particularly for infrastructural facilities (gas, water, electricity), where bottlenecks exist. There is some truth in these arguments. However, the policy of adding new investment incentives with each budget in order to maintain a certain rate of expansion of private investment also needs reconsideration. The private sector continues to ask for more and more and to wait for new measures rather than to respond to the present ones.

The ratio of gross fixed investment by private sector to public sector investment was 1.05 in 1969-70, 0.95 in 1972-3, 0.47 in 1974-5, and 0.48 in 1979-80.[15] As Table 7.7 shows, gross fixed investment by the private sector, which was 4.73 per cent of the GNP at current factor cost in 1977-8, only increased nominally to 4.89 per cent in 1979-80. Private savings also declined during the same period from 11.25 per cent of the GNP to 9.05 per cent. The composition of private investment (Table 7.8) shows that only 35 per cent of the total investment relates to agriculture and large-scale industry. Indeed the share of the large-scale industry has declined from 20.48 per cent in 1972-3 and 19.61 per cent in 1976-7 to 15.08 per cent in 1979-80.

Other elements in short-term management consist of attempts to correct price distortions and the re-introduction of medium-term planning. Price distortions were created through the subsidization of the use of a number of agricultural inputs and the consumption of certain food items. Despite great efforts to reduce the level of subsidy by the gradual enhancing of the prices of inputs like fertilizer, pesticides, tubewells, and seeds, as well as the urban supply price of wheat and sugar, the subsidy bill continued to rise from 0.85 per cent of the GNP in 1972-3 to 1.33 per cent in 1976-7 and 3.40 per cent in 1979-80.[16]

The present government is anxious to

Table 7.8: Sectoral share in Total Private Investment

	1972-3	1973-4	1974-5	1975-6	1976-7	1977-8	1978-9	1979-80
Agriculture	16.43	19.22	16.24	20.81	20.57	22.22	21.54	26.28
Mining and quarrying	0.51	0.60	0.58	0.51	0.48	0.46	0.45	0.41
Manufacturing large-scale	20.48	18.15	19.01	20.19	19.61	17.56	17.03	15.08
Manufacturing small-scale	6.87	8.49	8.58	7.87	7.52	7.23	7.26	6.53
Construction	0.64	0.70	1.19	0.77	1.53	1.20	1.25	1.20
Electricity and gas	3.01	0.03	0.02	0.03	0.03	0.02	0.02	0.07
Transport and communication	25.98	26.04	19.51	16.52	15.00	14.00	14.51	17.12
Banking, insurance, and other financial institutions	0.94	0.26	0.12	0.11	0.18	0.15	0.17	0.16
Ownership of dwellings	13.26	13.02	21.81	20.68	21.97	23.22	23.63	25.00
Services	11.92	13.52	12.92	12.54	13.12	13.93	14.13	14.16
Total	100.00	100.00	100.00	100.00	100.00	100.00	100.00	100.00

Source: State Bank of Pakistan, *Annual Report, 1979-80*, p. 12.

reduce its commitments to the public sector by completing on-going projects as soon as possible (for example, 88 per cent of the federal government programmes in industry in 1980-1 had been allocated for on-going projects) and also by reducing the involvement of the public sector in areas which can be taken up by the private sector. The overall policy is thus based on a consolidation of the existing structure rather than an expansion into new areas.

7.2.2 Long-Term Management

There is awareness of a long-term disequilibria existing in the economy in the form of (a) gaps between savings and investment, (b) balance of payments deficit, and (c) the budgetary deficit. There is a need for a more fundamental improvement in the level of savings in the country. As the situation exists at present, the public sector makes the major portion of investments while its share in total savings is quite small. There is hardly any mechanism for transferring private savings to the public sector except through government borrowings from the banking system. The market for government bonds and other papers is unorganized and small. Domestic savings can be increased primarily by reducing current consumption but with a high population growth rate there is little room for reduction in consumption. Price controls and rationing has been historically ineffective. The way out in the long run seems to be by restricting public spending and by encouraging private investment. This can reduce the existing imbalance between savings and investment. Long-term economic management, therefore, aims at making private investment in priority sectors more profitable and attracting investments made by private sector away from less desirable uses like trading and construction. But this will need flexibility in the pricing policy including a frequent review of prices in line with inflation and production costs.

The deficit in the balance of payments also tends to increase and a long-term strategy to create equilibrium seems to be emerging. A number of incentives have been offered for the promotion of exports while import policy continues to be restrictive. The government has been able to hold down imports in physical terms. During 1979-80, for example, the entire increase in the import bill was due to a price rise.[17] So far, part of the balance of payments deficit has been covered by remittances from abroad and these have shown a continuously rising trend. But equilibrium in this sector will have to depend upon more controlable and predictable elements.

The budgetary deficit also needs to be tackled on a long-term basis. The government is doing its best to phase out subsidies and to rely more on the improvement in support services to induce higher agricultural production. Privatization of the distribution of pesticides was a realistic step in this direction. In the long run an effort will have to be made to raise the marginal rates of taxation to fix the prices of various industrial and agricultural products and inputs at more realistic levels and to restrain any further growth in public expenditure.

Currently most of the government's effort in long-term management is concentrated on the process of Islamization which, in terms of the long-run impact on the economy, may surpass the restructuring of the development strategy and the Plan priorities. The process involves a basic transformation of the entire society and intra-social relationships in conformity with the tenets of Islam. Social justice in every walk of life by following the Islamic principles, especially in the distribution of income and wealth in favour of the poor, and the elimination of interest (*sood*) charged by banks are viewed as key features of the Islamization process.

The Islamic economic system is based on the principles of welfare and social justice, and the creation of wealth is seen as a way to achieve these goals. Economic activity is encouraged to the point of it being a moral obligation and individuals are given the right to own and use property but only to the extent of it being socially beneficial and ethically valid. Keeping means of production idle is not favoured and Muslims are obliged to use them in the best possible manner. Emphasis is also laid on the duty of the rich to provide assistance to the poor within an institutional framework in the form of *zakat.*

Zakat is a levy on wealth charged annually at the rate of 2.5 per cent. This is collected by the state from all those who own wealth above a certain minimum level specified in the Islamic *Shariah* (code). The resources thus mobilized are used to provide help to the absolute poor and to assist them in standing on their own feet.

The system was introduced in Pakistan in 1980 with the levy of *zakat* on all institutional savings of Rs 1,000 and above held for at least one year.[18] The total collection upto April 1981 was Rs 815 million. The distribution of this amount has been entrusted to a vast network of about 32,000 *Zakat* Committees duly elected by local communities throughout the country who prepared lists of those in need of help. The amount was distributed at the rate of Rs 40 per month per head. The committees are also authorized to collect voluntary payment of *zakat* on other assets from the affluent, and to distribute it within their own jurisdiction. The amounts involved so far are small but as more and more assets are brought under the coverage of the system, collections are bound to increase. But the main achievement so far in this regard is the creation of a credible machinery for its collection and disbursement.

Another levy enjoined by Islam is *ushr,* a tax on agricultural income at the rate of 5 per cent. The relevant law has been enacted but the collection of *ushr,* which will replace the existing land revenue, has not started as yet.

Steps have also been taken to eliminate interest and to gradually evolve an interest-free financial system. Islam strictly prohibits the charging of interest which violates the principles of social justice and social welfare. The idea of a fixed charge over and above the principal amount without sharing the risks involved in the use of the money by the borrower is repugnant to the Islamic norm of justice. Moreover, it distorts the investment pattern of the society channelling funds into interest-rate-determined, as against socially beneficial needs-oriented, lines of trade and production.[19]

A fixed and predetermined rate of interest, which is paid irrespective of the quality of the operating results of the enterprise, is also unjust to the entrepreneur if business suffers cumulative losses or if profits follow a declining trend. On the other hand, if the interest rate is kept artificially low, which is generally the case in developing countries, a fixed and predetermined interest rate is unjust to the savers and that is why an interest based economy encourages the inequitable distribution of income in favour of the entrepreneurs and discriminates against the savers/capitalists.[20] An interest-free system, if it can effectively link returns to savers with current levels of profits, can ensure justice to both the owners and the users of loanable funds.

Certain financial institutions like the National Investment Trust and the Investment Corporation of Pakistan are now operating on an interest-free basis. The interest-bearing securities and media of exchange have been replaced by the Participation Term Certificate (PTC) which embodies the Islamic principle of equitable risk-sharing between the borrower and the lender and enables the issuing company to raise capital for a specific period against the security of a legal mortgage on its fixed assets. The Bankers' Equity now provides equity capital to the corporate sector through the issue of PTCs instead of interest-bearing debentures. The House Building Finance Corporation, which advanced loans for the construction of houses, now operates on a rent-sharing basis.

In commercial banking, initial steps have been taken to shift operations to an interest-free system with the opening of interest-free counters in January 1981 and the acceptance of deposits under Profit and Loss Sharing Accounts.

Arrangements have also been made to float *mudaraba*, a business in which one person participates with his money and another with his efforts with profits distributed among the participants in agreed proportions. But any losses are borne by the person contributing the capital. His liability is unlimited while that of labour or management is limited to the extent of the reward of their services.

NOTES

1. For a detailed discussion on the impact of the land reform, and land resumed, and number of people who benefited, see Section 9.2.4.
2. R. Amjad, *Industrial Concentration and Economic Power in Pakistan*, South Asian Institute, University of the Punjab, Lahore, 1974.
3. See Government of Pakistan, *Pakistan Economic Survey, 1972-3*, Islamabad, pp. ix-xiii, for details.
4. Ibid., p. xiii.
5. Ibid., p. xi.
6. Government of Pakistan, *Pakistan Economic Survey, 1973-4*, Islamabad, pp. xi-xv.
7. See *Annual Plans* and *Pakistan Economic Survey*, Islamabad, for these years.
8. Government of Pakistan, *Pakistan Economic Survey, 1975-6*, Islamabad, p. xi.
9. Government of Pakistan, *Annual Plan, 1975-6*, Islamabad.
10. Government of Pakistan, *Pakistan Economic Survey*, 1973-4, Islamabad, p. xv.
11. Ghulam Ishaq Khan, *Budget Speech, 1979-80*, June 1979, Islamabad, p. 4.
12. Government of Pakistan, *Pakistan Economic Survey, 1979-80*, Islamabad, p. 43.
13. Ibid., p. 43.
14. Sultan Ahmed, 'Private Sector vs. Public Weal in Pakistan's Economy', *Dawn*, Karachi, 24 February 1981.
15. *Pakistan Times*, 'Editorial', 16 March 1980.
16. Government of Pakistan, *Pakistan Economic Survey, 1979-80*, Islamabad, p. 15 (Statistical Annexure).
17. Jawaid Azfar, Article in *Dawn*, Karachi, 30 June 1980.
18. Government of Pakistan, *Pakistan Economic Survey, 1980-1*, Islamabad, p. 262.
19. Mian M. Nazir, 'The Framework of an Islamic Economic System' in *Economic System of Islam*, published by National Bank of Pakistan, Karachi, 1980, p. 132.
20. For a more detailed discussion, see Mahfooz Ali, 'Some Aspects of an Interest-free Economy', *UBL Monthly Economic Letter*, Karachi, June 1980, pp. 4-18.

PART III

AGRICULTURE

8 | Agriculture: An Overview

The main challenge of development efforts in Pakistan lies in the rural sector which suffers from widespread poverty and a number of attendant problems encompassing social, economic and technological factors. The social problems arise mainly from a pattern of skewed distribution of land ownership which makes the rural society both rigid and iniquitous. The technological problems are the result of traditional cultivation methods perpetuated by pressures of population on land, the small size of cultivation units, and tenancy farming which block incentives for technological progress. The economic problems stem primarily from the inability of the agricultural sector to provide adequate opportunities for full employment and its resulting failure to yield incomes adequate for providing a satisfactory living standard to the rural population at large. Also, there is not enough saving capacity to enable capital formation for raising the productivity of both land and labour to optimize their potentials.

8.1 Major Trends

After Independence, the stagnation in agricultural production and the emergence of a food deficit in the fifties can be attributed not only to the existence of these problems but also to the absence of any integrated policy framework to tackle them. Except for the construction of a number of irrigation projects, the agricultural sector failed to stir itself out of a state of inertia. By the end of the fifties, however, pressing problems like food shortage, foreign exchange scarcity, and raw material constraints on industrial development were responsible for forcing the planners towards an agricultural policy. This policy aimed at achieving self-sufficiency in food, increasing production for both domestic use and export, reducing unemployment and underemployment, and restructuring land relationships.

The change in emphasis in government policy, which was initiated in the early sixties, coincided with the advent of the so-called 'green revolution'. This revolution started with scientific and technological breakthroughs in the form of inputs, like high yielding varieties of seeds (HYV), fertilizers, pesticides, and water, and it was accompanied by a greater spread of agricultural mechanization, mainly in terms of tubewells and tractors.

In (West) Pakistan the 'green revolution' period can be divided into two sub-periods with regard to the use of these inputs. During 1960-4, an increased water availability due to a greater supply of surface water and, more importantly, to an expansion in tubewell installations, mostly in the private sector, was the 'cutting edge of development'.[1] But in the second phase, i.e., 1964-9, high yielding varieties of seeds, fertilizers, pesticides, farm mechanization, and continued increases of supplementary water contributed to the agricultural breakthrough. The liberal subsidization of inputs and higher price incentives provided the needed motivation, in the form of higher profitability, for the adoption of the new technology package by the farmers.

The result of these economic means and technological improvements was that while the agricultural sector had experienced a growth rate of only 1.8 per cent per annum during the First Plan period, the average annual growth rate jumped to 3.8 per cent during the Second Plan, and to 6 per cent during the Third Plan period. The peak growth of 11 per cent was registered in the years 1967-8.[2]

Agricultural progress slowed down again in the seventies. The average annual compound growth rate of agriculture fell from 7.5 per cent during 1966-70 to 1.9 per cent during 1970-8. The reasons for this 'slow-down' were many. The 'green revolution' came riding in on a wave of significant increases in public expenditure on (productive and consumptive) subsidies which propelled the initial stage of the breakthrough. But the development of support services especially agricultural extension, research, education, and training had been almost totally neglected. Despite a greater availability of key inputs like fertilizers, high yielding varities of seeds, and water, the agricultural sector began to experience diminishing returns since enough attention had not been paid to the efficiency of their use. Thus, despite land reforms which were introduced in the early seventies, the institutional failure to supplement the 'magic formula' of the 'green revolution' proved crucial in slowing down agricultural growth. Only recently, in the late seventies, did agricultural production once again show an increasing trend mainly because of favourable weather conditions and a better distribution of inputs, but also because more appropriate price incentives were offered to the farmers.

8.2 The Role of Agriculture in Pakistan's Economy

The pre-dominance of the agricultural sector is usually one of the main characteristics of developing countries in the sense that agriculture is not only the largest contributor to the national income but also the major source of employment and foreign exchange earnings. It is also the provider of food grain especially for the growing urban population and for the generation of the investible surplus to finance development efforts.

It is thus evident that a programme for overall economic development must lay great emphasis on agricultural development. While it is necessary that other sectors should also grow in order to impart sectoral balance, it is the agricultural sector which must generate resources needed to finance the initial development effort. Any credible programme for growth, greater savings and investments, improved technology, and removal of social imbalances would be incomplete without agriculture making a major contribution to the entire effort and at the same time getting its due share of resulting benefits. While the proportionate contribution of agriculture in the national economic framework tends to diminish as other sectors emerge and expand, its role and functions continue to grow in both depth and range.

In a list of thirty-seven low-income countries (including Pakistan) having a per capita income of US$300 or less (in 1979 US dollars) the average contribution of agriculture to the GDP was 50 per cent in 1960 and 37 per cent in 1977.[3] On the average, agriculture provided employment to 73 per cent of the total labour force of these countries in 1976 as compared to 77 per cent in 1960. The percentage share in merchandise exports contributed by primary commodities (excluding fuels, minerals, and metals) was also very high being over 70 per cent in the case of nine of these countries.

Although Pakistan is still dependent on agriculture, it is in a position of relatively less dependence among this group of low-income countries. The share of agriculture in the GDP (at constant factor cost of 1959-60) was about 30 per cent in 1978-9, compared to almost 60 per cent in 1949-50. As regards employment, agriculture engaged 56.4 per cent of the total civilian labour force in 1978-9 as against 57.3 per cent in 1969-70 and 65 per cent in 1950-1. In export earnings, agriculture (which includes major and minor crops, fishing, forestry, and livestock) contributed 32.2 per cent in 1978-9 as against 44.8 per cent in 1971-2.[4]

Agriculture is not only the supplier of food grain for Pakistan's growing population, it must also meet an increasing demand for food which is the result of higher per capita incomes and increasing urbanization. However, failure of the agricultural sector to provide self-sufficiency in food has necessitated the import of food grain in the past years. This has resulted in the diversion of scarce foreign exchange to the import of wheat. This extra burden on the economy only serves to underline the importance of agriculture as the supplier of food grain.

The agricultural sector, especially during the fifties, contributed greatly to capital formation in the non-agricultural sector. Capital transfers have taken place from agriculture to other sectors, especially manufacturing, through the mechanism of taxation, direct purchase of farm products by the state for export and for supply to the urban market at less than market prices, channelizing of rural savings to non-agricultural sectors through banking and other financial intermediaries, and through government manipulation of the inter-sectoral terms of trade.

In the foreign trade sector, agriculture's contribution to export has been consistently high. It was 80 per cent in 1960-5, 82 per cent in 1972-3, and 66 per cent in 1977-8. Its share in total imports on the other hand was a modest 17 per cent in 1960-5, 29 per cent in 1972-3, and 21 per cent in 1977-8. This indicates that the net export earnings of agriculture contributed significantly to the financing of non-agricultural imports.[5]

8.3 Policy Framework for Agricultural Growth

Traditional agriculture as it exists in underdeveloped countries has been defined as the sector which has attained a particular long-run equilibrium with respect to the allocation of the factors of production at the disposal of the farmer, and with respect to investments to increase the stocks of such factors. It is also characterized, in most cases, by the pre-dominance of a small land-owning class, a dwindling class of small owner-cultivators and, at the end of the social scale, a large mass of marginal farmers, tenants, share-croppers, and landless labourers who are at the core of the poverty problem.[6] With little change in social relationships, no inducement to new investment, and widespread poverty of the rural masses, it is easy to understand why the traditional technology remained totally stagnant and also why it managed to survive over such long periods. Within the limits of this traditional technology and the state of technical know-how it is argued that the farmers have exhausted all possible economic opportunities inherent in it to increase production.

Many studies of peasant farming in underdeveloped countries conclude that traditional farmers are using their current resources very 'efficiently' and that any readjustments in the present factor combinations under existing traditional technology will provide very little growth. Additional savings and investments, in order to increase the present stock of factors under existing technology, offer very little growth opportunities due to low returns. The traditional farmers are thus 'poor but efficient'.[7]

The transformation of agriculture under these circumstances can take place mainly in response to new economic opportunities offered by the process of industrialization and expansion in infrastructural facilities. A greater need for raw materials for export and for use by indigenous industries, for higher food supplies to support rising standards of living, and for expansion of the domestic market for industrial products underline the compulsions for modernizing agriculture in developing countries. This can be done by introducing a new set of technology, know-how, and equipment. Transformation in agriculture is thus largely a product of developments in the non-agricultural segments of the economy though the process is hastened by a rising awareness and social consciousness of the rural masses which results in a building up of political pressures for social change.

Therefore, public policy aiming at achieving agricultural breakthroughs, generally seeks to create conditions within the rural sector which would bring about changes in the farmers' perceptions and preferences in favour of, and motivation to use, new factor-combinations pertaining to a higher level of technology. The external factors calling for basic changes in agricultural production pattern and productivity levels can be supplemented by helpful developments within the agricultural sector. The policy package generally comprises the following:

a. land reforms aimed at providing greater security to tenants and readjustment of land ownership pattern;
b. public investments for expanding infrastructural capacity in irrigation, power, transportation, and communication;
c. allocation of significant resources to provide and subsidize physical inputs, for example, fertilizers, pesticides, seeds, water, machinery, and credit;
d. imposition of a mix of low and premium prices for agricultural products to balance the conflicting demands for low urban food prices, high producer prices, and surplus for export;
e. creation of an institutional structure for encouraging local leadership and organizing the provision of various services like marketing extension and research through rural development and other programmes.

To what extent has Pakistan been able to break away from the traditional stagnant agricultural sector and put into operation institutional changes and the provision of key inputs to transform its agricultural sector? It is this important question to which we shall seek answers in subsequent chapters but first we must establish the agricultural resource base, output, and productivity trends to see both the magnitude of the resources available as well as the past performance of the agricultural sector.

8.4 Resource Base

8.4.1 Land

The total area of Pakistan is about 80 million hectares (nearly 197 million acres) of which 25.2 per cent is cultivated area, 10 per cent is culturable waste, and 3.6 per cent is under forests. The remaining 60 per cent of the area consisting of deserts, mountains, open water, and habitation is unsuitable for agriculture and forestry.[8]

Table 8.1 indicates changes in the pattern of land utilization since Independence. It shows that in the last three decades, the total cultivated area increased by 35.8 per cent and the cropped area by 58.2 per cent. Areas sown more than once registered a sharp increase of 241 per cent during this period thus indicating greater cultivation intensity.

Table 8.1: Land Utilization
(Million hectares)

				Cultivated area					
Year	Reported area	Forest area	Not available for cultivation	Cultivable waste	Current fallow	Net area sown	Total area cultivated/ sown (cols 6+7)	Area sown more than once	Total cropped area (cols 7+9)
1	2	3	4	5	6	7	8	9	10
1947-8	46.7	1.38	20.82	9.18	4.01	10.68	14.69	0.95	11.63
1957-8	48.48	1.30	20.50	10.44	3.69	12.55	16.24	1.38	13.93
1967-8	53.16	2.28	18.87	12.58	4.55	14.88	19.43	2.06	16.94
1977-8	54.97	2.86	21.47	10.69	4.79	15.16	19.95	3.24	18.40

Source: Finance Division, Government of Pakistan, *Pakistan Basic Facts, 1978-9*, Islamabad, 1980, p. 3.

8.4.2 Labour

The total civilian labour force in the rural sector was estimated to be 14.23 million in 1972 and 15.13 million in 1975. About 72 per cent of the rural labour force in 1975 was engaged in agriculture, forestry, and fishing, 9.0 per cent in manufacturing, 5.8 per cent in trade, 5 per cent in community, social, and personal services, and 3.4 per cent in construction.[9] Only 13.7 per cent in the rural labour force were paid workers while the rest consisted of self-employed workers (51.3 per cent), unpaid employees (34.1 per cent), and employers (0.8 per cent).[10]

In 1975 the rural labour force comprised about 72 per cent of the total civilian labour force compared to 78 per cent in 1961. In terms of marginal rate of labour absorption over time, out of an increase of a hundred persons in the total labour force in 1962, the rural sector absorbed sixty-seven persons. This declined to fifty-five persons in 1975. Indeed, except for a very brief period (1967-9), the marginal rate of absorption in the rural sector has been quite low.[11]

The employment picture in agriculture is rather complicated mainly because of the difficulty in making a clear distinction between employment, unemployment, and disguised unemployment. This stems from the special employment setting in Pakistan, particularly in the rural sector which is characterized by widespread under employment[12] of various forms, a preponderance of self-employed and unpaid family workers in the working population, and the fluid and intermittant nature of work patterns and economic activities.[13]

Disguised unemployment or underemployment is difficult to estimate. However, a recent estimate of 'chronic underemployment' in the rural areas puts it at over 2 million workers,[14] although in recent years emigration to the Middle East and other countries has improved the general employment situation and may have even created shortages in certain categories of skilled and semi-skilled workers.

As regards open unemployment in the rural sector, there are different estimates which put the unemployment rate generally between 1 to 2 per cent during the sixties and the seventies. These figures are based on a number of surveys conducted by the Statistics Division of the Government of Pakistan and other agencies.[15] These estimates seem to be surprisingly low, possibly due to the definition of 'unemployment' and the methodology employed in these surveys.

Another aspect of the employment situation in agriculture is the seasonal variation in the demand and the supply of labour. While during most of the year the labour supply is plentiful, both for permanent and temporary labourers, in more recent years shortages have been reported during critical periods of heavy work load, particularly during April-July and October-November, mainly due to wheat harvesting, and rice transplantation and harvesting.

8.5 Output and Productivity Trends

A general view of the progress made by agriculture in the last three decades can be obtained from the increase in value added in the agricultural sector from Rs 6,595 million in 1949-50 to Rs 15,814 million in 1979-80 (at a constant factor cost of 1959-60). This amounts to an overall increase of 139 per cent in thirty-five years. Decade-wise, the growth rate registered in agriculture, calculated on the same base, comes to 16.9 per cent in the fifties, 63 per cent in the sixties, and 18.8 per cent in the seventies.[16]

The index of agricultural production (1959-60=100) stood at 89 in 1948-9 which increased to 128 in 1964-5, 186 in 1969-70, and 239 in 1979-80.[17]

Agriculture consists of five sub-sectors: major crops, minor crops, livestock, fisheries, and forestry. Major crops usually contribute 50 to 60 per cent of the value added in the agricultural sector. In 1977-8, for example, the share of major crops in the total value added in agriculture (constant factor cost of

1959-60) was 57.57 per cent, while other sub sectors' contribution included 13.77 per cent by minor crops, 27.71 per cent by livestock, 0.64 per cent by fisheries, and 0.31 per cent by forestry.[18]

Rabi and *kharif* are the two main cropping seasons. Wheat, barley, gram, tobacco, rapeseeds, and mustard are grown in *rabi*, the winter crop, while in *kharif* the summer crops are cotton, rice, sugarcane, *bajra,* maize, and sesame.

The principal crops are classified into food crops and cash crops. Food crops include wheat, rice, *bajra, jowar,* maize, barley, and gram while cash crops include cotton, sugarcane, tobacco, rapeseed, mustard, and sesame. Taking the average annual output of the period 1950-5 as the base, (Table 8.2) the average annual production of food crops increased by 12.2 per cent in 1955-60, 26.3 per cent in 1960-5, 64 per cent in 1965-70, 103 per cent in 1970-5, and 153 per cent in 1975-80. The area under cultivation for food crops increased by 40.2 per cent in 1975-80 as compared to 1950-5. As regards cash crops, the rate of increase over the base year was 41.8 per cent in 1955-60, 114.6 per cent in 1960-5, 200 per cent in 1965-70 (the 'green revolution' years), and 194 per cent in 1970-5 when the growth in agriculture was somewhat subdued. But in the period 1975-80, the increase was 275 per cent higher than the base period.

Table 8.2: Trends in Principal Crops—Area, Yield, Production
(Area in 000 hectares, production in 000 tonnes)

	Food crops		Cash crops	
	(Annual average)		(Annual average)	
Years	Area	Production	Area	Production
1950-5	8,139	5,692	2,050	7,692
1955-60	8,158	6,390	2,376	10,912
	(2.23)	(12.2)	(15.9)	(41.8)
1960-5	9,385	7,190	2,426	16,507
	(15.3)	(26.3)	(18.3)	(114.6)
1965-70	10,403	9,350	2,842	23,111
	(27.8)	(64.2)	(38.6)	(200.4)
1970-5	10,449	11,566	3,126	22,666
	(28.3)	(103.2)	(52.5)	(194.6)
1975-80	11,415	14,401	3,196	28,883
	(40.2)	(153.0)	(55.9)	(275.5)

Note: Figures in brackets show percentage increase over 1950-5.

Source: Government of Pakistan, *Pakistan Economic Survey, 1980-1,* Islamabad, Statistical Annexure, pp. 24-7.

8.5.1 Wheat

Wheat is the most important food crop as it is the main diet of the people. Since 1950-5, wheat production has risen by 236 per cent (1979-80) while the total area under cultivation increased by 66 per cent and the yield by 103 per cent.

The average annual compound growth rate of wheat output between 1959-60 and 1977-8 was 1.63 per cent in area, 3.77 per cent in yield, and 5.42 per cent in production (Table 8.3).

The major reasons for the increases in total output and yield are the improvement in irrigation water supply during *rabi* season, a greater use of inputs especially fertilizer, use of better quality of seeds, and better cultural practices. In 1977-8, 74 per cent of the total area under wheat cultivation was sown with high yielding varieties of seed (HYV). Its lowest use was in Baluchistan (only 19 per cent) while its use was spread over 86 per cent of the cultivated wheat area in the Sind, 74 per cent in the Punjab, and 61 per cent in the NWFP. About 85 per cent of the total wheat output came from HYV. In 1977-8, the average yield in the country per hectare was 1,316 kilograms. This does not compare well with other countries like Turkey (1,774 kilograms), India (1,477 kilograms), Canada (1,999 kilograms), USA (1,774 kilograms), Mexico (3,483 kilograms), and France (5,057 kilograms) for the same year.[19]

The Fifth Plan targets for wheat are for 47 per cent increase in production, 11 per cent in area under cultivation, and 32 per cent in yield over 1977-8 by 1982-3. The total wheat output by the end of the Plan period is expected to be 13 million tonnes. The 47 per cent increase in output will be achieved through a greater use of fertilizer and seeds (27 per cent), an increase in area under cultivation (17 per cent), and the introduction of improved cultural practices (3 per cent).[20]

8.5.2 Rice

Rice is grown in 10.3 per cent of the total cropped area in Pakistan and on 18.5 per cent of the total area under food cultivation. Taking the average annual output for 1950-5 as the base, the production of rice rose by 253 per cent for the period 1975-80. The area under rice cultivation increased by 99 per cent and the yield per hectare by 79 per cent during the same period (Table 8.4). As in the case of wheat, the reasons for higher production are greater water supply, better seeds, and greater use of fertilizers. Of the total area under rice cultivation, 43 per cent is under HYV.[21] The two improved varieties of paddy

Table 8.3: Area Production and Yield Trends—Wheat

Years	Average total area (000 hectares)	Increase in average area as per cent	Average total production (000 tonnes)	Increase in average production as per cent of 1950-5	Average yield per hectare (kilograms)	Increase in average yield per hectare as per cent of 1950-5
1950-5	4,154	—	3,235.8	—	776.6	—
1955-60	4,736.6	14	3,677.6	14	782.2	1
1960-5	4,995	20	4,152.6	28	831.8	7
1965-70	5,774.2	39	5,716.2	77	977	26
1970-5	5,934	43	7,222	123	1,216.8	57
1975-6	6,111	47	8,691	169	1,422	83
1976-7	6,390	54	9,144	183	1,430	84
1977-8	6,360	53	8,367	159	1,316	69
1978-9	6,696	61	9,944	207	1,485	91
1979-80	6,886	66	10,870	236	1,579	103
1975-80	6,488	56	9,403	191	1,446	86

Source Government of Pakistan, *Pakistan Economic Survey, 1979-80*, Islamabad, Tables 3.2, 3.3, and 3.4.

Table 8.4: Area Production and Yield Trends—Rice

Years	Average total area (000 hectares)	Increase in average area as per cent of 1950-5	Average total production (000 tonnes)	Increase in average production as per cent of 1950-5	Average yield per hectare (kilograms)	Increase in average yield per hectare as per cent of 1950-5
1950-5	947	—	837.2	—	878.4	—
1955-6	1,078.8	14	909.6	9	846.8	(—)4
1960-5	1,246.4	32	1,158.8	38	929.6	5
1965-70	1,479.6	56	1,722.8	106	1,507.6	72
1970-5	1,511	60	2,311.8	176	1,531.6	74
1975-6	1,710	81	2,618	213	1,531	74
1976-7	1,749	85	2,737	227	1,565	78
1977-8	1,899	101	2,950	252	1,553	84
1979-80	2,033	115	3,204	283	1,576	79
1975-80	1,883.4	99	2,956	253	1,568	79

Source: Government of Pakistan, *Pakistan Economic Survey, 1979-80*, Islamabad, Statistical Annexure, pp. 24-7.

seeds are *basmati* and *irri*. In the Sind and Baluchistan, only *irri* is used whereas in the Punjab and NWFP both *basmati* and *irri* are used. Therefore, the national average was 1,553 kilograms which compares unfavourably with India (1,977 kilograms), Thailand (1,750 kilograms), Philippines (1,965 kilograms), USA (4,945 kilograms), and Japan (6,166 kilograms).[22]

In 1949-50, the total production of rice was only 800,000 tonnes. This rose to about 1 million tonnes in 1959-60, 2.40 million tonnes in 1969-70, 2.31 million tonnes in 1974-5, and 3.20 million tonnes in 1979-80. Rice is also an important exchange earner. About one third of the rice output was exported in 1972-3. In 1977-8, the share of export in total rice output was 29.8 per cent.

The Fifth Five Year Plan aims at increasing the area under rice cultivation by 9 per cent, production by 34 per cent, and yield by 24 per cent. Thus, the total output by 1982-3 is to be 3.9 million tonnes. This increase in production is to be achieved mainly through the improved use of seeds and fertilizers (18 per cent), an increase in area under cultivation (10 per cent), plant protection (4 per cent), and better cultural practices (2 per cent).[23]

8.5.3 Cotton

Cotton is the major cash crop and also an important foreign exchange earner. It is grown on 67 per cent of the area under cash crop cultivation and on 10 per cent of the total cropped area. About 25 to 32 per cent of the total output is generally exported, depending upon the level of internal production, domestic consumption, and external demand. Production trends in cotton have been erratic. Compared with 1950-5 figures, production decreased by 13 per cent in 1955-60 but then increased to 82 per cent above the base period during the Third Plan period and to 140 per cent during 1970-5. Since then cotton has suffered mostly from a lack of pest control and adverse weather conditions, with the result that production declined in the late seventies and it was only in 1979-80 that cotton registered a 177 per cent increase over the base period because of a record bumper crop. In 1979-80 the area under cotton cultivation increased by 59 per cent and the yield by 74 per cent over the 1950-5 figures. However, taking the average of 1975-80, the yield per annum was only 36 per cent higher than the base period (Table 8.5). From 212 kilograms per hectare in 1950-5, the

Table 8.5: Area Production and Yield Trends—Cotton

Years	Average total area (000 hectares)	Increase in average area as per cent of 1950-5	Average total production (000 tonnes)	Increase in average production as per cent of 1950-5	Average yield per hectare (kilograms)	Increase in average yield per hectare as per cent of 1950-5
1950-5	1,275.8	—	270.2	—	212	—
1955-60	1,393.2	9	236	(—)13	212	0
1960-5	1,400.2	10	357.8	33	254.6	20
1965-70	1,693.2	33	491.6	82	289.4	36
1970-5	1,917	50	649	140	339.6	60
1975-6	1,852	45	514	90	277	31
1976-7	1,865	46	435	61	233	10
1977-8	1,843	44	575	113	312	47
1978-9	1,891	48	473	75	250	18
1979-80	2,034	59	747	177	368	74
1975-80	1,897	49	549	103	288	36

Source: Government of Pakistan, *Pakistan Economic Survey, 1979-80,* Islamabad.

yield increased to 312 kilograms by 1977-8 which is higher than India (155 kilograms per hectare) and Brazil (259 kilograms per hectare) but lower than Egypt (681 kilograms per hectare), Turkey (740 kilograms per hectare), USA (583 kilograms per hectare), and Mexico (915 kilograms per hectare).[24]

By 1982-3, the Fifth Five Year Plan envisages a 33 per cent increase in yield and a 14 per cent increase in area under cotton cultivation. Total cotton production is expected to increase to 875,000 tonnes, i.e., 51 per cent over the benchmark figure. Most of the increase in output should originate from the use of seed-fertilizer packages (24 per cent) followed by an increase in area under cultivation (14 per cent), plant protection (10 per cent), and better cultural practices (3 per cent).[25]

8.5.4 Sugarcane

About 4.5 per cent of the total cropped area (which is 30 per cent of the area under cash crops) is under sugarcane cultivation. Sugarcane production showed a steady increase upto 1970 but since then production trends have zig-zagged mainly because of a shortage of irrigation water at sowing time and borer attacks. Both production and area under cultivation declined in the late seventies in spite of the rise in the minimum support prices for sugarcane, from Rs 0.15 to 0.16 per kilogram in 1977-8 to Rs 0.24 to 0.25 per kilogram in 1980-1. Sugarcane yield has shown stagnation, rising from 29 tonnes per hectare in 1950-5 to only 37 tonnes in 1975-80 (Table 8.6).

The Fifth Plan provides for a 23 per cent rise in production and a 23 per cent rise in yield. No increase in area under cultivation is envisaged and almost the entire increase in yield is expected to depend upon the use of better seeds and fertilizers. The total output is expected to rise to 34.3 million tonnes by the end of the Fifth Plan and the yield per hectare to 45,377 kilograms per hectare from the benchmark figure of 36,600 kilograms. Pakistan's yield per hectare is one of the lowest in the world. For the year 1977-8, the yield per hectare was 45,968 kilograms in Cuba, 53,383 kilograms in India, 68,783 kilograms in Equador, 73,443 kilograms in Mauritania, 79,201 kilograms in USA, and 83,041 kilograms in Egypt.[26]

Table 8.6: Production and Yield Trends—Sugarcane

Years	Average total area (000 hectares)	Increase in average area as per cent of 1950-5	Average total production (000 tonnes)	Increase in average production as per cent of 1950-5	Average yield per hectare (tonnes)	Increase in average yield per hectare as per cent of 1950-5
1950-5	245.6	—	7,192.6	—	29.18	—
1955-60	365.4	49	10,318.6	43	28.24	(—) 3
1960-5	468.5	91	15,849	120	33.58	14
1965-70	582.2	137	22,258.4	209	37.84	31
1970-5	607.8	147	21,646	201	35.72	24
1975-6	700	185	25,547	255	36.4	24
1976-7	788	221	29,523	310	37.5	24
1977-8	822	235	30,077	318	36.6	24
1978-9	752	206	27,326	280	36.3	24
1979-80	710	189	27,200	278	38.3	31
1975-80	954.4	289	27,935	288	37	27

Source: Government of Pakistan, *Pakistan Economic Survey, 1979-80,* Islamabad.

NOTES

1. Rashid Amjad, 'A Critique of the Green Revolution', *Pakistan Economic and Social Review*, June 1972.
2. Government of Pakistan, *Pakistan Economic Survey, 1980-1*, Islamabad, Statistical Annexure, p. 10 (compiled).
3. World Bank, *World Development Report, 1979*, Washington, August 1979, p. 130.
4. These figures relate to 'primary commodities' which include raw cotton, raw wool, rice, fish, hides and skins, and tobacco.
5. WAPDA *Revised Action Programme for Irrigated Agriculture*, Vol.I, May 1979, pp. 1-9.
6. Defining the rural poor as 'landless labourers, and owners and tenants with holdings of less than 5 acres', the total number of poor households in Pakistan in 1977 was 2 million and of poor population 13 million. See *Small Farmers and the Landless in South Asia*, World Bank Staff Working Paper No. 320, 1979, p. 1.
7. Schultz, *Transforming Traditional Agriculture*, Yale University Press, 1964, p. 44.
8. Government of Pakistan, *Pakistan Basic Facts, 1979-80*, Islamabad, p. 31 (compiled).
9. Statistics Division, Government of Pakistan, *Twenty-five Years of Pakistan in Statistics, 1947-72* and *Pakistan Statistical Year Book 1977*. Quoted in *Pakistan Economist*, Karachi, 16 May 1981, p. 19.
10. Statistics Division, Government of Pakistan, *Labour Force Survey, 1974-5*. Quoted in *Pakistan Economist*, Karachi, 16 May 1981, p. 20.
11. Mohammed S. Khan, 'Man on the Move', *Pakistan Economist*, Karachi, 16 May 1981, p. 18.
12. Underemployment can be defined as a situation in which the actual labour supply in a sector is in excess of the number required, had each worker been fully employed at the current level of technology, with the result that the marginal product of labour is zero, or near zero, and withdrawal of a large number of workers is not likely to cause any reduction in output.
13. S.S. Hoda, 'Statistics for Manpower and Employment Planning in Pakistan', article in *Manpower and Employment Statistics in Pakistan*, Pakistan Manpower Institute, Islamabad, 1977, p. 26.
14. Government of Pakistan, *Pakistan Economic Survey, 1979-80*, Islamabad, p. 4.
15. This is brought out in Pakistan Manpower Institute, *Manpower and Employment Statistics in Pakistan, 1977*, pp. 43 and 92. The surveys include annual Labour Force Surveys conducted by the Statistics Division and population census data for 1961 and 1972.
16. Government of Pakistan, *Pakistan Economic Survey, 1980-1*, Islamabad, Statistical Annexure, pp. 9-11 (compiled).
17. Ibid., p. 21.
18. Ibid., pp. 9-11 (compiled).
19. Ministry of Food and Agriculture, Government of Pakistan, *Agricultural Statistics of Pakistan, 1978*, Islamabad, 1979, p. 57.
20. Government of Pakistan, *The Fifth Five Year Plan*, Part II, Islamabad, p. 13.
21. Ibid., Part II, p. 19.
22. Government of Pakistan, *Pakistan Economic Survey, 1979-80*, Islamabad, p. 15.
23. Government of Pakistan, *The Fifth Five Year Plan*, Islamabad, p. 13.
24. Ministry of Food and Agriculture, Government of Pakistan, *Agricultural Statistics of Pakistan*, p.57.
25. Ibid., p. 57.
26. Ibid., p. 57.

9 Land Reforms

In agrarian societies, land is the primary productive asset and the tangible expression of economic and political power. Therefore, the struggle for control of land and its fruits is a constant one. Throughout history, patterns of land ownership and tenure have played an important, and at times decisive, role in shaping the political and social system. It has, in most cases, also helped to determine the possibility and pace of economic change. It was thus inevitable that as economic development became a major goal in these societies, and the principal concern of governments, that large concentrations of land ownership and the feudalistic pattern of social relationships came to be regarded as prime obstacles to sustained growth and development. Demands for radical changes in the land-tenure systems became more and more persistent both on grounds of social justice as well as a pre-requisite for economic development.

9.1 Land-Tenure

The land-tenure system determines the legal and customary relationship principally between the landlord and the cultivator but also between the different classes and other interest groups who live in the rural areas. Land-tenure is thus a crucial element in determining the framework of socio-economic relationships in the rural areas. The most important aspects of a land-tenure system are rights, titles, and obligations of the various parties —tenant, landowner, and the government— and permanent and periodical records are prepared to set down these rights.

It is obvious that a number of problems can arise in a system dominated by big landowners and characterized by a large concentration of land ownership. It breeds absentee landlordism whereby the landlord obtains a substantial share of the produce of the land without making any substantial effort or investment in the production process. He is, therefore, indifferent towards making his own contribution to land improvement or to better land management. The land is cultivated by tenants who suffer not only from social subordination to the landlords but also from different types of exploitation. The exploitation can take the form of high rents (in cash or kind) or insecurity of tenure which can lead to a lack of capacity as well as a lack of motivation for improving cultivation.

In addition to the existence of big landlords, which dominate the agrarian society, small independent cultivators also exist within the same socio-economic framework. As a result of the constant process of subdivision, which leads to a fragmentation of holdings, the small independent cultivators generally comprise one of the poorest sections in the rural society. Further subdivision may ultimately make some of them almost landless while others may subsist as part-owner-part-tenant. Another important characteristic of such a land tenure system is the existence of a large class of landless people in the rural sector who earn their living by working as labourers. It is these landless labourers, the insecure tenants, and those owning marginal subsistence farms who constitute the poorest of the poor in these countries.

9.1.1 The Concept of Land Reforms

In a general sense, land reform is regarded mainly as an attempt to redistribute the land in favour of the landless peasants and small farmers. In the over-populated countries of Asia, Africa, and Latin America, which suffer from under-development, stagnation in production, and an extremely low investment in agriculture, land reform understandably became a major social, political, and economic issue as development programmes in these countries were chalked out. Land being in fixed supply, it was considered consistent with the requirements of social justice to break large concentrations of land ownership and to establish a wider base of landholdings which should ensure a more intensive use of land resources, a greater motivation for hard work and investment in land improvement, and an increase in productivity through technological advancement. Land reforms in Pakistan, as in a number of other developing countries, sought to provide both a technological and motivational breakthrough by breaking down the rigidities of the existing land relationships.

Land-tenure is not, of course, the sole determinant of agricultural progress. It is one of many factors—including taxation policies and pricing, facilities for scientific research, credit, extension, transportation, and marketing—that together create an agrarian structure that promotes, or prevents, broadly-shared progress. Seldom can the tenure-system be isolated as the sole cause of poor productivity. Nor can the redistribution of land, or the reform of tenancy practices, alone guarantee dramatic rises in output. Appropriate changes in the array of support systems and policies that affect farmers' decisions are also crucial to production breakthroughs.

A decision to undertake land reforms often meets with strong resistance from landowners who constitute a powerful elite in agricultural societies. It is, therefore, preceded by political controversies and national debate. Even after a land reforms proposal passes through the legislative process, its implementation is a complicated task due to the lack of organization at the village level, a dearth of proper data, a faulty maintenance of land records, and lengthy and complex legal procedures. These obstacles can, of course, be overcome by a strong political will and the active support of the rural masses for the programme.

9.1.2 Pakistan's Land-Tenure System

The present land-tenure system inherited by Pakistan was the product of three distinct historical processes. The Mughals granted big *jagirs*, or landed estates, to their nobles and favourites in return for their loyalty and support, both military and political. When the Mughal empire disintegrated, a number of local and tribal chiefs occupied vast areas of land and became owners by virtue of occupation. The British made the problem more complicated by granting *jagirs* and land ownership rights to people whose support *they* needed. In Bengal, after unsuccessful attempts by the East India Company to collect revenue through its own officials, the rights of revenue collection were auctioned from 1772 onwards and in 1793 the revenue collectors were made proprietors of lands under the Permanent Settlement. When British control extended to other areas in the subcontinent, a more flexible approach was adopted and an attempt was made to base the land-tenure system on the pattern of existing relationships in each region between the landlord and the tenants on the one hand and the state and the landlord on the other. In the Punjab and the NWFP, the rights of large estate-holders, which were acquired during the period of political disintegration, were recognized. Land was also awarded to those who had rendered services to the British in the process of conquest.

As a result of these historical processes, three types of land-tenure patterns became established in present-day Pakistan.

i) *Private Landlordism*

This is the most common system of land-tenure and it exists in most areas of Pakistan. The proprietary rights are vested in individuals who pay revenue under periodical settlements. Before the 1959 land reforms, the holdings under this system varied considerably in size, ranging from a fraction of an acre to thousands of acres. While big landlords retain some of this land for self-cultivation, most of their holdings are parceled out in small lots to tenants. In the fifties there were two types of tenants: *occupancy tenants* (who were lesser in number) were those who enjoyed considerable security of tenure and whose right of tenancy was heritable whereas the vast majority of tenants were *tenants-at-will* who could be ejected at any time by the landlord and who thus suffered from insecurity of tenure.

ii) *Ryotwari System*

This is the system of direct holdings from the government without the intermediary of a landlord. The cultivator is treated as a peasant proprietor under this system. His rights are heritable and transferable. This system existed in most parts of Sind where, in the early part of this century, plenty of land was available but there was a paucity of cultivators. By fixing a nominal rent, the government encouraged people to settle on the land. This system was distorted when a canal network was constructed in the thirties following the completion of the Sukkur Barrage. As the land became highly productive and land values soared, many people occupied vast areas of land and became landlords in all but name. The land was actually cultivated by tenants, known as *haris*, who were given little protection under the law which, in fact, hardly recognized their existence.

iii) *State Landlordism*

Under this system, the state itself acts as the landlord and the cultivator is a tenant to the state and continues to cultivate, with heritable rights, as long as government dues are regularly paid.

In addition to these three patterns, small village communities were traditionally organized under the *Mahalwari* system in some parts of the Punjab and the *Bhaichara* system in the NWFP. Under this arrangement, in each village community, where land holdings are usually of small size, the owners of these holdings are individually as well as collectively responsible for the payment of government dues.

In addition, there were a number of *jagirs*, i.e., landed estates, which were exempted from land revenue in return for public services. The tenant-landlord relationship in Pakistan, unlike in the British feudal system, is not a market-oriented arrangement determined by bargains freely entered into but is the result of inherited status. Traditionally, the tenant paid 50 to 60 per cent of the produce to the landlord as rent-in-kind, or *batai*, and this system prevailed throughout most of the country. In some areas, however, cash rent was charged. The tenant was also made to pay a number of other charges including almost all the cultivation costs. Any sign of resistance to the landlord or reluctance to accept the *status quo* resulted in harassment and ejectment of the tenant. There was thus limited security against the unfairness and whims of the upper rural classes. According to the Food and Agriculture Commission (1960), 'when the terms of share-cropping permit an absentee-owner to get too large a share and bear too little of the cost and offer the tenant too little security, the tenant is discouraged from adopting improved methods which cost him more in money and effort'.[1] A more forceful indictment of the system was made by the Land Reforms Commission of 1959 which said, 'initiative and enterprise are absent; there is no security for those engaged in production; reward proportionate to effort is absent and incentive for greater production is lacking. There is no encouragement for capital formation and productive investment in agriculture. In many areas power is concentrated in the hands of a privileged few which hampers the free exercise of political rights and stifles the growth of democracy and democratic institutions.'[2]

9.1.3 Concentration of Land-Holdings

An idea about the extent of the concentration of land ownership can be had from some of the available data regarding land-holdings in the early fifties. In the Punjab, 0.6 per cent of the landowners owned 21.5 per cent of the total cultivated area while 31.8 per cent of the land was held by 78.7 per cent of the owners.[3] In the Sind, 3 per cent of the owners owned 48.6 per cent of the total cultivated area while 60 per cent of the owners had only 12 per cent of the land. In NWFP, 0.1 per cent of owners controlled 12.5 per cent of the land. After the establishment of One Unit, the consolidated picture of (West) Pakistan, as it emerged in the Agricultural census of 1960, showed that about 9 per cent of landowners held 42 per cent of the total farm area. Tenancy farming in the early fifties covered 56 per cent in NWFP.[4] By 1960, 45 per cent of the cultivated area in (West) Pakistan was under tenants, 32 per cent under peasant proprietors, and 23 per cent under tenants-cum-owners.[5]

9.2 Land Reforms in Pakistan

Historically, former East Pakistan was always considerably ahead of West Pakistan in the field of land reforms. Based on the recommendations of the Land Revenue Commission (1940) and the Bengal Administrative Enquiry Committee (1944), the East Bengal Estate Acquisition and Tenancy Act (1950) embodied a number of radical changes in the land ownership and tenure system. All sub-tenancies and subletting were prohibited, rent-receiving interest between the cultivating tenants and the state was abolished, a ceiling of 33 acres (13.35 hectares) was fixed for self-cultivation and tenants were given full occupancy rights including the right of transfer.

In the western wing, the focus of a series of land reforms has been on four aspects of land-tenure: (a) tenancy regulation; (b) the abolition of *jagirdari*; (c) the fixation of the ceiling on land ownership; and (d) the consolidation of holdings. Land reforms, mainly dealing with tenancy conditions, were introduced in the early fifties under separate laws in the Punjab, the Sind, and NWFP. This was followed by the 1959 Land Reforms which placed a ceiling on land ownership and attempted to make tenure conditions uniform throughout West Pakistan. Later, different land reform measures were introduced in 1972, 1976, and 1977. It is appropriate to discuss land reforms, which pertain to each of the four areas mentioned above, separately.

9.2.1 Tenancy Regulation

The earliest efforts in land reforms in (West) Pakistan dealt mainly with the regulation of tenancy conditions. The Muslim League Agrarian Reforms Committee (1949) suggested making occupancy tenants full fledged owners, providing security of tenure to tenants-at-will, reducing rents payable by tenants, and abolishing illegal exactions imposed on tenants by landlords. These recommendations were also supported by the Punjab Tenancy Laws Enquiry Committee. Accordingly, in the Punjab, tenancy legislation was enacted in 1950 which intended to abolish the various cesses (*Haboob*) which the tenants had to pay to landlords in addition to rent. Restrictions were imposed on the rights of landlords to eject their tenants. A tenant could be ejected only if he was not cultivating the land according to the specific or customary terms of his tenancy or if he did not pay the rent punctually. Areas up to 25 acres, under self-cultivation by an owner, were excluded from the scope of the law. The share of the landlords in *batai* was fixed at 40 per cent. Occupancy tenants were given proprietary rights without compensation to the landlords where no rent was being paid and with compensation (twenty times the annual rent) where rent was being paid. The law also reduced the burden of government dues on the tenants. It was laid down that the tenant shall be liable for the payment of government dues on the same basis as the *batai*.

In 1952, certain terms of the law were softened 'in favour of the owners who were allowed to exchange self cultivation areas with areas acquired subsequently by inheritance. Secondly, if at any time an owner disposed of any part of his self-cultivated holding, he could *de novo* eject tenants from his tenanted holding so as to secure 25 acres under self-cultivation'.[6]

In the Sind, where tenancy conditions were perhaps the most unfavourable, the Tenancy Laws Committee, which reported in 1945, suggested that occupancy rights should be granted to *haris* who had personally cultivated at least 4 acres of land annually for the same *zamindar* for an uninterrupted period of eight years. It also recommended giving greater security to the tenants. Another committee, known as the *Hari* Committee, was appointed in March 1947 and submitted its report in January 1948. The Committee, in its majority report, suggested only marginal adjustments in the system. While sympathizing with the *hari* for his hard life, the Committee devoted most of its report to defending the landlords. Its findings and recommendations were challenged in a note of dissent,[7] by one of the members who argued for radical changes in the land-tenure system so as to improve the conditions of the *haris*. Later, under the Sind Tenancy Act 1950, some attempt was made to provide relief to the *haris* by abolishing some statutory charges and fines and by giving permanent rights to cultivators of at least 4 acres of land for the same landlord for a continuous period of not less than three years.

In NWFP, security of tenure was given to all tenants for three years and full proprietary rights were conferred on occupancy tenants under the Tenancy Act of 1950.

In the Sind and the Punjab, these reforms did not achieve the professed aim of giving adequate protection to tenants in the desired manner. The laws were formulated in a way that left too many loopholes and these loopholes were fully exploited. Moreover, implementation of these reforms was at best halfhearted. In the Sind, the condition laid down for a *hari* to become a regular tenant was too strict and a careful landlord would not allow a *hari* to cultivate the same piece of land continuously for three years so that he could be entitled to permanent tenancy rights. Moreover, even the limited rights conferred on the *haris* could not be enjoyed by them because of the political and social influence of the landlords. Faulty and incomplete revenue records also made implementation difficult. The result was that instead of providing greater security, the reforms led to the ejectment of tenants on a large scale in the Sind and the Punjab. Of course, the reform effort made the tenants more conscious of their problems, and perhaps more determined to seek their full rights, and this led to tension between landlords and tenants. The only positive aspect of the reforms was that occupancy tenants became fulfledged landowners even though occupancy tenants were only a small part of the total number of tenants. As regards the abolition of illegal charges imposed by the landlords on the tenants, it is doubtful if the law achieved its purposes fully although it may have succeeded in limiting the extent of such exploitation. In NWFP, no serious tension was caused between the landlords and the tenants presumably because their respective rights were clearly defined in the tenancy law.

In the land reforms programme of 1959, insofar as tenancy rights were concerned, provisions were made to bring about uniformity in tenancy rights in (West) Pakistan. All occupancy tenants were made owners of land. Ejectment of tenants was allowed only if a tenant failed to pay rent, or if the cultivation of the land was such as to render it unfit for further cultivation, or if a tenant refused to cultivate or to sub-let. It also provided that as long as a tenant was cultivating some land, he could not be ejected from the house given to him by the landlord. In a case of ejectment, a tenant was to be compensated for disturbance and for any land improvements done by him.

In 1972, further legal provisions were made for the protection of the rights of tenants and for improving their share of the income from the land. The grounds for ejectment of a tenant were restricted to only one factor, i.e., failure to pay rent. The water rate and the cost of seeds were to be borne entirely by the landlord. In the case of the cost of fertilizers and pesticides, it was to be shared equally by the parties. Land revenue and other charges were to be paid by the landlord as in the past.[8] Levy of any cess and *begar* was banned. Another important concession to the tenant was his right to pre-emption in case the land under his cultivation was being sold by the owner. In December 1976, all occupancy tenants on state lands were made owners. In ejectment cases, after the appeals, a revision was open only to the tenants and not to the landlords.

What is the overall impact of these provisions, made by successive regimes, for the protection of tenancy? The degree of security and protection of tenure provided by any legislation depends upon the applicability and effectiveness of laws in the rural sector. To the extent that the law enforcing bodies in the rural areas are heavily biased in favour of the landed interests, the legal approach to strengthening the position of the tenants also remains ineffective. However, enactment of these measures, and the subsequent debates and controversies concerning them, have brought about a certain change in the outlook of all parties concerned. Thus, the final outcome of these measures is now dependent upon the ability of the tenants and the rural masses at large to organize themselves and to create an atmosphere in which the landlords can be made aware of the rights of the tenants as provided by the law.

According to a 1977 study, there was a spurt of ejectments for the first few years after the 1972 reforms. Ejectments are still continuing although they are far less numerous now, partly because the tenants who remain represent the minimum required for cultivation and partly because the new tenants are no longer being given the status of tenants. By using their influence with the bureaucracy, the landlords show the land the tenants cultivate as 'self-cultivated' through hired labour.[9] This allows the landlord to reduce the status of the tenant to almost that of a tenant-at-will who has virtually no protective rights as given in the more recent legislation.

9.2.2 The Abolition of *Jagirdari*

The grant of *jagir* means the transfer by government of some of its right to collect revenues in respect of a particular area and the enjoyment of the produce of any government land included in its limits. In some cases, the transfer of the right of revenue collection was also accompanied by a land grant. Most of these *jagirs* were in the Sind where the total area held by *jagirdars* in 1960 was over 1 million acres (0.45 million hectares).[10] The cultivation of *jagir* lands was usually undertaken by *zamindars*, some of whom existed even before the grant of *jagir* rights to the *jagirdars*. These *zamindars* either cultivated the land themselves or employed *haris*. Thus they became sub-lessees on the *jagir* land and were called *mukhadims*. The *jagirdars* had no power to evict the *mukhadims* from the land or to raise the rent beyond the fixed rates. Apart from *mukhadims* there were three types of *jagirdars:*

i) *Jagirdars* who were recipients of assignments of land revenues only with no interest in the land whatsoever;
ii) *Jagirdars* who had been given assignments of land revenue and were also granted *mukhadimi* rights without any payment;
iii) *Jagirdars* who were recipients of assignments of land revenues and who acquired *mukhadimi* rights after payment.[11]

In the Punjab all *jagirs*, except military *jagirs* or those connected with religious or charitable institutions, were abolished in

1952. In the Sind, the government issued orders for the abolition of *jagirs* in 1954 but they were challenged in the courts and the orders were never enforced.[12] In NWFP, the few *jagirs* in existence were abolished in 1952.

The final abolition of all types of *jagirs* came in the 1959 Land Reforms. *Jagirs* belonging to category (i) were abolished without any compensation. In the case of category (ii), the *jagirdar-mukhadims* were allowed to retain the permissible area and any excess lands were resumed with no compensation. With regard to category (iii), the *jagirdar-mukhadim* was compensated for any excess lands surrendered by him. *Mukhadims* who were not *jagirdars* were also allowed to retain permissible areas and were paid compensation for lands surrendered by them. The total *jagirs* land declared under this provision was 924,853 acres (374,275 hectares) out of which 332,607 acres (134,601 hectares) were resumed by the government. As a result of the abolition of *jagirs,* the total amount accruing to the government in terms of land revenue was estimated at Rs 3 million in 1960.[13]

9.2.3 The Ceiling on Land Ownership

The reason behind fixing a ceiling on land ownership is to assert the principle of owner-cultivation and to incorporate it in the agrarian structure thereby accelerating the transition from a feudal to an egalitarian society. Fixing a maximum limit also restricts, though it does not always eliminate, tenancy cultivation and its imperfections. A number of developing countries, including those where the right of private property is regarded as sacred, have introduced such ceilings. In Turkey, for example, the limit is 1,250 acres (about 506 hectares) whereas in Iran it is 1,000 acres (404 hectares) of irrigated and 2,000 acres (809 hectares) of unirrigated land. The ceilings in some other countries are : 7.5 acres of wet land (3 hectares) and 14 acres of dry land (about 6 hectares) in Taiwan; 12.5 to 37.5 acres (5 hectares to 15 hectares) of wet land and 50 acres (20 hectares) of dry land in Indonesia; 62.5 acres (25 hectares) for non-cultivating owners and 1.25 acres (0.5 hectares) for cultivating owners in Greece; 100 acres (40.5 hectares) in Cuba and Egypt; and 200 acres (81 hectares) of irrigated and 750 acres (303.5 hectares) of unirrigated land in Syria.[14]

In Pakistan, the Punjab Muslim League Agrarian Reforms Committee (1949) suggested the ceiling of 150 acres (61 hectares) of irrigated, 300 acres (121 hectares) of semi-irrigated, and 450 acres (182 hectares) of unirrigated land. The same proposal was included in the draft of the First Five Year Plan. However, in the revised version of the First Plan, it was stated that these figures 'were not sacrosanct' even though it was asserted that 'ceilings are an essential part of any programme to improve the land tenure system'.[15] It was recommended that individual holdings should be subject to both a ceiling and a floor limit. No action was taken prior to 1959 in this direction.

In the Land Reforms of 1959, the principle of placing a ceiling on individual ownership was accepted 'in order to break concentration of land and wealth, to narrow down income inequalities, and to encourage a more intensive land-use and productive investment'. The ceiling was 500 acres (202 hectares) of irrigated or 1,000 acres (495 hectares) of unirrigated land or 36,000 product index units (PIU)[16] whichever is more. In addition, a landowner could retain up to 150 acres (61 hectares) of orchards, if it was in blocks of not less than 10 acres each, and he could transfer to his heirs the equivalent of 18,000 PIU unless he had already done so between 14 August 1947 and 8 October 1958. Owners of existing stud and livestock farms and *shikargahs* were allowed to retain such additional areas as the government considered necessary. The landlord could also give 6,000 PIU to his dependent female relations.

9.2.4 Implementation

Compensation to the landowners for excess lands resumed by the government was provided at a rate varying from Re 1.00 to Rs 5.00 per PIU depending on the area of land to be resumed. The payment was to be made in fifty half-yearly equated instalments in transferable but non-negotiable bonds bearing 4 per cent per annum interest on unpaid balance. The resumed land was to be sold to new owners at the rate of Rs 8.00 per PIU payable in fifty half-yearly equated instalments including an annual interest of 4 per cent on unpaid balance. The entire reform programme was self-financing in the sense that the difference between the price realized and the compensation paid was used to meet the cost.

In a separate measure, under the Land Utilization Ordinance promulgated in August 1959, it was provided that private lands which remained uncultivated for a period of two years or more would be requisitioned by the government. The lands would be utilized and managed on approved lines after the owner had been given due notice to bring it under cultivation within a reasonable period.

The results of the 1959 Reforms, obtained up to June 1980, are summarized in Table 9.1.

The Land Reform Commission of 1958, whose comprehensive report was the basis of the 1959 Land Reforms, also dealt with the problem of what the First Plan described as the 'floor limit'. The existence of a large number of very small cultivation units is a serious problem and as worthy of attention as that of large estates. If the cultivation unit is small the resources of the farmer are inefficiently utilized thereby causing the production cost to rise and reducing the net profit of farm operation.

The Commission identified and defined two types of holdings:

i) Economic holdings, i.e., areas in which the current techniques of production can be profitably cultivated. (According to the Commission, an area of 64 acres in Hyderabad and Khairpur Divisions, or 50 acres elsewhere, whichever is more, should be regarded as an economic holding.)
ii) Subsistence holdings, i.e., areas which ensure subsistence to an average cultivator family with the current cultivation methods. (This was estimated to be 16 acres in Hyderabad and Khairpur Divisions or 12.50 acres elsewhere, whichever is more. The size corresponds to a unit which can be efficiently cultivated by one plough.)

The Commission recommended that efforts should be made to maintain economic or subsistence units at their current status and that a limitation should be put on their further subdivision or alienation. Holdings already below the subsistence level, the Commission proposed, could be sold, in parts if the buyer belonged to the same village, or as one unit if the buyer was from outside the village. With regard to those units which have several shareholders, it was recommended that the shareholders either cultivate the land jointly or elect one of themselves as the manager and share the produce so that the farming unit remained as it was. Another alternative was that one of the shareholders become the

Table 9.1: Progress of 1959 Land Reforms up to 30 June 1980 Under MLR 64

Province	Area resumed (acres)	Area allotted (acres)	Balance (acres)	Persons benefitted
Punjab	12,43,335	10,70,523	1,72,812	1,09,889
Sind	9,32,461	7,73,690	1,58,771	42,842
NWFP	2,40,406	2,40,406	–	24,314
Baluchistan	1,31,631	1,31,631	–	6,221
Total	25,47,833	22,16,250	3,31,583	1,83,266

Source: Government of Pakistan, *Agricultural Statistics of Pakistan, 1980*, Islamabad, 1981, p. 99.

owner purchasing the land from the others. If the shareholders fail to agree on any arrangement, the government may acquire the land on payment of compensation. However, little action has been taken so far by the local authorities which 'hardly ever take over land for this purpose'.[17]

The land reforms of 1972 further slashed the ceiling on land ownership to 150 acres (unirrigated) or 12,000 PIU, whichever is more. No exemptions were allowed for the retention of orchards, stud or livestock farms, and *shikargah*. The only exemption was for owners of tractors and tubewells (of not less than 10 HP) who could retain an additional 2,000 PIU. Thus all exemptions and concessions given under the 1959 Reforms were withdrawn except for recognized educational institutions. All land transfers after 20 December 1971 by way of gifts etc., were declared void. In addition, all land in the Pat Feeder area of Baluchistan were resumed and, similarly, land over 100 acres (40.5 hectares) which was acquired by a government servant during his tenure of office, or within two years after his retirement, was also taken over. The titles of all land acquired by exchange from the area of the defence belt to the interior were also cancelled. All state land was reserved exclusively for landless peasants, tenants, and owners of below-subsistence holdings.

No compensation was paid for land resumed. These lands were distributed among the tillers free of cost. Any balance of instalments being paid by owners who obtained land under the 1959 Reforms was also waived. Only state lands were sold to new owners and the price was realized in easy instalments. The allotment ceiling to new owners was 12.5 acres (5 hectares) for the Punjab and NWFP, 16 acres (7 hectares) for the Sind, and 32 acres (13 hectares) for Baluchistan. The restriction on the subdivision of holdings below the subsistence level, and on the partitioning and alienation of joint holdings, which was imposed under the 1959 Reforms, was continued.

In 1976, in another series of reforms, all culturable and cultivable state land was transferred to landless peasants or to those owning below-subsistence holdings.

In 1977, the ceiling on land ownership was further reduced to 100 acres (40.5 hectares) irrigated or 200 acres (81 hectares) unirrigated land or 8,000 PIU. This time the resumed land was acquired on payment of a compensation of Rs 30 per PIU. But the resumed land was given free, as before, to tenants and other cultivators.

Table 9.2: Progress of 1972 Land Reforms up to 30 June 1980 Under MLR 115

Province	Area resumed	Area allotted	Balance	Persons benefitted
Punjab	3,31,268	2,42,840	88,428	36,948
Sind	3,17,896	2,38,637	79,259	16,497
NWFP	1,41,877	1,32,860	9,017	12,639
Baluchistan	5,15,105	1,98,295	3,16,810	9,129
Total	13,06,146	8,12,632	4,93,514	75,213
Progress of 1977 Land Reforms up to 30 June 1980 Under Act II of 1977				
Punjab	93,806	23,426	70,380	1,543
Sind	31,741	19,966	11,775	1,496
NWFP	23,787	4,162	19,625	781
Baluchistan	17,502	269	17,233	14
Total	1,66,836	47,823	1,19,013	3,834

Source: Government of Pakistan, *Agricultural Statistics of Pakistan, 1980*, Islamabad, 1981, p. 99.

The progress of implementation of these Reforms up to 30 June 1980 is given in Table 9.2.

A comparison of the land reforms of 1959 and of the seventies with regard to the ceiling on land ownership is interesting. From the viewpoint of distributive efficiency, the land reforms in the seventies were definitely a step forward. There was general agreement that the ceiling fixed in 1959 was too high and the exemptions granted too generous. By 1977 the ceiling had been reduced by 80 per cent in terms of acreage and by 77.8 per cent in terms of PIU. Moreover, no compensation was paid in the seventies (except under the 1977 reforms) for land resumed. The land was given to small peasants and tenants free of cost (except on state lands) whereas under the 1959 reforms the new owners had had to pay a price recoverable in instalments. While the reforms in the seventies were more egalitarian regarding the limit on ceilings and other exemptions as compared to the 1959 reforms, they were more generous to heirs in two ways. First, in the 1959 reforms, transfers could be made only to the extent of half of the ceiling, i.e., 18,000 PIU, but in the seventies it was up to the full extent of the ceiling. Second, the 1959 reforms allowed transfers only if transfers had not been made previously but the reforms in the seventies did not place any such restrictions. What it amounted to was that landlords who took anticipatory action and divided their holdings among their heirs before 20 December 1971 were at a great advantage, compared to those who did not do so, since the family holdings of a farmer remained more or less unchanged.[18]

The major positive impact of the reforms in the seventies was mainly that no compensation was paid for lands resumed and resumed land was transferred free of cost to the land-poor. It is generally found that when land reforms with compensation are carried out, they tend 'to become little more than an episodic redistribution of wealth. This is because the transfer of ownership in such a case does not raise the position of the farmers financially as they are burdened with the obligation of paying over long periods for the land'.[19]

The financial requirements in the 1959 reforms for the purchase of land, coupled with that for initial investment in basic inputs, was so heavy that in many cases the new owners could not really become owners and after sometime they lost their land in one way or the other. On the other hand, landlords giving up their worst lands were well paid and this seriously impaired the welfare impact of these reforms.[20]

It is difficult to present statistical evidence regarding the impact of land reforms on the size of cultivation units or on the extent of tenancy farming in the last two decades. So far there have been two Census Reports (1960 and 1972) on agriculture. Unless another census, which is due in the near future, is completed, it will not be possible to have an accurate idea of the changes in agriculture which have taken place under the land reforms. A comparison of data compiled in 1960 and 1972 would only partially indicate the effect of the 1959 reforms. Since the implementation of land reforms is a very com-

Table 9.3: Number and Area of Farms Classified by Size, 1960-72

Size of farm (acres)	Farms (percentage)		Farm area (percentage)		Cultivated area (percentage)	
	1960	1972	1960	1972	1960	1972
Under 1.0	15	4	1	—	1	—
1.0 to under 2.5	18	10	3	—	3	1
2.5 to under 5.0	16	14	6	4	7	4
5.0 to under 7.5	12	15	7	7	8	8
7.5 to under 12.5	16	24	15	18	17	20
12.5 to under 25.0	15	21	26	27	29	29
25.0 to under 50.0	6	8	19	19	20	19
50.0 to under 150.0	2	3	13	15	10	13
150.0 and over	—	—	10	9	5	5

Source: (i) Summary Report, *Pakistan Census of Agriculture, 1960*, p. 58. (ii) All Pakistan Report, *Pakistan Census of Agriculture*, 1972, p. 1.

plicated matter, its pace is extremely slow. An idea can be had from the fact that 13 per cent of the land resumed under the 1959 reforms still remains undistributed after two decades while the area distributed as a percentage of the area resumed was, in 1980, 62 per cent in the case of the 1972 reforms and 29 per cent in the case of the 1977 reforms. However, changes in statistical terms, which took place between 1960 and 1972, may indicate some direction as shown in Table 9.3.

As pointed out earlier, the focus of land reforms was on limiting the extent of, and not eliminating, tenancy farming. Between 1960-72, the number of farms under tenants declined from 42 per cent of the total number of farms to 34 per cent. While this has only increased marginally, the number of owner-farms from 41 per cent to 42 per cent, major increases have taken place in owner-cum-tenant farms from 17 per cent to 24 per cent. In absolute terms, the number of tenant farms has declined from 2 million to 1 million. With regard to area, 39 per cent of the total area was under tenancy cultivation and this was reduced to 30 per cent between 1960 and 1972. The area under owner-farms has increased from 38 per cent to 40 per cent and the area under owner-cum-tenant farms has increased from 23 per cent to 30 per cent. It can be safely assumed that the impact of the land reforms introduced in the seventies will be more significant in terms of expansion of owner-cultivation and contraction of tenancy farming (Table 9.4).

Some further comments need to be made on the way the entire land reform effort was conceptualized and implemented. In the first phase of the land reforms in the early fifties, the initiative came from the prov-

Table 9.4: Number and Area of Farms, classified by Tenure and by Size 1960-72

Size of farm (acres)	Number of farms percentage (acres)							Farm area (acres) percentage						
	Total	Owner-Farms		Owner-cum-tenant farms		Tenant-farms		Total	Owner-farms		Owner-cum-tenant farms		Tenant-farms	
		1960	1972	1960	1972	1960	1972		1960	1972	1960	1972	1960	1972
Total	100	41	42	17	24	42	34	100	38	40	23	30	39	30
Under 1.0	100	62	77	5	2	33	21	100	60	76	6	3	34	21
1.0 to under 2.5	100	49	67	11	7	40	26	100	48	66	12	8	40	26
2.5 to under 5.0	100	41	53	18	17	41	29	100	40	52	18	18	42	30
5.0 to under 7.5	100	35	39	21	24	44	37	100	35	39	21	25	44	36
7.5 to under 12.5	100	30	29	23	26	47	44	100	30	29	23	27	47	45
12.5 to under 25.0	100	30	31	23	32	47	37	100	30	31	23	33	47	36
25.0 to under 50.0	100	33	38	25	34	42	27	100	33	38	25	36	42	26
50.0 to under 150.0	100	45	49	26	35	29	16	100	46	49	26	36	28	15
150.0 and over	100	64	63	19	28	17	9	100	69	62	18	30	13	8

Source: (i) *Pakistan Census of Agriculture*, 1960, p. 60. (ii) *Pakistan Census of Agriculture*, 1972, p. 3.

incial governments. The socio-economic objectives of the reforms were not articulated expressly or elaborately and the scope of the reforms was confined to security of tenure. The larger question of land ownership was not dealt with. In the second phase (1959-77), the initiative came from the federal government and the objectives were outlined in detail. The 1959 reform measures mentioned 'social justice and removal of institutional defects in the agrarian structure' as objectives, while in 1972 the objectives were spelled out in greater detail: 'social justice, the need to change the oppressive and iniquitous agrarian structure, increase in production, laying down foundations of a relationship of honour and mutual benefit between landlords and tenants'.[21]

However, no attempt was made to organize the farming community into any national or local organization nor was a proper social climate prepared for the implementation of the land reforms. Indeed, such organizations are conspicuous by their absence in Pakistan. As a result, the entire task of implementing the land reforms fell on the bureaucracy. Even the judicial and semi-judicial work was done by a bureaucracy concerned with land administration in the provinces. The Deputy Commissioner of the district was given the additional designation of Deputy Land Commissioner, the Divisional Commissioner also became the Land Commissioner, and the Member, Board of Revenue, was also made the Chief Land Commissioner. The special supporting staff to man the administrative side of the land reform was also drawn from revenue departments. They, therefore, brought with them not only their attitudes and backgrounds but also the old contacts and influences of the rural elites. It was therefore to be expected that there were cases of mishandling of records and attempts to escape the impact of land reforms.

Because the landowners had a choice in the retention of areas within the ceiling, the surrendered areas turned out to be far less utilizable than expected. Land not utilizable comprised over 20 per cent of the land resumed under the 1959 reforms and over 16 per cent of the land resumed under the 1972 reforms.

The concession given to the tenants in the form of the first right of pre-emption in the sale of land by the landlord was meant to provide a new forum through which the tenants could become landowners. In practice this objective has not been achieved because most tenants 'use it for securing hush-money to allow sale to genuine purchasers'. Some of the new owners of resumed land, though not allowed to sell for twenty-five years, are indulging in 'future sales' and either continue to be landless labourers or shift to urban areas.[22]

9.2.5 Consolidation of Holdings

Along with the continuous subdivision of holdings, a major problem which adversely affects the scale of operations in agriculture is the process of fragmentation. This relates to the manner in which land held by an individual is scattered throughout the village area in plots separated by land owned or possessed by others. This scattering of holdings undermines the foundation of a sound agricultural economy since it involves a wastage of time, money, and effort and gives inadequate returns on investments made by the peasants. It causes a wastage of water since unnecessarily long and badly laid water courses are used. It makes drainage, levelling, and other operations difficult and it is not easy to employ better equipment or improved cultivation practices.

Fragmentation, like subdivision of holdings, is caused by the operation of the laws of inheritance and the heirs' exercise of the right of alienation. Differences in the productivity levels, or different kinds of land under one ownership, may lead the inheritors to demand a share in each type of land.

This problem of fragmentation attracted the government's attention long before Independence. The situation was relatively more serious in the Punjab and NWFP. In the twenties and the thirties, various laws were enacted for the consolidation of holdings to be undertaken on a voluntary basis. But progress has been extremely slow. In the NWFP, between 1930 and 1955, a little over 100,000 acres, out of a total cultivated area of 3 million acres, was consolidated. The slow progress was due to the voluntary character of the programme and a lack of adequately trained staff. In 1946, the NWFP government passed the Consolidation of Holdings Act providing that if at least two-third of the owners possessing not less than three-fourth of the cultivated area agreed to accept a scheme of consolidition, it could be imposed on others. Implementation of this law could not take place due to a number of reasons. In the Punjab, the necessary law for the consolidation of holdings was passed in 1920 which provided that the peasants, if they wished, could revert to 'pre-consolidation' holdings after cultivating the consolidated holdings for four years. In 1936, an element of compulsion was introduced providing that if at least two-third of the owners in an area apply for consolidation, it should be imposed on others. In 1952, the government acquired the power to carry out consolidation compulsorily in any notified area. Progress in the Punjab was also very slow. Only about 2 million acres, out of a total cultivated area of 20 million acres in the Punjab, was consolidated in about thirty-five years, i.e., between 1920 and 1955.

The land reforms of 1959 recommended that a province-wide programme of consolidation should be launched on a compulsory basis. The reforms provided that consolidation could be undertaken on the initiative of the Board of Revenue or if any two or more landlords in an estate, or subdivision of estate, together holding not less than the minimum area of land prescribed in this behalf applied for it. The new laws also applied to evacuee lands where fragmentation had assumed serious proportions. Provision was also made to associate the representatives of landowners in the consolidation process.

Table 9.5: Consolidation of Holdings

	000 (hectares)	000 (acres)
Area consolidated upto 1955	651	1,607
Area consolidated between 1955-60	338	835
Area consolidated between 1960-5	3,356	8,289
Area consolidated between 1965-70	2,032	5,019
Area consolidated between 1970-5	1,086	2,682
Area consolidated between 1975-8	959	2,368
Total	8,422	20,800

Source: Government of Pakistan, *Agricultural Statistics of Pakistan*, Islamabad, 1978, p. 66.

By 1970, the total land consolidated in (West) Pakistan was 5 million acres. The units held by landowners before consolidation were 2 million which were reduced to 91,000. The average size unit was increased from 3 acres to 5.5 acres. The cost of consolidation, recoverable from the landowners, was about Rs 5 per acre.

The extent of fragmentation can be judged from the data compiled in the two agricultural census reports of 1960 and 1972. A comparison between the two shows that whereas 61 per cent of the total number of farms were affected by fragmentation in 1960, in 1972 it affected 62 per cent of the farms. However, as regards total farm area, the area affected by fragmentation declined from 81 per cent to 75 per cent. Between 1960 and 1972, the fragmentation situation worsened in farms below 1 acre. In 1960, fragmentation affected 30 per cent of farms below 1 acre but in 1972 it went up to 33 per cent. The situation has improved slightly on farms between 12.5 to 25 acres (from 80 per cent to 73 per cent) and those between 25 to 50 acres (from 87 per cent to 81 per cent). Thus it can be seen that while larger holdings are receiving slightly higher benefits from consolidation, the situation in the case of smaller holdings is not very good.

NOTES

1. Government of Pakistan, *Food and Agriculture Commission*, 1960, p. 42.
2. Government of West Pakistan, *Land Reforms Commission*, 1959, p. 11.
3. Government of Pakistan, *First Five Year Plan*, p. 308.
4. Ibid., p. 309.
5. Government of Pakistan, *Pakistan Census of Agriculture*, 1960, p. 58 (summary).
6. Abdul Qayyum, 'Policies and Implementation of Land Reforms–Macro Level Study for Pakistan', in *Land Reforms : Some Asian Experiences*, Inayatullah (ed.), APDAC, Kuala Lumpur, 1980, p. 64.
7. Government of Pakistan, *First Five Year Plan*, p. 315.
8. It was estimated that share-croppers (who operate about 89 per cent of the tenanted land) had to pay about 70 per cent of the production costs in the Punjab and about 60 per cent in Sind. This would be reduced to 44 per cent in case of farmers cultivating 8 acre farms and 56 per cent in case of farmers cultivating 10 acre farms in the Punjab. The position in the Sind for small peasants remained almost unchanged. See Yasmin Mohiuddin, *Attempts to Agricultural Development in Pakistan.* Paper in *Economic Reconstruction in Pakistan,* Rafiq Ahmed et al. (ed.), 1973, p. 298.
9. Abdul Qayyum, 'Policies and Implementation of Land Reforms–Macro Level Study for Pakistan', in *Land Reforms: Some Asian Experiences,* Inayatullah (ed.), APDAC, Kaula Lumpur, 1980, p. 85.
10. Malik Khuda Bux, *Land Reforms in West Pakistan*, Vol. I, 1960, p. 140.
11. Ibid., p. 143.
12. Government of Pakistan, *First Five Year Plan*, p. 316.
13. Ibid., p. 452.
14. Yasmin Mohiuddin, *Attempts at Agricultural Development in Pakistan*, p.309.
15. Government of Pakistan, *First Five Year Plan*, p. 318.
16. The Produce Index Units *generally* represent the annual gross produce value of an acre of land, separately calculated according to various classes of soil and other conditions.
17. Abdul Qayyum, 'Policies and Implementation of Land Reforms–Macro Level Study for Pakistan', in *Land Reforms: Some Asian Experiences,* Inayatullah (ed.), APDAC, Kuala Lumpur, 1980, p. 86.
18. Yasmin Mohiuddin, *Attempts at Agricultural Development in Pakistan,* paper in *Economic Reconstruction in Pakistan,* Rafiq Ahmed *et al.* (ed.), 1973, p. 296.
19. Ibid., p. 296.
20. Ibid., p. 297.
21. Abdul Qayyum, 'Policies and Implementation of Land Reforms–Macro Level Study for Pakistan' in *Land Reforms: Some Asian Experiences,* Inayatullah (ed.), APDAC, Kuala Lumpur, 1980, p. 84.
22. Ibid., p. 86.

10 Agricultural Inputs

In the initial stages of development in Pakistan, the use of modern inputs in agriculture did not receive the necessary attention since, in most cases, irrigation facilities could be expanded and new land brought under cultivation. In the early sixties, as the possibilities of extensive cultivation were seen to be reaching exhaustion level, there was a rapid shift in priorities in favour of the new input packages despite some initial doubts regarding their adoption by the tradition-bound farmers. But experience has shown that once a new technology has been developed, tested, and made available to the farmers, with appropriate price adjustments in the case of inputs and outputs in order to ensure its profitability, the farmers are quite responsive. Of course, agriculture is a location-specific activity and the yield potential of inputs like high yielding varieties of seed (HYV), fertilizers, and modern equipment varies with such characteristics as soil structure, water supply, and moisture level.

A vigorous extension and research effort is therefore needed to work out the optimal input combination for each set of agronomic conditions. Some of these inputs have the added advantage of divisibility so that even small farmers, given credit and access to supplies, can use them profitably. In the following sections we review the use of the various components of the input package, i.e., water, fertilizers, seeds, and pesticides.

10.1 Water

Water is the basic component of any combination of modern agricultural inputs. A greater availability of water at farmgate and a higher manoeuvrability of its inter-seasonal distribution were critical to the wide adoption of the new farm technology in the sixties and its significance has not diminished since then.

Some of the factors responsible for depriving agriculture of the full benefits of the extensive Indus basin irrigation system and the large underground water reservoir were an institutional failure to increase the efficiency of water delivery at the intermediate level and water use at the farm level, and an inability to formulate long term policies for flood control and land reclamation combined with water-logging and salinity. In the absence of a long-term perspective regarding the role of water in agricultural development, outlays and efforts in producing water as an end-product were not matched by similar outlays and efforts in ensuring the efficiency of its use as an input.

While temperatures in various regions allow for year-round cropping, rainfall is very low in most of the country. Artificial irrigation is therefore of crucial importance in agricultural development.

Most of the country lies in the Indus basin region irrigated by the Indus, its tributaries, and a large canal network. Outside the Indus basin is the coastal tributaries and Desert Streams region, covering most of Baluchistan, and consisting of desert and semi-desert valleys and barren surfaces with rugged mountains and scanty rainfall. Here agriculture is located in isolated pockets where the water source is perennial and non-perennial streams or diversion of flood water or ground water. About 70 per cent of the cultivated area is under artificial irrigation. The major irrigation sources can be classified into surface water (canal) and ground water (tubewells, wells, etc.).

10.1.1 Surface Water

The surface water supply through the canals is based on the Indus River System. The irrigation system of the Indus river, with a total culturable commanded area of 35 million acres, is perhaps the largest integrated system in the world. It comprises two large dams, dozens of small dams, twenty barrages and headworks, forty-five canals, about 200,000 tubewells, and about 88,600 water courses. The total length of the canals is about 35,500 miles and of water courses and farm canals about 1 million miles.

Historical Development

Given the extreme importance of the irrigation system, its development over the last century needs to be looked into in some detail. Before 1856, irrigation was done by inundation canals which functioned only during periods of high river flow providing water for *kharif* crops and some soil moisture for *rabi*. Controlled year-round irrigation started with the construction of the Upper Bari Doab Canal from Madhopur Headworks on the river Ravi. This was followed by the gradual construction of more such canals on the rivers Sutlej, Chenab, and Jhelum. By the turn of the century, it became apparent that the water resources of the individual rivers were not in proportion to the irrigable land served by them. The rivers Ravi and Sutlej were deficient in supply while the Jhelum had a surplus. Therefore the Triple Canal Project, linking the Jhelum, Chenab, and Ravi rivers, was constructed during 1907-15 for the transfer of surplus water from the Jhelum and Chenab to the Ravi, and ultimately to the Sutlej. The Triple Canal Projeot was a landmark in interbasin water resource management and it also provided the key concept for the resolution of the Indo-Pak water dispute in 1960.

The Sukkur Barrage (1931) and the Sutlej Valley Project (1933) followed by the Haveli and Rangpur canals from Trimmu headworks on the Chenab (1939) and the Thal Project (1947) completed the system as it existed at the time of Independence.

After Independence, the water dispute between India and Pakistan arose largely because the irrigation system, originally conceived as an integrated unit, was divided regardless of irrigation boundaries. The headworks of a number of canals irrigating Pakistan's territory were inexplicably assigned to India under the Radcliffe Award. This led to considerable controversy and conflict over the use of water facilities. The dispute ended in 1960 with the Indus Water Treaty according to which the flow of three eastern rivers (Ravi, Beas, and Sutlej), with a total mean annual flow of 33 million acre feet (*maf*), were assigned to India and the three western rivers (Indus, Jhelum, Chenab), with a total mean annual flow of 148 *maf*, were assigned to Pakistan. The Treaty also provided for the transfer of irrigation supplies from the western rivers to areas in Pakistan formerly served by the eastern rivers and provided auxiliary development potential to compensate for the additional burden of the maintenance of replacement works. Accordingly, the Indus Basin Project, including the construction of Mangla Dam, five barrages, one syphon, and eight link canals, was completed in 1971 while the last project, i.e., Tarbela Dam, went into partial operation in 1975-6.

Other ventures outside the Indus Basin Project, which were completed after Independence, were Kotri (1955), Taunsa (1958), Gudu (1963) and three more link canals.

Up to the sixties, surface water received a higher priority in development outlays, since in the fifties, the major task in water resource management was the capturing of natural river flows for irrigation by constructing barrages and associated canals. During the First Plan, the surface water subsector had received 76 per cent of the total allocations to the water sector. This declined to 51 per cent in the Second Plan, 18 per cent in the Third Plan, 38 per cent in the Fourth Plan, and 30 per cent in the Fifth Plan.

Changes in the Irrigation System

As the Indus Basin Project moved towards completion, the character of the irrigation network began to undergo a basic change from an unregulated system to an increasingly regulated one (particularly at the reservoir level). This trend was further accelerated by fresh ground water supplies from public and private tubewells during the same period which ensured a timely and adequate water supply for crop needs. The original design of the irrigation system was based on the need for opening up new lands which were sparsely populated in the second half of the nineteenth century, raising revenue from the sale of crown lands, settling of nomadic tribes, and alleviating chronic famines.

Thus the system was designed to bring a maximum area under cultivation at low cost and with minimum opportunity for human interference. The canal system was operated with the help of a small staff and limited means of communication over long distances. A simple and effective design was evolved for the distribution of water. Water courses operated through ungated outlets which provided automatic and proportional water supply. These outlets operate whenever the main distributory is operating. Only minimum canalflow regulation structures were devised to turn the flow on and off and to prevent overflow. Very few escapes near canal heads and major junctions were provided and there was no provision for tail escape with the result that any overflow had to be absorbed by the farmland. This arrangement had considerable validity in the past but now it constitutes a serious constraint on water management at the intermediate level, i.e., the distribution of canal water between various localities served by it.

The construction of reservoirs under the Indus Basin Project brought about, first, the capability to transfer low-value *kharif* water to high-value *rabi* water (Mangla, Tarbela, and Chashma have increased *rabi* supply by about 38 per cent of the average *rabi* flow) and, second, the ability to adjust the timings of both natural flows and storage releases to match actual crop needs.

However, this change in the basic character of the irrigation system was neither pre ceded nor followed by detailed planning for the utilization of the controlled supplies of this valuable additional water nor was the ground prepared for it by the construction of surface and subsurface drainage in the command areas. Furthermore, enough effort was not made in the direction of such follow-up activities as reducing water delivery losses and proper co-ordination between canal water supply and ground water supply. According to a number of studies, the water losses in delivery from canal outlet to farm are estimated to be 40 to 50 per cent. Some programmes for the improvement of the water courses were carried out but the situation is no better due to poor maintenance of the improved channels.

In the past, very little attention was paid to the problem of water use efficiency at the farm end and it was somehow assumed that it was fairly high. However, surveys conducted in the seventies showed a low efficiency in the use of irrigation facilities. The farmers have a tendency to over-irrigate particularly when fertilizers are used. There is also considerable under-irrigation which occurs late in the season when water requirement is at the highest. There is a great need for follow-up assistance in water application at various stages of crop growth.

The Allocation of Resources to the Water Sector

Water is an agricultural input and, therefore, it is highly instructive to compare allocations to the water sector with those to agriculture. The water sector received either higher or equal allocations throughout unless expenditure on the Indus Basin Project (which is a replacement work and not regarded as a development expenditure) is added in which case the percentage of water allocation rises considerably. Table 10.1 gives the allocations to water and the Indus Basin Project in rupees both at the current value as well as at the 1978 value.

Table 10.2 shows the percentage of total Plan allocations to agriculture, water, and the Indus Basin Project.

In the pre-Plan period, 1947-55, emphasis was laid mainly on the extension of irrigated areas through the conversion of inundation canals into weir-controlled canals. Little attention was paid to drainage and flood control. The Rasul Tubewell Scheme was started to intercept canal seepage. The First Five Year Plan, however, gave a long-term perspective for the water sector and emphasized the development of ground water for both primary and supplementary irrigation, the construction of link canals, the efficient use of the existing irrigation system, and the reduction of delivery losses. Attention was drawn to the conjunctive use of surface and ground water for intensive cultivation. Provision was also made for extension in irrigated areas, and for reclamation and drainage. Work was initiated on the Mangla reservoir, the Warsak, Thal, and Kotri projects, and continued on Gudu and Taunsa during the Plan period.

In the Second Plan period, Gudu, Taunsa, and Kotri projects were completed, and stress was laid on the extension of irrigated areas as well as the improvement and replacement of the existing canal network. SCARP-I was also started during this period.

During the Third Plan, expenditure on the Indus Basin Project reached its peak and allocations to the water sector were also higher than its combined allocations during the First and Second Plans. Greater attention was paid to ground water development where the target was an addition of 20 maf in surface

Table 10.1: Total Plan Budgets—in 1978 Rupees[1]
(Rs million)

Sector	First 1955-60	Second 1960-5	Third 1965-70	Fourth 1970-5	Fifth 1978-83
Total Plan allocation (water)	22,582	23,621	54,175	50,788	145,881
Indus Basin Project (IBP)	—	10,575	14,160	11,448	2,289
Total Plan Budgets—in Current Rupees					
Total Plan allocation (water)	5,381	6,216	16,220	17,696	145,881
IBP	—	2,924	4,552	4,859	2,289

1. Escalated by Wholesale Price Index.
Source: WAPDA, *Revised Action Programme for Irrigated Agriculture,* 1979, pp. VI-6.

Table 10.2: Agriculture, Water, and Indus Basin Project Allocations
Per cent of total Plan Allocation[1]

Sector	First 1955-60	Second 1960-5	Third 1965-70	Fourth 1970-5	Fifth 1978-83
Agriculture	12	15	14	10	10
Water	24	14	17	15	10
Indus Basin Project	—	(45)	(26)	(23)	(1.5)

1. Per cent of Plan allocation exclusive of Indus Basin Project Works.
Source: WAPDA, *Revised Action Programme for Irrigated Agriculture,* 1979, pp. VI-6.

water supply. More than half of the total allocation was for SCARP projects[1] since there was great concern about water-logging and salinity. Provision was made for tubewell installation in the private sector but no subsidy was granted. It was also proposed that the capacities of a number of canals be increased but little work was done in this direction. The construction of Tarbela Dam was begun during the Third Plan period.

In the Fourth Plan, emphasis was laid on 'complementary works necessary to utilize the supplemental water from tubewells'. A subsidy was provided for private tubewells. The need for the maximum utilization of existing irrigation facilities was also felt. Provisions were made to enlarge existing canals but no work could be done due to financial stringency. The Chashma and Greater Thal projects were also deferred since low priority was attached to new irrigation facilities.

The Fifth Plan aims at a 'massive assault' on water logging and salinity, and at increasing the water availability from 92 maf at farmgate to 103 maf, with an average annual growth of 2.4 per cent. The proportion of regulated supplies (reservoirs plus tubewells) are to increase from 42 per cent of the water supply to 47 per cent.

10.1.2 Ground Water

Ground water has gained in importance as an irrigation source—its share in the total water supply at farmgate increased from 14 per cent to 33 per cent between 1966-7 and 1979-80.[2] Its role in providing much-needed water in *rabi* is even more important, its contribution increasing from 12 per cent to over 40 per cent in the same period.

Pakistan has a large underground water reservoir whose average capacity is estimated to be 40 maf. This is being recharged every year and it thus seems to be a perennial source of water. Furthermore, it offers three distinct advantages. Its volume is far in excess of all the existing and potential surface reservoirs; it is immune to sedimentation and evaporation; its location is close to the areas of use. Extensive investigations and surveys were conducted by WAPDA and the US Geological Survey in the sixties. A number of reports, including the Lower Indus Report (1966), were prepared. Outside the Indus plain, there are isolated aquifers, which are small and less economical, but of great local importance, particularly in Baluchistan, where the only sources of water, besides the Pat Feeder Canal, are the *Karezes* which number 1,734 and irrigate 170,000 acres. A survey jointly conducted by UNDP and WAPDA is at present underway in the region.

Before controlled irrigation began in the mid-nineteenth century, the ground water system was in a state of equilibrium—water discharge from evaporation was balanced by recharge from rivers and rainfall. This natural balance was upset by the perennial irrigation system. Seepage from unlined canals, water channels, and farms increased the recharge in areas away from rivers and led to a rise in the water table which brought up dissolved salts in the root zone and at the surface mostly in the central parts of *doabs* in the Punjab and the Sind. Therefore, recharge exceeded water discharge in these regions until the fifties and created the 'twin menace' of water-logging and salinity which is discussed later in this chapter.

The potential of this huge underground water reservoir depends largely upon the quality of the water which is subject to deterioration over time. The continuous leaching of salts accumulated in the soil and those brought in by surface irrigation supply increase the salt content of the water, particularly in the absence of any salt export mechanism. Detailed investigations through the regular monitoring of the water quality are needed in order to gain the full benefits of this great asset. Another factor which may determine the benefits of this water resource is the introduction of appropriate water management and water-use practices which take into account soil, water, and plant relationships. There is a need for establishing suitable guidelines for different environments and for extension services to advise farmers on the best way of utilizing this water.

Major development efforts in ground water started with SCARP-I in Rachna Doab in 1959-60. Total water pumpage in the Basin increased from 3.27 maf in 1959-60 to 32.75 maf in 1976-7. At present a total number of 11,000 public tubewells (of 2 to 5 cusec average capacity) and over 154,000 private tubewells (of an average capacity of 1 cusec)[3] are operating to make use of this water and this is now a major supplement to canal water supplies. The availability of fresh ground water presents an ideal opportunity to match irrigation supplies to crop water requirements because it gives water supply a much needed flexibility. However, its potential has not been fully exploited because of institutional weaknesses such as a lack of co-ordination between concerned agencies. Tubewells and pumps in the public sector also suffer from poor maintenance since allocations for maintenance are generally low in view of the overall lack of financial resources. Very little research has been conducted in tubewell design and construction and there is hardly any arrangement for feedback for improvements therein.

i) *Water Subsidies*

Another issue in water management is the high recurring cost of operating the irrigation system. The cost rose from Rs 213 million in 1971-2 to Rs 567 million in 1977-8 while water revenues lagged behind rising from Rs 96 million to Rs 498 million in this period. Thus, in addition to the huge cost of construction of irrigation works, the entire burden of accelerated implementation of anti-waterlogging and salinity programmes falls on public revenues even though some of the operational cost of the irrigation system is borne by the taxpayers. According to calculations made in WAPDA Revised Action Programme (1979) the implicit subsidy per acre comes to a little over Rs 3 in non-SCARP areas and Rs 114 in SCARP areas for 1976-7.[4]

ii) *Inter-Provincial Water Allocations*

Another issue relates to the problem of competing demands of various provinces for irrigation supplies, particularly in *rabi* and in early and late *kharif*. The problem of water allocation between different user areas has existed since long before Independence. In 1920, a system for river discharge measurement at key locations in the river system was established in order to work out an allocation system. In 1934, the province of Sind raised an objection against the proposed irrigation projects at Thal, Bhakra, and Trimmu which, in its opinion, would be detrimental to the inundation canals in the Sind, particularly to *rabi* supplies at Sukkur Barrage. The Anderson Committee (1936), however, was able to establish allocations between various provinces. But as adverse affects on inundation canals were felt in due course, the problem of allocation continued to generate controversy and this led to the establishment of the Indus Commission in 1945. The Commission undertook an elaborate exercise in fixing priorities for both existing and projected canals. The report was presented to the government but could not be given formal approval by either the central government or the concerned provincial governments. However, further allocations of canal water were based on the formula devised by it.

After Independence, the Indo-Pak water dispute and the Treaty of 1960 changed the whole situation, with the loss of three eastern rivers and the construction of new reservoirs and link canals, and a need was felt to reallocate water rights. The Fazal-e-Akbar Committee was appointed in 1970 for this purpose. The committee submitted its report in 1971 but its recommendations remained under examination and no firm decisions were taken. Meanwhile, water allocations were made annually on an *ad hoc* basis. In 1977, another Commission under the chairmanship of the Chief Justice of Pakistan was appointed but its report is yet to be finalized.

The whole controversy revolving around water allocations and concomitant water rights has so far been treated as a 'regional' problem. But it is now time to consider whether the specific allocation of water according to regions is appropriate considering the national goal of maximizing agricultural output. Alternate criteria for flexible water allocations need to be developed. It is quite understandable that for a very long time the old formula of regional allocations operated even though no one province was fully satisfied with its working. Under conditions of unregulated river flows perhaps the old formula had considerable validity. But now, with the availability of substantial reservoir discharge and ground water, the need for those historically unchangeable rights can be questioned. There is a need to co-ordinate cropping patterns in various regions, not essentially on the basis of provincial boundaries but on geographical divisions, so that water allocation to different regions and zones are matched with their actual cropping patterns.

iii) *Waterlogging and Salinity Control*

Waterlogging and salinity have been described as the 'twin menace'. The basic cause of this menace is a sustained rise in the subsurface water table. Prolonged over-irrigation and poor drainage may cause the water table to rise so that in some areas saturation of the soil (*sem*) occurs thereby creating small ponds. Over-irrigation in certain areas causes the salts in the soil to rise up with the result that salt concentrations in the upper layer of the soil (*thur*) appear on the surface.

The data regarding the extent of damage wreaked by these two diseases is collected through regular surveys carried out by many agencies. The First Five Year Plan estimated the affected land at 6 million acres with an addition of 50,000 acres per year.[5] In the Second Plan it was reported that over 50 per cent of the irrigated land, an area of some 12 million acres, was affected by the twin menace.[6] The Third Plan estimated that (West) Pakistan was suffering an annual loss of 70,000 to 100,000 acres due to waterlogging and salinity.[7] Since 1959-60, when SCARP-I was launched as a pilot project for land reclamation, almost a dozen such projects have been in operation installing a large number of public tubewells for drainage of excess water supply and lowering the water table. The effort is supplemented by an increasing number of private tubewells in both SCARP and non-SCARP areas.

The SCARP projects suffered from a number of limitations such as a lack of sufficient financial support for the operation and maintenance of tubewells, a failure to improve and enlarge water courses, and a fragmentation of responsibility. Frequent tubewell breakdowns in the public sector resulted in low capacity utilization of public tubewells (40 to 50 per cent) and led to compensatory developments in the private sector.

The entire burden of waterlogging and salinity control now rests on the regular operation of public and private tubewells.

The real question which arises is : how far has the effort to control waterlogging and salinity succeeded? Have these programmes been able to reverse the trend and reclaim land at a pace faster than the loss of land? Unfortunately, the data which could throw light on these questions is limited to certain surveys conducted by the WAPDA Master Planning Division. Table 10.3 shows the position regarding overall salinity status and the changes which occurred between 1960 and 1976-8.

Table 10.3 refers to the profile chemical status of the soil samples in the root zone. In the Master Planning Survey, conducted by WAPDA, profiles were taken to a depth of seventy-two inches while making chemical analysis. Surface salinity refers to the presence of salt on the surface. Thus the Table shows substantial improvement in both profile chemical status and surface salinity. According to the *Pakistan Economic Survey (1979-80)*, 15 per cent of saline land has been reclaimed so far.[8] Table 10.4 shows that only 21 per cent of the area surveyed can be classified as difficult or very difficult to reclaim.

Apart from using tubewells to pump out excess water, a number of other remedies for controlling waterlogging have been suggested. The lining of canals was considered but the idea was rejected as too expensive and time consuming. Another course is to use 'vegetative' pumps. On every canal, six times the width of the canal is taken as the seepage zone. If this zone is put under suitable plantation, it may check the on-slaught of flow lines and also reduce the subsoil water accumulation to a reasonable depth. This method, however, is preventive rather than curative.

But, as most authors agree, suitable water management and better use efficiency of irrigation facilities is the long-term answer which alone can prevent both over-irrigation and under-irrigation and thus foreclose the process of waterlogging and salinity. This requires renewed efforts on the part of the poorly-financed and low-priority-receiving agricultural extension services. Soil conservation and drainage also seem to have received less attention than deserved. Greater investments in drainage will help not only in controlling waterlogging and salinity but also in preventing floods.

iv) *Flood Management*

The Indus Basin has a long history of flood recurrence causing heavy damages to the economy. The floods are caused by a combination of factors such as a lack of heavy silting in river beds causing erosion, de-

Table 10.3: Overall Salinity Status *circa* 1960 and 1976-8[1]
(Per cent)

Profile chemical[2] status	Not affected	Saline	Sodic	Saline-sodic	Other
1976-8	77	4	5	13	1
ca 1960	48	4	24	23	1
Surface salinity	**Salt free**	**Slightly saline**	**Moderately saline**	**Strongly saline**	**Other**
1976-8	67	12	8	10	3
ca 1960	53	18	11	16	2

1. Area Surveyed 21.1 million acres.
2. Includes the Punjab only, 12.2 million acres. Earlier data in Sind and NWFP not surveyed or not comparable.
Source: WAPDA, *Revised Action Programme for Irrigated Agriculture*, 1979, pp. III-13.

Table 10.4: Soil Reclaimability Potential by Provinces
(Per cent)

Province	Area surveyed (million acres)	Reclaimability class				Miscellaneous
		R 1	R 2	R 3	R 4	
NWFP	0.334	95	–	1	–	4
Punjab	9.545	86	4	6	2	2
Sind and Baluchistan	6.756	28	28	39	1	4
Total	16.635	62	14	19	2	3
Area (million acres)	—	10.393	2.276	3.192	0.314	—

Note: RI = Reclamation not required; R2 = Easily reclaimable; R3 = Difficult to reclaim; R4 = Very difficult to reclaim.
Source: WAPDA, *Revised Action Programme for Irrigated Agriculture,* 1979, pp. III-21.

position and rapid changes in course, and rapid denudation of catchment area hills.

Flooding in Pakistan takes place through excessive discharges in major rivers mostly during the months of July-September. These floods have caused wide scale damage to irrigation works and communication lines as well as cultivated areas. In the Punjab, spilled water generally returns gravity to the river but in the Sind the flood stages in the river are higher than in the adjoining areas so that the flood water does not recede back to the river and consequently the inundation period is long and losses are higher. In addition, there are flash floods in hill torrents and small tributaries caused by heavy rains in catchment hills. This causes water to rush down bringing along coarse sediment. The damage by these floods is more intense but localized. Another type of flooding is through heavy rainfalls in poorly drained irrigated areas which causes the *nallah* tributaries to the Chenab and Ravi to overflow. These *nallahs* spill over a very large area within a short time causing heavy damage to human life and crops.

The common method of flood protection is by construction of embankments. Some *bunds* were constructed in the last century for the protection of newly-built irrigation works. Thus irrigation and flood protection developed together and are now under the same department, i.e., Irrigation, although the Federal Flood Commission has now been charged with the planning and execution of flood control programmes. The total length of these embankments exceeds 2,500 miles.[9]

In the Sind, *bunds* now exist along almost all the Indus but in the Punjab and NWFP they are only at locations of higher risks. During major floods *bund* breaches are frequent due to poor construction and poorer maintenance. Even the practice of patrolling the *bunds* monitor their behaviour seems to have declined.

Flood control received very low priority during the relatively flood-free period of 1959-73. Allocations were very low and reached their lowest level in the Fourth Plan. The heavy floods of 1973, however, caused a rethinking. Allocations for flood control in the Fifth Five Year Plan amounted to Rs 1,795 million as against only Rs 41 million (for West Pakistan) in the Fourth Plan.

A major programme for *bund* improvements and re-enforcement was launched after a series of *bund* failures in 1973. This programme paid dividends during the equally large floods of 1976 and 1978. A number of *bunds* were also built parallel to the original *bunds* as a second line of defence in highly vulnerable areas in order to contain flood damages to limited areas. An attempt is also being made to make improvements in flood forecasting. Flood forecasting and warning centres are being established and made more effective.

There are a number of non-structural flood control measures which may supplement the overall effort. These measures include the identification of hazard areas and the appropriate adjustments in land use in those areas. The planting of forests in hazard areas also needs to be closely examined.

Before 1977 there was no single institution responsible for flood management planning at the national level. Most of the work was done by the provincial irrigation departments. As the need for comprehensive flood control planning increased with the three major floods in the seventies, it was felt that a federal agency should oversee this task and the Federal Flood Commission (FFC) was established for flood control planning at the national level. In 1979, the National Flood Protection Plan was prepared by the Commission. Local plans, prepared by provincial irrigation departments, railways, and highways departments also require the approval of the FFC if federal financing is needed or if there should be a possible impact on flood conditions elsewhere.

Flood planning should be viewed as a part of the overall water management system. Surface drainage, proper maintenance of flood protection works, and long-term planning for the prevention of floods need to be integrated with water management in general. The tendency to pay attention to floods only after the occurance of a major flood results in the underfunding of flood protection works and a deterioration in their conditions, as in the relatively flood-free period between 1959 and 1973, on the one hand and overfunding, after a major catastrophe has taken place, on the other. Flood occurance should be accepted as part of the geophysical environment of Pakistan and planning should proceed on that basis so that priorities are established through systematic analysis and deliberation.

10.1.3 Conclusion

Heavy investments had to be made for infrastructural works, especially in big projects like Tarbela (Tables 10.1 and 10.2), but it seems that enough planned effort has not been made to utilize the additional water supplies in the most effective manner. The result is that the increase in water availability at farmgate has far exceeded the increase in irrigated cropped area as shown in Table 10.5.

The gap between increased water supply and extension in irrigated cropped area can partly be attributed to such factors as rectification of previous under-watering and of seasonal supply imbalances which may be reflected in higher productivity of irrigated land. Increased water losses, particularly between the irrigation outlet and the farm, may also account for a small part of the gap. But the remaining gap remains unexplained.

The major problem relates to a failure to undertake complementary farm level measures which could enable the farmer to make effective use of increased water supply at the farm inlet.[10] These complementary measures include improvement in water courses and the water delivery system, and a better interaction between the water supply and the quality of land and water. This can be accomplished only through the revitalization of the agricultural extension services. It may also be pointed out that the water distribution system needs major changes. Most rights to water were established prior to the large-scale tubewell developments and present allocation practices, for this and other reasons, do not fully reflect the major changes that have taken place. Established distribution practices will have to be modified in order to obtain the optimum conjunctive use of surface and ground water resources and to ensure that water is used where it produces its highest social return.[11]

Table 10.5 : Increases in Water Supply and Irrigated Area (Per cent)

	Kharif		*Rabi*	
Period	Increase in water availability	Increase in irrigated cropped area	Increase in water availability	Increase in irrigated cropped area
1960-1–1964-5	15	10	22	5
1965-6–1969-70	44	15	52	23
1970-1–1974-5	46	32	54	20

Source: Government of Pakistan, *Fifth Five Year Plan*, Islamabad, p. 82.

10.2 Fertilizer

Because of the semi-arid tropical climate in most parts of the country, the soil is generally low in nutrients and organic material. It also requires nitrogen to support high yield. Most soils are also low in phosphorus contents. It is therefore essential that a greater use of fertilizers should form part of the strategy for achieving greater productivity in agriculture. This is especially so after the introduction of HYV since the range of increase in output due to fertilizer use is higher in the case of HYV than traditional seeds. Fertilizers also offer the advantage of divisibility since they allow farmers to make marginal adjustments in their application regardless of the size of the farm. Fertilizers have shown very good results particularly for wheat, rice, and sugarcane. Primary types of fertilizers in use are urea for nitrogen and DAP for phosphate. Very few farms use any other types of fertilizer.

Let us take stock of consumption trends in fertilizers. Since the early sixties, consumption per cropped hectare has increased at a very impressive rate. Compared with only 4.57 nutrient kilograms in 1965-6, it increased to 18.59 nitrogenous kilograms in 1969-70 and 54.10 nitrogenous kilograms in 1979-80.[12] Table 10.6 shows the position regarding local production, imports, and total consumption trends for fertilizer. It shows that domestic production of fertilizer went up from 41,000 nitrogenous tonnes in 1962-3 to 133,000 nitrogenous tonnes in 1969-70 and 433,000 nitrogenous tonnes in 1979-80. Imports also went up from 3,000 nitrogenous tonnes in 1962-3 to 624,000 nitrogenous tonnes in 1979-80. Total consumption increased from 40,000 nitrogenous tonnes in 1962-3 to 308,000 nitrogenous tonnes in 1969-70 and 869,000 nitrogenous tonnes in 1979-80.

An interesting comparison can be made between the local production of fertilizer and its import. In 1962-3 the ratio of local production to import was 13:1. During the 'green revolution' period, when local production failed to cope with the rapidly rising domestic demand, imports increased sharply and the ratio of local production to import was 0.42:1 in 1966-7, 0.34:1 in 1967-8, and 0.52 1 and 1968-9. The ratio improved to 3:1 in 1971-2 and 2.4:1 in 1974-5. However, in the late seventies, it again declined to 0.60:1 in 1977-8 and 0.68:1 in 1979-80.

The Fifth Five Year Plan estimated that the total fertilizer consumption will rise to 1.3 million nitrogenous tonnes by 1982-3 at an average annual growth rate of 14.9 per cent during the Plan period.[13] Compared to the average annual growth rate of fertilizer consumption of 23 per cent during the Second Plan and 29 per cent during the Third Plan, this seemed to be a low target. But it represented a substantial improvement over 1970-7 when fertilizer consumption increased at an annual rate of 10.6 per cent due mainly to distribution bottlenecks and frequent price changes. The higher target envisaged in the Fifth Plan was based on the assumptions of an increased availability of water, the extension of seed-based technology to new areas and crops, the launching of proposed programmes for spreading the improved technology in the *barani* areas, and improvements in the supply and distribution system.[14]

An important aspect of fertilizer use is the maintenance of an appropriate balance between different types of fertilizers. The

Table 10.6: Production, Imports, and Consumption of Fertilizers
(000 N/Tonnes)

	Production				Imports				Consumption			
Year	N	P	K	Total	N	P	K	Total	N	P	K	Total
1962-3	39.95	1.07	–	41.02	3.11	–	–	3.11	40.00	0.20	–	40.20
1964-5	46.61	1.44	–	48.05	3.20	–	–	3.20	85.00	2.20	–	87.20
1969-70	129.27	4.15	–	133.42	292.19	11.45	–	303.64	272.56	33.80	1.34	307.70
1972-3	274.52	8.22	–	282.74	115.59	72.11	–	187.70	386.39	48.73	1.38	436.50
1974-5	320.60	6.30	–	326.90	105.53	21.88	5.96	133.37	362.83	60.57	2.09	425.49
1976-7	312.30	13.40	–	325.70	132.81	139.16	2.49	274.46	510.63	118.21	2.46	631.30
1979-80	389.90	43.00	–	432.90	485.10	138.09	19.16	642.35	682.67	178.52	7.95	869.14

Note: N = Nitrogenous; P = Phosphatic; K = Potassic
Source: Government of Pakistan, *Pakistan Economic Survey, 1980-1*, Islamabad, p. 31.

farmers in Pakistan mostly use nitrogenous fertilizers without paying due attention to the use of phosphatic and potassic fertilizers. This unfavourable ratio of phosphatic and nitrogenous fertilizers partly explains the decline in wheat yields since it led to a failure to replace residual soil phosphate that was exhausted during the early years of the 'green revolution'.[15] The N:P (nitrogenous : phosphatic/potassic) ratio was 220:1 in 1962-3, 8:1 in 1969-70, and 4:1 in 1977-8,[16] whereas the desirable ratio is 2:1 or 3:1 depending upon the type of the soil. During the Fifth Plan an effort has been made to popularize the use of phosphatic and potassic fertilizers which is expected to bring the N:P ratio to 2.3:1.[17]

The sale of fertilizers was subsidized in the early sixties mainly because the consumption of fertilizers was very low and farmers were unfamiliar with its use while the government was extremely keen to increase agricultural productivity. The amount of subsidy has steadily increased from Rs 103 million in 1972-3 to Rs 326 million in 1974-5, Rs 617 million in 1977-8, and Rs 2,500 million in 1979-80.[18] This increase in the total amount paid as subsidy took place in spite of a government decision to raise the price in February 1980 from Rs 63 per bag to Rs 93 per bag for urea and from Rs 67 per bag to Rs 100 per bag for DAP.

In view of the changed circumstances, it is difficult to justify the continuation of the subsidy programme and the commitment of larger and larger amounts of money for this purpose. A subsidy is justified if the demand is low and highly price-responsive. At present, the demand for fertilizer far exceeds its availability and there are shortages particularly at critical times. The farmers are not only familiar with its benefits they are becoming extremely conscious of them. The demand for fertilizer responds not so much to the actual price as to the net returns expected from its use which appear to be fairly high. Indeed the major constraint on the consumption of fertilizer now is supply. Moreover, the distribution system is also a bottleneck. Fertilizer supplies are not available at the proper time and at convenient locations. The dealers and those responsible for distribution delay the supply of fertilizers in order to extract higher black market prices. The present artificially low fertilizer prices not only make this scarce input even more scarce, they also result in the careless use and wastage of fertilizer by those who are fortunate enough to obtain supplies. A better use of the resources now committed to subsidies would be to improve the credit situation, extension services, and the input distribution system.

In the final analysis, the greatest harm which heavy investment in subsidization can do is to divert attention away from long-term programmes for institutional development and towards short-term solutions to agricultural problems through greater input consumption. In this particular case, allocation of funds for subsidies and inputs push into the background such important and difficult programmes as agricultural research, extension, and education. For example, over 41 per cent of the total public sector allocation to agriculture in the Fifth Plan is for improved seeds and fertilizers while research, education, and extension services receive only 8 per cent in all.[19]

10.3 High Yielding Varieties

Improved seed is the primary and cheapest input for effecting responses from more expensive inputs, such as water and fertilizers, and is fundamental to increasing per acre productivity. The use of improved varieties of seeds (HYV) is becoming more and more popular. Most of the improved varieties are the result of cross-breeding between native and foreign varieties and sometimes within native varieties. The use of better seeds offers the advantages of greater productivity through higher response to more water and fertilizer, and greater crop intensity. However, continuous research is needed in order to retain the advantages and the productivity of the improved varieties.

The development of quality seeds is achieved in three stages : (a) the production of nucleus seeds at research stations; (b) the multiplication of nucleus seeds into foundation seeds at government farms under the supervision of experts; and (c) the multiplication of foundation seeds into certified seeds under the overall supervision of the agricultural departments. The crops whose improved varieties are being produced and distributed include wheat, cotton, rice, maize, and gram. The introduction of Mexi-Pak seeds in wheat and Irri-Pak in rice were particularly instrumental in bringing about the breakthrough in agricultural production in the late sixties.

Table 10.7 shows the distribution of improved seeds in Pakistan during the seventies. Starting from a low base in the early seventies, the distribution of improved seeds reached fairly high levels during 1975-7 but shows declining trends in the later seventies.

However, unless supplemented by better cultural practices and a greater commitment of water and fertilizers, the introduction of improved seeds can produce only a limited increase in production. In the case of wheat, for example, the yield per acre is only about 213 kilograms per acre (553 kilograms per hectare) higher, in the case of the improved varieties, than the traditional varieties in the case of all farmers. Leading farmers (those who use better practices and complementary inputs) are, however, able to obtain 727 to 1,091 kilograms per acre (1,845 kilograms to 2,767 kilograms per hectare) higher.

Table 10.7: Distribution of Improved Seeds
(000 tonnes)

Crop	1970-1	1972-3	1975-6	1976-7	1979-80
Wheat	8.32	0.85	26.35	50.84	41.01
Paddy	3.88	1.27	1.31	2.91	0.78
Maize	0.22	0.37	1.53	0.97	0.39
Cotton	6.57	5.94	12.45	34.54	17.20
Gram	0.15	0.56	–	0.15	0.60
Potato	1.12	0.11	1.16	0.71	1.04
Oil seed	–	–	0.15	–	–
Others	–	–	0.21	3.43	0.04
Total	20.26	9.10	43.16	93.55	61.06

Source: Government of Pakistan, *Agricultural Statistics of Pakistan, 1980*, Islamabad, 1981, p. 104.

The need for constant research and effort exists because improved seeds, when grown over a long period of time under ordinary farming conditions and without being replaced at intervals, deteriorate in quality. This necessitates the replacement of old seeds at regular intervals and a constant supply of the breeder seeds. It was possibly due to this reason that a decline or stagnation was noticed during 1972-7 in the productivity of HYV. A study of trends in the Punjab found that major reverses in wheat took place in regions with a relatively better resource base and productivity per hectare declined from 2,212 kilograms in 1972-3 to 1,844 kilograms in 1976-7. In the case of rice, also, productivity fell, in the leading rice tracts of the Punjab, from the peak levels in 1969-71 of 2,518 kilograms to 1,844–2,120 kilograms in 1976-7.[20]

The World Bank data regarding acreage and production of the two major crops, i.e., wheat and rice, for Pakistan, demonstrate that productivity per acre of improved varieties showed impressive results in the initial years of introduction but in later years signs of stagnation were evident as examplified by the Mexi-Pak variety of wheat and the Irri-Pak variety of rice.[21]

The distribution of improved seeds is being subsidized at rates ranging from Rs 0.18 to Rs 0.40 per kilogram for various crops.[22]

10.4 Pesticides

A warm climate and high humidity in various parts of the country generally make crops vulnerable to different types of pests and plant diseases. However, only a small percentage of farmers practice any kind of pest or disease control. The result is that crop damage was fairly high, particularly in rice, during 1966-70 and 1976-7, in cotton in 1973-4, and in sugarcane since 1971-2. The problem has become more acute in recent times due to the expansion in the use of modern inputs and the increasing intensity of cropping. Chemical fertilizers make the plant more succulent and vulnerable to pests. Some of the HYV, particularly Mexi-Pak, are delicate and susceptible to pest infestation. Attempts to develop insect and disease-resistant varieties are ineffectual because some of the major pests tend to develop new bio-types. The Fifth Plan estimated crop losses due to pests and plant diseases to be 20 to 30 per cent of the total output in normal years.

Compared to the magnitude of the problem, the resources available for fighting this menace are extremely inadequate. Plant protection falls within the purview of agricultural extension services which make arrangements for aerial and ground spray. Tables 10.8 and 10.9 show the area covered by aerial and ground plant protection operations during 1978-9.

It can thus be seen that in 1978-9 aerial and ground spray operations covered 8.9 per cent of the total cropped area. This repre-

Table 10.8: Crop-wise Area Covered by Aerial Plant Protection Operation (1978-9)
(Area 000 hectares)

Crops	Cropped area	Area sprayed	Percentage of area sprayed	Spray hectares	Number of sprays
Cotton	1,891	155	8.2	246	1 to 2
Paddy	2,026	377	18.6	377	1
Sugarcane	753	87	11.6	157	2
Maize	650	55	8.5	55	1
Fruits/vegetables	432	—	—	—	—
Tobacco	48	22	45.8	22	1
Oil seed	578	20	3.5	20	1
Miscellaneous	12,782	10	0.1	11	1 to 2
Total	19,160	726	3.8	888	

Source: Government of Pakistan, *Agricultural Statistics of Pakistan,* 1979, Islamabad, p. 87.

Table 10.9: Crop-wise Area Covered by Ground Plant Protection Operation (1978-9)
(Area 000 hectares)

Crops	Cropped area	Area sprayed	Percentage of area sprayed	Spray hectares	Number of sprays
Paddy (nursery paddy)	2,025.6	217.1	10.7	284.1	1 to 2
Cotton	1,891.2	287.1	15.2	1,051.9	1 to 4
Sugarcane	752.5	120.7	16.0	236.4	2
Maize	649.9	35.3	5.4	59.3	1 to 2
Oil seed	577.9	6.2	1.1	6.2	1
Fruits/vegetables	432.0	115.6	26.8	301.7	1 to 3
Tobacco	47.7	13.7	28.7	27.7	2
Others	12,783.2	171.9	1.3	173.2	1
Total	19,160.0	967.6	5.1	2,140.5	

Source: Government of Pakistan, *Agricultural Statistics of Pakistan, 1979*, Islamabad, p. 88.

sents only a small improvement over the sixties. For example, in 1965-6 ground and aerial sprays covered 6.6 per cent of the total cropped area.[23] It should also be noted that greater reliance is now placed on ground spray. Up to 1979-80, ground spray was subsidized to the extent of 75 per cent and aerial spraying was free of cost. But now farmers, except in Baluchistan, are required to pay for pesticides although they can purchase sprayers at a 50 per cent subsidy.

Plant protection activities have not been very effective for a number of reasons including an insufficient quantity and defective methods of spraying and the inferior quality and unsuitability of pesticides. The government has recently allowed the private sector to import and sell pesticides and to phase out government involvement in plant protection.

NOTES

1. Government of Pakistan, *Third Five Year Plan*, 1965, p. 312.
2. Government of Pakistan, *Agricultural Statistics of Pakistan*, Islamabad, 1980, pp. 105-8.
3. WAPDA, *Revised Action Programme for Irrigated Agriculture*, Vol. 1, May 1979, pp. V-34.
4. Ibid., pp. 15, Annexure.
5. Government of Pakistan, *First Five Year Plan*, p. 356.
6. Government of Pakistan, *Second Five Year Plan*, p. 209.
7. Government of Pakistan, *Third Five Year Plan*, p. 399.
8. Government of Pakistan, *Pakistan Economic Survey, 1979-80*, Islamabad, p. 35.
9. S.M.H. Bokhari, *Case Study on the Demand/Supply Relationship for the Indus River Water Supply and Management*, Vol. 3, 1979. UK, p. 96.
10. World Bank, *Pakistan, Development Issues and Policies*, Vol. I, report No. 1924-PAK, April 1978, p. 21.
11. Ibid., p. 23.
12. Government of Pakistan, *Pakistan Basic Facts, 1979-80*, Islamabad, p. 29.
13. Government of Pakistan, *Fifth Five Year Plan*, Islamabad, p. 64.
14. Ibid., *Sectoral Programmes*, p. 16.
15. Gotsch and Brown, *Prices, Taxes and Subsidies in Pakistan Agriculture, 1960-1976*, The World Bank Staff Working Paper No. 387, 1980, p. 18.
16. Government of Pakistan, *Agricultural Statistics of Pakistan*, Islamabad, 1979, p. 25.
17. Government of Pakistan, *Fifth Five Year Plan*, Islamabad, p. 64.
18. Ibid., p. 28.
19. Ibid., p. 526.
20. Dilawar Ali Khan, *New Technology and Rural Transformation: A Case Study of Pakistan*, Punjab, UNCRD, 1979, p. 114.
21. IBRD, *Pakistan Economic Development and Prospects*, 1980, pp. 125-6.
22. Government of Pakistan, *Annual Plan, 1979-80*, Islamabad, p. 114.
23. (a) Cropped area data: Government of Pakistan, *Twenty-five Years of Statistics in Pakistan, 1947-72*, p. 82.
    (b) Plant Protection data: Government of Pakistan, *Pakistan Economic Survey, 1966-7*, Islamabad.

11 Some Key Issues in Agriculture

In the last three chapters we have looked at major trends in agricultural production, changes in structural relationships, and the increased use of agricultural inputs. In this chapter we take up some key issues in agriculture which have a direct impact on the pace and the quality of agricultural development. We will first take up two inter-related issues, i.e., agricultural pricing policies and taxation in agriculture. These issues seem to lead to a number of complications stemming from a lack of (or low) taxation of agricultural incomes, the subsidization of inputs, and the low procurement prices of agricultural produce. Such policies are necessitated by considerations of keeping the urban cost of living as low as possible, minimizing the fiscal burden of agricultural subsidies, and encouraging greater agricultural productivity. They show that we are still in the process of learning the art of using agricultural pricing as an instrument for producing general incentives effect on agricultural productivity and relative incentives effect on cropping patterns. We will also take up the provision of two essential facilities for agriculture, i.e., credit and marketing, and look at how the government is attempting to remove marketing bottle-necks and control the volume, distribution, and cost of credit to the farmers.

We also take up the very important issue of the mechanization of agriculture, the subject of a debate which still continues. We will also discuss the role of the financially starved areas of agricultural extension, research, and education. The role of agricultural extension, in particular in optimizing the use of agricultural resources and know-how and in increasing productivity levels, has been underestimated. A revitalized agricultural extension service can perform many tasks presently under-taken not so successfully by such costly programmes as IRDP and agricultural subsidies.

11.1 Agricultural Price Policy

An agricultural price policy refers to the government's role in determining or influencing the prices of agricultural outputs and inputs. The price mechanism can, if used judiciously and systematically, prove to be an effective supplement to efforts towards the revitalization of agriculture and increased agricultural productivity based on an appropriate package of technology and inputs. However, this will require an integrated approach towards the pricing of inputs and outputs so that higher agricultural production, as a policy objective, is viewed within a context of maintaining a balance in terms of trade between agriculture and other sectors.

In the first two decades, the agricultural price policy in Pakistan followed the development strategy of that time which sought to 'channel resources away from the massive agricultural population to the urban industrial entrepreneurs'.[1] This was done by keeping the prices of manufactured goods above the world level through import controls and the prices of agricultural products below the world level through the compulsory procurement of major agricultural crops at pre-determined prices and the imposition of domestic taxes and export duties on agricultural commodities thereby making the inter-sectoral terms of trade unfavourable to agriculture.

However, this policy has been adjusted and modified in response to a number of other considerations which included the need for export promotion, the domestic availability of industrial raw materials, the maintenance of an adequate domestic food supply, the encouragement of a greater use of improved technology and inputs, and the stabilization of the urban cost of living.

It is appropriate to divide the subject into two broad areas relating to (a) output pricing which includes the fixation of support or procurement prices of different agricultural crops; (b) input pricing which refers to the subsidies made available on seeds, fertilizers, plant protection, tubewells, agricultural machinery, and water. But this division of price policy into output pricing and input pricing does not suggest that these two aspects of a price policy are independent of each other or that decisions regarding them are made in isolation from each other. Indeed, output pricing has to take into consideration the overall cost structure in agriculture, which includes input prices, and part of the justification for subsidizing the sale of inputs flows from a policy designed to keep agricultural output prices within certain limits. It is only more convenient to take up various issues in a certain sequence.

11.1.1 Output Price Policy

This involves three types of pricing decisions:

A. The fixation of procurement prices for wheat, rice, and other food grain;
B. The determination of support[2] prices for export crops like cotton, rice, potato, and onions;
C. The fixation of sale prices of commodities required by indigenous industries as raw materials, for example, sugarcane, cotton, and seed cotton.

A. Wheat has been subjected to a most comprehensive price control system. It is procured from the cultivators at fixed prices usually announced before the sowing of the *rabi* crop, and according to targets laid down by the government. The control system also covers the milling process and the distribution channels for urban areas through rationing. The objectives of such an operation are somewhat contradictory since the government attempts to keep the urban cost of living and urban wage levels as low as possible and at the same time provide enough inducement to the farmers to increase the area, production, and productivity of wheat (which is the main diet and the price of which influences the prices of other wage goods).

The procurement price of wheat remained almost stagnant during the fifties and the early sixties rising from Rs 0.26 per kilogram in 1947-8 to Rs 0.38 in 1966-7 (Table 11.1). It is therefore not surprising that the wheat output also remained stagnant during this period. It was generally assumed in policy-making circles that agricultural production does not respond to price changes and that low prices, resulting from compulsory government procurement or high export duties on agricultural products, would not effect the output level.[3] Even the deteriorating food situation (the per capita availability of food grain declined from 16 ounces per day in 1948-9 to 13 ounces per day in 1962-3)[4] failed to create much anxiety due to the easy availability of food aid under PL-480 which might even have 'blurred the government's vision of the seriousness of the agricultural situation in Pakistan'.[5] Griffin also found a clear association between PL-480 imports and stagnating wheat production.[6]

In 1960, as part of a policy of general liberalization and relaxation of economic controls, 'voluntary' procurement of food grain replaced the system of 'compulsory' procurement. Controls on the prices and movement of wheat were lifted. There was also growing pressure on the government to pursue a price policy more favourable to agriculture. The reduced local production in the mid-sixties also coincided with reduced availabilities under PL-480.[7] Agricultural stagnation was perceived as responsible for the worsening balance of payments position, low savings, and low demand for indigenous industrial goods. It was also realized, as borne out by a number of studies,[8] that agricultural production does respond to price incentives through increases in area and yield of individual crops and changes in the cropping pattern spread over a number of years. The price incentive also changes the farmers' long-run expectations of profitability and this influences their decisions regarding investment and use of labour inputs and technology. The stability of net returns, rather than relative prices, is also an important aspect of production incentives because of inherent risks in agriculture, uncertainties of production, and the small size of cultivation units which reduce the farmers' abilities to bear losses.

The procurement price of wheat was raised to Rs 0.4 per kilogram in 1967 and Rs 0.63 per kilogram in 1972-3. Since then, it steadily went up to Rs 1.31 per kilogram in 1979-80 (Table 11.1.).

While wheat is procured mainly to regulate its availability to urban consumers, rice is an important export item. Prior to 1971, rice procured in West Pakistan was shipped to East Pakistan which had a deficit in rice production. During the seventies, rice became a major export item. Except for a few years during the fifties, the procurement of rice has been a regular feature. Procurement prices for

Table 11.1: Procurement/Support Prices of Agricultural Commodities
(Rupees per 37.324 kilogram)

Commodities	1947-8	1948-9	1959-60	1962-3	1966-7	1967-8	1972-3	1974-5	1975-6	1977-8	1979-80
Wheat	9.50	9.75	12.50	13.50	13.50	17.00	22.50	37.00	37.00	37.00	46.65
Rice											
Basmati	22.06	20.50	23.00	26.00	28.00	31.00	46.00	90.00	90.00	95.00	110.00
Permal	21.06	18.50	18.00	18.00	17.50	20.00	21.00	40.00	40.00	–	–
Begmi	14.31	13.43	15.00	16.00	17.50	18.50	21.00	40.00	40.00	–	–
Kangni	–	–	15.00	16.00	17.50	19.00	20.50	39.00	39.00	39.00	39.00
Joshi	15.31	13.75	14.50	15.50	17.00	19.00	20.50	39.00	39.00	–	–
Irri-6	–	–	–	–	–	–	21.00	48.00	48.00	46.00	49.00
Irri-8	–	–	–	–	–	–	19.50	38.00	40.00	38.00	38.00
Sugarcane (mill gate)											
NWFP	–	–	–	2.25	2.00	2.25	3.10	5.00	5.50	5.50	6.75
Punjab	–	–	–	2.25	2.00	2.42	3.35	5.25	5.75	5.75	7.00
Sind	–	–	–	2.25	2.00	2.56	3.50	5.40	5.90	5.90	7.15
Cotton (Lint)											
Desi	–	–	–	–	–	–	–	–	–	335.00	350.00
AC-134, NT	–	–	–	–	–	–	–	–	–	335.00	383.00
B-557,149-F	–	–	–	–	–	–	–	–	–	388.00	416.00
Sarmast, Qalandri	–	–	–	–	–	–	–	–	–	421.00	449.00
Deltapine, MS-39/40	–	–	–	–	–	–	–	–	–	421.00	449.00
Seed Cotton (*Phutti*)											
Desi	–	–	–	–	–	–	–	–	–	132.00	134.00
AC-134,NT	–	–	–	–	–	–	–	–	–	138.00	138.00
B-557, 149F	–	–	–	–	–	–	–	–	–	149.00	149.00
Sarmast, Qalandri	–	–	–	–	–	–	–	–	–	160.00	160.00
Deltapine, MS-39/40	–	–	–	–	–	–	–	–	–	25.00	25.00
Potato	–	–	–	–	–	–	–	–	–	–	–
Onion	–	–	–	–	–	–	–	–	–	18.00	13.00

Source: Government of Pakistan, *Pakistan Economic Survey, 1979-80*, Islamabad, Statistical Annexure, pp. 36-8.

basmati were fixed at Rs 0.57 per kilogram in 1948-9 which rose to only Rs 0.73 per kilogram by 1962-3 and Rs 0.87 per kilogram by 1967-8. Since then it has been raised to Rs 1.07 per kilogram in 1968, Rs 1.29 per kilogram in 1972-3, Rs 2.63 per kilogram in 1974-5, and Rs 3.09 per kilogram in 1979-80 (Table 11.1).

The policy of procurement of food grain usually seeks to stabilize food prices by building up buffer stocks. However, such a policy can succeed only to the extent of storage facilities available to the government. In many years, for example in 1962-3, when there was a particularly good harvest, the government was not able, or willing, to procure large food stocks due mainly to storage limitations. The result was that the farmers were unable to sell their produce quickly and reap the benefits of higher production. It also made them suspect that the government procurement policies worked only during bad years when higher prices could have compensated them for low production.[9]

Inspite of these setbacks, a recognition of the role of prices in agricultural development did provide much needed incentives to the growers and may have partly contributed to the high growth rates in the late sixties.

A word on the level of procurement prices. Admittedly these are low when compared to world prices. One may question the use of world prices as the criteria in this matter. However, it does have some relevance since, in the case of wheat, part of the total quantity consumed in Pakistan is imported and, in the case of rice, procurement is primarily meant for export. Table 11.2 shows that the gap between procurement prices and world prices of the two commodities was very large during

Table 11.2: Wheat and Rice: Domestic vs. World Prices
(Rupees per 35.5 kilogram)

Foodgrain	1969-70	1973-4	1974-5	1975-6	1976-7	1977-8	1978-9
Wheat							
Procurement price	17	26	37	37	37	37	45
World price (FOB)*	23	78	68	56	48	45	49
Rice							
Procurement price	35	62	90	90	95	95	110
World price (FOB)*	54	202	135	95	100	107	125

*World Bank Commodity Price Projection, 1977.
Source: WAPDA, *Revised Action Programme for Irrigated Agriculture*, 1979, pp. 1-18.

Table 11.3: Rice and Wheat: Domestic Prices
(Rupees per 35.5 kilogram)

Foodgrain	1971-2	1972-3	1974-5	1975-6	1978-9	1979-80
Wheat						
Issue price (at ration depot)	18.35	18.35	21.50	32	37	45
Procurement price	17	20.50	37	37	45	46.65
Open market price	28	25	37	52	58	57
	1973-4	1974-5	1975-6	1976-7	1977-8	1978-9
Rice						
Procurement price	62	90	90	95	95	110
Open market price	86	95	99	110	145	123

Source: Government of Pakistan, *Pakistan Economic Survey, 1979-80*, Islamabad, pp. 38, 99-101.

the mid-seventies but is now diminishing. The procurement prices are also low in comparison with their domestic open market prices (Table 11.3). The procurement price of wheat is higher than its issue price at ration depots because its sale to urban consumers is subsidized. However, budgetary constraints now seem to be compelling a reduction in the subsidy and, therefore, this gap is narrowing. Good harvests since 1979 also seem to have restrained the open market prices of wheat.

The policy of food provision at low prices to urban consumers and the generation of public revenues from the export of procured commodities at higher than purchase prices has also imposed an implicit commodity tax on the growers which constitutes a disincentive for higher production.[10]

In the case of rice, for example, the total profits earned by the state-owned Rice Export Corporation, which holds the monopoly for the procurement and export of rice, stood at Rs 1,173 million in 1979-80.[11] This is indicative of the extent of the hidden taxation on rice growers.

It would be worth investigating if higher procurement prices, by encouraging production and export and by making farmers more willing to sell to the government, would bring in more exchange earnings (and higher profits to the public sector which monopolizes its export) than the money saved by paying below market prices to the growers.

However, a policy of low procurement prices also offers certain advantages. It offsets the absence of agricultural income taxation and the existence of subsidies on agricultural inputs. However, the level of procurement prices must also take into account price movements in the non-agricultural sectors.

B. Minimum support prices have been fixed in the case of seed cotton, cotton lint, oilseeds, maize, onions, potatoes, and pulses in order to protect the producers against steep price declines, particularly in the international market, so that a certain profit margin could be guaranteed to them. In the case of potatoes, onions, pulses, and oilseeds, the Pakistan Agricultural Storage and Services Corporation is charged with the responsibility of maintaining their prices above the support level.

Cotton prices were indirectly controlled through the imposition of export duties on all varieties of raw cotton. The export duties remained in force from 1947 to 1967 except during the post-Korean recession year of 1952-3.[12] Since the world market for cotton is highly competitive, the export duty could not be transferred to the foreign buyers.[13] It therefore served in most of the years only to depress the domestic prices and thus acted as a disincentive to the producers.[14] The duty was reimposed following the devaluation of the Pakistan rupee in 1972. However, *desi* cotton has been exempted from duty since 1976.[15] In 1976-80, the export duty on raw cotton yielded Rs 260 million or 7.6 per cent of the total export earnings from raw cotton.[16]

In addition to the export duty, the overvaluation of the rupee before 1972 also constituted a tax on exports and as such on the growers.[17]

Since 1973, cotton is purchased by the state-owned Cotton Export Corporation which monopolizes its export and also arranges for its local sales. It is also responsible for maintaining cotton prices at the level determined by the government. It thus seems that, in addition to the export duty, there is an implicit tax on cotton growers represented by the excess of export price of cotton over its domestic purchase price. The magnitude of this tax can be gauged by the profits earned by the Cotton Export Corporation (Rs 151 million in 1979-80).[18]

C. The sale price of sugarcane was introduced in 1961, apparently in order to accommodate the interests of both the sugarcane growers and the indigenous sugar industry. In most of the sugarcane growing areas, the local sugar mill is the single buyer and, particularly during the years of high production, the sale-price really functions as a support-price protecting the growers' interest while, during low output seasons, it functions as a price-ceiling to protect the interests of the sugar mills. During the sixties, sugarcane support prices remained stagnant around Rs 0.07 per kilogram but increased in the seventies to Rs 0.15 per kilogram in 1975-6 and Rs 0.19 per kilogram in 1979-80 (Table 11.1). Sugar-cane prices remained below the world price level during the early seventies in spite of a rise in support prices but in the late seventies prices remained substantially higher than the world level. In 1978-9 the sugarcane support price was 180 per cent higher than the world price.[19]

11.1.2 Input Pricing Policy

During the sixties and seventies, an elaborate structure of agricultural inputs subsidies was evolved covering fertilizers, improved seeds, plant protection, tubewells, and agricultural machinery. The objective of subsidizing inputs was to provide greater production incentives and to encourage the use of superior technology. It has been argued that while high output prices may or may not lead to greater investment in better technology, and may be diverted to higher consumption, subsidization of inputs, which comprises the new technology, would ensure its rapid adoption. Also, while higher output prices may benefit only those farmers who already have marketable surpluses, low input pricing may enable subsistence farmers to produce such surpluses. Subsidizing inputs also stabilize the prices of agricultural produce and consequently does not effect the urban cost of living except through higher taxation to finance the subsidy programme.

But, in many cases, the cost of the inputs may only be a small part of the total cost of production of agricultural commodities and, therefore, even a liberal subsidy may not have an appreciable impact on the farmers' profit margin and production incentives. Inputs subsidies may also lead to certain undesirable substitution effects, for example, subsidized fertilizers may discourage the use of organic manure; subsidized credit may encourage capital-intensive techniques; and a subsidy on water supply may lead to over-irrigation and a wastage of water. A subsidy programme must also examine the opportunity cost of the funds being allocated for this purpose.

It should also be pointed out that the subsidy should be regarded as a strictly temporary form of assistance. There is always a need for a constant review of the subsidy level and for making adjustments according to the demand, cost, and supply situations which tend to change quite rapidly. A policy based on subsidies would lose its effectiveness if it does not possess a high degree of flexibility.

The subsidy on fertilizer was made available on a modest scale during the fifties through a federal grant to the provinces. The annual subsidy during the fifties remained below Rs 20 million.[20] The amount involved in subsidy increased steadily in the early sixties and quite rapidly in the late sixties when the scope of the programme was extended to the sale of improved seeds, the installation of tubewells, and plant protection. In fact, plant protection, which included both insecticides (all imported) and spray operations, was free up to 1966. Later, during 1966-72, the subsidy covered 88 per cent of the total cost. In 1972 it was further reduced to 50 per cent in the Punjab and 75 per cent in other provinces. However, in 1979, the subsidy was withdrawn in all provinces except Baluchistan. The import and spray of pesticides has now been transferred to the private sector but the sale of sprayers is still substantially subsidized. Inputs subsidies rose quite steadily during the fifties and the sixties with a rapid increase in the subsidy bill during the seventies. Table 11.4 shows consolidated (federal plus provincial government) subsidies during the seventies for food (which is included in non-development expenditure) and agricultural inputs (which is part of development expenditure). It is worth noting that the subsidy bill for agricultural inputs has amounted to 14.1 per cent of the consolidated development expenditure in 1979-80 as against 6.7 per cent in 1972-3.

The supply to cultivators of such other inputs as electricity, which is made available for agriculture at concessional rates, and canal waters is also considerably subsidized. The emergence of the canal water subsidy is of recent occurrance. A comparison of water receipts and expenses on irrigation show that during the sixties and the early seventies the income from water revenue exceeded the current expenditure of the irrigation department in various provinces. From 1974-5, however, the trend was reversed as the rise in

Table 11.4: Consolidated (Federal and Provincial) Government Subsidies, 1972-3 to 1979-80
(Rs million)

	1972-3	1973-4	1974-5	1975-6	1976-7	1977-8	1978-9	1979-80
Food	920	2,186	2,562	1,552	1,111	1,655	3,179	2,582
Wheat	920	1,917	1,551	1,552	1,107	1,634	2,575	1,582
Edible oil	–	269	443	–	–	–	577	973
Sugar	–	–	–	–	4	21	27	27
Agricultural inputs	381	203	454	897	562	1,026	2,100	3,367
Fertilizers	228	118	326	607	87	617	1,692	2,985
Plant protection	128	63	112	241	421	347	376	326
Tubewells	22	10	16	43	48	37	24	48
Wheat seeds	3	12	–	6	6	25	8	8
Non-development consolidated expenditure	12,473	15,764	21,672	26,800	26,085	29,426	41,763	49,354
Food subsidies as percentage of non-development consolidated expenditure	7.38	13.87	11.82	5.79	4.26	5.62	7.61	5.23
Consolidated development expenditure	5,636	8,021	13,172	16,368	19,510	19,405	22,744	23.793
Agricultural subsidies as percentage of consolidated development expenditure	6.76	2.53	3.45	5.48	2.88	5.29	9.23	14.15

Source: (i) Federal and provincial Budgets of various years for subsidies. (ii) Government of Pakistan, *Pakistan Basic Facts, 1979-80*, Table 18.8, pp.224-5 for consolidated development and non-development expenditure. Computed by eliminating increase/decrease in cash balances from capital receipts and capital disbursements, and also not including capital disbursements to private sector.

Table 11.5: Irrigation Receipts and Irrigation Expenditure
(West) Pakistan (1962-71)
(Rs million)

	1962-3	1963-4	1964-5	1965-6	1966-7	1967-8	1968-9	1969-70
Receipts	51	75	113	113	58	69	102	109
Expenditure	19	13	13	21	14	19	24	27

Pakistan (1971-9) Combined Figures for all Provinces

	1972-3	1973-4	1974-5	1975-6	1976-7	1977-8	1978-9
Receipts	259	397	253	376	431	497	532
Expenditure	229	273	403	565	627	646	787

Source: Government of Pakistan, *Pakistan Basic Facts, 1979-80*, Table 18.4, pp. 205-7.

expenditure was much faster than in irrigation revenues (Table 11.5). Calculating on the basis of the total area irrigated by government canals in 1978-9 (about 11 million hectares)[21] and Rs 225 million being the excess of irrigation expenses over revenues (Table 9.5) the subsidy per hectare amounts to Rs 24 per hectare (Rs 9.75 per acre). On the same basis, the subsidy for 1974-5 turns out to be Rs 15.40 per hectare (Rs 6.27 per acre).

11.1.3 Inter-sectoral Terms of Trade

The terms of trade between agriculture and other sectors have followed a fluctuating path. Gotsch and Brown[22] have divided these trends into several identifiable periods. Period 1 coincides with the fifties when Pakistan was still feeling the impact of partition. Before partition, agricultural goods from Pakistani regions were exchanged for industrial goods from Indian regions. The destruction of that relationship led to significant changes in the rates at which the agricultural–non-agricultural exchange took place.

Period 2 relates to the Second and part of the Third Plan periods when the policy-makers' approach to agriculture was 'more positive'. The terms of trade improved appreciably for agriculture as agricultural prices showed an upward trend. But the very success of agriculture in the late sixties led to pressures for a reversal of the terms of trade and for agriculture to share its prosperity with the rest of the society. As such, input prices were allowed to rise in the late sixties and early seventies (Period 3) while major exports (cotton and rice) continued to be taxed via an over-valued exchange rate and specific export cesses. However, the farming lobby reacted promptly and produced the usual 'cost-price squeeze' argument. They also strongly criticized the export duties and higher charges for inputs and water. The government responded by raising the price of wheat, rice, and maize. Thus the terms of trade for agriculture began to look up during 1972-4. However, these increases in agricultural prices were not sufficient to remain ahead of the rapidly rising prices in the non-agricultural sector. There was a sharp decline in the agricultural terms of trade in the mid-seventies. Figure 11.1 shows three-year moving averages of the gross barter terms of trade while Table 11.6 shows the year to year trends in terms of trade between agriculture and other sectors.

11.1.4 Price Policy and Income Distribution

The impact of agricultural price policies on income distribution within agriculture also needs to be examined. So far as output pricing is concerned, procurement policies affect almost all farmers except the subsis-

Table 11.6: Indices of Output, Prices, and Income for Pakistan Agriculture
(FY 1960 = 100)

FY	Output (1)	Terms of trade (2)	Real income (3)	Rural population (4)	Income per farmer (5)
1960	100	100	100	100	100
1961	100	115	115	103	112
1962	109	113	123	105	117
1963	119	108	129	108	119
1964	118	111	131	111	118
1965	128	115	147	114	129
1966	127	108	137	117	117
1967	135	114	154	120	128
1968	157	109	171	123	139
1969	168	102	171	126	139
1970	186	106	197	129	153
1971	174	104	181	133	136
1972	183	108	198	136	146
1973	188	112	211	140	151
1974	196	121	237	143	166
1975	187	108	202	147	137
1976	199	102	203	151	134

Source: (i) Government of Pakistan, *Pakistan Economic Survey, 1976-7,* Islamabad, Statistical Appendix, p. 20. (ii) C. Gotsch, *Working Note No. 1,* 2 December 1976. Output prices deflated by index of all manufactured goods. (iii) = (1) x (2). (iv) Constructed assuming 2.6 per cent per annum growth of rural population. (v) = (3) ÷ (4). Assumes number of farmers growing at same rate as rural population.

tence farmers. In the years when production is low and procurement prices are below the scarcity value of the crops, it can be assumed that the government has to pursue procurement policies more energetically in order to ensure domestic availability. It can also be assumed that big farmers, due to their social influence, can easily evade the procurement policies so that the burden of these policies is borne by farmers at the other end of the scale. On the other hand, during the years of high production when procurement prices seem attractive and farmers are in a hurry to sell their produce, the benefit will again go to the larger farmers. In a highly differentiated social structure it is only natural that the procurement process seems to favour the big farmers at the cost of the small farmers under all types of conditions.

In the case of input pricing also, a number of studies[23] have shown that most of the benefits of the subsidies accrue to the big farmers who have easier access not only to the inputs but also to water, credit, and agricultural extension services.[24]

This situation thus seeks to widen the gaps in productivity and income between large and small cultivators. The only difference is that while procurement prices relate to all farmers, except subsistence farmers, input subsidization, supported by improvement in supply and a more efficient distribution system, may make it possible for small and subsistence farmers to have access to these inputs and to become capable of entering the market.

Fig. 11.1: Three-Year Moving Average of the Gross Barter Term-of-Trade for Pakistan Agriculture:1950-75

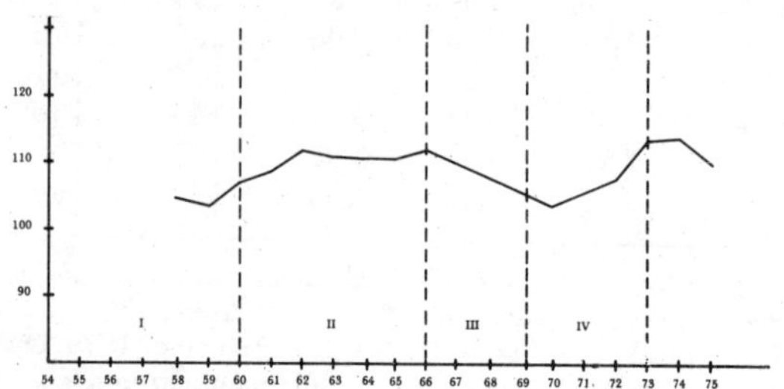

Source: Gotsch and Brown, *Prices, Taxes and Subsidies in Pakistan Agriculture, 1960-76*, World Bank Staff Working Paper No. 387, 1980, p. 36.

11.1.5 Conclusion

The determination of the prices of agricultural crops by the government, along with other administrative and economic controls on their processing, distribution, and export, amount to the suppression of the market mechanism. But markets in Pakistan, as in other developing countries, are hardly perfect. Imperfections in the form of under-developed transport and communication facilities, a high degree of heterogeneity among both the buyers and the sellers, and the division of the market into small isolated sub-markets, make the market system incapable of generating a substantial degree of competition. The farmers belong to a highly differentiated structure of interests in land, ranging from sharecroppers and tenants to owner-cultivators and still further to capitalist farmers and absentee landlords. Most farmers have little contact with the market either because they are subsistence owners-cultivators without a marketable surplus or because they are sharecroppers whose surplus is taken away by a non-cultivating class.[25]

State intervention under these circumstances is essential in order to create a mutually accomodating price-structure. This could allocate land and other resources among competing crops and also reconcile prices of agricultural output with the overall cost structure within agriculture. Inter-sectoral terms of trade between agriculture and other sectors also need to be maintained at levels which would eliminate causes of social frictions and distortions in development priorities.

It is quite obvious that in the foreseeable future the agricultural price policy will have to be framed in such a way so as to achieve conflicting objectives like incentives for the farmers, stability of the urban cost of living, easy domestic availability of food grain and industrial raw materials, and adequate exportable surplus. In addition, small cultivators, including subsistence farmers, have to be given access to new inputs and technology and also to the benefits of the subsidy programmes so that these large public outlays do not become the cause of widening social disparities.

The pressing need to cater to all these requirements calls for a highly flexible approach to agricultural prices. But it seems that the government, in spite of a commitment to a policy of gradual reduction in subsidies,[26] is unable to reverse the trend. Substantial amounts are now involved in subsidies (over 15 per cent of the consolidated development expenditure and over 6 per cent of the consolidated non-development expenditure in 1979-80) whose opportunity cost may be quite high (Table 11.4). For example, the total subsidy bill for food and agricultural inputs for one year (1976-7) was 33 per cent higher than the entire Fifth Plan allocation for agricultural research, education, and extension.[27]

What is required in this situation is to look beyond subsidies as a policy instrument, and to pay serious attention to such matters as improving the overall supply position of the inputs, particularly such divisible inputs as seeds, fertilizers, and pesticides, and to ensure their timely availability. Attention should also be paid to the extension of rural outlets, the encouragement of multiple market channels, and the improvement of the farmers' ability to make efficient use of the inputs. As the supply position improves, it would be easier to reduce the subsidy level and to allow prices to rise gradually. If the farmer has access to institutional credit and is able to increase his net returns, an increase in input prices may not inhibit his demand for them.

There is also a need to gradually raise output prices so that resources now tied to consumer subsidies are released for other purposes on the one hand and, on the other, the farmer can confidently look forward to larger cash flows and can plan his investments for a longer period than one or two crop seasons. It is imperative that the price signals sent to the farming community should be unambiguous and have a certain amount of continuity.

Finally, an agricultural price policy by itself cannot necessarily serve as a grand design for major institutional or technological changes. It can serve limited goals and its success will depend upon it being supplemented by co-ordinated efforts in other related areas. It can heighten the effectiveness of various other tools of economic policy rather than become a substitute for them. In other words, it can function as a 'fine tuner' and not as a 'prime mover'.

11.2 Agricultural Taxation

Four types of land revenue assessment systems were prevalent in (West) Pakistan after Independence:

a. fixed assessment;
b. fluctuating assessment;
c. fluctuating assessment with a sliding scale;
d. fluctuating assessment with a sliding scale for certain crops and fixed rates for others.[28]

The first three types prevailed in the Punjab where assessment varied from district to district, *tehsil* to *tehsil*, and assessment circle to assessment circle according to a detailed soil classification. Under the fourth type, which functioned in the Sind, assessment varied from crop to crop according to the nature of irrigation. The sliding scale system was brought in after Independence because of the continuous rise in prices, resulting in a decline of the real income of the government. In 1967, the system of land revenue all over (West) Pakistan was consolidated. The (West) Pakistan Land Revenue Act 1967 provided that land revenue shall be assessed:

a. as a fixed annual charge payable in lump sum or by instalments; or
b. in the form of prescribed rates per acre according to the area recorded as sown, matured, or cultivated, during any harvest or during any year.

The period of assessment was fixed at twenty-five years. The average rate of assessment cannot exceed the rate fixed in the previous assessment by one-fourth for any assessment circle and one-half in the case of an estate.

Two major controversies exist in the field of agricultural taxation. These relate to (a) the land revenue and the system of its assessment and (b) agricultural income tax. A number of commissions and committees, appointed by the Pakistan Government, have looked into these areas. In addition, fairly intense public debates have taken place during the last three decades. Mention must be made here of the Taxation Enquiry Committee (1959), the Food and Agriculture Commission (1960), the Fact Finding Committee on Agricultural Taxation (1964), and the Commission on Taxation and Tariff (1967). The controversies revolve around the period of settlement and the assessment system.

It is generally agreed that the period of settlement is too long. Forecasting the course of prices for a period of twenty-five years is 'an exercise in speculation' particularly in view of the rapid changes in technology, productivity, and the prices of both the land and its products. Also 'in a period of rising prices, statistical average of price data of historically distant years,' according to one study, 'can give misleading results. If the duration of settlement is ten years, the trend of the past ten years can be statistically projected over the next five years and the resulting prices can be adopted for settlement!'[29]

But a shorter assessment period may create administrative problems. Land revenue assessment is a time-consuming and complicated process. Before Independence, assessment was done after every thirty to forty years and this period was reduced in 1967. The period can be further reduced by speeding up the settlement process through a simplification of the soil classification, a reduction in the number of soil categories, and the separation of revenue settlement from correcting records of rights.

The relative merits of fixed and fluctuating systems of assessment have also provoked debate. The fixed assessment system has been criticised on grounds of income and price-and-yield-inelasticity. However, by keeping the land revenue fixed for a considerable period, it allows the cultivators to gain the full benefits of higher productivity. It also provides less scope for corruption since the discretion of petty bureaucracy is limited. Fluctuating assessment is relatively elastic but the scope for corruption in this case is fairly wide since lower officials of the Revenue Department have considerable discretion in assessing its liabilities.

It must, however, be noted that land revenue is now about to fade away. It may be replaced by *usher* in the near future. Small cultivators were exempted from land revenue in 1975 while the rates have been raised for big farmers.

The issue relating to agricultural income tax was debated with considerable intensity in the mid-seventies. The discussion took place partly with regard to the conveniences and inconveniences of replacing land revenue with agricultural income tax and partly with regard to the wider issue of the balance between taxable capacity of, and actual tax burden on, the agricultural sector. The arguments advanced against extending the cover of income tax to agricultural income was the following:

1. It would be inconvenient to both the tax-collectors and tax-payers since farming in Pakistan is generally of the subsistence type and not of the commercial type. Farmers do not maintain standardized accounts of their costs and returns and, therefore, it is difficult to assess their net incomes.
2. The number of farmers is very large and they are scattered all over the country, many in remote inaccessible areas. It would cause considerable loss of time and money to even contact the potential taxpayers.
3. Agricultural incomes being uncertain, depending upon the vagaries of nature, it is quite probable that a large number of farmers may frequently move across the tax exemption limit thus making it difficult and laborious for tax authorities to keep tabs on them.

But there are strong arguments in favour of extending income tax to agriculture:

1. It is unfair and illogical to make a distinction between agricultural and non-agricultural incomes for purposes of taxation. Just as incomes below a certain level are exempted from tax in case of non-agricultural incomes, the same principle should be extended to agricultural income. This would take

care of the large majority of subsistence farmers who would be automatically excluded.

2. There is considerable evasion of income tax by those having both agricultural and non-agricultural incomes. Part of their non-agricultural income is shown by them as accruing from agriculture, thus evading the tax. Extending income tax to agriculture would reduce tax evasion.
3. Agricultural income tax would be more income-elastic than land revenue. With a greater yield per acre, higher procurement prices, and mechanization, the benefits of which are mainly confined to large farmers, incomes in the agricultural sector have risen considerably but yield, in terms of direct taxes from agriculture, has not risen so fast. Between 1972-3 and 1978-9, the yield from direct taxation on agriculture (land revenue and irrigation charges) increased by 78 per cent (from Rs 472 million to Rs 762 million) while value-added in agriculture at current factor cost increased by 157 per cent (Rs 21,907 million to Rs 56,370 million).[30]

The larger issue of whether agriculture is under-taxed or over-taxed both with regard to its own taxable capacity and in comparison with other sectors should also be looked at. The view-point of the agriculturists is summarized below:

1. Agriculture is subject to a large number of direct, indirect, and hidden taxes. Indirect taxes constitute over 85 per cent of the total revenues of the federal government.[31] Since these taxes are paid by all, it can be safely assumed that the agricultural population (being about three-fourth of the total population) bears a heavy burden. There are also hidden taxes in the form of low procurement prices paid by the government for many agricultural products, export duties on agricultural commodities, and the mechanism of terms of trade between industry and agriculture.
2. Increase in agricultural incomes has been off-set by a rise in population and higher expenditure on agricultural inputs and equipment.
3. Higher taxation on agriculture will adversely affect the motivation for savings and investments at a time when farmers must make larger investments in order to increase productivity.
4. Agricultural income has increased not only due to higher income per acre but also due to the increase in area under cultivation. Higher taxation will discourage farmers from bringing new land under the plough.

Some strong arguments, however, support the contention that agriculture has considerable capacity for additional taxation:

1. Direct taxes on agriculture have risen at a slower pace than growth in agricultural incomes, as shown in Table 11.7.

But the introduction of subsidies to agricultural producers on inputs (Table 11.1) and to urban consumers on wheat, edible oil, and sugar provides further complications. Subsidy is a 'negative tax' and should be taken into account while calculating relative tax burdens. Gotsch and Brown have attempted the calculation of subsidy transfers between the agricultural producers, the urban consumers, and the government (which includes both the federal and provincial governments), which are shown in Table 11.8.

Negative figures in the Table should be added to the tax burden while positive figures should be deducted. The data supports the view that the rural sector has (a) received much less subsidy from the government than the urban sector, and (b) contributed a substantial share to the consumer

Table 11.7: Burden of Direct Taxes on Agriculture
(Rs million)

	1972-3	1973-4	1974-5	1975-6	1976-7	1977-8	1978-9
Land revenue	168	186	188	198	136	117	230
Irrigation charges	259	397	253	376	431	497	532
Total (direct taxation on agriculture)	427	583	441	574	567	614	762
Value-added in agriculture (current factor cost)	21,907	28,084	33,533	38,338	43,686	49,370	56,370
Percentage of direct taxes on agriculture to value-added in agriculture	1.9	2.0	1.3	1.5	1.3	1.2	1.3

Source: (i) Government of Pakistan, *Pakistan Basic Facts, 1979-80*, Table 18.4, pp. 205-7 for land revenue and irrigation charges. (ii) Government of Pakistan, *Pakistan Economic Survey, 1979-80*, Table 2.2, Islamabad, Statistical Annexure, p. 13, for value added in agriculture.

subsidies. However, these figures do not show the full effect of the subsidy transfer due to, apart from other reasons, the fact that Gotsch and Brown did not include in their calculations such implicit subsidies to agriculture as canal water, power supply, institutional credit, and the benefits of extension services.

The argument, therefore, remains inconclusive and in need of further inquiry.

2. Any comparison of an aggregate tax burden on agriculture with another sector will have little meaning in terms of equity unless a large number of variables are considered and given due weightage. However, a simple comparison between direct taxes on agricultural and non-agricultural incomes will be instructive (Table 11.9).

The Table shows that while direct taxes on agricultural income have increased by 78 per cent between 1972-3 and 1978-9, direct taxes on non-agricultural incomes have risen by 182 per cent.

Direct taxes, of course, do not tell the whole story. Indirect taxes provide the bulk of the total consolidated tax revenue of the federal and provincial governments. But it is difficult to calculate their incidence separately on agriculture and other sectors.

3. The population argument is weak because the urban population has increased even faster than the rural population due to both natural factors and migration from the rural sector.
4. The major benefits of a rise in incomes due to higher yield in agriculture went to larger farmers.[32] This has intensified inequities in income distribution in the rural sector and would indicate additional taxable capacity.
5. The rise in incomes has not been accompanied by any corresponding increase in the level of domestic savings which has remained low. The failure of the

Table 11.8: Subsidy Transfers between Sectors
(Rs million)

	1966	1970	1972	1973	1974	1975	1976
Producer Subsidy Value	–310	–651	–289	–343	–1,356	–1,925	–1,237
from consumers	–348	–710	–329	–447	–1,495	–2,088	–1,540
from government	38	59	40	104	139	163	303
Consumer Subsidy Value	651	895	583	1,053	2,750	3,779	3,280
from producers	348	710	328	446	1,495	2,088	1,540
from government	303	185	255	607	1,255	1,691	1,740
Government Budget Cost	341	244	295	711	1,394	1,854	2,043
to producers	38	59	40	104	139	163	303
to consumers	303	185	255	607	1,255	1,691	1,740

Source: World Bank, *Prices, Taxes and Subsidies in Pakistan Agriculture, 1960-76*, World Bank Staff Working Paper No. 387, p. 100.

Table 11.9: Comparative Burden of Direct Taxes on Agricultural and Non-Agricultural Incomes
(Rs million)

	1972-3	1973-4	1974-5	1975-6	1976-7	1977-8	1978-9
Direct taxes on agricultural income (land revenue and (irrigation charges)	427	583	441	574	567	614	762
Direct taxes on non-agricultural incomes (Corporation tax, wealth tax, worker's welfare tax, gift tax, estate duty)	1,210	1,390	1,580	2,310	2,850	3,011	3,415

Source: (i) Table 11.7 for direct taxes on agriculture. (ii) Government of Pakistan, *Taxation Structure of Pakistan, 1976*, p. 2, for 1972-3, and *Taxation Structure of Pakistan, 1980-1*, p. 3, (for 1973-4 to 1978-9), for direct taxes on non-agricultural incomes.

government to expropriate this surplus has resulted in a considerable increase in consumption expenditure of the rich farmers.[33] According to Alavi, even when there are adverse changes in terms of trade (for agriculture) the rural elite enjoy considerably enhanced real incomes.[34]

11.3 Agricultural Credit

In backward economies, credit has a wide range of uses in agriculture. It is needed by the farmers for production marketing and consumption even if no organized effort for the development of agriculture is under way. However, in an economy going through a process of development, greater provisions of credit will be needed for the purchase of inputs, livestock, and implements.

The farmers also require credit for financing long-term developments like land improvement, the installation of tubewells, the construction of storage facilities, embankments, and the improvement of drainage and irrigation channels. Since there is a gap of six months to one year between the two incomes of a farmer, depending upon the relative crop intensity, his consumption needs may also have to be met through credit. However, the existence of subsistence farming makes the provision of credit a highly complicated task where conventional banking institutions and practices do not have much relevance. Organizing a viable structure of rural credit institutions calls for considerable innovative skill, imagination, and risk-taking. The clientele consists of millions of small cultivators operating all over the country. The rural credit set-up will have to disorient itself from urban pulls and environments (which is more difficult to accomplish in reality than in appearance) and to penetrate the remotest rural habitation. It has to serve farmers who are easy victims of fraud and exploitation and who are often unable to safeguard their interests (though they are gradually becoming highly conscious of them). While a conventional financing institution deals with people who are credit-worthy, or very close to it, the rural credit institutions must aim at dealing with poor illiterate farmers (most of whom probably do not have any conventionally acceptable security to offer) and transforming them into credit-worthy and self-relient entrepreneurs.

These credit institutions will also need to maintain a delicate balance between financing the farmers' production and marketing needs and their consumption requirements since the dividing line between them is often vague and somewhat unreal since agriculture is more a way of living than an occupation for most of the farmers. Of course, one of the long-term objectives of development is to transform agriculture into a profit-conscious and profit-making venture but, until this is actually accomplished, the institutional set-up in the rural sector must recognize existing reality.

11.3.1 Classification

Rural credit is usually classified as short-term (upto one year), medium-term (one to five years), and long-term (exceeding five years). Short-term loans are needed for meeting annual production costs (for example, seeds, pesticides, fertilizers,) and for the replacement of a portion of the farmer's fixed capital (for example, bullocks, sheds, implements, and the cost of consumption needs up to harvesting). Thus these loans can be treated as part of the working capital requirements. Medium-term loans are needed for the purchase of livestock, implements, the construction/improvement of water courses, and for equipment not expected to last more than five years.

Long-term loans are needed for improvements of a more lasting character like the sinking of wells and tubewells, the purchase of additional land, or for repayment of old debts.

Loans can also be categorized into productive loans and unproductive loans. According to the conventional definition, a productive loan is a loan which is utilized in such a way that it leads directly to an increase in the income of the farmer and adds to his capacity to repay. These loans may finance current production, i.e., meeting current cultivation costs, and future development, i.e., increasing future returns. Unproductive loans are those which do not directly increase the efficiency of cultivation or the farmers, income. But, as pointed out above, it is sometimes difficult to separate productive loans from unproductive loans.

It is generally believed that most of the loans borrowed by the farmers are for unproductive purposes, or for household expenditure, or for repayment of old debts. The CSO Survey of Agricultural Credit in the early sixties indicated that in (West) Pakistan 44.9 per cent of the cultivators were in debt and received an average cash loan of Rs 598. The loans were mostly borrowed for household expenditure (45 per cent) and livestock (35.4 per cent). Other uses were for land development (6 per cent), the construction of storage facilities (5.6 per cent), and the purchase of seeds (5.2 per cent), fertilizers (1.1 per cent) and tools and implements (0.8 per cent).[35]

11.3.2 Total Credit Needs and Gaps

The Fifth Five Year Plan estimates that the credit availability per cropped acre increased from Rs 4.75 in 1970-1 to Rs 44 in 1977-8, and will further increase to Rs 89 by 1982-3.[36]

But is this supply level of rural credit sufficient for meeting the requirements of the agricultural sector particularly in view of the rising demand for more sophisticated agricultural equipment and inputs? The subcommittee on Agriculture and Credit (1973) appointed by the Agricultural Credit Advisory Council estimated that '53.5 per cent of total cash requirements in agriculture can be identified as credit needs'.[37]

According to this criterion, the total credit requirement for 1975-6 was estimated at Rs 2,140 million whereas the total availability of institutional credit in that year was only Rs 1,255 million.

Another formula for calculating the credit requirements was suggested by the Credit Enquiry Commission of 1959. According to this Commission, the ratio of credit to the total output flow in agriculture should be 25 per cent. Calculated on the basis of the value added in agriculture at constant factor cost of 1959-60, the results obtained are given in Table 11.10.

As seen in Table 11.10, the credit gap was fairly large in the early seventies but is now progressively diminishing. The size of the credit gap also indicates the scope for the operation of unorganized sources of credit.

Sources of agricultural credit can be categorized as institutional and non-institutional.

Table 11.10: Credit Gap
(Rs million)

Year	Value added in agriculture (constant factor cost of 1959-60)	Credit requirements (at 25 per cent of real value added in agriculture)	Total credit supply from institutional sources	Credit gap
1972-3	12,821	3,205.25	306.82	2,898.43
1973-4	13,357	3,339.25	913.25	2,426.00
1974-5	13,074	3,268.50	909.34	2,359.16
1975-6	13,659	3,414.75	1,254.74	2,160.01
1976-7	13,998	3,499.50	1,717.65	1,781.85
1977-8	14,348	3,587.00	1,868.59	1,718.41
1978-9	14,948	3,737.00	2,223.78	1,513.22
1979-80	15,851	3,962.75	2,927.00	1,035.75

Source: Government of Pakistan, *Pakistan Economic Survey, 1979-80*, Islamabad, pp. 9-11 and 32.

Institutional sources include the provincial government (revenue department), Co-operative credit societies and banks, the Agricultural Development Bank of Pakistan, and commercial banks. Non-institutional channels are identified as 'friends and relatives, private money lenders, traders and landlords.'

11.3.3 Non-Institutional Sources of Credit

No comprehensive data is available for the amount of credit advanced by non-institutional sources. As such it is difficult to find solid evidence regarding the relative share of these two categories in the total credit supply. The First Five Year Plan suggested that a national credit survey be conducted to determine the state of indebtedness, the general credit supply situation, and the farmers' total credit requirements. The same suggestion was repeated in the Second Plan but unfortunately little action was taken in this direction. A number of sample surveys conducted during the fifties and early sixties reported a predominance of unorganized sources particularly of 'friends and relatives'. According to Donald, only 14 per cent of the total agricultural credit in Pakistan comes from institutional sources.[38]

However, a recent study at governmental level in 1977 revealed a slightly different picture. It showed that large farmers realized about 75 per cent of their credit requirements from institutional sources while informal sources provided most of the credit for middle (80 per cent) and small farmers (86 per cent).[39]

The survey conducted by the National Bank of Pakistan in five districts, sampling farmers owning 12.5 to 25 acres, found that the share of institutional sources in credit was 45 per cent in Faisalabad, 60 per cent in Lahore, 50 per cent in Gujranwala, 55 per cent in Gujrat, and 20 per cent in Rawalpindi.[40]

Given the problems of collecting data in the villages on a subject like credit, about which people generally do not like to divulge much, the sample surveys should not be taken as concrete evidence of either the relative shares of various sources of credit or the overall credit situation in the rural sector. Sometimes certain biases also creep in both from the side of the organizers of the survey as well as the respondents. However, the surveys might indicate a certain trend of expansion in the share of institutional sources.

Before 1947 the private money-lenders consisted almost entirely of non-Muslims. After Independence, with the exodus of non-Muslims from Pakistan, the money-lending class disappeared from the scene and the rural credit system was left wide open. Since then, some Muslims have taken up this business, mostly in a clandestine manner, since interest-taking is strictly prohibited by Islam. Their share in the credit supply was reported to be 1.3 per cent in the 1949 Survey by the Punjab Board of Economic Enquiry and 1.1 per cent in the 1954 Survey by Punjab University.[41]

Private money-lending is also done by commission agents, village traders, landlords, and well-to-do farmers. After the land reforms, the role of landlords and big farmers in this field may have diminished. Usually loans advanced by these sources are sanctioned on personal security and are for short durations, payable at the time of the next harvest. In many cases a farmer borrowing from a trader has to return the favour by selling his produce to, or through, him. The lender in such cases has a strong bargaining position *vis-a-vis* the borrower and the lower prices paid to the farmer may be an indirect form of charging interest. In other cases interest is charged, openly or not so openly, and rates are probably very high.

'Friends and relatives' emerged as the major informal source of credit according to some surveys shortly after Independence. A large number of refugees were in the process of settling down and, in a period of rapidly shifting population, personal security could hardly be offered by the new settlers or accepted by the lenders. Thus they could only fall back upon those whom they knew and who could afford to spare some money.

The non-institutional sources are generally regarded as exploitative and undesirable for many reasons. First, the lender is usually indifferent to the use of the borrowed amount and as such the system encourages borrowing for unproductive purposes. However, it would be too simplistic to assume that all loans from non-institutional sources are utilized for consumption purposes. Donald (1976) reports that 27 per cent of non-institutional credit in Pakistan was for 'commercial' and 73 per cent for 'non-commercial' purposes.[42] Second, the cost may be very high. The unorganized sources do not have standardized interest rates and regulations, and conditions attached to the loans are subject to bargaining. Naturally the borrower's is the weaker side. The farmer, therefore, often has to pay usurious interest rates. Moreover, a credit market dominated by unorganized sources tends to operate outside, and often at cross purposes with, the overall framework of economic policy. It is therefore difficult for the government to enforce its policy choices in such matters as the size of the total credit supply and the terms and conditions, uses, and cost of credit.

However, these informal sources are still the major suppliers of credit. Any attempts to drive them out, or at least to compete with them, principally by lowering the interest rates, have not been particularly successful. This suggests that policy-makers tend to think exclusively in terms of rates of interest often over-looking other credit traits essential for the farmer such as simple procedures, adequacy, and timeliness. These informal sources are easily accessible and the service is available virtually at the farmer's doorstep. These are some of the characteristics that organized agencies with their immense resources could do well to emulate. The very fact that a large number of farmers prefer to borrow from informal sources in spite of the high cost shows, that the demand for agricultural credit is highly service-elastic, a significant factor which is often overlooked.

11.3.4 Institutional Sources

Institutional sources comprising the ADBP, commercial banks, provincial governments, and Co-operative institutions are presently emerging as major credit suppliers in the rural sector particularly in financing production

Table 11.11: Institutional Sources of Agricultural Credit
(Rs million)

Year	Agricultural Development Bank of Pakistan	*Taccavi*	Co-operatives: Individuals	Co-operatives: Societies	Commercial banks	Total
1953-4	0.06	7.70	12.26	3.24	–	23.26
1959-60	24.80	17.90	42.11	2.77	–	87.58
1964-5	40.50	30.50	50.60	5.94	–	127.54
1969-70	91.30	10.60	47.38	6.07	–	155.35
1972-3	168.80	10.80	34.74	7.28	85.20	306.82
1973-4	415.20	67.50	95.70	48.45	286.40	913.25
1974-5	395.60	12.20	68.24	13.30	420.00	909.34
1975-6	532.20	25.70	79.54	12.30	605.00	1,254.74
1976-7	638.80	13.30	88.17	7.28	970.10	1,717.65
1977-8	430.53	9.10	110.00	28.04	1,290.92	1,868.59
1978-9	416.94	11.96	363.53	50.25	1,381.00	2,223.68
1979-80(Targets)	1,000.00	11.00	353.00	65.00	1,498.00	2,927.00

Source: Government of Pakistan, *Pakistan Economic Survey, 1979-80*, Islamabad, 1980, Statistical Annexure, p. 32.

and development costs. With the government increasingly committed to a policy of inputs-based technology for agricultural advancement and the farmers themselves realizing the benefits of investing in the acquisition of new technology, the role of institutional sources underwent a major change, both qualitatively and quantitatively, particularly in the seventies. The total amount of credit from institutional sources in 1953-4 was only Rs 23 million but since then it has increased rapidly particularly in the late sixties when, under the 'green revolution' impetus, the demand for outlays in inputs was high and after 1972 when commercial banks were encouraged to enter this field as shown in Table 11.11.

The Fifth Five Year Plan provides for the supply of credit from institutional sources amounting to Rs 16,800 million during 1978-83. This means that the average annual credit flow should be Rs 3,360 million. In the first year of the Plan, the performance of institutional sources fell short of the target and therefore the targets for 1979-80 were fixed at a lower level.

In 1972, the National Credit Consultative Council was established. This high-powered body formulates policies regarding the size and distribution of the total credit supply in the country. One of the tasks of this Council is to set specific targets for agricultural loans to be provided by commercial banks. Another body, which is more directly concerned with rural credit, is the Agricultural Credit Advisory Committee which was also established in 1972. It is charged with the task of assessing credit requirements in the agricultural sector, improving credit availability, strengthening the institutional framework for rural credit, and co-ordinating the activities of agricultural credit agencies.

11.3.5 Co-operative Credit Institutions

The Co-operative movement in Pakistan is largely a rural credit movement since agencies specializing in rural credit dominate its structure. The primary Co-operative credit society lends directly to farmers, mostly against personal security. A primary society has a membership of ten to a hundred members living within a small area generally a village. Its working capital is derived from deposits, share capital, and borrowing from other Co-operative institutions. Preference in their lending policy is for consumption purposes like family needs and repayment of old debts. Most of these societies have unlimited liability particularly in the rural areas. Since 1972, traders are prohibited from becoming members of the society. The total number of primary societies has shown a modest increase over the years—from over 9,000 in 1948-9 these societies increased to over 16,000 in 1977-8 though a large number of them are not in an operational condition. The Credit Enquiry Commission (1959) reported that over 40 per cent of the societies were defunct or near defunct in 1956-7.[43]

The primary societies are supported by a hierarchy of Co-operative banking institutions like the Central Co-operative Banks, the Provincial Co-operative Banks, and the Federal Bank for Co-operatives.

Co-operative organizations have certain distinct advantages over other credit sources. They exist at grassroots level and are financed and managed at the village level by the farmers themselves. They also have the advantage of accessibility but, for a number of reasons, the Co-operative movement has stagnated. Their working is criticized on the following accounts:

1. Even after almost eight decades, the Co-operative movement has failed to cover the entire country or the entire population. While the total number of villages in Pakistan is about 45,000, the number of societies in 1978, including those not functioning, was less than 17,000. In a total rural population of over 55 million, the total number of their members was still less than 1 million.[44]
2. The size of the primary societies is too small to have resources to finance agricultural development through greater use of inputs and equipment.
3. The appeal of these societies has been reduced because their liability is unlimited.

4. The standard of management is generally low as examplified by the high percentage of defunct societies. This is due mainly to uneducated and faction-ridden leadership.
5. Co-operatives tend to become part of the establishment, as their leadership is usually taken over by the rural elite, with the result that the small farmer's interest is abandoned which defeats their initial purpose. Unless the government itself is free of the influence of the rural power structure and strong enough to make Co-operatives a viable mechanism for protecting the interests of small farmers, the Co-operative sector as a positive element has little prospects.

Before Independence, it was claimed that one of the major reasons for the lack of satisfactory progress of these societies was competition with money-lenders. With this class removed after Independence, the Co-operative societies had a valuable opportunity to capture the rural credit market. However, because of operational rigidities, they found it difficult to fill the gap[45] (as reflected in various credit surveys). Nevertheless, among the institutional sources, the Co-operatives contributed a major share, for example, 66.6 per cent in 1953-4, 51.2 per cent in 1959-60, 44.3 per cent in 1964-5, and 34.4 per cent in 1969-70.[46] The reason for the decline in their percentage of contribution is understandable. The Co-operatives are essentially short-term lending agencies while, during the sixties, the demand on the production side was mainly for long and medium-term loans. This explains the rapid growth of the ADBP and the lesser role of the Co-operatives. As commercial banks entered the field, the share of the Co-operatives in the total institutional credit in 1978-9 was reduced to 18.6 per cent.

One major problem with the Co-operative organization is the nature of their relationship with the official controlling authority. Ideally a Co-operative society is an enterprise promoted, financed, and managed by the shareholders themselves. However, the history of Co-operatives in the sub-continent shows a different trend. The movement started with the initiative and guidance provided by a Co-operative bureaucracy. The original idea was a happy compromise of initiative at the grass-roots level and general guidance and discipline exercised by the controlling authority. However, things did not work out as envisaged in this ideal plan. The right degree of initiative at the village level and of guidance from the department could not be worked out. 'Where too much guidance has been given, there has been no sense of participation on the part of the membership; where too little has been given, the people may have merely participated in failure!'[47]

The lending policies of the Co-operatives may also possibly contain a bias against small farmers insofar as loans are granted by them in proportion to the share capital purchased by the members. In a study by Gotsch, it was found that most programmes aimed at improving the capital markets faced by small farmers have left the majority of the small farmers untouched. 'Even where there has been a willingness to absorb the cost of small farmer credit programmes, creating local institutions which are responsive to the weaker sections of the farming community, it has been exceedingly difficult'. He found that the direct distribution of government-subsidized credit 'invited extra-market activities by the socially and politically powerful aimed at securing available funds for themselves. Where credit was indirectly disbursed through organizations made up of farmer representatives, due to the disparity of power even credit programmes aimed expressly at the small farmer were unsuccessful'.[48]

11.3.6 The Agricultural Development Bank of Pakistan

The Agricultural Development Bank of Pakistan was established as a result of the merger of two institutions which had been created in the fifties : the Agricultural Development Finance Corporation (1952) and the Agricultural Bank of Pakistan (1957). This institution advances short, medium, and long-term loans to farmers, for a very broad range of farm and off-farm activities, and to agro-based and farm-related processing industrial units.

The Bank advances loans on personal security or on the basis of land mortgage. Short-term loans are also advanced on the basis of crop hypothecation (in the case of sugarcane and cotton) to small farmers who have no other security to offer. The rate of interest charged is 11 per cent on all loans above Rs 5,000, and 9 to 10 per cent on smaller loans. Although the Bank accepts deposits, these form only slightly over 9 per cent of its total liabilities.[49]

Most of the Bank's advances are of long-term duration. In 1978-9, 80.6 per cent of the amount advanced was for long periods, 10.6 per cent for short periods, and the rest for medium terms.[50]

As regards the uses of the loans, the largest amount was advanced for tractors, power tillers, and attachments. In 1978-9, 74.4 per cent of the total credit was issued for this purpose followed by seasonal inputs (10.5 per cent). Other purposes for which credit was advanced are livestock, tubewells, poultry farming, fisheries, and dairy farming, etc.[51]

A study of loans advanced by the ADBP according to the size of holdings shows that most of the loans are advanced to owners owning 12.50 to 50 acres. They received 56.8 per cent of the total credit in 1977-8, followed by owners of 50 to 100 acres (23.3 per cent), landless farmers (10.7 per cent), and owners of below 12.50 acres (6.5 per cent). It is interesting to note that this is a pattern which took shape since 1974-5. Credit distribution in 1973-4 shows 47.7 per cent of the credit to landless farmers, 24 per cent to owners of less than 12.50 acres, 11.8 per cent to owners of 12.5 to 50 acres, 8.7 per cent to owners of 50 to 100 acres, and 7.8 per cent to owners of over 100 acres. This change is connected with a switch-over by the Bank from short-term to long-term lending. (In 1973-4 the Bank advanced 46.8 per cent of the loans for short-term, 24.6 per cent for medium-term, and 28.6 per cent for long-term).[52]

The Bank's advances (Rs 458 million in 1978-9) are far in excess of its paid-up capital (Rs 319 million) and deposits (Rs 106 million). Its lending operations are thus dependent upon heavy borrowing from the Rural Credit Fund of the State Bank of Pakistan and credit lines from IDA, SIDA, and ADB.[53]

11.3.7 Commercial Banks

Before 1972, commercial banks in Pakistan did not take any interest in agriculture except for the financing of trading in agricultural products. In 1972, the government showed a keenness to expand agricultural credit and to tap all possible resources in fulfilling this purpose. The State Bank of Pakistan therefore introduced an Agricultural Loans Scheme making it mandatory for commercial banks to provide short, medium, and long-term loans to farmers on the security of land, crops, or other fixed assets including personal surety. Their task was further facilitated by a guarantee given by the State Bank of Pakistan covering up to 50 per cent of their bona fide losses in agricultural financing. The State Bank also offered refinancing facilities to cover the greater commitment of funds by the banks to rural credit. Loan recovery on rural credit advanced by commercial banks was also made recoverable as arrears of land revenue.

The entry of commercial banks in this field was accompanied by a number of innovative efforts. Compared to the rigid procedures and static approach of the Co-operative credit institutions, the commercial banks attempted a number of new schemes. They experimented with a supervised credit scheme and tried to offer technological assistance along with finance. They also introduced mobile banking in rural areas. Thus, a number of steps, described by one eminent banker[54] as 'institutional engineering', have been introduced.

A very important effect of the commercial banks' entry in rural financing may have been on resource transfer from rural to urban areas. Before 1972, commercial banks already had a wide network of branches in market towns. These branches collected substantial deposits from their rural clients but the money was invested almost exclusively in urban areas. Thus rural savings were used for urban investment. A commitment of the commercial banks' finances for the rural sector may negate this resource transfer, at least in part.

11.3.8 Government Loans

Provincial governments also advance credit to farmers through the revenue department. Originally these loans, called *Taccavi*, were distress loans given to farmers in times of calamities. But at present *Taccavi* loans are governed by the West Pakistan Agriculturalists Loans Act 1958 which provides for lending for the purchase of livestock and inputs, improvements of land, flood protection, drainage, reclamation, etc. The rate is 5.5 per cent. These loans are a relatively minor source of credit providing only 3.5 per cent of the total institutional credit in 1972-3 and only 0.54 per cent in 1978-9 (Table 11.11).

The commitment of funds, however small, for *Taccavi* lending makes little economic sense. The *Taccavi* loans are not popular with borrowers due to long delays in the issue of the loans and the exactions of petty officials. The revenue officials are more concerned with the mechanics of lending rather than with its utilization. There is a tendency on the part of those who manage to borrow to squander the funds received considering it as some kind of grant.

11.3.9 The Role of the State Bank of Pakistan

The charter of the State Bank of Pakistan at the time of its establishment in 1948 did not envisage a major role for it in agricultural finance. It was only allowed to advance short-term loans (upto nine months) to Co-operative banks. However, in 1956, important changes were made in order to give the State Bank a greater opportunity to participate in the financing of agriculture. It was allowed to advance credit to agriculture for longer periods including loans through the discounting of bills of exchange for a period of up to fifteen months, medium-term loans up to five years through promissory notes issued or guaranteed by scheduled banks, and long-term loans to specialized rural credit institutions for periods to be determined according to the purpose of the loan. An Agriculture Credit Department was also established for research, assessment of credit needs, and supervision of rural credit operations. A special Rural Credit Fund was also created in 1961. The Fund is fed from the profits of the State Bank. In 1978-9, Rs 170 million were transferred to it which stood at Rs 940 million in June 1979.[55] This money is made available to rural credit agencies at 2 per cent below the Bank Rate for lending for agricultural purposes only.

11.3.10 Rate of Interest

Rates of interest charged by various credit agencies range from 5.5 per cent (on *Taccavi* loans) to 11 to 14 per cent charged by the commercial banks. Are these interest rates high or low? The interest rate structure in Pakistan is controlled by the State Bank of Pakistan. Apparently the rates fixed are low compared with those charged by the informal credit sector. The purpose behind keeping interest rates low is to encourage the farmers to borrow and invest and also to keep the institutional credit cheap in relation to non-institutional credit. The credit supply is not interest-elastic since funds available with credit institutions originate mostly from the government.

But is this viable in the long run? The view that farmers, specially small farmers, need subsidized credit in order to borrow for productive purposes has been challenged by some evidence showing that if institutional interest rates are raised there would be few losses in terms of programme goals. Farmers are willing to invest whenever profitable opportunities are made available to them. They are accustomed to, and undeterred by, higher rates charged by informal credit sources. For credit institutions, on the other hand, artificially low interest rates do not cover operating expenses. This results in portfolio losses so that credit institutions are unable to finance their research, extension, and technical supervision programmes properly. This induces credit institutions to focus on prosperous farmers, particularly on those with collateral, and thus the bulk of the small farm sector is excluded.[56] High interest rates may also encourage financial savings in the rural sector so that agriculture is able to generate some of its own capital requirements. The subsidizing of credit tends to distort the credit market, leads to opportunity costs way below what they truly are, and induces large farmers to invest in virtually useless enterprises. However, subsidies to credit institutions do play a useful role in covering institutional deficits, at least in the initial stages.[57]

11.3.11 Conclusion

In the field of rural credit, important changes are taking place as agricultural output is increasing and there is a greater demand for agricultural equipment and inputs. It is thus obvious that, in such a situation, the role of institutional sources is bound to expand at the cost of non-institutional sources. The demand for productive loans is also rising, so much so that, at times and for certain purposes, even the big credit institutions are unable to meet the entire demand. In the case of tractors, for example, the major lending institutions offer credit in kind. But there are long waiting lists and buyers have to wait for one to two years before delivery. The annual demand, it seems, is higher than the availability of tractors. A number of schemes have been introduced by credit institutions in order to answer the peculiar needs of farmers, particularly small farmers. The effectiveness of credit institutions and the schemes introduced by them will depend upon a number of factors including the degree of accessibility of small farmers to short-term lending facilities, procedures, terms and conditions, and facilities like technological advice and credit supervision. However, at present there are a number of problem areas in the field of credit which can be identified as follows:

a. The recovery rates are low mainly because the credit institutions themselves have little role to play in the recovery process. Their loans are at present recovered as arrears of land revenue through the revenue administration. It has been assumed so far that declaring rural credit recoveries as arrears of land revenue solves most of the recovery problems. But the assumption is not well founded. The revenue administration has its own limitations and difficulties. At times there have been complaints of accumulation of arrears of land revenues. So far, no alternative arrangements have been explored or envisaged but it is time this problem is looked into. Bad recoveries may hamper the credit flow in the long run, hurt the liquidity position of the credit institutions, and ultimately disrupt the whole system.

b. There is a considerable duplication of efforts between the Co-operative societies, the commercial banks, and the ADBP who advance loans for the same purposes to the same clientele and for almost the same periods. It would be more logical and economical to have each institution specialize in certain types of loans. But since the coverage of each institution is limited in terms of area and population, there are practical problems in specialization. The ideal solution suggested by many is for Co-operative societies to specialize in seasonal credit, commercial banks in medium-term credit, and the ADBP in long-term credit. But unless all these institutions are accessible to the entire peasantry, specialization would not solve the existing problem. Accessibility, it seems, remains a constant problem. The major credit institution, i.e., the ADBP, has only 170 branches throughout the country to serve over 45,000 villages, about 54 million people, and 4 million farms.

c. The major lending institutions, i.e., the commercial banks and the ADBP, have serious shortages of technological personnel who could offer know-how and guidance for supervised credit.

d. Land mortgage as security for rural credit is preferred neither by the borrower, for whom land is a symbol of status, nor by the lender since there is no organized land market in the country and there are complicated procedures for acquisition of land by the lender in case of default. Crop hypothecation may be a better alternative but so far it has been tried only by the ADBP and only in the case of cotton and sugarcane.

However, besides the short-term problems and difficulties mentioned above, certain questions about the long-term strategy of rural credit remain. First, how far should the credit institutions go in offering extension services? There is no doubt that extension services are important as a supplement to credit. They can help farmers raise their incomes, even with their present resources, if they follow better cultivation practices and make better use of the land. There is an agricultural extension service provided by the provincial departments of agriculture. While the credit institutions cannot replace this service totally, it must not compete with it either. A workable system of co-ordination between agricultural extension authorities and the credit institutions may be the answer in the long-run though not necessarily the easiest. Second, many small and middle farmers are now producing more marketable surpluses, or may be doing so shortly, as more investments are made and new technologies are employed. They are bound to have problems in managing seasonal cash surpluses and deficits, comprehending market trends, managing farm accounts, and calculating profits and losses. But, apart from that, they are likely to form their own perception of risk while making decisions regarding cropping pattern, land-use, borrowing, and the use of credit. Inputs and know-how offered by the credit agencies as determined by their extension and research services may not always answer the questions arising in the minds of the farmers. The credit package reflects the country's economic needs and requirements as seen by the government and the credit institutions. It may also be governed by considerations of overall economic policy like yield maximization and encouraging food production. However, the farmer may have his own objectives of income maximization, discounting for risk, and a strong consumption preference which is not unnatural in a society living for long at subsistence level. A credit programme not taking the farmers' preference into consideration is not likely to go far. Thus neither interest-subsidies, nor input-subsidies, nor systems to control input-use are likely to prove of much value in encouraging the use of credit. The credit package must promise higher returns at reasonable risk in order to induce the farmers to borrow for higher purposes.

11.4 Agricultural Marketing

As agricultural production becomes commercialized and greater surpluses are available with the farmers, the marketing of farm products becomes an indispensable part of the whole production process. An orderly marketing system supported by an adequate storage capacity and proper product standardization could strengthen the farmers' staying power and ensure better prices for their produce.

The agriculture-dominated economies of developing countries are usually semi-monetized and characterized by an atomistic structure of production which creates certain imperfections in the rural marketing framework. The well-being of the vast mass of small farmers depends as much on productivity levels and use of inputs and advanced technologies as on the price obtained by them for their marketed surpluses. Indeed the farmers' motivation to use better inputs and cultural practices, to work out optimal cropping patterns, and to make further investments in land improvements will ultimately depend upon their ability to sell their produce at a price which ensures economic returns to them. Thus, the evolution of better marketing conditions will go a long way towards the modernization and commercialization of agriculture and the ensuring of adequate capital inflow into this vital but capital-starved sector.

11.4.1 The Market System in Operation

In Pakistan, the marketing of agricultural produce takes place primarily to meet urban consumer demand and, in the case of many commodities with larger surpluses, for export. The produce is assembled from widely scattered villages by government and semi-government procurement agencies in the case of some specific commodities (mainly food and export items) and by brokers, travelling representatives, traders, and commission agents in the case of other products. The stocks congregate into a wide network of town markets (*mandis*) through a large number of brokers and wholesale and retail dealers and from there they head for their final destinations in large urban centres for internal consumption or for export.

An indication of how market constraints distort cropping patterns is given by the discovery that such important crops like fruits and vegetables receive the least importance in farmers' cropping sequence despite the fact that these enjoy a relatively higher net income per acre than principal crops like cotton and wheat. According to a 1975 study, the net income per acre was Rs 67 for cotton, Rs 102 for wheat, Rs 320 for *guara*, and Rs 1,056 for vegetables.[58] One of the major constraints on the adoption of fruit and vegetable cropping patterns was inadequate market logistics.

The marketing system can be judged on the basis of four standards:

a. The level and quality of competitive conditions.
b. The relative predictability and stability of prices.
c. Product standardization.
d. The effectiveness of market regulation.

The discussion on the agricultural marketing system in Pakistan will, therefore, concentrate on these four aspects.

11.4.2 Competitive Conditions

Fair prices can be ensured for all (consumers, producers, middlemen) only if a certain degree of competitiveness exists in the market. Buyers and sellers must also have access to a number of selling or buying alternatives and information about prevailing prices. The staying power of the parties must have some balance so that a mutually agreeable price is arrived at in an open manner. This will require an efficient and relatively inexpensive transport system, the availability of sufficient and safe storage accomodation, and the existence of a credible market information mechanism.

The transport system in rural areas in Pakistan is, to say the least, inadequate. Except for villages in close proximity to major towns and cities, the farm-to-market roads are either non-existent or of very low quality. According to the Fifth Five Year Plan, only 16 per cent of the villages lie on all-weather roads and only about 20 per cent have all-weather connections to wholesale markets. According to a generally acceptable criteria (2 miles per square mile of cultivated land and 0.5 mile per square mile of other areas) the requirement of all sorts of roads in Pakistan works out to be 240,000 miles of primary roads, 60,000 miles of secondary roads, and 180,000 miles of rural roads.[59] But the total road length (high and low types) in Pakistan in 1980 was only 95,776 kilometres (59,525 miles).[60] There is provision in the Fifth Plan for rural road construction of 4,020 miles of new *katcha* roads and black topping of 3,000 miles of existing *katcha* roads.[61] The immense benefit and importance of farm-to-market roads is indicated by an estimate that the construction of 8 miles of farm-to-market road in the Sind will provide access to 15,840 persons and connect 10,766 acres of cultivated land with *mandi* towns.[62] The inadequacy of the road net-work and transport facilities forces the farmers, especially small farmers, to rely on local traders or brokers for the disposal of their produce.

Non-availability of storage accommodation compels the farmer to sell his produce immediately after harvest and thus reduces his staying power. The farmers' income can increase substantially only if they could hold back part of their produce for obtaining better off-season prices. But storage accommodation is extremely limited. Even the government's own storage capacity, inspite of its requirements for storage of rice and wheat and a number of other commodities, is extremely limited amounting to about 3 million tonnes at present. This is inadequate when compared to the total output of over 15 million tonnes of food crops and over 43 million tonnes of principal crops (1978-9).[63] Warehousing capacity in the private sector is not known but it is generally believed to be insufficient and of low quality which results in wastage of valuable crops. Moreover, even this storage accommodation generally belongs to big and middle farmers.

11.4.3 Market Intelligence

As far as the dissemination of market intelligence is concerned, the Central Statistical Organization (CSO) and provincial marketing directorates issue periodic reports giving the retail and wholesale prices of important agricultural products in different markets. The daily price situation is also broadcast from Radio Pakistan which covers 88 per cent of the total population. This has been helpful in providing useful information to the farmers especially after the popularization of transistors in the villages.

The competitive conditions in the rural marketing structure are thus far from satisfactory and it is the producer who usually suffers by failing to get a profitable price for his output. The consumer also suffers because the price he is made to pay is inflated by the profits of the long chain of middlemen. In the case of vegetables, according to a survey, the producer receives only 44 per cent of the price paid by the consumer in the Punjab, 34 per cent in NWFP, and 22 per cent in Baluchistan while the middleman receives 37 per cent, 57 per cent, and 70 per cent respectively, the balance being covered by marketing expenditures at various stages. Another study conducted by the Sind Agricultural University reports that the producer obtains 31 to 46 per cent of the final price of onions, chillies, and potatoes and 22 to 32 per cent of mangoes, dates, and bananas. The reasons, as pointed out by the Planning Commission, for the producer's low share in the final price is the lack of warehousing facilities and cold storage for perishable goods, the lack of grading, the poor road system, and the long distances from the market.[64] It can thus be seen that the producers do not receive the full benefits of any post-harvest rise in the prices of agricultural products which can motivate them to increase production.

The large number of middlemen and the high profits earned by them have often provoked comment and criticism. Since their number is large, they obviously do not have the advantage of monopolistic conditions unless all the functionaries of a market act in collusion. Their high profits can, therefore, be the result of the large scale of their operations, their command over capital which is a scarce resource in isolated rural communities, and their own skill and knowledge of market trends and conditions in which they have a definite edge over the farmers.

11.4.4 Price Stability

In relative terms, a certain degree of price stability is desirable for planning future investment and production programmes. Erratic price variations are extremely frustrating for the producers and the consumers as well as the policy-makers and analysts. Markets in Pakistan are characterized by wide seasonal variations which deprive producers of the benefits of higher off-season prices and only add to the already substantial profit margins of the middleman. It also encourages hoarding and speculation particularly in durable commodities. The price variations are caused by high supply variations since the vast majority of farmers tend to sell immediately after the harvest and there is very little additional supply coming into the market during the off-season. According to some sporadic data available for price variations, their magnitude ranges between 20 to 24 per cent for poultry eggs, 25 to 35 per cent for vegetables, and 15 to 20 per cent for fruits.[65]

11.4.5 Product Standardization

Most of the produce sold in the rural markets in sub-standard and ungraded primarily because the market does not reflect price differential for quality nor does the farmer perceive significant advantages in improving the quality of his produce.[66] This leads him to, first, indifference towards producing high quality varieties and, second, to adulterate high quality with low quality. This may not do any damage in small local markets but it discourages expansion in the size of the market and is positively disastrous insofar as export prospects are concerned.

Some efforts have been made to improve the situation. In the sixties, the government introduced compulsory grading in such commodities as wool, hides and skins, and potatoes. According to the administrative arrangements at present, commodities for internal consumption are graded at the provincial level while grading export items is the responsibility of the federal government. The Third Five Year Plan recommended that all grading standards should be set at the federal level and that provinces should be responsible for the checking and supervision of the standardization work. But this recommendation does not seem to have been accepted. Progress in this field has been slow. In the seventies only oil cakes, citrus fruits, and fish were brought under the compulsory grading system. The effort seems to be limited to exportable goods only although even in that category major commodities like cotton and rice have not so far been brought under grading and marketing rules. This is programmed for the Fifth Plan period[67] but items for internal market remain on the whole ungraded.

11.4.6 Market Regulation

Rural markets in Pakistan grew up in a haphazard manner with very little regulation or control at any governmental level. A number of malpractices, therefore, became rampant in due course of time. There are widespread complaints about sub-standard weight and measures, levying of various unjustified charges on farmers by market functionaries, and price fixation in an underhand manner. These rural markets were originally run and dominated by traders and brokers with the farmers having very little say in their management.

In 1939, the Punjab Agricultural Produce Act was passed and market committees were established to supervise and regulate the *mandis*. This Act was extended to other regions in 1966. The market committees appointed under this Act consist of representatives of farmers, traders, and other interested parties, and they work under the supervision of the district authorities. The law also provides for the mandatory display of daily price lists by traders and it prohibits the levying of undue charges on the farmers. It also requires all market functionaries such as brokers, commission agents, weighmen, etc., to obtain licenses and their charges are fixed by the law.

According to the Fourth Five Year Plan, the total number of regulated markets in (West) Pakistan was 146 in 1968-9. The number is obviously too small but, curiously enough, the Fourth Plan did not set any targets for bringing more markets under the cover of this law and the Fifth Plan has followed suit. It seems that there is very little faith in the current market legislation for improving market conditions although the situation remains as bad as ever. The market legislation, according to one study, did not ensure the proper functioning of market committees in the context of the regulation of market charges and the adulteration of products. On the contrary, fraudulent practices are rampant and the farmer, especially the small farmer, is completely at the mercy of the middlemen.[68]

11.4.7 The PASSCO

An attempt to improve marketing conditions is now being made through the Pakistan

Agricultural Storage and Services Corporation (PASSCO). This organization, which started operating in 1974, was charged with ensuring a better return to the farmer by increasing his holding power and by minimizing post-harvest losses by extending the facility of scientific storage. It also procures agricultural commodities on behalf of the government in order to stabilize prices besides providing farm machinery on hire and indulging in processing agricultural produce. So far its main operations include the procurement of agricultural products and the construction of cold storage facilities. It is responsible for the procurement of wheat, paddy, pulses, and potatoes. But except for potatoes, in which case PASSCO entered the market to ensure support prices to the growers after the bumper crop of 1978-9, its operations seem to be more consumer-oriented than producer-oriented. Pulses are procured for supply to the Utility Stores Corporation, Co-operatives, Jails Departments, Defence Services, and the World Food Programme.

Government procurement efforts are not a boon to small farmers if procurement prices are less than the open market prices. While large farmers may succeed in evading procurement, the politically less powerful small farmers tend to become its main targets. Thus the small farmers may be selling their produce cheaper for the benefit of higher-income urban consumers (see also Chapter 9).

11.4.8 Co-operative Marketing

Is Co-operative marketing the answer to Pakistan's marketing problems? Co-operation offers a number of advantages. Managed and financed basically by the farmers themselves, the Co-operatives can look after the interest of their own members rather effectively. There is no problem of inaccessibility so common in the case of big government organizations and, located within the rural areas, they have the flexibility to deal with a variety of situations. However, the success of Co-operative institutions in agricultural marketing would depend upon a number of factors. Since average cost tends to decline as the quantity marketed increases, the number of members of the society should be large in order to derive maximum benefit. The society must be able to command the loyalty of its members so that they sell their produce exclusively through it. It must have adequate storage capacity and arrangements for grading, packing, processing, transportation, and insurance, as well as market information, all of which very obviously requires not only financial resources but also a certain level of administrative ability. The Co-operative marketing society should be able to function more as a multi-purpose society rather than a purely marketing organization.

Immediately after partition, when the non-Muslim trader class migrated, the Co-operative marketing societies in Pakistan were extremely helpful in providing marketing facilities to the farmers. It was almost a break-through in the Co-operative movement in the sense that for the first time the Co-operative marketing organizations handled a big task successfully. However, as new trading classes emerged in the rural sector, the Co-operatives withdrew to their traditional role of relative inactivity. But throughout the fifties great faith was placed in the potentialities of Co-operatives in marketing. The Co-operative Enquiry Committee of 1955 suggested an entire hierarchy of marketing institutions at the village level (primary societies), *mandi* (secondary societies), and the provinces (apex Co-operative marketing federations). The First Five Year Plan suggested that Co-operative marketing institutions should act as a direct link between the producer and the final consumer, and marketing was described as being the most important Co-operative activity after credit. Similarly, the Second Five Year Plan also suggested a prominent role for Co-operatives and supported the recommendations of the 1955 Committee. In fact, Co-operative marketing was regarded as being so important that the lack of marketing facilities provided by the Co-operatives to farmers was mentioned as one of the main reasons for the slow progress of the Co-operative movement.

However, after the Second Plan, in which a fairly ambitious target was set for a network of Co-operative marketing societies, the Planning Commission's enthusiasm seems to have cooled down and since then Co-operative marketing received much less attention in subsequent Plans.

Because they are tied to private marketing channels due to credit and other service obligations, the farmers are generally reluctant to make use of official agencies. The traders function in the least accessible areas and meet the farmers' credit needs including their consumption needs. The timeliness and flexibility of service provided by them can hardly be matched by the government agencies which is why the farmers turn to traders even when government or Co-operative channels are available. In addition, marketing margins incurred by governmental and semi-governmental agencies are almost invariably higher than those incurred by private traders. Since the government agencies have to appoint agents all over the country, one wonders if they have even been able to reduce the number of intermediaries.

11.5 Farm Mechanization

Labour intensive methods of cultivation are common in labour-abundant economies. These methods, although simple, are less productive both in terms of land and labour as well as in the time needed for various farming operations. With the increase in population and a greater need for resources to finance development programmes, an increase in agricultural production and a greater intensity of cultivation assume very high priority. The shift of labour from the farm sector to the non-farm sector creates shortages particularly at sowing and harvest times. Thus the need for mechanization and for increasing the productivity of land and of labour during the busy seasons becomes crucial.

However, a basic change in technology cannot take place without creating imbalances. Much of the mechanical farm technology which has been transferred directly from the developed countries has not proved useful as it was designed to maximize output per worker and was thus labour-displacing. In some cases capital-intensive mechanical technology may have been adopted due to underpricing of capital and foreign exchange or because the more appropriate labour-intensive machines had not as yet been developed. Sometimes policy-makers themselves tend to equate efficiency with the labour-saving mechanical technology used in developed countries.

It is proposed to take up some related issues regarding mechanization in this section. These include (a) the case for and against mechanization; (b) the mechanization process in Pakistan; (c) the appropriate form of technology for Pakistan; and (d) the impact of mechanization on productivity, employment, and income distribution.

11.5.1 The Mechanization Debate

The debate on farm mechanization is a distinctive feature of under-developed countries. The arguments for and against mechanization are summarized in the following paragraphs.

The First Five Year Plan mentioned widespread unemployment and underemployment, small and fragmented individual holdings, scarcity of foreign exchange for importing farm machinery, and absence of facilities for its maintenance and servicing as the major arguments against mechanization. In recent times, some more arguments, partly in elaboration of the above arguments, against mechanization have been forwarded. They are as follows:

1. Farm mechanization is basically capital-intensive. This has so far thrived in developing countries on

the basis of direct subsidies and subsidized credit since scarcity of capital is not reflected in its price.

2. Mechanization of farming will divert capital and foreign exchange from non-agricultural sectors to agriculture where labour-intensive alternatives are available.
3. The argument that mechanization increases the productivity of land (except through multiple cropping) has not been conclusively proved.
4. Mechanization not only displaces labour but also induces landlords to cultivate land through hired hands hence the social cost in terms of tenants converting into landless labourers.
5. Farm technology has a big-farmer bias and accentuates social disparity particularly in the case of assets having lumpy investments.

Arguments advanced in favour of farm mechanization are summarized as below:

1. Mechanization encourages multiple cropping and greater intensity of cultivation and is thus land-saving.
2. It reduces the dependence upon draught animals whose number is not increasing as fast as the availability of water. One reason why the cropped area has not increased in proportion to the water supply is the inadequacy of farm power.[69] Mechanization will free land from growing fodder for draught animals.
3. Mechanization will make dry-farming possible and will in this way counterbalance the regional bias of the package of modern inputs in favour of irrigated areas.[70]
4. The new package of modern inputs and greater water supply can attain their highest potential yield only with the help of mechanization.
5. Mechanization lowers the cost of production by allowing more efficient utilization of land, labour, irrigation, and other inputs.[71]

The arguments on both sides are fairly strong but there is general agreement on one point—there is need for the development of an appropriate form of technology suitable for developing countries like Pakistan.

The First Plan mentioned certain cases in which mechanization would be desirable. These included the reclamation of culturable waste land, the rapid development of land in the new irrigation project areas, anti-erosion and flood control work, dry-farming and moisture conservation work.[72]

The public policy of 'selective mechanization' must encourage a form of technology that (a) increases yields or the yearly production of food crops; (b) reduces losses in processing, storage, and handling; and (c) increases the utilization of labour. The encouragement of different forms of mechanization will, of course, vary with time, location, soil conditions, and the quality of water. For instance, tractors are more suitable in areas where sweet ground-water is available but are not so suitable for saline ground-water areas where threshers seems to be the appropriate form of mechanization.[73]

11.5.2 The Process of Mechanization in Pakistan

Mechanization in Pakistan has so far meant the greater use of tractors and threshers.

The number of tractors in operation in 1975 was 35,714 of which 33,621 were in the private sector. The regional distribution of tractors was 81 per cent in the Punjab, 11 per cent in Sind, 7 per cent in NWFP, and 1 per cent in Baluchistan. The average annual import of tractors numbered 3,613 during 1965-70 and 4,471 during 1970-5 but during 1975-80 the average annual import increased sharply to 14,262.[74] The tractor is especially useful in the reclamation of water land, for increasing cropping intensity, for deep ploughing, levelling, clearing, and transportation and, according to a World Bank study, the annual financial return on a tractor in Pakistan is 57 per cent.[75]

Another type of machinery fast becoming popular is the wheat thresher. The conventional method of threshing is costly and time consuming and increases the risk of weather hazards and loss of grain. The thresher, a supplement to the tractor, reduces the tractor's fixed cost per hour as its working hours increase. The internal rate of return, calculated on the basis of a 50 acre farm in the Punjab, comes to 46 per cent in the case of a tractor alone and 63 per cent in the case of a tractor plus thresher.[76] Another study has worked out the comparative cost of conventional threshing and mechanical threshing. Assuming a yield of 710 kilograms per acre, the cost with conventional methods is Rs 0.22 per kilogram while with a mechanical thresher it is Rs 0.14.[77]

11.5.3 Appropriate Farm Technology

We can now discuss the type of technology appropriate for Pakistan. Obviously, the viable form of technological progress should be low cost (especially in terms of capital investment and purchased inputs), should minimize risk, should have a significant impact in a relatively short period, and should be such as can be popularized without the necessity of a sophisticated support system.

The major question is the choice between a large and small tractor. The purchase of tractors was highly subsidized during the sixties through an overall exchange rate and subsidized interest rates on credit. This enabled large farmers to earn windfall profits. Now, after the 1972 devaluation, the subsidy is lower. Most of the tractors in Pakistan are between 40 to 100 HP range. It is only recently that some 15 to 20 HP tractors and two-wheeled power tillers have been imported.

Obviously this kind of technology does not match the farm size and capital base of the small cultivators, i.e., those who cultivate farm units of below 50 acres. A study in the early seventies made a strong case for fractional technology in the form of small tractors particularly the two-wheeled power tiller. The usual argument advanced against small tractors is that, because the soil in Pakistan is hard, these tractors are unsuitable. Arguments in favour of the small tractors are as follows:

1. Only 10 per cent of Pakistan's soil can be classified as hard. And if cultivators can till the land with the help of a wooden plough and bullocks, why not a power source 20 to 30 times stronger?
2. A small tractor has the advantage of high profitability with an internal return rate of 45 per cent.
3. As regards factor intensity, it will replace draught animals and increase the demand for labour while the large tractor is labour-displacing.
4. The small tractor, by increasing the small farmer's income, will reduce disparities within the rural sector while the large tractor will accentuate it. The real objective of land reforms (the establishment of a more egalitarian social structure in the rural sector) can be achieved through fractional technology and not through lumpy technology.[78]

11.5.4 The Impact of Mechanization on employment, productivity, and income distribution

Contrary to the common apprehension that mechanization results in the replacement of labour by capital, some studies have shown that mechanization has resulted in an increasing demand for seasonal labour and, consequently, rural wages have become more or less at par with urban wages.[79] Insofar as the small-farm sector is concerned, tractorization has taken place only marginally and farming operations continue mostly with the use of bullocks. Therefore, the labour displacement effect of farm mechanization is of

Table 11.12: Impact of Mechanization on Agricultural Labour

Farm size (acres)	Number of tractor-owners	Number of tractors reporting change in labour requirements			
		Increased	Decreased	No change	Net change
Under 12.5	2,060	460	423	1,177	+ 2 per cent
12.5 to 25	3,627	842	989	1,796	− 4 per cent
25 to 100	16,366	4,723	2,717	8,926	+ 12 per cent
Over 100	32,083	9,381	6,728	15,974	+ 8 per cent

Source: WAPDA, *Revised Action Programme for Irrigated Agriculture*, pp. III-36. Based on: *Census of Agricultural Machinery*, 1975, Agricultural Census Organization.

minor significance in their case. So far as seed, fertilizer, and pesticide technologies are concerned, they are generally labour-augmenting.

Table 11.12 shows the impact of mechanization on agricultural labour.

The demand for labour will increase if tractors are assembled or manufactured within the country and if maintenance and servicing units for agricultural machinery are set-up in rural areas.

Another study shows that the influence of mechanization on employment varies with the system of irrigation and the package of mechanization used. In the canal-irrigated areas with a tubewell, employment per cultivated acre decreases when bullocks are replaced by a tractor. Adding a thresher to the mechanization package further reduces employment. But if the thresher is used with bullocks, labour use increases to 367 man-hours per cultivated acre as compared to 344 with bullocks only. In the tubewell areas, all forms of mechanization, i.e., tractor alone, tractor plus thresher, bullocks plus tractor, and bullocks plus thresher, lead to an increase in employment when compared to the traditional form of cultivation.[80]

A number of studies report higher productivity as a result of mechanical cultivation. An FAO study[81] estimated around 20 per cent increases in productivity through mechanization. Bose and Clark have also reached the conclusion that the yield of corn and wheat will increase by about 30 per cent through mechanized cultivation as against traditional farming with bullocks although they also contend that similar increases could be achieved through improvements in the traditional cultivation methods. Another study reports an increase of 16 to 33 per cent due to mechanization.[82] A World Bank study shows about 140 to 200 per cent increase in

Table 11.13: Distribution of Farms by Size, Owner, and Capital Assets: 1972

Size (acres)	Under 7.5	7.5 to 12.4	12.5 to 24.9	25.0 to 49.9	50.0 to 149.9	150.0 and above	Total
Number of farms ('000)							
Owner	879	270	248	111	51	10	1,569
Owner and tenant	263	244	250	99	36	5	897
Tenant	497	407	296	79	16	1	1,296
Total	1,639	921	794	289	103	16	3,762
Area: ('000acres)							
Owner	2,771	2,577	4,085	3,516	3,653	2,798	19,400
Owner and tenant	1,240	2,363	4,268	3,299	2,665	1,325	15,160
Tenant	1,981	3,968	4,708	2,400	1,085	359	14,501
Total	5,992	8,909	13,061	9,215	7,402	4,482	49,061
Number of tubewells	16,259	18,285	33,733	28,654	22,865	7,754	127,550
Number of tractors	1,049	1,763	4,272	7,182	11,443	4,804	30,513
Percentage of total number of farms	43.6	24.5	21.1	7.7	2.7	0.4	100.0
Area	12.2	18.2	26.6	18.8	15.1	9.1	100.0
Number of tubewells	12.8	14.3	26.4	22.5	17.9	6.1	100.0
Number of tractors	3.4	5.8	14.0	23.5	37.5	15.8	100.0
Acres per tubewell	368	487	387	321	324	578	385
Acres per tractor	5,712	5,053	3,057	1,283	647	933	1,608

Source: Ministry of Food and Agriculture, Government of Pakistan, *Pakistan Census of Agriculture 1972*, 1975, p. 26.

cropping intensity on irrigated farms in the Punjab due to mechanization.[83]

As regards the impact on income distribution, the tractor-tubewell technology is lumpy and scale non-neutral. As such, prima facie, it seems that only big farmers would have used this technology. However, the actual situation reveals different results. The big farmer seems to have the major share in tubewells but they have been made use of by both small and large farmers (Table 11.13). In the case of tractor technology, due to labour displacement, agricultural labourers and tenants seem to have suffered. However, many small and medium farmers, who had the financial liquidity, were able to buy tractors (Table 11.13) and use them as additional sources of income by hiring them out.[84]

While the debate on mechanization continues, it is obvious that the limitations and the potentialities of mechanical technology are not general but specific to the irrigation system, the quality of water and soil, and the agronomic conditions. The appropriate technology for each set of agronomic situation will be different particularly when looked at from the viewpoint of its social impact. However, fractional technology, in a labour-abundant country like Pakistan, is socially preferable to lumpy technology. No technological progress can produce any meaningful results unless the small-farm sector is deeply involved and motivated to participate in the effort. A mechanized revolution in agriculture is one which seeks to reduce, not accentuate, social disparities in the rural sector.

11.6 Agricultural Extension, Research, and Education

Research and education is a continuing requirement for agricultural development not only in developing better seeds, improving cultivation practices, and better use of other physical inputs, but also for finding out their best combinations under different conditions and for matching them with water availability, moisture levels, and soil conditions. But research and education must reach the cultivators speedily through a well planned and co-ordinated agricultural extension programme. Unfortunately, these crucial areas of agricultural policy have not received due attention and suffer from financial and personnel constraints.

11.6.1 Extension

In Pakistan, the agricultural extension service has mostly been dormant. Despite a fairly rapid increase in ADP allocations in recent years, the coverage of the extension service is extremely limited due mainly to poor service conditions and the inadequate provision of extension aids. The expenditure per cultivated acre on extension remains extremely low (it was only Rs 3 in 1977-8). The total number of extension workers was 6,588. On the average, each extension worker has to look after 7,335 acres of cultivated land and 570 farming families.[85] Of course this situation is better than in 1957 when, according to the First Plan, the total number of extension workers in (West) Pakistan was only 365 and each worker had to look after, on the average, 104 villages and 16,000 cultivators.[86] The problems faced by extension workers, as spelled out in the First Plan,[87] like low salaries, poor service conditions, and lack of residential and transport facilities, have been restated in the Fourth Plan[88] and the Fifth Plan.[89] This is indicative of the lack of sufficient progress in this field. No wonder that the extension service has been criticized as being 'of dubious quality and unequally distributed'.[90]

An agricultural extension service aims at providing the farmers with systematic access to knowledge about farming practices, multiple cropping, and use of physical inputs, and ensuring that the knowledge provided is appropriate to the kind of farming being practised. The conventional pattern of an extension service is the stationing of extension agents in rural areas, frequent visits to farmers to offer technical advice and guidance, the setting up of demonstration farms, and the holding of agricultural fairs.

A new approach to agricultural extension has been recommended by Benor and Harrison.[91] The basic concept underlying their system is to motivate farmers to do simple things that could increase their output immediately and which extension workers could be easily taught to carry to the farmers. The initial concentration is on improving agricultural management practices such as better land preparation, improved seed-beds preparation, better tilling methods, and the weeding and proper spacing of plants. The reason for the initial stress on better farming practices is that, first, these practices produce quick results and the farmers face little risk and, second, these require little cash outlay. Better cultural practices also prepare the farmers to derive the full benefits of new production technology. These practices are at first recommended only for a small part of the farmer's land so that they do not appear unduly risky and their results can be compared to those of traditional practices in the farmer's own field. Benor and Harrison's approach is thus more management-intensive than cash-intensive.

This methodology has been tried in three pilot projects in India as well as in Turkey and the results obtained are quite impressive.[92] The approach, however, is relatively new and it has not been tried under all technological environments and in all geographical regions. A similar programme is being launched in Pakistan during the Fifth Plan with the World Bank's assistance.

11.6.2 Research

Insofar as the number and range of research institutions is concerned, agricultural research is fairly well organized. There are multi-disciplinary Agricultural Research Institutes in Faisalabad (Punjab), Tandojam (Sind), Tarnab (NWFP), and Sariab (Baluchistan) and monocrop research institutions dealing with rice (at Dokri and Kala Shah Kaku), maize and millet (Yousafwala and Pir Sabbak), cotton (Multan and Sakrand), and horticulture (Mirpurkhas). In addition, the Agricultural Research Centre at Islamabad and the Arid Zone Research Institute at Quetta are in the process of being set up.

All these research institutions function at the federal level under the overall supervision of the Pakistan Agricultural Research Council which has now been given the status of a Division.

The research effort is supplemented by Agricultural Universities and other institutions dealing with agricultural education. While the Universities concentrate on such subjects as agricultural planning and evaluation, land tenure, taxation, supply and demand projections of agricultural commodities, marketing, and input-output relationships, the specialized research institutions have made significant contributions to agricultural development by developing high yielding pest-resistant and fertilizer-responsive seeds. Their achievements particularly in the field of wheat and rice are known the world over. Research effort has also concentrated on the introduction of new crops in various ecological zones, the development of *barani* cultivation technology, and such sub-sectors as livestock, dairy farming, poultry farming, and fisheries.

11.6.3 Education

One of the major causes of the farmers lack of acres to research and extension facilities is their low level of education. While educated farmers can press the system to deliver the required knowledge, make sure that it is appropriate to their needs, and use it in an effective manner, the uneducated farmers are unable to do so. The lack of education also reduces the farmers' ability to operate the complex agronomic systems resulting from the use of modern technology. Widespread illiteracy is thus a major factor in the low capacity of the farming sector to absorb technological change. In countries like Japan, China, and Korea, impressive results have been attained by spreading education which has enabled farmers to improve cultural practices and farm management.

Thus education, even if limited to making the farmers merely literate, is of great importance. It is even more important to introduce an angro-technological bias in education in the rural areas. Some attempts have already been made in this respect. At the school level from class VI to class X, agrotechnical education is being progressively included in the curricula.

Specialized agricultural education is needed to train agricultural extension personnel, researchers, and educators. For this purpose, five agricultural training institutions are functioning in various parts of the country. They provide both pre-service and in-service training to personnel working in agricultural extension and related fields. The Fifth Plan also suggests that leading farmers be trained in these institutions.

At the higher level there are two Agricultural Universities at Tando Jam and Faisalabad, one Agricultural College at Peshawar, and a Barani Agricultural College at Rawalpindi.

But success in programmes in the agricultural education service will depend upon its ability to train people in various categories of higher and intermediate skills. Their demand is increasing with technological changes in agriculture. Educational institutions must maintain a certain correlation between the demand for and the supply of various skill levels and categories.

11.6.4 Conclusion

Undoubtedly extension, research, and education are poorly financed, as pointed out in earlier sections, even though the ADP allocations to them show an impressive increase from Rs 10 million in 1972-3 to Rs 193 million in 1979-80.[93] However, it is still less than 6 per cent of the total ADP allocations for 1979-80. But, in addition to more finances, there is a need for greater co-ordination between them so that farmers have easy and speedy access to the results of agricultural research. At present this task is being performed by radio and various journals and pamphlets issued by research and educational institutions. But the main channel of communication, i.e., the extension worker, must be strengthened and more resources and information placed at his disposal.

Determination of support prices of Agricultural Commodities

Support prices for agricultural commodities can be determined either on the basis of the cost of production or by what is termed as the 'parity approach'.

The cost of production approach aims at guaranteeing a fair return of a certain crop to the farmers and establishing a balance between a number of competing crops so that an optimum cropping pattern is achieved. Subject to soil, climatic, and other agronomic conditions influencing crop substitution in certain areas, cropping patterns can be moulded to correspond to planned production targets. For instance, wheat competes for area with both cotton and rice so a certain balance between the prices of the three commodities can help in attaining their required production levels.

However, there are certain problems in the cost of production approach. Agricultural production requires a number of inputs which are not marketed and whose valuation will, therefore, present difficulties. Such inputs include labour, management, and land. Labour and management costs, which should be the share of the entrepreneur, are difficult to assess. Similarly land rent, which may be the single largest cost item, is difficult to determine in a country where there is no organized land market.[94]

The regional variations in physical resource

endowments also have to be taken into account in the choice of samples for calculating cost. Moreover, with rise in prices, the cost of production has to be periodically adjusted.

The cost of production is also related to technology. For purposes of price support the cost of production may either pertain to old traditional technologies, which means a higher level of support price, or to the new technologies where costs may be low. A support price based on the new technology cost structure will have adverse equity effects particularly if the new inputs are subsidized or a large number of farmers have no access to the new technology. Large holdings with lower production costs may get higher net returns compared to small holdings. Thus the higher the support price, the greater the transfer of income to large holdings from the general revenues. It is now believed that the support price programme in Pakistan has operated in contradiction to the original intent of better income distribution among various segments of the rural farm sector[95] since, mainly, the cost of production approach has been followed while determining the structure of support prices.

In addition to the problem of identifying the technology, and the cultivators using that technology, there is another question: which cost should be taken into consideration? Average or incremental? In a production system as varied as Pakistan's agriculture in technology as well as scale, both types of unit costs are bound to create complications.

The 'parity price' approach is used in order to correct imbalances in terms of trade between the agricultural and the non-agricultural sectors. The 'parity price' is an output price that will yield income which will buy the same quantity of other products as it would in some specified base period. Thus a balance can be maintained between the prices of commodities sold by the farmers and the commodities which they purchase. It can be calculated through a comparative index of agricultural and non-agricultural prices. In this approach, the effects of inflation which keep upsetting the income and expenditure structure of the farm household are accounted for. Although it is free from the usual objections of lack of scientific rigour and bias in favour of transfer of resources to a particular category of land holding, the choice of the base year for working out the parity ratio may introduce some distortion in the income distribution pattern of different tenure and size farm categories.[96]

The choice between the two approaches depends upon the relative importance of various objectives of the price support programme. If the major objective is providing production incentives for particular crops or crop combinations, the cost of production approach may serve the purpose at least in the short-run. Parity prices, on the other hand, provide a range within which prices may be located in order to reflect the influence of the forces of demand and supply as well as the long-run objective of equity between urban and rural sectors.

In addition to the two approaches mentioned above, three other criteria are sometimes used for determining support prices : (i) open market prices; (ii) inter-crop parity index; and (iii) world prices.

An assessment of the open market price, as determined by the supply-demand interaction, is essential and should be kept in mind while making decisions regarding the support price. It serves as a restraining factor since too much deviation from the open market price may make the price support programme unrealistic and ineffective. It is, however, difficult to make an accurate assessment of the open market price since the markets are highly imperfect, unstable, and dominated mostly by a few buyers (*arhtis*/sugar mills). In fact, an agricultural price policy itself represents an attempt to escape from the uncertainties and distortions of the so-called 'open market'.

The inter-crop parity index reflects the relative positions of various agricultural products and the rates at which these are exchanged. Their main utility lies in monitoring the use of scarce resources for competing crops and calculating optimal resource allocation.

World prices are relevant in the case of export commodities or those commodities which are partly supplied from abroad. But world markets are not equally competitive for all commodities. Their use is further restricted by the fact that while a certain product and some of the inputs (for example, pesticides and fertilizers) may have relevance to world market conditions, major elements in the cost structure (for example, canal water and labour) may have no linkage.

NOTES

1. Griffin, 'Financing Development Plans in Pakistan'. Paper in *Readings in Strategy and Techniques of Development Planning*, edited by A.R. Khan, PIDE, 1969, Karachi, p. 27.
2. The support price is the minimum level of a commodity's price below which the government would not allow it to fall. At times, procurement prices may also tend to function as support prices, i.e., after bumper harvests when open market prices are declining. On the other hand, during periods of bad harvest, procurement prices may resist sharp price increases.
3. Papanek, *Pakistan's Development—Social Goals and Private Incentives*, Oxford University Press, 1968, pp. 148-9.
4. Griffin, 'Financing Development Plans in Pakistan'. Paper in *Readings in Strategy and Techniques of Development Planning*, edited by A.R. Khan, PIDE, 1969, Karachi, p. 31.
5. Beringer and Ahmed, *The Use of Agricultural Surplus Commodities for Economic Development in Pakistan*, PIDE, 1964, p. 59.
6. Griffin, 'Financing Development Plans in Pakistan'. Paper in *Readings in Strategy and Techniques of Development Planning*, edited by A.R. Khan, PIDE, 1969, Karachi, p. 40.
7. Government of Pakistan, *Fiscal Policy in Pakistan*, Vol. II, Budget Speech (1967-8) by the Finance Minister, Islamabad, p. 557.
8. (a) Bauer and Yamey, 'A Case Study of Response to Price in an Under-developed Country', *Economic Journal*, December 1959.
   (b) Clark, 'The Economic Detriments of Jute Production', *Monthly Bulletin of Agricultural Economics and Statistics*, September 1959.
   (c) Fulcon, *Farmer Response to Price in an under-developed area : A Case Study of West Pakistan*, Harvard University, 1962.
   (d) Sayed Mushtaq Hussain, *The Effects of Growing Constraint of Subsistence Farming on Farmer Response to Price : A Case Study of Jute in Pakistan*, PDR, Autumn 1969.
9. Papanek, *Pakistan's Development—Social Goals and Private Incentives*, Oxford University Press, 1968 pp. 153-4.
10. Mohammad Ali Chaudhry, 'Pricing and Performance—Special Report', *Pakistan Economist*, Karachi, 21 February 1981, p. 18.
11. See Federal Budget for 1980-1.
12. Government of Pakistan, *Pakistan Economic Survey, 1970-1*, Islamabad, p. 121.
13. Government of Pakistan, *Taxation Inquiry Committee—Interim Report (Central Taxation)*, 1959, p. 66.
14. G.M. Radhu, 'The Rate Structure of Indirect Taxes in Pakistan', *Pakistan Development Review, Vol. IV, No. 3*, Autumn 1964, p. 533.
15. Government of Pakistan, *Taxation Structure of Pakistan, 1980-1*, p. 47.
16. Government of Pakistan, *Government Sponsored Corporations, 1979-80*, p. 275.
17. Lewis, 'Aspects of Fiscal Policy and Resource Mobilization in Pakistan', *Pakistan Development Review, Vol. IV, No. 2,* Summer 1964, p. 277.
18. Government of Pakistan, *Government Sponsored Corporations*, 1979-80, p. 276.
19. World Bank, *Pakistan Economic Developments and Prospects*, 1980, p. 12.
20. Government of Pakistan, *Pakistan Basic Facts, 1979-80*, Islamabad, p. 219.
21. Government of Pakistan, *Agricultural Statistics of Pakistan*, 1970, p. 67.
22. Gotsch and Brown, *Prices, Taxes and Subsidies in Pakistan Agriculture, 1960-1970*, World Bank Staff working Paper 387, 1980, pp.35-7.
23. See (i) Rashid Amjad, 'A Critique of the Green Revolution', *Pakistan Economic and Social Review*, June 1972, (for the period of the sixties).
    (ii) Mohammad Ali Chaudhry and Nuzhat Iqbal, 'Support Price Policy Impact on Rural Farm Sector Income Distribution', *Local Government and Rural Development Review*, April-June 1979.
    (iii) Dilawar Ali Khan, *New Technology and Agricultural Transformation*, UNCRD, 1979.
24. Mohammad Ali Chaudhry, 'Support Price Policy Impact on Rural Farm Sector Income Distribution' *Local Government and Rural Development Review*, April-June 1979, pp. 15-7.
25. Mahmood Hassan Khan, 'Private Surplus at

Public Cost', *Pakistan Economist*, 13 June 1981, p. 19.
26. Government of Pakistan, *Fifth Five Year Plan*, Islamabad, p. 62.
27. Ibid., p. 218 for Plan allocations and Table 9.4 for subsidies.
28. B.A. Azhar, 'Agricultural Taxation in West Pakistan', *Pakistan Economic and Social Review*, Autumn 1973, p.288.
29. B.A. Azhar, 'Land Revenue Settlement', *Pakistan Development Review*, Autumn 1973, p. 239.
30. See Table 11.7.
31. Government of Pakistan, *Pakistan Economic Survey, 1979-80*, Islamabad, (Statistical Annexure) p.183.
32. Dilawar Ali Khan, and Haider Ali Chaudhri, 'Income Impact of the Green Revolution', *Pakistan Economic and Social Review*, Spring 1973, p. 80.
33. Rashid Amjad, 'A Critique of the Green Revolution in (West) Pakistan', *Pakistan Economic and Social Review*, June 1972.
34. Hamza Alavi, 'The Rural Elite and Agricultural Development in Pakistan', Paper in *Pakistan Economic and Social Review*, special issue on Income Inequalities in Pakistan, Vol.XIV, No. 1-4, 1970, p. 206.
35. US AID, *Pakistan Agriculture, Resource, Progress, and Prospects*, Karachi, 1967, p. 91-2.
36. Government of Pakistan, *Fifth Five Year Plan*, Islamabad, p.36.
37. Aftab Ahmed, 'Agricultural Credit—Availability—Need Gap in Pakistan', *Quarterly Economic Journal*, National Bank of Pakistan, October-December 1977, p. 46.
38. Donald, 'Credit for Small Farmers in Developing Countries', quoted in *Small Farmers and the Landless in South Asia*, p.94.
39. A.D. Butt, 'Mechanism of Agricultural Credit', *Pakistan Economist*, Karachi, 19 November 1977, p. 22.
40. Aftab Ahmed, 'Agricultural Credit—Availability—Need Gap in Pakistan', *Quarterly Economic Journal*, National Bank of Pakistan, October-December 1977, p.46.
41. Andrus and Mohammad, *Trade, Finance, and Development in Pakistan*, Oxford University Press, 1966, p. 135.
42. Donald, 'Credit for Small Farmers in Developing Countries', in *Small Farmers and the Landless in South Asia*, p. 94.
43. Andrus and Mohammad, *Trade, Finance, and Development in Pakistan*, Oxford University Press, 1966, p. 142.
44. Ministry of Food and Agriculture, Government of Pakistan, *Agricultural Statistics of Pakistan, 1978*, 1979, p. 102.
45. S.K. Qureshi, *The Performance of Village Markets For Agricultural Produce : A Case Study of Pakistan*, PDR, Autumn 1974, p. 284.
46. Government of Pakistan, *Pakistan Economic Survey, 1979-80*, Islamabad, Statistical Annexure, p. 32.
47. Ministry of Food and Agriculture, Government of Pakistan, *Food and Agriculture Commission*, 1960, p. 181.
48. Quoted in *Small Farmers and the Landless in South Asia*, p. 99.
49. Finance Division, Government of Pakistan, *Government Sponsored Corporations, 1978-9*, 1980, p. 19.
50. Government of Pakistan, *Agricultural Statistics of Pakistan*, Islamabad, 1979, p. 94.
51. Ibid., p. 95.
52. Ibid., p. 97.
53. Finance Division, Government of Pakistan, *Government Sponsored Corporations*, pp.19-21.
54. Jamil Nishtar, Chairman ABDP, *Pakistan Economist*, Karachi, 5 November 1977.
55. State Bank of Pakistan, *Annual Report, 1978-9*, 1979, pp. 102 and 112.
56. *Small Farmers and the Landless in South Asia*, pp. 106-7.
57. Ibid., p. 108.
58. M.Aslam Chaudhary, 'Market-Oriented Growth in Agriculture', *Quarterly Economic Journal*, National Bank of Pakistan, October-December 1977, p. 41.
59. Government of Pakistan, *Fifth Five Year Plan*, Islamabad, p. 430.
60. Government of Pakistan, *Pakistan Economic Survey, 1979-80*, Islamabad, Statistical Annexure, p. 169.
61. Ibid., p. 226.
62. Government of Pakistan, *Annual Plan, 1979-80*, p. 349
63. Government of Pakistan, *Pakistan Economic Survey, 1979-80,* Islamabad, Statistical Annexure, p. 25.
64. Government of Pakistan, *Fifth Five Year Plan*, Islamabad, p. 32.
65. Directorate of Agriculture (Economics and Marketing), *Punjab Bulletins*, 1973-4 and 1974-5.
66. M. Aslam Chaudhary, 'Market-oriented Growth in Agriculture', *Quarterly Economic Journal*, National Bank of Pakistan, October-December 1977, p. 41.
67. Government of Pakistan, *Fifth Five Year Plan*, Islamabad, p. 34.
68. M. Aslam Chaudhary, 'Market-oriented Growth in Agriculture', *Quarterly Economic Journal*, National Bank of Pakistan, October-December 1977, p. 42.
69. Government of Pakistan, *Fifth Five Year Plan*, Islamabad, p. 24.

70. Nigar Ahmed, 'The Contradictions of Capitalism and Marginal Solution', paper in *Economic Reconstruction in Pakistan*, edited by Rafique Ahmed et al., 1973, p. 145.
71. Javed Hamid, 'A Case for Fractional Technology', *Pakistan Economic and Social Review*, December 1972, p. 138.
72. Government of Pakistan, *First Five Year Plan*, p. 233.
73. Bashir Ahmed, *The Economics of Tractor Mechanization in the Pakistan Punjab*, Food Research Institute Studies, 1975.
74. Government of Pakistan, *Agricultural Statistics of Pakistan*, 1978, Islamabad, pp. 110 and 113.
75. The Consequence of Farm Tractors in Pakistan, *World Bank Staff Working Paper No. 210*, 1975.
76. Bashir Ahmed, *The Economics of Tractor Mechanization in the Pakistan Punjab*, Food Research Institute Studies, 1975.
77. A. Matin, 'Financing of Agricultural Progress by ADBP', *Local Government and Rural Development Review*, April-June 1979.
78. Javed Hamid, 'A Case for Fractional Technology', *Pakistan Economic and Social Review*, December 1972.
79. *Employment and Occupational Change in Rural Punjab—Consequences of Green Revolution*, Economic Research Institute, 1978.
80. Bashir Ahmed, *The Economics of Tractor Mechanization in the Pakistan Punjab*, Food Research Institute Studies, 1975.
81. *Indicative World Plan for Agricultural Development*, 1969.
82. Gill, 'Economics of Farm Mechanization', *West Pakistan Journal of Agricultural Research*, July 1962.
83. IBRD, *Third Credit for the ADBP*, June 1969.
84. Dilawar Ali Khan, 'Reflections on Agricultural Transformation in West Pakistan—Implication for Future Agricultural Development Strategy', Paper in *Economic Reconstruction in Pakistan*, edited by Rafique Ahmed, 1973, p. 269.
85. Government of Pakistan, *Fifth Five Year Plan*, Islamabad, p. 42 (the figures relate to 1977-8).
86. Government of Pakistan, *Fifth Five Year Plan*, Islamabad, p. 273.
87. Ibid., p. 276.
88. Ibid., pp. 294-5.
89. Ibid., p. 42.
90. Mahmood Hasan Khan, 'Is Small Farmer the Problem? *Pakistan Economist*, 13 May 1978, p. 7.
91. Benor and Harrison, *Agricultural Extension—Training and Visiting System*, World Bank, 1977.
92. World Bank, *Small Farmers and the Landless in South Asia*, p. 24-5.
93. Government of Pakistan, *Annual Plan, 1979-80*, p. 131.
94. M. Afzal, *Parity Pricing as an Approach to Price Support Programmes*, PDR, Autumn 1977.
95. Mohammad Ali Chaudhary and Nuzhat Iqbal, 'Support Price Policy Impact on Rural Farms Sector Income Distribution', *Local Government and Rural Development Review*, April-June 1979, p. 17 and 18.
96. Ibid., p. 16.

12 Rural Development: Past Policies and Programmes

12.1 Introduction

The existence of extreme poverty in the rural areas has compelled economic planners to suggest different schemes and programmes throughout the last three and a half decades whereby the economic plight of the rural population could be improved especially that of the small farmers, the tenants, and the landless labourers.

A review of these programmes is important to help us understand the basic approach the planners have adopted in their attempts to improve the condition of the rural economy. Most of these programmes had a number of common assumptions and goals. The limited success of each programme which was implemented only led planners to suggest new approaches, in many cases without seriously considering the factors responsible for their failure.

An interesting fact is that despite the considerable importance which has been given to these programmes, the actual amount of funds allotted to them have throughout been extremely meagre. Table 12.1 shows the funds spent on the major programmes in the last thirty-five years and that even at their highest level they never exceeded 4 to 5 per cent of total development expenditure. During the seventies they were less than 2 per cent of the total.

In the sections below, we review the major programmes bringing out their obiectives and their achievements.

12.2 The Village Agricultural and Industrial Development Programme (Village AID)

The Village AID Programme was initiated in 1953 to improve the social and economic condition of villages through community development methods. The First Five Year Plan (1955-60) gave a very high priority to rural development and strongly supported the Village AID Programme to achieve it. It was stated in the Plan document:

> 'The Village AID Programme is of crucial importance as the means for bringing better living standards and a new spirit of hope (and) confidence to the villagers where, according to the 1951 census, about 90 per cent of the people of the country live.'[1]
>
> 'The enrichment of life in the villages and rural areas of the country is in our view the most important objective of the Plan, because about 90 per cent of the country's people live in rural areas, often in poor and primitive conditions. The major instrument for accomplishing this is the Village Agricultural and Industrial Development Programme which aims at increasing the production from agriculture and village industries thereby increasing the incomes of the rural people. The programme also seeks to provide more schools and health centres, better water supplies, and other social and recreational facilities for the villages.'[2]

All this was to be done mainly through the 'initiative and energy of village people themselves, co-operating and pooling their own resources'. The government was to provide the assistance of 'village workers' under the leadership of development officers who were to help the villagers in making plans for local development and in organizing themselves to carry them out. The government was also to provide the services of specialists from different government departments—agriculture, animal husbandry, health, and so on—and some funds and materials to enable the villagers to carry out work which otherwise they could not do.

Some rural areas called 'development areas' were to be selected for intensive development. Each development area was to consist of 150 to 200 villages with a population of about

100,000 and placed in charge of a development officer who was to have at his disposal the services of specialists in farm management, animal husbandry, co-operation and marketing, and health and sanitation. He was also to direct the activities of the 'village workers' each of whom were to be responsible for five to seven villages.

It was emphasized that the programme would be successful if it realizes and organizes the very large, and frequently unrecognized, resources that exist in the villages and 'stimulates the spirit of self-help and co-operation'. The key to the whole programme was the assistance and advice of the village worker trained to help the villagers to find ways to solve their own problems, and directed and guided by the development officer.

During 1955-60, about one quarter of the rural population was to be covered by Organized Village AID development areas, i.e., about 26,000 villages and 17 million people. It was hoped that by 1965 it could cover the whole country. The most important objectives the Village AID Programme set itself were:[3]

a. To rapidly raise the output and income of the villagers through better methods of farming and to expand cottage industries;
b. To create a spirit of self-help, initiative, and co-operation among the villagers, a spirit that can be the basis for continuing economic, social, and political progress;
c. To multiply the community services available in rural areas such as schools, health centres, pure water supplies, etc.;
d. To create conditions for a richer and higher life through social activities including recreation for men and women.

The Village AID Programme was also to channelize badly needed technical and material assistance to cottage and small-scale industries in the rural areas.[4] Village industries were divided into two kinds needing two distinct types of workers. The first were those industries which were producing for the immediate vicinity, serving the ordinary needs of the area, and employing village artisans like weavers, blacksmiths, carpenters, and potters. It was felt that there should probably be a specialist in each development area or *tehsil* to serve this type of industry supported at the district or provincial level by a specialist for each of these main industries. The second type of industries were the more highly skilled arts and crafts supplying wider markets with sports goods, fine textiles, metal work, basket and straw work, furniture, ceramics, and so on.

It was felt that these industries may face special problems in marketing their products and a specialist in each craft, in a district or province, could render valuable services. It was recommended that training courses for the village industrial workers and for the various kinds of specialists should be organ-

Table 12.1: Expenditure on Rural Development Programmes
(Rs million)

Programme	Years	Total Expenditure (Rupees in million)	Percentage of public sector Development Programme
Village AID[1]	1955-60	298	3.2
Rural Works Programme[2]	1960-5	650	3.71
Rural Works Programme[2]	1965-70	1,136	4.48
Integrated Rural Development Programme[3]	1972-7	131.1	
Peoples Works Programme[3]	1972-7	887.8	1.99
Agrovilles Development Programme[3]	1972-7	22.75	
Rural Development Programme[4]	(Projected) 1978-83	1,500	1.5

1. Government of Pakistan, *First Five Year Plan,* Planning Board, 1957, p. 75.
2. Government of Pakistan, *Fourth Five Year Plan,* Planning Commission, July 1970, p. 37.
3. A.S. Bokhari, 'Review of Direct Employment Creation Schemes and Rural Development Programmes in Pakistan', Bangkok, 1978, p. 176, for Expenditure on Programmes. For total Public Sector Expenditure Programme during these years *Annual Development Programme,* Planning Commission, (different years).
4. Government of Pakistan, *Fifth Five Year Plan,* Islamabad, 1978.

ized in co-operation with the central and provincial education, labour, and Village AID authorities.

The development of small and rural industries was also to be stimulated by a 'research and demonstration approach'. A Ford Foundation team, which had visited Pakistan in April 1957, had recommended the setting up of two demonstration projects on rural and small industry development, one in each wing of the country for two major purposes: (i) research and planning; and (ii) demonstration operations. The research function would comprise such matters as selection of areas and projects, industry, outlook reports, evaluation of pilot project results, and dissemination of results. The demonstration function was to include specific experiments on production techniques and credit mechanism, marketing scheme, raw materials, purchase plans, business management, and training programmes.

The planners recommended that the administrative responsibility for the Village AID Programme should vest in the Planning and Development Department. This was to be done by appointing the Director of Village AID as Deputy Development Commissioner with the status of Joint Secretary in that capacity.[5] The reason why these measures were thought necessary was because in the earlier years the Village AID Programme had to face serious problems of departmental adjustment and co-ordination. It was hoped that by these measures it would be possible to ensure day to day co-ordination between policy and execution in an activity which was meant to be a representative cross-section of the whole field of planned development. The district administration through the district officers in the development fields were also to take principal responsibility for the implementation of the Village AID Programme.[6]

12.2.1 Progress under the First Plan (1955-60)

The Village AID Programme achieved a fair degree of overall success during the First Plan period. The Programme was introduced into 176 development areas as against the Plan target of 172 areas. In terms of money and labour, the village communities contributed about Rs 12 million for education, health, construction and improvement of roads, and other services. Some 150,000 agricultural demonstration plots were laid out, 1,000 miles of canals were dug, 3,000 miles of unmetalled roads were constructed, and 4,000 miles of old roads were put in serviceable condition. According to the Second Five Year Plan, 'the adoption of farm practices was faster in the development areas than elsewhere although accomplishments in agriculture were in general short of expectations'.[7] The major weakness of the Programme had been a lack of proper co-operation between the Village AID organization and the nation-building departments.[8] Village workers, supported by departmental technicians, had been intended to work as extension agents of all departments at the village level. However, although this arrangement worked reasonably well in East Pakistan it did not do so in West Pakistan where the existence of a good deal of unhealthy rivalry necessitated strong intervention by the central government.

During the Second Five Year Plan it was hoped that, with the creation of Basic Democracies,[9] a new dimension would be added to community development and, in cooperation with these institutions, the Village AID organization would in future have an even greater opportunity for promoting an integrated social and economic advancement of the rural community. It was stated that 'the Second Plan treats the Village AID Organization as a significant instrument of rural development in all its aspects and especially in relation to agricultural production'.[10] During 1960-5 it was hoped that all areas will be served by a development officer and at least 85 per cent of the rural population will have access to the services of village workers. The plan made a provision of Rs 484 million to cover the cost of the Village AID Programme and the number of development areas was to be increased from 176 to 435 by 1965.

12.2.2 End of Village AID Programme

The Village AID Programme was discontinued in 1962 when its work for agricultural development was transferred to the Provincial Agricultural Departments and the Agricultural Development Corporations whereas its community development and other responsibilities were taken over by the Basic Democracies institutions.

In the Final Evaluation of the Second Five Year Plan, it was stated that 'the Village AID Programme has been successful in fostering spirit of self-help and co-operation among the villagers'.[11] By 1960-1, about 2,650 village councils were established, 1,011 new school buildings were constructed, and 1,014 existing school buildings were repaired in the 202 development areas in the country. Besides, 9,200 poultry farms were opened, 4,200 adult education centres were started, 6,500 miles of new *kutcha* roads were constructed, and 5,900 miles of existing *kutcha* roads were improved. Furthermore, two Academies for Village AID development were established, one in each province, to train Village AID officers in community development.

The major short-coming of the Programme and its limited success was attributed to a shortage of technical personnel and lack of proper co-ordination amongst the various government departments at the local level. 'Moreover the Programme expected too much from the people in the form of voluntary work (and the) whole of the leadership was imposed from outside rather than evolved from within the village community.'[12]

12.3 Rural Works Programme/Basic Democracies (1962-9)

It was now argued that the missing link in the Village AID Programme was the absence of local leadership and the development and growth of institutions within the rural society. These institutions would bring the rural areas into direct contact with the process of development originating in urban centres, provide a channel for the communication of the needs and desires of the village population regarding patterns of development to higher levels in the administrative hierarchy, and relay back the decision supported by necessary financial allocations. It was emphasized that this gap was filled by the creation of the Basic Democracies in 1959 and that the basic idea of the Rural Works Programme could not have been translated into reality without the foundation of this political and administrative institution.[13] The Rural Works Programme had been evolved in 1961 to utilize the concealed unemployment in the agricultural sector through the institution of Basic Democracies. The Rural Works Programme was started as a project outside the Second Five Year Plan as it was feared that the injection of additional purchasing power, in the form of wages, into the relatively non-monetized economy of the village might create inflationary pressures. The Rural Works Programme was backed by supplies of food-stuff under the PL-480 Programme. A Pilot Project was undertaken in 1961 by the Academy of Rural Development at Comilla to determine the efficacy and feasibility of such a programme and to formulate a procedure of work. The Project showed encouraging results and demonstrated that given the necessary training and assistance the Basic Democrats were capable of planning and executing development projects of local significance in co-operation with government officials.

The Programme was started in 1962-3 in the former East Pakistan and in the following year in West Pakistan. The basic objectives of the Rural Works Programmc were:

a. To provide greater employment by creating work opportunities in the rural areas on local projects not requiring large capital investment.
b. To create an effective nucleus of planning and development at the local level, and to associate a much larger segment of the population in the country's development effort.
c. To create rural infrastructure such as roads, bridges, irrigation canals, flood protection embankments, water supplies facilities, etc., in the rural areas.

d. To raise additional monetary and manpower resources for central programmes that may be available for local projects through taxation or voluntary labour.

The underlying assumptions behind these objectives were:

i) Existence of surplus rural working force;
ii) Zero marginal cost of their transfer;
iii) Labour-intensive forms of local projects and harnessing of surplus labour to accelerate the growth in the agricultural sector;
iv) Availability of local leadership.

The Rural Works Programme contemplated an outlay of Rs 1,600 million during the Second Plan. As the Programme was actually put into operation in the third year of the Plan in East Pakistan, and with another year's delay in West Pakistan, only Rs 650 million was utilized. In West Pakistan, in physical terms, 112 miles of metalled roads, 410 miles of treated roads, 2,810 miles of *kutcha* roads, 1,500 miles of village tracks, 2,000 culverts and bridges, and about 3,000 schools were constructed and repaired. In East Pakistan, on the other hand, 76,883 miles of *kutcha* road, 6,056 *pucca* roads, 5,754 miles of embankment, 7,525 miles of drains and canals, 4,049 Union Community Centres, and over 400,000 (Rft) of bridges and culverts.

During the Third Plan, it was decided that the Rural Works Programme would form a separate sector in the Plan concerned with the growth and development of the rural economy. An allocation of Rs 2,500 million was provided in the Third Five Year Plan out of which Rs 1,500 million was for East Pakistan and Rs 1,000 million for West Pakistan. PL-480 counterpart funds were to continue to finance the Programme but it was estimated that only Rs 1,000 million may be available out of these funds and therefore the balance was to be financed out of the government's own funds. Besides, it was proposed to initiate an Urban Works Programme during the Third Plan so as to offer employment opportunities to people living in urban areas and to provide them with low cost housing, community centres, recreational facilities, and social welfare services. In terms of broad sectoral priorities in West Pakistan emphasis was on link roads (50 per cent of the total allocation) and rural water supply schemes (25 per cent) leaving 25 per cent for other schemes. In East Pakistan emphasis was on training centres, village co-operatives, and improvement of communication and irrigation facilities.

The Programme was considered fairly successful in terms of the physical achievements made during the Third Plan. In East Pakistan, 63,752 miles of *kutcha* roads, 3,118 miles of *pucca* roads, and 41,745 bridges and culverts were constructed under the Programme. Besides, 395 Thana Training and Development Centres, 3,000 Union Community Centres, 188 Coastal Community Centres, and a large number of marketing and shopping centres were built. Construction of 6,750 miles of embankments and 7,700 miles of canals and drainage were undertaken in the flood control and irrigation sector. In West Pakistan, the main physical achievements were the construction of 536 miles of metalled roads, 2,086 miles of treated roads, 3,399 miles of *kutcha* roads, 110 bridges, and 6,700 culverts. In the health and sanitation sector, construction of 586 civil dispensaries, 196 drains, excavation of 436 tanks, and installation of 9,518 handpumps was completed. In the water, power and irrigation sectors, 185 tubewells, 1,296 open surface wells, and 445 *Karazes*. Besides these 3,170 schools, 930 community centres, and 258 veterinary dispensaries were opened.

With the overthrow of Ayub's Government, in the spring of 1969, the Basic Democracy system was abolished and the Rural Works Programme associated with it was abandoned.

12.4 The 'Comilla' Approach to Rural Development

Any account of the rural development programmes undertaken by the government in the fifties and sixties would be incomplete without mentioning the approach evolved by the Academy for Rural Development in

Comilla (former East Pakistan) which was set up in 1958 and headed by a remarkable Director, Akhtar Hameed Khan. The Academy adopted the administrative unit in which it was located, the Thana of Comilla, as a laboratory. The approach was also tried successfully in groups of Thanas in the districts of Comilla, Chittagong, and Dinajpur and in four agricultural estates established by the East Pakistan Agricultural Development Corporation.

When the Academy was set up, its first aim was to improve the quality and scope of rural administration. To achieve this end, the Thana Training and Development Centre was established with offices of the so-called nation-building departments–Agriculture, Animal Husbandry, Fishery, Health, and Education were housed together. For planning and co-ordination, a local government council was created at the Thana level and also located at the Centre. Chairmen of the next lower tier, the Union Councils, and the departmental officers were the constituent members. The assumption was that the people should be mobilized through their elected leaders and that the government officials should co-ordinate with each other as well as the councillors. The Centre was also to be a training ground and special meeting halls and class-rooms were added and officers were encouraged to teach.

The first task which the Thana Council set for itself was the construction of a drainage and roads network which was financed through PL-480 counterpart funds as part of the government's Rural Works Programme. This was followed by an irrigation works programme whose objective was to mobilize village groups to find and use surface or ground water wherever it was available. Its several compartments–formation of groups, operation of lift pumps and tubewells, field channels and distribution of water, maintenance of machines, training of drivers and managers–required prolonged testing. But after several years, it began to function very effectively and, within a comparatively short period with few costly construction and with low capital expenditure, several hundred thousand acres were irrigated which increased both production and farm employment.

The Academy's most ambitious action research was the Co-operative Project which was an attempt to organize the peasant proprietors, who constituted 70 per cent of the agriculturists in the area, for production as well as protection. These grass-roots or primary village Co-operatives were organized preferably around concrete innovating implements requiring group action such as pumps and tubewells. The primary societies elected representatives as managers as well as 'model' farmers who participated in training courses held once a week at the Thana headquarters. They would learn and then come back and demonstrate appropriate cultivation techniques, procure and distribute inputs, manage credit, and keep books. They were what one could term as down-to-earth agents. To quote Akhtar Hameed Khan,

> 'in the light of our research we discarded the orthodox notions of an outsider, a missionary, or guide-philosopher-friend, or a multipurpose worker, or an agricultural assistant, coming to convert or rescue or reclaim the village. Instead we found that it was more fruitful to rotate village representatives between the nascent urban centre and their rural habitations'.[14]

These primary village Co-operatives were grouped at the Thana level as a supporting Thana Co-operative Federation. The Thana federations had the size and resources to back up the primary societies with essential inputs–credits, supplies, and services. They could employ supervisory and extension personnel to continuously help the village groups. The Thana federation procured resources from various government agencies and supervised the use of these facilities by the village societies. They maintained and hired out machinery and distributed fertilizer, insecticides, etc. Profits out of such operations were added to the financial resources of the federations and enabled them to extend services in other needed fields.

To quote from the Fourth Plan:

> 'In areas where the programme has been implemented, there has been visible improvement in

farmers' motivation, adoption of innovations, productive utilization of credit, timely repayment of debts, and savings out of increased ineome. This confirms that the farmer is willing and able to take a path of planned change. But he has to be carefully and continuously assisted. In the Fourth Plan, the Agricultural Co-operatives part of the Comilla model is intended to be multiplied throughout the province.'[15]

The Plan went on to state that whereas the programme will not directly improve the lot of landless labourers, or of families with extremely small plots of land, these groups will benefit indirectly from the increased demand for agricultural labour and increased welfare services around them.

12.5 Integrated Rural Development Programme

The IRDP, which was formally launched by the Government of Pakistan in July 1972, was built on the model of the Shadab Pilot Project which had been started slightly earlier (August 1971) in ten Union Councils of Lahore *Tehsil.* The basic concept underlying the Pilot Project had been defined as follows:

'To select a production area comprising 50 to 60 villages, mostly with small and medium size farmers, with a view to improving their socio-economic status by intensive rural development programmes with an initial thrust to increase productivity by providing technical guidance, supervised credit, supply of inputs, machinery on hire, storage and marketing facilities, etc., based on sound physical, organizational, and institutional infrastructure, by intensification, diversification, and commercialization of agriculture through a social co-operative system under a total approach.'[16]

The Shadab Project envisaged achieving its objective by co-ordinating the activities of the nation-building departments/agencies together with private enterprise in a planned way. In order to perform its functions, the project had been provided with a Project Manager and ten Development Agents, one in each Union Council. The Development Agents, who were agricultural graduates, were responsible for providing technical guidance to the farmers, making arrangements for supervised credit, supply of agricultural inputs, guidance in farm planning and management, laying of demonstration and experimental plots, making arrangements for storage and marketing, formation of farmers' Co-operative associations, and development of fishery and forestry with other nation-building departments and agencies. During 1971-2, the officials of the Project held over a thousand group meetings with the farmers, all of whom were contacted individually several times. Sixty model farms were built up, one in each village, where farming was done according to the latest agricultural methods. About 167 demonstration and experimental plots were laid to help convince the farmers to adopt new techniques. Improved inputs were provided to the farmers through sales depots established at Union Council level. Steps were taken to make it easier for the farmers to get loans from the Agricultural Development Bank. A community development centre was established with a social welfare officer who, along with his field staff, helped in the area of maternity and child health, adult education of both males and females, industrial and household affairs training, and creating social awareness among women.[16]

A study carried out by Ali and Khan[17] in 1978 to evaluate the success of the Shadab Project came to the conclusion that

'cropping and land use itensities had increased more in "with project" area as compared to "non-project" area but the increase was not statistically significant. Average yield of different crops in the "with project" area had shown an increasing trend resulting thereby in higher gross and net incomes per acre. Increased productivity also developed the financial resources of the farmers in the "with project" area. Moreover, general awareness of the farmers of this area about improved varieties and techniques of farming had also been increased by Shadab workers—one can safely conclude that the Shadab Project has achieved success both by increasing productivity as well as social justice by improving relative economic position of the small farmers but this increase was not significant'.[18]

After an operational period of one year, in July 1972, the Project was considered successful and extended to the country as a whole as the IRD Programme.

12.5.1 Institutional Framework

The IRDP envisages an institutional arrangement from the village upward whereby the felt needs of the rural community are identified by the people themselves and met through the process of the integration of nation-building departments and other agencies concerned with the development of rural economy. To serve the target group more effectively, the programme suggests two types of organizations to operate concurrently in the rural areas viz., (i) a local government set-up which would contribute to political stability, generate a sense of participation among the people, and provide a structure for the articulation of local needs and their subsequent transfer to provincial and federal governments; (ii) a Co-operative system which would enable the people to organize themselves at the village and *markaz* levels to meet their immediate economic needs.

The institutional set-up of the local government to implement the IRD Programme is as follows:

i) *Primary Unit:* The lowest unit, where farmers can get together for operational performances, is the village or group of villages. This unit forms a homogenous community which can meet frequently for the discussion of prodution plans and development schemes. At this level, the main task is to organize the people for the purpose of identification of felt needs, formulation of action plans, and development of local resources for self-management of the projects.

ii) *Markaz:* The hub of development activities is the *markaz.* It is established at a focal point which has the potential to develop into an agrovile for providing necessary support facilities to the surrounding villages. It is here that the activities of various nation-building departments, peoples' organizations, private sector, and other agencies operating in the rural areas are integrated for area planning and development. The *markaz* is the co-terminus with the basic tier of the local government system to ensure popular participation at the grass-root level. The village Co-operatives are federated at the *markaz* to carry out economic activities for the benefit of the primary units.

iii) *District Level:* The selected District Council is responsible for financing, supervising, co-ordinating, and evaluating the development projects in the District. At the District level, the technical departments have the responsibility of back-stopping their functionaries in all the *marakiz* of the district.

iv) *Provincial Level:* The local government and Rural Development Department at the provincial headquarters is responsible for laying down operational targets, formulating policies, allocating required funds for rural development, and monitoring *markaz* plans in the provinces. The Rural Development Board, presided over by the Provincial Chief Executive, co-ordinates and evaluates the work of various departments in the field of Rural Development. The Board is also responsible for policy-making, budgeting, and approval of plans in keeping with national priorities.

v) *Federal Level:* The local government and Rural Development Division is responsible for policy guidance, co-ordination, follow-up actions, evaluation, and international assistance for provincial programmes of rural development. The Division is also responsible for planning and execution of rural development programmes in the federal capital area. A high-powered National Council for Rural Development and Local Government (NCRD and LG) has been constituted under the Chief executive to enable the representatives of the farmers to sit with federal and provincial executives and concerned senior officials to review the progress of rural development and to formulate policy guidelines for speedy implementation of IRDP in the country within the framework of local government institutions.

To meet immediate economic needs, the arrangement envisaged in the IRDP is to organize multi-purpose village Co-operatives that would initiate group action to secure economic and social services for their members. Although these societies are named on the pattern of traditional Co-operatives, they are basically different. They not only receive and distribute loans but they also act as grass-root forums for discussing problems and spelling out felt needs. As the villages get organized and registered into primary Co-operatives, they will federate into a bigger unit at the *markaz* called the Markaz Co-operative Federation. The Federation would act as a link between the farm and the remote market.

A hundred and thirty-seven *marakiz* were set up all over the country during 1972-7. In the absence of local government institutions, efforts were also made to organize the people into village Co-operatives so as to ensure their participation in developmental activities. Over 2,000 Co-operative societies were organized in ninety-one *marakiz*. The primary Co-operatives federated themselves into *markaz* federations in twenty-three *marakiz*.

The main activity of the *markaz* federations in the Punjab was to arrange farm inputs for the member societies besides providing a link between the people and government. In NWFP, however, the *markaz* federations have also undertaken land development operations such as providing wells for both drinking and irrigation purposes, constructing diversion spurs, etc.

Table 12.2: Evaluation of the IRD Programme

Programme Dimension	Manawala (Punjab)	Battal (NWFP)
Centrality	No significant change in Manawala town's role except for the location of *markaz* offices.	No significant change in Battal village's role except for the location of *markaz* offices.
Integration of public services:	Not many departmental representatives posted at the *markaz*.	Many departmental representatives seconded to *markaz*. No significant change in availability of services.
Simultaneous delivery of agricultural inputs.	*Markaz* supplementing market channels for the supply of seed and fertilizer. Many essential farming needs remain unattended. Farm planning non-existent.	Little visible effort to deliver agricultural inputs. Farm planning non-existent.
Organization and mobilization of people.	Initial success in setting up or adopting existing Co-operative societies. Little follow-up and petering out of enthusiasm.	Co-operative societies very popular and more being demanded. These are *ad hoc* groups mainly interested in obtaining public funds for civil works.
People's awareness and local leadership.	Fairly high level of general awareness about rights and needs. The IRDP is only a coincidental factor in the emergence of this feeling.	High level of awareness. Considerable interest in *Markaz* civil works. Most of the Co-operative societies' leaders belong to the rural bourgeoisie. Generally, they are small shopkeepers-cum-farmers with some education and considerable influence.
Improving living conditions infra-structural development.	No civil works undertaken on behalf of *markaz*. Health, education, and welfare services expanding generally and incrementally. The IRDP has not given any special stimulus to these efforts.	Numerous schemes for building village roads field terracing, and water supply underway. Health, education, and welfare services not affected much by the IRDP. No overall plan for civil works.
Target population and beneficiaries.	Farmers are in general beneficiaries though middle class and influential persons benefitting more directly.	Possibilities of general public benefitting from civil works. More direct benefits for leaders of Co-operative societies.

Source: M.A. Qadeer, *An Evaluation of the Integrated Rural Development Programme*, Monograph No. 19, PIDE, Islamabad, 1977.

12.5.2 Evaluation of the IRD Programme

The only evaluation of the IRD Programme is Qadeer (1977)[19] which is based mainly on two *marakiz* (one each in Punjab and NWFP) and it is therefore difficult to generalize from these findings for the entire programme. He has presented a summary Table on his findings which is reproduced as Table 12.2. He states that, 'agricultural production processes are undergoing changes under the influence of farmers' initiative and a variety of public and private channels of supply. The IRDP has not made any notable contribution to this trend, (rather) it has coasted along with it'.[20]

As regards non-agricultural job opportunities, he states that the two *marakiz* could not initiate new productive activities which might have increased job opportunities. However, the rural economies of the *marakiz* were being diversified through focus of commercialization and public investments. In Manawala (one of the *marakiz*) a rigorous carpet weaving cottage industry had emerged spontaneously but the IRDP did not take any systematic measures to either reinforce or accelerate these trends. In conclusion he states,

> 'the IRDP has attracted the same class of rural bourgeoise, *safaid posh*, which normally appropriate any public development programme. In this case, the voluntary association with a Co-operative group further reinforced cliquish tendencies. Co-operative societies were *ad hoc* functional groups which could seldom be credited with local representatives. Whatever little benefits the IRDP confers (are) most (probably) being appropriated by the middle and upper classes.'

12.6 People's Works Programme (PWP)

The People's Works Programme was introduced by the People's Party Government in 1973 as a joint enterprise of the government and the people and its success, like the IRDP, depended on the motivation of the masses on a national scale. The aim was to undertake such labour-intensive projects as could be completed quickly through self-help with some financial support from the government. It aimed at enhancing employment opportunities and improving rural infrastructure. Under the PWP, priority was given to such productive projects of short duration as would build up the economy through the provision of basic capacities and amenities in as many sectors as possible. The main fields included in this programme were: link roads, school buildings, small irrigation works, health units, drinking water facilities, tree plantation, industrial homes for women, and cottage industries, etc.

The total allocation during 1972-7 (including non-development) was Rs 1,004 million of which only Rs 888 million showed a utilization rate of 88.5 per cent.

On an average, 50 per cent of the funds were spent on improving communication network, 1.86 per cent on expanding irrigation facilities, 0.21 per cent on housing, 4.55 per cent on the extension of education and adult literacy, 2.03 per cent on the construction of health dispensaries, and 31.13 per cent on miscellaneous infrastructure works such as village sanitation, drinking water supply, etc.

It has been estimated that the number of man-years created through PWP for the three provinces of Punjab, Sind, and NWFP during 1973-4 were equal to 22,000 of which 12,000 were regular employees of PWP including 6,000 *Sipah-i-Khidmat* volunteers in the Punjab. The main reason for the low employment generation was the overwhelming reliance, for the construction of roads and buildings, on contractors who preferred to use capital-intensive methods to avoid labour management difficulties.

12.7 Agrovilles Development Programme

The pattern of urban development during the last two decades indicated a rapid increase of population in a few large cities and a weakening of the traditional distribution of population in small urban settlements. In order to arrest the rapid migration from villages to large cities, it was considered necessary to develop small towns and medium size cities through the location of new productive enterprises and the provision of educational, health, water supply, waste disposal, energy, transport, and other facilities. The successful development of small towns in rural environments was expected to reduce the movement of population, prevent large-scale transfer of people to metropolitan areas, and underpin smaller urban settlements. For this purpose a new programme called the 'Agrovilles Development Programme' was launched in 1973.

The financial allocations made to the Agrovilles Development Programme during 1972-7 amounted to Rs 34 million of which Rs 23 million or 66.1 per cent was utilized.

The achievements of this programme have been extremely modest. So far only five sites including the 'Badin Agroville' in Sind are reported to have been developed.

When the scheme was launched in 1973, it was contemplated that under the IRDP the *markaz* will ultimately develop into agrovilles and absorb surplus farm labour from the surrounding rural areas by providing employment opportunities in various pursuits. However, because of organizational and financial constraints, the programme was not able to take off properly. Although reliable statistics are not available to indicate the employment opportunities generated by this programme, Badin Agroville which is reported to have been partially completed has created roughly 150 jobs, in terms of man-years, on regular basis and 1,300 jobs on casual basis.

12.8 Rural Development Strategy for the Fifth Five Year Plan (1978-83)

The Fifth Plan emphasized rural development as a major constituent of total national effort with the following major objectives:[21]

a. To meaningfully integrate rural development with the national socio-economic development effort.
b. To reduce the burden of underemployment.
c. To increase the density of services provided to agriculture and other rural activities.
d. To improve rural infrastructure.
e. To make a beginning towards providing social amenities to target groups.
f. To create an institutional framework to ensure community participation in the implementation of the rural development programme.

As regards rural industries it states that small-scale enterprises based on agricultural raw materials will be located in the rural areas. These industries include rice and wheat milling, *gur* and sugar making, oil crushing, cotton ginning, hoisery and other textile crafts, carpets, leather, and footwear. Efforts are also to be made to develop new industries based on agricultural by-products and waste products like molasses, wheat, and rice straw, etc. On the basis of a review of the IRDP and People's Works Programmes, new institutional arrangement is being suggested at the local level to support the rural development strategy.

There are two alternative models both viable in different local circumstances. The first model will be a two tier system. The top tier will be the district council, at the district level, with the *markaz* council providing the bottom tier. The *markaz* council, having jurisdiction over twenty to thirty villages, will be headed by a Rural Development Officer with all the line departments at the *markaz* level represented on it.

The second model consists of a three tier system. At the lowest level there will be a union council with about ten villages. The intermediate tier will be the *markaz* covering an area equivalent to about fifty to seventy-five villages.

The main functions of the proposed institutions will be the following:

a. Construction and maintenance of primary and secondary schools, basic health units, rural health centres, rural roads, drinking water supply and sanitation systems, and miscellaneous small-scale local schemes.
b. Co-ordination and overall monitoring of the total development programme for the district *markaz*.
c. Facilitating the formation of associations to per-

form tasks that can only be done collectively or can be performed better collectively, for example, consumer associations for distribution of electricity, farmers' associations for water course management, associations for distribution of agricultural inputs, Co-operative marketing associations, etc.

d. Mobilization of local resources through voluntary contributions, taxes on property, consumption, and other sources identified by the community (except trade) and fees and charges for the use of utility services provided by the councils such as water supply, sanitation.

12.9 Conclusion

The limited success of the programmes so far implemented has been shown clearly. The IRDP and Rural Works Programmes are still in operation although some modifications have been suggested.

It is difficult to generalize about the programmes' limited achievements. As was shown earlier (Table 12.1) the funds allocated to them have been extremely meagre. Also none of the programmes were implemented for long enough to be given a reasonable chance of success.

However, we have come a very long way from the simple idealism of the planners as reflected in the Village Aid Programmes. The realization that transforming the rural structure will need more than a few selfless village workers has finally dawned. The argument that the existing social structure and property relations in the rural areas are factors which have never seriously been taken into consideration when either formulating or analysing the success or failure of these programmes is certainly very correct and this has played a very important role in the limited success of these programmes.

NOTES

1. Government of Pakistan, *First Five Year Plan*, National Planning Board, 1957, p. 16.
2. Ibid., p. 29.
3. Ibid., Chapter 14, pp. 192-212.
4. Ibid., section entitled 'The Special Problems of Rural Industries', paras 44-8, p. 205.
5. Ibid., pp. 99-100.
6. Ibid., p. 102.
7. Government of Pakistan, *Second Five Year Plan*, Planning Commission, 1960, p. 393.
8. Ibid., p. 394.
9. The institution of Basic Democracies was created by Ayub Khan in 1959. It was to be a form of elected local self-government entrusted with limited development activities to be undertaken in their areas. The system comprised of four tiers viz., Union Council, *Thana/Tehsil* Councils District Councils, and Divisional Councils. Ayub Khan used the Basic Democracies as the electoral college for the elections of President and National and Provincial Assemblies in the 1962 Constitution. The fact that they were excessively politically oriented is normally cited as the major cause for their failure in developmental efforts.
10. Government of Pakistan, *Second Five Year Plan*, Planning Commission, 1960, p. 394.
11. Government of Pakistan, *Final Evaluation of the Second Five Year Plan*, Planning Commission, 1966.
12. Government of Pakistan, *Third Five Year Plan*, Planning Commission, 1965, p. 594.
13. Ibid., p. 596.
14. Akhtar Hameed Khan, 'The Ghost of Comilla', *Integrated Rural Development Review*, December 1975, Vol. I, No. 1, Rural Development Wing, Government of Pakistan, 1975, p. 76.
15. Government of Pakistan, *Fourth Five Year Plan*, Planning Commission, 1970, p. 345.
16. Ministry of Food and Agriculture, Government of Pakistan, IRDP, *A Revolutionary Approach*, March 1973, Chapter 4.
17. Asghar Ali and Ahmed Saeed Khan, 'An Economic Evaluation of Integrated Rural Development Programme with Special Reference to Shadab Pilot Project', *Pakistan Economic and Social Review*, Vol. XVII, Autumn-Winter 1979, No. 3-4.
18. Ibid., p. 262.
19. M.A. Qadeer, *An Evaluation of the Integrated Rural Development Programme*, Monograph No. 19, PIDE, Islamabad, 1977.
20. Ibid., p. 67.
21. Government of Pakistan, *Fifth Five Year Plan*, Planning Commission, 1978.

PART IV

INDUSTRIAL AND COMMERCIAL POLICIES

13 Pakistan's Industrialization Experience

13.1 Introduction

Pakistan's growth experience over the last thirty-five years bears testimony to the pursuit of economic policies which were heavily biased in favour of the industrial sector and against the agricultural sector, especially during the fifties and sixties. Before we examine Pakistan's industrial record in some detail and analyse critically the factors which have influenced industrial growth, let us first raise a more basic issue: why should a developing country, predominantly agricultural at the time of independence, have made such a great effort, at considerable cost, to achieve rapid industrialization? The answer to this question, although deeply rooted in most developing countries' perception of the principal causes of their underdevelopment, is no longer as simple and straightforward as it had seemed in the early fifties.

As a starting off point, most developing countries, especially those which had been colonialized, viewed their past history as one of economic 'exploitation' by the colonial powers. This they attributed, to a large extent, to the economic strength of the colonial country gained after the 'industrial revolution' which had made it possible to gain control of the colonies as well as to exploit their economic resources. The mechanism of resource transfer between the colonial power and the colony was seen to take place mainly through the transformation of the latter into an agricultural hinterland to supply raw materials for the industries of the former and to serve as a market for their industrial goods. The enforcement of 'free trade' policies led in many cases to the destruction of the indigenous local small-scale industries leading to unemployment and impoverishment for those who were dependent on it for a living.[1] Also, the inequitable terms of trade between raw materials and manufactures led to the transfer of real economic resources from the agricultural based to the industrialized economy. It was mainly because of this that both the theory of 'comparative advantage', which advocated that the developing countries should specialize in agriculture, and the prescription of 'free trade' advocated by the advanced industrialized countries began to be viewed by most developing countries as leading to an unfair international division of labour. These theories baised the gains of trade heavily in favour of the industrialized countries and perpetuated underdevelopment and poverty in the backward ones.

With these 'historical' factors serving as a background, a number of other important arguments were put forward which further reinforced the case for the industrialization of developing countries. An important reason was the need to create employment especially as the process of development would, with the introduction of modern technology, lead to labour displacement from the agricultural sector. In many developing countries this sector was already overpopulated and it would be difficult to create employment even for the increasing rural population. Another reason was the need to reduce the dependence on the agricultural exports of a few commodities to earn.badly needed foreign exchange. These exports were seen to be subject to sharp cyclical fluctuations in prices in international markets as well as to suffer from declining terms of trade in relation to manufactured goods. Another important factor in favour of industrialization was, as had been seen from the development process in the industrialized countries, that it was only within the industrial sector that the gains of sustained productivity growth over time, the so-called 'dynamic economies of scale', were to be found which were the result of technological progress and increasing returns to scale and which were found to a far lesser extent in other sectors of the economy.[2]

With these strong arguments given in favour of industrialization it was not surprising that most developing countries at the time of independence identified the process of industrialization as a prerequisite for economic development and rapid economic growth, to reduce technological dependence on industrialized countries, to achieve genuine self-reliance, and to reap the gains of sustained productivity growth over time.

In most cases, and this was especially true of Pakistan, this was sought to be achieved through import substitution. Although this strategy was initially successful in achieving rapid industrial growth, it contained certain inherent difficulties. In most cases import substituting industrialization was promoted by a policy of heavy protection, low interest rates and over valued currency, and fiscal concessions. This led to a marked bias in favour of capital-intensive large-scale industries with the excessive use of scarce capital and inadequate participation of small-scale industries. There was hence little expansion in the demand for labour and the strategy did little to solve the pressing problems of unemployment and underemployment with which most developing countries, including Pakistan, were faced. Furthermore, the pro-industrial policies were implemented mainly at the expense of the agricultural sector which was squeezed (through adverse terms of trade) to finance industrial development. This neglect of the agricultural sector led to the gradual exhaustion of the domestic market for the easy import substitutes and resulted in a slowing down of industrial growth. These two factors, together with the rural sectors' inability to provide increased employment (a situation worsened by the adoption of labour displacement technology), became crucial in causing underemployment, real wage stagnation, and inequality of income distribution.

The major attacks against this strategy of industrialization came mainly from three directions. The first were the so-called 'efficiency arguments' which put forward strong evidence to show that as a result of protection (and/or import controls) the industrial structure was highly 'inefficient' when valued in terms of 'international' or 'world' prices and that a substantial portion of value added (between one-half to two-third) was the result of the protection given to the domestic industry. The second (and their arguments in many cases followed from the first) were those who argued that the neglect of the agricultural sector and the small-scale manufacturing sector in favour of the large-scale industrial sector had been a mistake and that the continuing poverty and the lack of impact of industrial growth on the living standards of the vast majority of the people could be traced to the pro-industrial bias in the development strategy. The third view was diametrically opposed to the first two in that it argued that the industrialization process which had unfolded was one which led to further dependence on the advanced industrialized countries and that the institutional framework in which industrial development had taken place had made it impossible for the country to achieve genuine self-reliance which had been the argument for industrialization in the first place.

Our aim in this and the subsequent chapter on industrialization is to critically evaluate Pakistan's industrial record over the last thirty-five years and to see to what extent the criticisms levelled against its industrial experience are justified and what are the major strengths and weaknesses of the industrial structure which has emerged.

13.2 Important Features of Pakistan's Industrial Development

Pakistan's industrial experience, shown mainly in terms of the large-scale manufacturing sector (defined as units employing more than ten people and using power in its operations), for which reliable statistics are available, is viewed in terms of growth rates over different sub-periods, the breakdown of industrial goods produced between capital, intermediate, and consumer goods and the production of major industries.

13.2.1 Growth

Growth rates were exceedingly high during the fifties and the sixties although in both decades there was a distinct slowing down in the second half as compared to the first. Although growth rates in the fifties must be viewed keeping in mind the small industrial base from which the economy started, this was certainly not true of the sixties when high industrial growth rates were achieved from a substantial base built up in the fifties (Table 13.1). During 1972-7, with the impact on the economy of the break-up of the two wings of the country, the increase in oil prices and the international recession, the attempt to create a substantial base of heavy and basic industry in the public sector, and the reduced role of the private sector in industrial development, the growth rate of large-scale manufacturing declined substantially. In the last five years there has been substantial recovery mainly as a result of a better export performance and a more liberal import policy, which improved the levels of capacity utilization, and also because a number of long gestation industrial projects established in the earlier years of the seventies has started production.

The growth in the small-scale industry till 1969-70 may well be under-estimated as the data compiled by the CSO was based on an indirect estimation technique which equates the growth in small-scale industry to the growth rate of population. Growth rates for the seventies are based on the Statistics Division's Survey of Small and Household Manufacturing Industries, 1969-70, and Punjab SHMI Survey 1975-6. However, certain other studies suggest that the growth

Table 13.1: Growth Rates in Manufacturing
Pakistan (West)

	1949-50 to 1954-5	1954-5 to 1959-60	1959-60 to 1964-5	1964-5 to 1969-70	1972-3 to 1976-7	1976-7[1] to 1981-2
Large-scale	23.6	7.7	16.9	9.9	1.5	9.4
Small-scale[2]	2.3	2.3	2.9	2.9	7.4	7.3

1. Since 1976-7 was an unusually bad year (because of political unrest) the average for the years 1974-5 and 1975-6 were taken for the large-scale sectors.
2. Till 1969-70, the growth rate of the small-scale sector was assumed to be the same as the population growth rate.
Source: Government of Pakistan, *Pakistan Economic Survey, 1981-2,* Islamabad, 1982.

Table 13.2: Structure of Value Added in Large-Scale Manufacturing
(At 1959-60 prices)
Pakistan (West)

	1959-60	1964-5	1969-70	1975-6
Total large-scale manufacturing	100.0	100.0	100.0	100.0
Consumer goods	71.0	61.8	70.8	64.7
Intermediate goods	10.3	15.5	12.8	16.1
Capital goods	18.7	22.7	16.4	19.2

Source: J. Hamid, *Choice of Technology, Employment and Industrial Development,* PIDE, Monograph, 1978.

rate may in fact be even higher at around 12 per cent in the seventies.[3]

13.2.2 Structure of Output

From 1950 to the mid-sixties, the expansion in industry was largely in the light consumer goods and easy processing category (Table 13.2). After this there was a shift, especially during the seventies, towards intermediate and capital goods industries. This change does not emerge clearly from Table 13.2 mainly because capital goods have long gestation periods and therefore the impact of investment in the seventies is not clearly reflected in the data available.

The production of major manufacturing

Table 13.3: Production of Selected Manufacturing Industries

	1949-50	1959-60	1969-70	1981-2
Cotton yarn (million kilogram)	12.1	160.4	273.2	324.9
Cotton cloth (million square metres)	46.3	455.0	606.5	307.9
Sugar (000 tonnes)	17	84	610	851
Vegetable ghee (000 tonnes)	4	29	126	505
Cigarettes (million)	1,488	8,172	22,369	35,891
Cycle tyres/tubes (000s)	112	3,079	6,727	9,409
Cement (000 tonnes)	395	982	2,656	3,538
Fertilizer urea (000 tonnes)	–	–	206.3	828.4
Bicycles (000s)	–	na	160.1	327.3
Iron and steel products (000 tonnes)	–	–	196.1	494.7
Paper board (000 tonnes)	–	7.9	25.6	27.3

Source: Government of Pakistan, *Pakistan Economic Survey, 1981-2,* Islamabad, 1982.

Table 13.4: Manufactured Exports
(Rs million)

	1965-6	per cent	1969-70	per cent	1977-8	per cent	1980-1	per cent
Textiles								
Cotton and cotton products (excluding cotton garments)	250.1	63	511.6	61	2,871.3	52	4,539.9	44
Garments and hosiery	9.1	2	24.9	3	138.7	2	745.1	7
Synthetic textiles	5.0	1	14.8	2	154.0	3	1,272.3	12
Non-textiles								
Leather tanned	74.9	19	107.0	13	636.5	12	891.9	9
Footwear	8.2	2	29.0	3	71.6	1	100.8	–
Cement	0.2	2	20.5	2	3.2	–	–	–
Tobacco raw and manufactured	0.7	–	14.4	2	126.1	2	53.7	–
Carpets and rugs	23.2	6	64.7	8	1,170.8	21	2,243.3	22
Surgical instruments	7.1	2	18.4	2	160.5	3	264.0	3
Sports goods	19.1	5	32.7	4	194.9	4	312.3	3
All manufactured exports	397.6	100	838.0	100	5,527.6	100	10,423.3	100

Source: Government of Pakistan, *Pakistan Economic Survey, 1981-2,* Islamabad, 1981.

industries for selected years is shown in Table 13.3. Considering the fact that industrial production was almost non-existent at the time of Independence, the growth of output, especially in consumer goods, has been substantial. This was especially true of the growth of the textiles, food, and tobacco manufactures in the fifties and sixties and the growth of output of cement, chemicals, engineering, and paper and board during the sixties and the seventies.

13.2.3 Manufactured Exports

The structure of Pakistan's manufactured exports is given in Table 13.4. It is quite clear that industrial exports, like the whole industrial structure, have been heavily dominated by textiles especially cotton textiles. This tendency has remained unchanged since the early sixties and the cotton textile group has always represented from one-half to more than two-thirds of manufactured exports.

The major increase in manufactured exports took place during 1965-6 and 1969-70 when they grew at over 20 per cent per annum. There was a boost in exports after 1972 mainly because of favourable international conditions and a shift from East Pakistan to the world market. However, exports stagnated after 1974 because of international recession and a stagnation in domestic production. After 1978, there has been substantial improvement although the growth of individual manufacturing goods has been unstable and suggests that manufactured exports may have grown irrespective of government policies.

13.2.4 Employment

Employment in the manufacturing sector had increased from 900,000 in 1950-1 to about 3

Table 13.5: Employment in Industry

	1950-1	1960-1	1971-2	1977-8	1982-3
Manufacturing (million)	0.9	1.84	2.28	2.82	3.37
Large-scale (million)	na	0.34	0.48	0.58	0.69
Small-scale (million)	na	1.50	1.80	2.24	2.68
Large-scale manufacturing (per cent)	na	18.5	21.0	20.6	20.5
Small-scale manufacturing (per cent)	na	81.5	79.0	79.4	79.5

Source: (i) J. Hamid, *Choice of Technology, Employment and Industrial Development*, PIDE, Monograph, 1978 for 1950-1. (ii) For other years, ILO/ARTEP, *Employment and Structural Change in Pakistan—Issues for the Eighties*, Mimeograph, Bangkok, 1983.

Table 13.6: Capital Intensities in Large-Scale Manufacturing
(At 1959-60 prices)

	Capital labour ratio (Rs per man)				Capital output ratio			
	1959-60	1964-5	1969-70	1975-6	1959-60	1964-5	1969-70	1975-6
Consumer goods	10,015	11,308	10,045	10,890	3.07	1.90	1.18	1.59
Intermediate goods	20,363	23,800	45,115	40,336	3.14	1.93	4.27	3.87
Capital goods	8,841	7,702	8,122	14,080	2.58	1.76	1.90	1.91
Total large-scale manufacturing	10,361	11,126	12,660	14,842	3.00	1.87	1.70	2.02

Source: J. Hamid, *Choice of Technology, Employment and Industrial Development*, PIDE, Monograph, 1978.

million in 1977-8 (Table 13.5). Almost three quarters of this employment was in the small-scale sector.[4] There was little increase in the total employment in the large-scale manufacturing sector in the seventies reflecting both a slowing down in growth rates of output and the highly capital-intensive nature of the industrial investment which took place during this period. The increase in employment in small-scale manufacturing in the seventies was the result of much higher growth rates of output in this sector as a result, amongst others, of the drastic devaluation in 1972 which reduced the effective protection given to the large-scale sector and increased the protection for the small-scale sector.

13.2.5 Capital Intensities

In Tables 13.6 and 13.7 estimates of capital intensities in both the large-scale and small-scale manufacturing sectors are provided. Data on estimates of the capital stock are not very reliable given the difficulties of measuring capital stock over time. However, the data do provide us with some basis of comparisons between the large-scale and small-scale for creating a job in these respective sectors (capital labour ratios) as well as the average capital cost of output in the two sectors. If we were to convert the capital labour ratios in the large-scale manufacturing sector for 1975-6 into current prices, it would come to Rs 19, 457 per man as compared to Rs 5,158 per man for the small-scale sector. Similarly, the capital output ratio for the large-scale sector in 1975-6 was 0.82 as compared to 0.45 for the small-scale sector.

In the large-scale manufacturing sector the highest capital intensities are for the intermediate goods industries mainly because three industries included in it (fertilizer, paper, and petroleum products) have unusually high capital intensity. The reason for the much lower capital intensity of the large-scale capital goods sector is that most of the existing industries in this sector were in fact in the nature of small engineering works producing to job orders rather than being highly automated works capable of mass production. On the other hand, a large number of consumer goods industries were process industries with substantial automation.

The bias in favour of the large-scale industrial sector can be seen from estimates of investment in industry divided between large-scale and small-scale (Table 13.8). From

Table 13.7: Capital Intensities in Small-Scale Industry (At current prices)

	Capital labour ratio (Rs per man)		Capital output ratio	
	1966-7	1975-6	1966-7	1975-6
Consumer goods	1,959	5,411	0.80	0.45
Intermediate goods	2,367	3,110	0.61	0.33
Capital goods	2,484	5,249	0.91	0.46
Total small-scale manufacturing	2,100	5,158	0.81	0.45

Source: J. Hamid, *Choice of Technology, Employment and Industrial Development*, PIDE, Monograph, 1978.

Table 13.8: Investment in Industry (Public plus Private)

	1949-50	1964-5	1969-70	1977-8	1981-2
Total fixed capital formation	100.0	100.0	100.0	100.0	100.0
Investment in industry	14.0	24.4	23.0	30.4	16.9
(a) Large-scale	12.6	22.1	20.3	28.2	16.88
(b) Small-scale	1.4	2.3	2.7	2.2	0.02
Small-scale investment as a per cent of total investment in industry	10.4	9.3	12.1	7.4	13.8

Source: (i) J. Hamid, *Choice of Technology, Employment and Industrial Development*, PIDE (Monograph), 1978 for 1949-50 and 1964-5. (ii) Government of Pakistan, *Pakistan Economic Survey, 1981-2*, Islamabad, 1982, for other years.

1964-5 till the early seventies, investment in industry was between 20 to 24 per cent of the total fixed investment for the economy as a whole and the share of the small-scale sector was between 9 to 12 per cent. During the seventies, the share of industry, mainly large-scale, increased substantially as investments in intermediate and capital goods peaked (especially the steel mill). More recently, the share has fallen to almost half this figure as these investments have been completed and no new major projects have been initiated.

13.2.6 Wages of Production Workers

What has been happening to the level of real wages in the economy during this period of substantial industrial development? The answer to this question is important for it would help us to determine whether there has been any improvement in the living standards of the production workers employed in the manufacturing sector. The overall period can be divided into three distinct sub-periods (Table 13.9). Between 1954 and 1962-3 there was hardly any increase in the real wages of workers in the large-scale sector. There was a significant increase between 1962-3 and 1965-6 but real wages again fell sharply over the next two years and in 1967-8 were at the same level as they had been in 1962-3. After

Table 13.9: Real and Money Wages of Production Workers in Large-Scale Manufacturing
(Rs) 1959-60 = 100

	Money wages		Real wages	
1954	981	90	1,122	103
1959-60	1,091	100	1,091	100
1962-3	1,189	109	1,110	102
1965-6	1,464	134	1,245	114
1967-8	1,536	141	1,116	102
1970-1	2,094	192	1,384	127
1974-5	4,953	454	1,730	159

Source: S. Guisinger, *Wages, Capital, Rental Values, and Relative Factor Prices in Pakistan,* Washington, IBRD, Staff Working Paper No. 287, 1978.

1967-8, the data does show a substantial increase till 1974-5 and, although it may not have been as significant as the data indicates, there was still an increase during this period.

Time series data for small-scale industries are not available. However, based on the information available, an IBRD study concludes, 'what is more surprising is the fact that average wages in large-scale firms are below those in the small and medium factories. This may be explained by differences in skill mix and industrial composition. Pakistan certainly does not conform to the pattern of a modern sector elite labour force widely separated in earnings and working conditions from the traditional sectors which characterized some developing economies'.[5]

13.3 Some Important Issues

Let us list some of the important preliminary issues which arise from our description of Pakistan's industrial development in the last thirty-five years.

a. The pace of industrial development which has led to the country acquiring a substantial industrial base by the end of the seventies.
b. The fluctuations in the growth rates between the fifties, sixties, and seventies as well as the significant differences between the first and second half of the fifties and sixties and the last three years of the seventies.
c. The very high level of protection afforded to the domestic industry and the 'efficiency' of the industrial structure which has emerged.
d. The high capital intensity as reflected in capital labour and capital output ratios of the large-scale manufacturing sector which has resulted in low employment generation in this sector.
e. The major share of industrial investment (which has been a significant portion of the total gross fixed investment in the economy) has been in the large-scale manufacturing sector with the small-scale sector receiving only about 10 per cent of the total.
f. Finally, the level of real wages of production workers did not see any significant increases during the period of high industrial growth in the fifties and sixties and the increase which did take place was in the seventies, a period of low

industrial growth. Also, the little evidence that exists does not support the proposition that the level of wages are higher in the large-scale sector as compared to the small-scale sector. In fact, there is evidence presented by certain agencies to show that average wages in large-scale firms are below those in the small and medium factories.

Some of the features mentioned above, especially the growth rate of the industrial sector, fluctuations in growth rate over time, and the bias in favour of consumer goods industries, have already been covered in the overall review in the earlier chapters. However, a number of important and specific issues as regards the growth of the industrial sector still remain and it is these that we will turn to in the next chapter. But before doing so, we review briefly the existing government policies which help determine the growth and pattern of industrial investment in the country.

13.4 | The Industrial Policy Framework

The industrial structure which has emerged has been mainly the result of government policy measures which created incentives for industrial investment. Some of the main features of the industrial policy framework are outlined so as to analyse the incentive system as it exists at the present. These consist mainly of the protection system, fiscal, and export incentives.

13.4.1 The Protective System

Quantitative Restrictions

In Pakistan the amount of protection given to an industry is determined not so much by the tariff structure but the quantitative restrictions which are generally the effective constraint on imports. The import licence system is based on a Free List and a Tied List. The Free List contains three parts: Part A covers those goods that can be imported by both commercial and industrial importers and includes various types of consumer goods as well as some raw materials and capital goods; Part B items are mainly raw materials and can only be imported by industrialists; and Part C imports are reserved for public sector agencies. The Tied List covers those items which can only be imported under country-specific agreements. All those goods not included in either the 'Free' or 'Tied' lists are, in practice, banned. Moreover, some Part C imports have at times been limited *de facto* through restrictions in foreign exchange allocations to public sector agencies or through limitations on value or volume. In addition, quantitative restrictions or licence entitlements for permitted items are imposed in accordance with foreign exchange availability.

The total number of items on the Import List is extremely large. In 1981-2, the Free List contained 505 items although the actual number would be larger as this reflects the count of products only by their common names. The number of items on the Tied List were twenty.[6] This system of listings originated in the early sixties and has evolved over the years mainly through consultations with commercial importers and industrialists. The combined effect of this mechanism of import control together with that of tariffs discussed below makes it exceedingly difficult (if not impossible) to determine the actual level of protection being applied to the industrial sector at any moment of time.

The Present Protective Tariff

Tariffs are imposed on both industrial finished goods and inputs. They are also used in the form of rebates as a major incentive for export promotion and the development of particular industries. In 1980-1, the incidence of import duties on all imports was 37 per cent with a 67 per cent average for consumer goods, 31 per cent for raw materials for consumer goods, 34 per cent for raw materials for capital goods, and 38 per cent for capital goods. While industrial tariffs reach a level of 200 per cent on some consumer goods, most rates fall in the range of 40 to 100 per cent.[7]

There has been no recent comprehensive investigation of the level of effective protection in Pakistan. But the low proportion of value-added in most of Pakistan's manufactured goods coupled with a wide range of tariff rates makes it almost certain that (a) the level of effective protection has been high on most commodities and (b) the rate of effective protection varies widely among individual goods. This important issue is taken up in more detail in Section 14.1.

13.4.2 Tax Incentives

The basic system of corporate income tax in Pakistan has been fairly stable over the years with an income tax of 30 per cent and a super tax of 30 per cent on profits. From 1977 onwards the government has introduced a number of general tax incentives including:

a. a reduction in the basic rate of corporate tax (income and super taxes combined) from 60 to 55 per cent;
b. elimination of the tax on bonus shares at the shareholder's level;
c. a tax credit (until 1983) equal to 15 per cent of the cost of machinery purchased for Balancing, Modernization, and Replacement (BMR);
d. reduction in the super tax on inter-corporate dividends from 15 per cent to 10 per cent for public companies and from 50 per cent to 30 per cent for private companies;
e. five year tax exemption for capital gains and dividend income declared by a new public company engaged in an industrial undertaking; and
f. an increase in the rate of initial depreciation on plant and machinery from 25 to 40 per cent.

Besides the above general tax incentives, additional tax incentives are provided at different rates and for different regions to direct industrial investment towards the less developed regions of the country. These include:

a. a five year exemption from corporate income tax and super tax on company profits;
b. tax credit of 15 to 30 per cent of the investment made in the share capital of another company; and
c. complete or partial exemptions from custom duties on plant and machinery.

At the moment there are thirteen regions or districts in the provinces of Baluchistan and NWFP which can benefit from all or some of these concessions.

The success of the general tax incentives in attracting private industrial investment in the past has been mixed as discussed in Section 7.2 although more recently there seems to have been a significant improvement. As regards location incentives, though in some areas the number of sanctioned projects has increased, most areas have failed to attract new investment mainly because the required manpower and infrastructure are not available.

13.4.3 Export Incentives

In order to encourage and diversify manufactured exports,[8] the government offers the following export incentives:

Custom Rebates

Export industries are entitled to a refund for all custom duties, and sales taxes paid on imported inputs, at rates between 3 to 35 per cent of total export value. Rates have been standardized for each industry and only firms exporting a new item need to authenticate duties and taxes paid.

Compensatory Rebates

Certain export industries are compensated for indirect taxes paid at rates varying between 7.5 to 12.5 per cent of the FOB value of exports. Originally these rebates were given only to the cotton textile industry but have now been extended to cover engineering goods, canvas footwear, acetate yarn, cutlery, sports goods, and surgical instruments.

Income Tax Rebate

Profits on exports qualify for a tax rebate of 55 per cent of the amount of income tax and super tax payable. The rebate applies to all types of exports except raw cotton and a few other specified items.

Balancing, Modernization, and Replacement Scheme

Export industries are allowed duty free import of machinery and equipment for balancing, modernization, and replacement.

Raw Material Replenishment Scheme

Exporters are allowed to import, duty free, raw materials used in the production of export and import inputs that would otherwise be banned.

Export Finance Scheme

Export finance is provided by scheduled banks at a concessional rate of 3 per cent per annum. The State Bank, in turn, provides refinancing to the banks at zero interest.

13.4.4 Other Incentives

Two incentive schemes which do not involve any tax or cash benefits but which may be considered as real incentive measures, because the volume of investments flowing through them has increased dramatically, are the Non-Repatriable Investment Scheme and the Pay-As-You-Earn-Investment Scheme. These are discussed briefly.

Non-Repatriable Investment Scheme (NRI)

This scheme is composed of a number of procedures basically directed at attracting savings and funds owned, and hitherto not repatriated, by Pakistanis living abroad. One of the measures grants non-repatriable foreign investment the same protection in terms of nationalization and compensation as given to other foreign investment under the Foreign Private Investment (Promotion and Protection) Act, 1976. Procedures have been modified to ensure rapid sanctioning of investment proposals. The sponsors are allowed to bring in non-repatriable investments without producing certificates to prove that the funds have not originated from direct or indirect transactions with Pakistan. Submission of a surveyor's certificate, normally required for import of second-hand rebuilt machinery, has also been dispensed with in the case of non-repatriable investment. The Investment Promotion Bureau, while examining cases of non-repatriable investment, does not insist on firming up rupee financing arrangements before approving a project. Investors under the NRI also receive the incentives given to other industries.

Pay-As-You-Earn-Investment Scheme (PAYE)

PAYE was originally introduced in 1962 but was greatly modified in 1967 and 1973. Under the scheme, plant machinery and equipment may be imported from suppliers who are willing to accept payment from the export earnings of the industrial unit over a period of time. The government may allow advance payment in foreign exchange for purchase of a plant and machinery (up to 15 per cent of the C and F value of the machinery) provided that sponsors will repatriate the foreign exchange to Pakistan or pay to the government a penalty of 27 per cent of the advance payment plus 9 per cent interest from the date of remittance if machinery is not imported. Projects established under PAYE are allowed a maximum of 50 per cent of the FOB value of their foreign exchange earnings for meeting debt liability and other foreign exchange payments on account of royalty, technical fees, and incidental charges.

There are a number of important issues regarding the industrial policy framework which presently exists in the country.

The first is regarding the combined effect of the system of import controls and tariffs on the level of protection afforded to the domestic manufacturing sector. This important question regarding the 'efficiency' of the industrial structure is discussed in Section 14.1 although, as we shall see, there are no studies presently available for the seventies.

The other important question, which in many ways is closely related to the first, is whether the present system of incentives favours import substitution industries as compared to those industries which produce a substantial output for exports. This again requires a comprehensive review of the import tariff and export taxes on all Commodities. A partial study[9] carried out in the mid-seventies on major exports indicated that many important exports do not have positive effective protection, while others (for example, cloth, canvas, carpets, shoes, sports goods, and surgical instruments) are effectively taxed by the protection system (effective protection rates are less than unity). Thus the export incentives may have turned into disincentives.

What is most urgently required is a comprehensive review of the incentives system including taxes, subsidies, non-tariff controls, and tariffs. Recognizing this urgency, the government has commissioned the Pakistan Institute of Development Economies (PIDE) to undertake a study to assess the levels of effective protection[10] (and related measures) and to gauge the efficiency of production for export or for import substitution.

NOTES

1. The classical illustration of this was the destruction of the weaving industry in India in the nineteenth century through the imports of textiles from Britain mostly duty-free or at payment of a nominal duty. (See R. Dutt, *The Economic History of India,* London, 1901, for a more detailed account of this process and the hardships faced by the weavers as a result of these measures.)
2. For the argument that in industry not only increasing returns but also the dynamic economies of scale are to be found, see N. Kaldor, *Causes of The Slow Rate of Economic Growth of the United Kingdom,* Cambridge, 1966 and by the same author, *Strategic Factors in Economic Development,* Ithaca, 1967.
3. N. Hamid, *Growth and Development of Small-Scale Industries in Pakistan,* Report submitted to ILO/ARTEP, Bangkok, 1982.
4. ILO/ARTEP, 'Employment and Structural Change in Pakistan—Issues for the Eighties', Bangkok, 1983.
5. IBRD, *The Role of Small-Scale Sector in Pakistan's Development : Opportunities and Constraints,* Washington, 1975.
6. IBRD, *Pakistan Economic Developments and Prospects,* Washington, 1982, Report No. 3802-Pak, p. 32.
7. Ibid., p. 31.
8. M. Zubair Khan, *The System of Export in Manufacturing Sector of Pakistan,* IBRD study, Washington, 1978.
9. Ibid.
10. The PIDE study is entitled, *Effective Protection and Incentives Reform.*

14 Important Issues in Industrial Development

In this chapter, we deal with some of the important issues regarding industrial development in Pakistan. The issues cover a wide range of subjects and touch upon some of the major controversies and debates which have figured prominently in recent literature. We start by analysing the criticism that the industrial structure which emerged in Pakistan, especially during the fifties and sixties, was highly 'inefficient' and was a result of the import substitution strategy pursued. The second issue which we look at is one which was very prominent in the late sixties and which focused on the question of concentration in the industrial sector especially in the pattern of ownership. The third important issue that we deal with is the performance of public sector enterprises during the People's Party government of which there has been considerable criticism though the arguments and evidence have never been substantiated. The fourth issue deals with the growth of the trade union movement in Pakistan and how the relative strength of labour and the existing labour laws have affected industrial relations and the level of real wages of the industrial workers. The fifth and last section deals with the development of small-scale industries mainly to show how government policy has been biased against it and has favoured the large-scale sector.

14.1 The Efficiency of Pakistan's Industrial Structure

During the fifties and sixties, the industrial sector was said to be thriving in that it was able to achieve very high industrial growth. It is, however, now argued that the problems which the industrial sector found itself facing in the seventies had its roots in the industrial structure established in the preceding two decades. It is alleged that the policies pursued during this period—generous fiscal incentives, high rates of protection, export subsidies, favourable exchange rates—led to the creation of an industrial structure that was highly 'inefficient' both economically and technically. A number of studies[1] found exceedingly high effective protection for most industries in Pakistan and negative value added at 'world prices' for a number of these in the mid-sixties. It is also suggested that management, operating in a highly profitable environment, had little incentive to control costs or to improve quality with the result that the general standard of management was extremely poor. Industrial performance in terms of output growth, exports, and investments may have given the 'appearance' of being highly satisfactory but this was more a reflection of strong incentives rather than actual efficiency. In the seventies, these basic industrial inefficiencies were laid bare by the abolition of the export bonus scheme, a considerable reduction in investment incentives, and changes in the pattern of world trade including the advent of recession and competition from Korea and Taiwan in the textile market in the Far East.

This 'inefficiency' of the industrial structure is illustrated by converting the share of the GDP of value added in manufacturing at domestic prices into 'world' prices. The results of an earlier exercise reduces it from 7 to 0.4 per cent in 1963-4 and shows that, compared to a number of other developing countries, value added in manufacturing in Pakistan was mainly the result of the high rates of protection which the industrial sector received (Table 14.1). Although the results of these studies are rough and outdated, a number of other studies[2] also found very high effective protection for most industries in Pakistan (higher for consumer goods than for capital and intermediate goods industries) and 'negative' value added at world prices for a number of these industries in the mid-sixties. In fact, it has also been suggested that many of the problems faced by the public sector in the seventies reflected the inefficient state of the enterprises taken over.

How valid are these criticisms forcefully put forward ever since the end of the sixties? Before we go into this it might be appropriate to go over the basic methodology used in the calculation of effective rates of protection and how we come up with such concepts as 'negative value added' by certain manufacturing industries. Basically, these exercises calculate the cost of inputs and the value of outputs first at 'market' or 'domestic' prices, which include protection and other subsidies, and compare these with the costs of inputs and the value of outputs of similar (or nearly so) goods at what they would be in the 'world' market or 'trading prices', i.e., if they were bought and sold in the open world market. The rate of effective protection is then defined as the per cent of value added due to protection.

Table 14.1: Value Added in Manufacturing Industries at Domestic and World Prices in Selected Developing Countries

Country	Year	Share of GDP at domestic prices	Share of GDP at world prices	(2)÷(1)
		(1)	(2)	(3)
Argentina	1958	31.3	22.5	.718
Brazil	1966	27.9	21.3	.763
Mexico	1960	19.0	17.2	.095
Philippines	1965	19.0	15.2	.800
Taiwan	1965	18.7	16.0	.855
Pakistan	1963-4	7.0	0.4	.057

Source: I.M.D. Little, D. Scotovsky, and M. Scott, *Industry and Trade in Some Developing Countries*, OECD, 1970, p. 75.

A simple version of this concept may be shown as follows:-

Value added in industry 'i' at 'market' or 'domestic' prices
= w = sale value of output minus cost of inputs
Value added in industry 'i' at 'world' or trading prices
= ŵ = sale value of output minus cost of inputs
Effective rate of protection or value added due to protection $= \frac{w - \hat{w}}{w}$

Let us illustrate by taking three different cases. Suppose value added at 'domestic' prices is a hundred but at 'world' prices is only ten. Then value added due to protection or the effective rate of protection is 90 per cent. In the second case, suppose value added at 'domestic' prices is again a hundred but at world prices is negative, i.e., sale value of output is less than the cost of inputs (say minus ten). In this case then, as the rate of effective protection is > 100, it would imply *negative value added* by that industry. What this means is that rather than add value to the inputs it uses, it actually 'loses' value when we evaluate the inputs and outputs at world prices. Finally, suppose value added at 'world' prices is greater than value added at domestic prices, then this would indicate that the protection system is discriminating against the output of that industry (for example, tariffs, on inputs exceed tariffs on output).

The result of such an exercise calculating the effective rate of protection for the sixties is available for 1963-4 only and some of the results of that study are reported in Table 14.2. The results show that five industries (edible oils, sugar refining, motor vehicle assembly, silk and artificial silk textiles, and wearing apparel) have effective protection in excess of 90 per cent. Of these, the first three show the value of output at 'world prices' to be less than the value of tradable inputs at 'world prices'. The other two have virtually no value added when both output and tradable inputs are valued at 'world prices'. Five more industries (rubber goods, plastic goods, metal products, cotton textiles, and jute textiles) show that more than two-thirds of value added was due to protection. In the case of a number of other important industries effective protection varied between 20 to 50 per cent.

The evidence put forward clearly showed the basic 'inefficiency' of the industrial structure, which had emerged by the mid-sixties, when compared to 'world prices'. Although it can be argued that any country starting the process of industrialization behind tariff barriers would show considerable 'inefficiency' in terms of 'world prices', there is still no doubt that the industrial structure in Pakistan was extremely inefficient even after fifteen years of industrialization. The reason for this was the incentive structure, created for the manufacturing sector, which put little or no pressure on the producers to cut down on costs especially capital costs of production. Also, little attention was given to the question of whether it was really beneficial for the country to set up an industry which would never really ever become internationally competitive and whose value added would in the extreme case continue to be negative even after many years of production behind highly protective barriers.

To what extent did this situation change in the seventies? This question becomes all the more important as far-reaching reforms, especially the abolition of the export bonus scheme and the devaluation in 1972, altered the incentives offered to the manufacturing sector. It is indeed unfortunate that no detailed study to see the effects of these reforms on the level of effective protection is available for this period. The only available evidence is for the levels of nominal protection (i.e., protection afforded by the tariff structure alone) for 1963-4, 1970-1, and 1972-3 as shown in Table 14.3. While the nominal rates of protection give us a very general idea of the structure of incentives, they do show that they had fallen significantly for all groups of industries. The drop is greatest for the consumer goods industries group (which nevertheless was still more highly protected than either the intermediate or the capital goods industries).

Table 14.2: Levels of Effective Protection from All Sources
Pakistan 1963-4

Industry (consumption goods)	Protection	Industry (intermediate goods)	Protection	Industry (capital goods)	Protection
Sugar	167	Jute textiles	65	Non-metallic mineral products	42
Edible oils	205	Thread and Thread-ball	45	Cement	33
Tea	–6	Saw milling	48	Basic metals	66
Cotton textiles	68	Tanning	49	Metal products	73
Silk and artificial silk	99	Rubber products	84	Non-electrical machinery	63
Footwear	37	Fertilizer	65	Sewing machines	45
Wearing apparel	95	Paints and Varnishes	57	Electrical machinery and equipment	42
Printing and publishing	14	Chemicals	53		
Soaps	69	Petroleum products	–5		
Matches	8	Paper products	59		
Plastic goods	77				
Sports goods	43				
Pens and pencils	65				
Electrical appliances	42				
Motor vehicles	105				
Simple average	68		52		58

Source: S.R. Lewis and S.E. Guisinger, 'The Structure of Protection in Pakistan', in *The Structure of Protection in the Developing Countries*, edited by B. Belasca.

However, as pointed out in Section 13.4, an idea of the present efficiency of the industrial structure and its bias in favour of import substitution industries, as compared to export industries, will be possible only after the results of the PIDE study are available.

14.2 Monopoly Power and the Concentration of Industrial Ownership in the Sixties

One of the most important and controversial issues to emerge during the sixties was the question of concentration in the ownership pattern of industrial and financial assets. The so-called slogan of the 'twenty-two families' owed its origin to a statement made by Mahbub-ul-Haq in April 1968, then Chief Economist of the Planning Commission, that twenty-two families controlled 66 per cent of the industrial assets and 87 per cent of the banking and insurance assets in the country. Haq, however, never substantiated the study on which these figures were based.

In this section we explore critically two broad areas of monopoly power. The first is

Table 14.3: Comparison of Protection Rates: Manufacturing Activities 1963-4, 1970-1, and 1972-3
(Per cent)

Sector	1963-4 Nominal Protection	1970-1 Nominal Protection	1972-3 Nominal Protection
Consumer goods			
Sugar	215	266	57
Edible oils	106	54	62
Cotton textiles	56	76	0
Other textiles	350	141	88
Printing and publishing	28	43	57
Soaps	94	43	34
Motor vehicles	249	270	61
Simple average	157	128	63
Intermediate goods			
Wood and lumber	73	85	108
Leather tanning	56	76	0
Rubber products	153	55	48
Fertilizers	15	25	na
Paints and varnishes	102	56	34
Chemicals	81	56	34
Petroleum products	107	121	65
Paper products	94	57	69
Simple average	85	66	43
Investment and related goods:			
Non-metallic mineral products	154	76	70
Cement	75	76	70
Basic metals	66	96	32
Metal products	95	102	64
Non-electrical machinery	89	81	44
Electrical machinery	60	83	47
Simple average	90	86	50
All industries simple average	110	92	52

Note: nva = negative value added at international prices;
nc = not calculable because of presence of negative value-added industries.

Source: S. Guisinger, 'Trade Policies and Employment: The Case of Pakistan', in *Trade and Employment in Developing Countries*, edited by Anne O. Krueger, NBER, 1981, p. 313.

the exercise of monopoly power at the industry level, i.e., to what extent was there concentration in the production of industrial goods and what influence did that have on prices. The second is to see to what extent was Haq's statement of the extreme concentration in the ownership of industrial and financial assets a true reflection of the situation as it existed by the end of the sixties.

Figure 14.1:

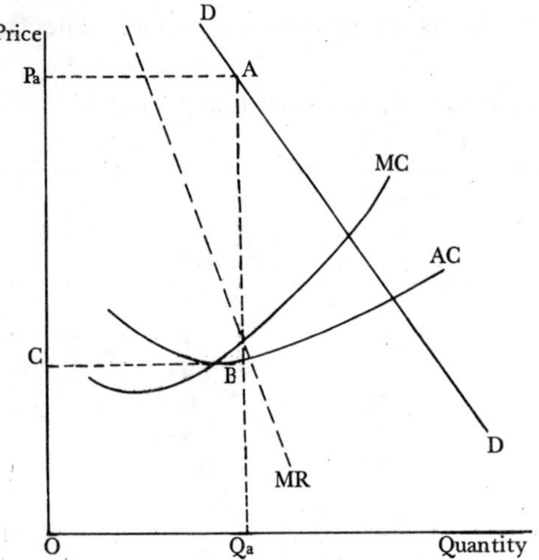

Source: L. White, *Industrial Concentration and Economic Power in Pakistan*, Princeton, 1974.

Figure 14.2:

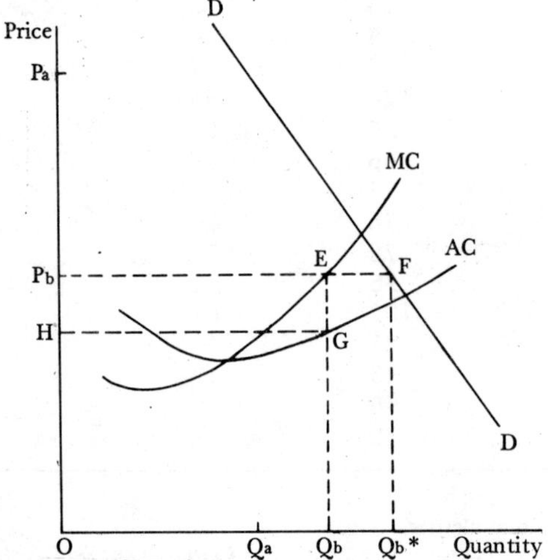

Source: L. White, *Industrial Concentration and Economic Power in Pakistan*, Princeton, 1974.

14.2.1 Monopoly Pricing

The effect of monopoly on prices in conventional economic theory is illustrated in Figure 14.1. Prices would be higher and production lower in a monopoly as compared to the competitive situation. However, in the manufacturing sector in Pakistan in the sixties, there were a number of other factors which also influ-

Figure 14.3:

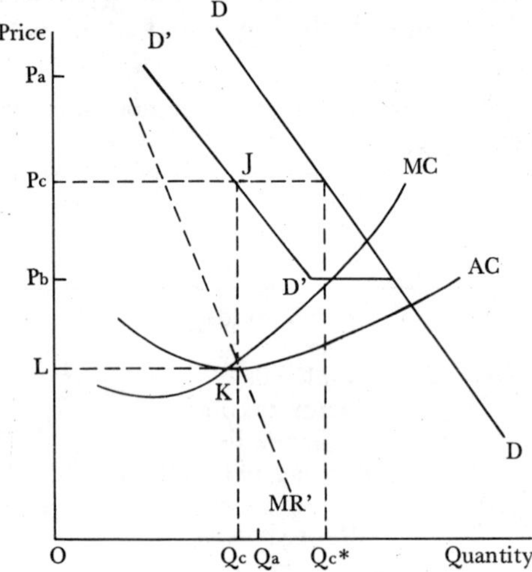

Source: L. White, *Industrial Concentration and Economic Power in Pakistan*, Princeton, 1974.

Figure 14.4:

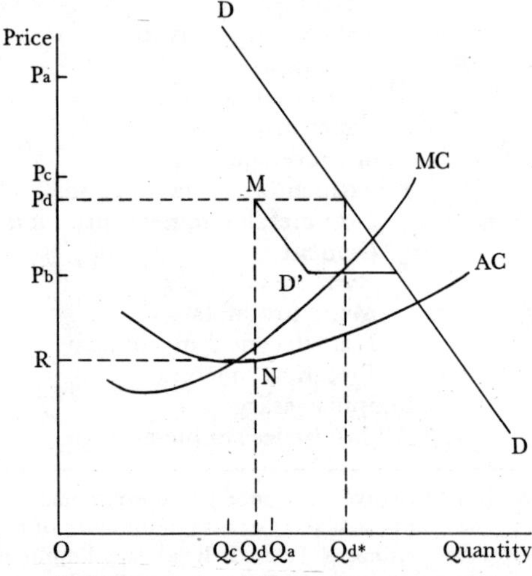

Source: L. White, *Industrial Concentration and Economic Power in Pakistan*, Princeton, 1974.

enced the prices of manufactured goods in the domestic market the most important of them being import restrictions and the terms and conditions of the availability of industrial raw materials. How this would influence monopoly power is illustrated in White's Model[3] (Figures 14.2 to 14.4) based on assumed situations in which (a) foreign goods were freely importable, (b) there were restrictions on the amount that could be imported, and finally (c) further additional imports could be made through bonus vouchers (as was the situation in the sixties).

These situations are illustrated by White with the aid of simple geometry. Figure 14.1 depicts the standard textbook monopoly equilibrium. The monopolist faces a demand curve DD and perceives a marginal revenue curve MR. He operates with marginal costs MC and average costs AC. He maximizes his profits by expanding his production to quantity Q_a where marginal costs equal marginal revenues. He charges a price P_a and he makes monopoly profits equal to the area P_aABC.

In Figure 14.2, foreign competing goods are freely importable at a CIF plus tariff price of P_b. The monopolist cannot raise his price above P_b and thus is prevented from exploiting his monopoly power. The effective demand curve that he faces is P_bFD. Price P_b is the price that rules in the market, quantity Q_b is produced domestically, and quantity Q_bQ_b* is imported. The monopolist's profits have been limited to P_bEGH. With a higher tariff, price P_b would be higher, more would be produced domestically, less would be imported, and the monopolist's profits would increase.

In Figure 14.3, import licences for only Q_cQ_c* in foreign goods are available at an importer's price (CIF plus tariff) of P_b. The demand schedule D'D' now facing the monopolist is parallel to the original but is shifted to the left by the amount Q_cQ_c* since, at all prices above the CIF plus tariff price of P_b, the demand for the monopolist's product is reduced by the amount of the licenced imports. But he is free to charge any price on the new demand schedule since only Q_cQ_c* can be imported. He will thus produce up to the point where he equates his marginal costs and his new marginal revenue curve MR'. He produces Q_c at a price P_c. His monopoly profits are P_cJKL. The more stringent the import licencing, the higher will be the monopolist's output, price, and profits. Those holding import licences make a windfall gain of P_c minus P_b on each unit of their imports. Import duties only absorb part of their windfall gain but do not affect the monopolist's output, price, or profits, until the duties get high enough to restrict the demand for imports below the licenced level.

In Figure 14.4, import licences for Q_dQ_d* in foreign goods at price P_b are available but additional goods can be imported at the CIF plus bonus vouchers plus tariff price of P_d. This places a price ceiling of P_d on the monopolist and restricts his demand curve to P_dMD'. In the figure, he chooses to produce Q_d with a price P_d that just forestalls the bonus voucher imports. His profits are P_dMNR. The height of the tariff, the price of bonus vouchers, and the stringency of licencing, all affect the monopolist's action.

White also points out that if the domestic producers themselves held the licences for the competing imports, then imports would no longer serve as any kind of check on the market power of the domestic producers. The entire market demand would be available to the domestic producers and the imports would be part of their supply.

Empirical Findings

Two studies have tried to test empirically the relationship between profitability and concentration across different industries during the sixties.

The first study was done by White[4] who examined the relationship between industrial profitability and three independent variables namely concentration, the dependence of an industry on imported raw materials, and the protection given to the industry from foreign competition. As a proxy for dependence on raw materials, White used the degree of capacity utilization to measure both the terms on which firms could get imported raw materials as well as their ability to get them freely. For the measure of protection, which was intended to represent the stringency of licencing for competitive imports, White used the figures given by Lewis and Guisinger (Table 14.2) to measure the difference between domestic and the CIF import price of various industrial goods for the year 1963-4.

White tested his model using cross-section data primarily from 1964 and 1965 and used a measure of industry profitability based on firms listed on the Karachi Stock Exchange (KSE). Due to the limited variety of firms listed on the KSE and the limited number of industries listed by Lewis and Guisinger, the sample was restricted to seventeen industries.

$$P = -0.37 + \underset{(0.68)\ (1.74)}{0.16C^{c}} + \underset{(2.25)}{0.08W^{b}} + \underset{(0.73)}{1.19CU} - \underset{(0.70)}{0.81CU^{2}}$$

$$R^2 = 0.42$$

Where P = Industry profitability ratio, measured as the weighted average of net pre-tax profits to net worth for 1964 and 1965 for firms quoted on the KSE
C = Four-firm concentration ratio
W= Average difference between domestic price and imported price
CU= Capacity utilization for each industry

Note : Figure in parentheses are t-ratios
[b]: significant at the 5 per cent level
[c]: significant at the 10 per cent level

White concluded from his result 'that there seems to be a positive relationship between profit rates, industrial concentration, and import licencing stringency'. According to him 'the sample is small, the data are spotty, the results are not wholly satisfactory, but the basic tendencies seem to be present'.[5]

The second study was done by Amjad[6] who used the price-cost margin as the indicator of profitability and data from the Census of Manufacturing Industries to measure it. He carried out the study for four years between 1965 and 1970 (excluding 1967) for West Pakistan using a sample of twenty-five industries and found a significant relationship between price-cost margins and concentration ratios. For the average of the price-cost margin he was able to obtain the following regression results:

$$PC = \underset{(4.236)}{0.24\, CR_4^{a}} + \underset{(1.509)}{4.61\, K/O^{c}} \qquad R^2 = 0.60$$

Where PC = Price-cost margin
CR_4= Four-firm concentration ratio
K/O= Capital output ratio

Note: Figure in parenthesis are t-ratios
[a]: significant at the 1 per cent level
[c]: significant at the 10 per cent level

The results of these two studies therefore clearly did show the existence of a positive and significant relationship between profitability in the manufacturing sector and concentration in the production of manufactured goods.

14.2.2 The Extent of Concentration of Industrial Economic Power

The domination of the industrial sector by a small number of monopoly houses was clearly evident by the end of the fifties. Papanek[7] had shown that in 1969 sixty industrial groups (out of a total of 3,000 firms) controlled 60.6 per cent of all private industrial assets and 43.5 per cent of all private industrial sales. Out of these sixty, only seven controlled 24.4 per cent of the total private industrial assets and 15.6 per cent of the total private industrial sales.[8]

Throughout the sixties, the concentration of industrial wealth in the country was an important political issue and its existence was widely accepted even by the government. Haq's claim[9] that twenty-two families controlled 66 per cent of the total industrial effort in the country, 70 per cent of the total insurance, and 80 per cent of the total banking assets was, however, never substantiated.

More recently, however, certain attempts have been made to estimate the actual extent of the concentration of economic power as it existed by the end of the sixties.[10]

The results of a study done by Amjad are presented in Table 14.4. The extent of concentration was measured in terms of control over gross fixed assets by the monopoly houses. The concentration was first measured in terms of all non-financial companies listed on the Karachi Stock Exchange (KSE), then in terms of only manufacturing companies listed on the KSE, and finally in terms of the entire large-scale manufacturing sector. Each of these sectors was further subdivided into private companies (i.e., excluding government controlled companies) and private domestic companies (i.e., excluding the government controlled and foreign controlled companies).

The results show that, in 1970, forty-four monopoly houses controlled about 77 per cent of the gross fixed assets of all the manufacturing companies listed on the KSE and about 35 per cent of all assets for the entire large-scale manufacturing sector. In terms of only private domestic companies, these forty-four monopoly houses controlled 80 per cent of assets for companies listed on the KSE and about 48 per cent of the assets of the total large-scale manufacturing sector.

Out of these forty-four monopoly groups, eighteen, with assets of more than Rs 100 million, controlled over 60 per cent of assets of private domestic companies quoted on the KSE and about 35 per cent of the domestic assets of the entire large-scale manufacturing sector.

The monopoly over industrial assets is also shown separately for the two provinces. In East Pakistan, sixteen monopoly houses controlled 50 per cent of the private domestic assets of the province's large-scale manu-

Table 14.4: Control of Assets[1] by Monopoly Houses in 1970

		Non-financial companies listed on the KSE*			Manufacturing companies listed on the KSE			Large-scale manufacturing sector		
Size[2] (Rs million)	Number	All	Private[3]	Private domestic[4]	All	Private	Private domestic	All	Private	Private domestic
All Pakistan										
Over Rs 100	18	40.0	55.2	62.4	53.9	55.8	62.7	25.4	31.8	34.8
Rs 50 to Rs 100	13	7.3	10.1	11.4	10.6	11.0	12.4	6.0	7.5	8.2
Less than Rs 50	13	3.6	5.0	5.6	5.3	5.4	6.1	2.4	3.0	3.2
Total	44	50.9	70.3	79.4	69.8	72.2	81.2	33.8	42.3	46.2
West Pakistan										
Over Rs 100	12	31.1	46.5	54.3	44.7	46.7	54.6	23.7	26.3	28.7
Rs 50 to Rs 100	13	9.5	14.2	16.6	15.0	15.7	18.4	8.9	9.9	10.8
Less than Rs 50	17	6.4	9.5	11.1	8.6	9.0	10.5	4.6	5.1	5.6
Total	42	47.0	70.2	82.0	68.3	71.4	83.5	37.2	41.3	45.1
East Pakistan										
Over Rs 100	6	53.8	53.8	55.1	57.6	57.6	57.6	19.9	33.9	37.0
Rs 50 to Rs 100	4	11.7	11.7	11.9	12.6	12.6	12.6	4.4	7.5	8.2
Less than Rs 50	6	4.5	4.5	4.6	4.8	4.8	4.8	2.6	4.4	4.8
Total	16	70.0	70.0	71.6	75.0	75.0	75.0	26.9	45.8	50.0

1. Gross fixed assets at cost.
2. All manufacturing companies.
3. Excluding government controlled companies.
4. Excluding foreign owned and government controlled companies.
* Karachi Stock Exchange.
Source: R. Amjad, *Private Industrial Investment in Pakistan, 1960-70*, Cambridge, 1982.

facturing sector as compared to 45 per cent of the assets controlled by forty-two monopoly houses in West Pakistan. In terms of the number of monopoly houses controlling a given share of industrial assets, there was much greater concentration in East Pakistan. This reflected the fact that a number of monopoly houses did not invest in East Pakistan and the industrial sector there was dominated by the few monopoly houses that did.

These estimates confirm a high degree of concentration in the manufacturing sector even though the figure is not as high as claimed by Haq. The control of the monopoly houses, however, was not limited to the manufacturing sector and extended also to the financial sector.

The close link between industrial and finance capital was another important aspect of the corporate environment existing in Pakistan in the sixties. The monopoly houses controlled both the Banks and Insurance Companies and were influential in the running of the main aid disbursing agency, PICIC (Pakistan Industrial Credit and Investment Corporation).

The monopoly over banks is shown in Table 14.5 in terms of the proportion of total deposits and total loans and advances made by those banks in 1970. Of the seventeen banks incorporated in Pakistan, seven were under the direct control of the monopoly houses. These banks accounted for about 50 per cent of the total deposits and 50 per cent of the loans and advances made by all banks operating in Pakistan, i.e., including nineteen foreign banks.

If we exclude the banks incorporated outside Pakistan and one state-controlled bank (the National Bank of Pakistan) the

Table 14.5: Control of Banks by Monopoly Houses: 1970
(Rs million)

Bank	Controlling group	Deposits	Loans and advances
Habib Bank	Habib	4,270.8	2,622.7
United Bank	Saigol	3,234.5	2,032.4
Muslim Commercial Bank	Adamjee	1,326.4	843.7
Commerce Bank	Fancy	375.4	312.9
Australasia Bank	Colony (F)	338.8	245.0
Premier Bank	Arag	41.9	23.7
Sarhad Bank	Faruque	20.2	7.1
(a) Total controlled by Monopoly Houses		9,608.0	6,087.5
1 (a) as per cent of all banks, domestic and foreign		59.3	51.0
2 (a) as per cent of all domestic banks		65.4	57.0
3 (a) as per cent of all domestic private banks (i.e., excluding those which were state-controlled)		86.9	84.2

Source: R. Amjad, *Private Industrial Investment in Pakistan, 1960-70*, Cambridge, 1982. Calculated from the State Bank of Pakistan, 1972.

Table 14.6: Control of Insurance Companies by Monopoly Houses: 1969
(Rs million)

Insurance company	Controlling group	Total assets
Eastern Federal	Arag	332.8
Habib	Habib	152.8
New Jubilee	Fancy	72.9
Adamjee Insurance	Adamjee	67.2
Premier	Premier	39.4
Central Insurance	Dawood	23.4
United	Valika	15.5
Eastern Insurance	A.K. Khan	14.0
International General Insurance	Wazir Ali	12.1
Crescent Star	Millwala	9.9
National Security	Colony (N)	9.8
Khyber	Zafar-ul-Ahsan	8.7
Union	Nishat	6.0
Universal	Ghandara	4.4
(a) Total		768.9
1 (a) as per cent of all insurance companies, domestic and foreign.		50.4
2 (a) as per cent of domestic insurance companies		76.1

Source: R. Amjad, *Private Industrial Investment in Pakistan, 1960-70,* Cambridge, 1982. Based on Controller of Insurance, Karachi, 1971, pp. 334-9 and 512-27.

figure for the monopoly houses comes to over 86 per cent of deposits and over 84 per cent of all loans and advances made by private domestic banks in 1970.

A large share of the assets of the insurance companies was also concentrated in a few hands (Table 14.6). There were forty-seven Pakistani insurance companies and thirty foreign insurers in 1969. Of these companies, fourteen were controlled by the monopoly houses and their share came to over 50 per cent of the entire assets of the insurance sector (i.e., those incorporated in Pakistan or abroad) and 76 per cent of all the assets of the Pakistani insurance companies.

From the above results we can conclude that there was a high degree of concentration in the ownership of industrial assets and that a major portion of both the banking and the insurance assets in the country was controlled by the same monopoly houses. Also, the monopoly in the production of manufactured goods led to high profits because of higher prices being charged by the producers.

14.3 Nationalization and the Performance of Public Sector Enterprises

One of the most important economic issues is concerning the economic performance of the industries nationalized in the early seventies by the previous government. There has been considerable criticism, especially in the last few years, of the economic performance of the public sector enterprises taken over by the People's Party government. In more recent years, i.e., from 1977-8 to 1979-80, it is said that the performance has improved considerably and that this is due to the reforms, both financial and administrative, introduced by the present government.

Two broad sets of issues are discussed in this section. The first reviews the performance of the public sector enterprises during the years of the People's Party government and the second evaluates their performance in more recent years.

14.3.1 Performance of Public Sector Enterprises between 1972-3 and 1976-7

How well or badly did public sector enterprises perform during the years between 1972-3 and 1976-7? If we were to quote official government sources for these years or for later years, they could be said to be considerably biased—the first source would give extremely favourable comments while the second might be unjustly harsh. For this reason we have relied on neither of these two sources but mainly on a World Bank Report,[11] published in 1978, which reviewed the performance of public sector enterprises between 1972-3 and 1976-7. The analysis which follows relies almost exclusively on that Report and its analysis of the performance of public sector enterprises.

a. *The Background*

Until 1972, Pakistan Industrial Development Corporation (PIDC) was virtually the only public sector entity involved in manufacturing. A number of its projects were running at a loss which was not surprising since PIDC was established to promote regional growth in the backward areas and to develop industries wherever it was felt that private investment was inadequate. The more successful projects were sold off to the private sector. As of June 1972, PIDC had completed fifty-eight industrial and mining projects (with a total project cost of over Rs 1 billion) of which forty projects remained under PIDC management. The largest share of PIDC investment went to fertilizers (34 per cent), followed by gas (22 per cent), cement (14 per cent), and shipbuilding, coal mining, and sugar (about 6 per cent each). In regional terms, Punjab accounted for 60 per cent of the total, Sind 28 per cent, NWFP 6 per cent, and Baluchistan 5 per cent (Baluchistan had a higher share in completed PIDC projects than in the country's total industrial activities). The major portion of PIDC investment (in projects completed by June 1972) in Punjab was concentrated in fertilizers

(57 per cent) whereas in Sind the cement industry accounted for the major share of investment (42 per cent). In Baluchistan, PIDC's investment was concentrated in collieries which accounted for 92 per cent of the total capital investment in that province. In NWFP the principal investment of PIDC was in sugar factories (56 per cent).

As part of its package of social, economic, and political reforms, in January 1972 the People's Party government took over the management of thirty-one major manufacturing enterprises covering ten sub-sectors. The Board of Industrial Management (BIM) was established in August 1972 with the Minister of Production as Chairman to control these enterprises. In September 1973, the government took over, from these enterprises, the entire equity of the private limited companies and acquired a majority ownership in the public limited companies. In December 1973 the government, after studying the experience of Italy in organizing its public industrial sector under the Industrial Reconstruction Institute (IRI), created twelve Sector Corporations under the BIM. These became holding companies for the government's shares in the nationalized enterprises. PIDC too became a sector corporation. It was left with the projects in the textile, sugar, forestry, and natural gas industries; its mining projects were transferred to the Pakistan Mineral Development Corporation (which was set up in 1974) and projects pertaining to cement, fertilizers, chemicals, heavy engineering, and ceramics were transferred to the other newly created sector corporations concerned.

In 1974, the number of sector corporations was reduced from twelve to ten by merging tractors and automotives and by putting the State Electrical Corporation under the control of the State Heavy Engineering and Machine Tool Corporation. The ten sector corporations were:

Federal Chemical and Ceramics Corporation (FCCC);
Federal Light Engineering Corporation (FLEC);
National Design and Industrial Services Corporation (NDISC);
National Fertilizer Corporation of Pakistan (NFCP);
Pakistan Automobile Corporation (PACO);
Pakistan Industrial Development Corporation (PIDC);
Pakistan Steel Mills Corporation (PASMIC);
State Cement Corporation of Pakistan (SCCP);
State Heavy Engineering and Machine Tool Corporation (SHE and MTC);
State Petroleum Refinery and Petrochemical Corporation (PERAC).

The BIM group included fifth-three units in production and twenty-three major projects under implementation. Within the BIM group, the most important sector, in terms of sales in 1975-6, was the automotive sector (37 per cent of total group sales) followed by light engineering (15 per cent) and cement (14 per cent). In terms of employment in 1975-6, light engineering came first (21 per cent of total group employment) followed by automotives (16 per cent), heavy engineering (15 per cent), and cement (14 per cent).

b. *Performance from 1972-3 to 1975-6*

The BIM inherited from the private sector and the PIDC a productive apparatus that was, in general, economically inefficient to a large extent either because the projects had been chosen for social or political reasons or because of the economic policies pursued in the sixties which resulted in very high effective protection and seriously distorted relative prices. The very high profits of the private sector in the sixties, which had basically been paid for by consumers and government revenues through various forms of protection and subsidy, gave rise to high expectations at the time of nationalization. The public manufacturing sector was consequently burdened with a number of tasks and objectives which made it impossible for it to earn much profit. Prices were to be reduced or held down despite inflation, and workers and shareholders were to be given 'a fair deal'. The resulting depressed profits, coupled with the sharply rising investment programme for the public manufacturing sector, led to insignificant internal financing and a heavy burden on the government. At the same time, the scope for improving efficiency was limited by the nature of the productive apparatus that was inherited, the inability to close plants or reduce the work-force, the initial lack of management autonomy and flexibility, and a host of factors outside the control of management (separation from the former East Pakistan, labour unrests, shortage of raw materials, fuel or transportation, shortfalls in demand, emigration of skilled personnel to the Gulf States, droughts and floods, etc.). While many of the social goals that the public sector was required to pursue may have been laudable in themselves, there could be no real or permanent achievement of these goals without the economic and financial improvements to pay for them.

i) *Productivity Performance*

Table 14.7 indicates the growth of labour productivity in BIM units compared to the manufacturing sector as a whole. While BIM units appear to have done better than the latter, most of the increase took place between 1972-3 and 1973-4. Although productivity in BIM units stagnated thereafter (largely because of the increase in employment) productivity in the manufacturing sector as a whole appears to have actually fallen in the same period.

Table 14.7: Output, Employment, and Productivity Indices of BIM Units and the Manufacturing Sector

BIM units	1972-3	1973-4	1974-5	1975-6
Weighted production quantum index	100	133	163	170
Employment index	100	111	132	142
Productivity index	100	120	123	120
Manufacturing sector in Pakistan[1]				
Weighted production quantum index	100	107	106	106
Employment index	100	103	115	118
Productivity index	100	103	92	90

1. Includes small-scale sector.

Source: IBRD, *Pakistan Development Issues Policies, Vol. 1*, Washington, 1978, p.115.

While detailed statistics are not available, it appears that management had taken on or retained more labour than was needed and that over-manning was a problem in many units.

ii) *Financial Performance*

In evaluating the financial performance of public sector enterprises, it should be kept in mind that the situation was radically different from that prevailing before the nationalization in 1972. Before 1972, the government had allowed private sector industry to operate behind high tariff walls, import controls, and multiple exchange rates and had provided them with generous investment incentives and fiscal exemptions. By charging high prices, high profits were made. With the changed conditions, the various burdens placed on the public manufacturing sector, and the inherited productive apparatus, it was unreasonable to expect the public sector to earn the same level of profits as before or to make any significant contribution to financing the high and rising level of investment. Besides, in the event of protection from imports, government control of prices, or distorted factor prices, it is also self-evident that financial profit cannot be taken as a good indicator of economic efficiency or social profitability. However, financial profitability is still important if only because it has a direct bearing on the public manufacturing sector's ability to finance its investment expenditure (which is of major concern in view of resource limitations in Pakistan and the role assigned to the public sector in industrial development). Moreover, although high profits may be the result of high import protection, the combination of high protection and poor profitability warrants the suspicion of economic inefficiency.

A number of points should be made regarding the measurement of financial profit-

Table 14.8: Profits and Profit Margins of BIM Operating Units[1]
(Rs million)

Sector	1973-4	1974-5	1975-6
Automotive			
a. Net profit before tax	48.4	91.8	34.5
b. Sales	848.8	2,000.4	1,942.0
c. Percentage of profit margin	5.7	4.6	1.8
Cement			
a. Net profit before tax	40.7	96.5	78.4
b. Sales	489.1	701.9	724.8
c. Percentage of profit margin	8.3	13.7	10.8
Chemicals and Ceramics			
a. Net profit before tax	31.0	15.4	33.3
b. Sales	349.2	344.0	411.5
c. Percentage of profit margin	9.0	4.5	8.1
Light Engineering			
a. Net profit before tax	30.3	57.4	10.5
b. Sales	430.8	735.1	766.4
c. Percentage of profit margin	7.0	7.8	1.4
Heavy Engineering			
a. Net profit before tax	– 47.7	– 40.5	– 60.3
b. Sales	46.6	49.8	191.9
c. Percentage of profit margin			
Fertilizers			
a. Net profit before tax	25.1	12.9	18.2
b. Sales	196.6	186.8	197.5
c. Percentage of profit margin	12.8	6.9	9.2
Petroleum			
a. Net profit before tax	9.0	12.5	33.4
b. Sales	332.9	622.3	712.8
c. Percentage of profit margin	2.7	2.0	4.7
PIDC			
a. Net profit before tax	22.9	16.5	15.5
b. Sales	246.2	327.1	337.9
c. Percentage of profit margin	9.3	5.0	4.6
Total BIM			
a. Net profit before tax	159.8	262.5	217.7
b. Sales	2,893.6	4,967.4	5,284.8
c. Percentage of profit margin	5.5	5.3	4.1

1. Profit after interest and depreciation but before tax.
Source: IBRD, *Pakistan Development Issues Policies*, Vol. 1, Washington, 1978, p. 115.

ability. One year measures, such as Return on Investment or Return on Capital Employed, compare a flow (profit) with a stock (assets). Much depends on the valuation of the assets base which is linked to its age. Secondly, profit is a residual in the income statement and much depends on the accounting practices being followed. In fact, profit figures published by the BIM were often changed in subsequent presentations. The fifty-three operating enterprises in BIM group probably followed different accounting methods. Thirdly, in calculating return on capital, one should compare like with like. Thus, if the denominator is the value of total assets, the numerator should be profit before interest since interest is the return on that part of total assets that is financed by borrowing; whereas profit after interest (the shareholders' part) should be compared with capital employed or net worth.

Since nationalization, accounts indicate that profits after interest, but before tax, of BIM operating units as a whole improved from Rs 23 million in 1972-3 to Rs 160 million in 1973-4 and Rs 262 million in 1974-5 but declined to Rs 218 million in 1975-6. Table 14.8 gives the breakdown by sectors and the profit margins for the three fiscal years. The consistent loss-maker was the heavy engineering sector. In 1975-6, the largest contributor to overall profits was the cement sector followed by automotives, petroleum, fertilizers and chemicals, in the given order. For the BIM units as a whole, profit margins appear to have been declining. In 1975-6, the highest profit margin was shown by the *cement sector* and since cement in Pakistan was sold below world market prices, this would suggest that the sector was economically efficient as well. After cement came fertilizers, a priority sector for industrial investment. The profit margin of the automotive sector declined in the last three years shown in the Table despite an increase between 1973 and 1976 in import duties on motor vehicles (which range from 50 per cent to 200 per cent), an increase in capacity utilization, and a more than doubling of the value of sales. While demand did suffer as a result of the economic recession in 1975-6, the basic problem was that the sector was not economically efficient because of the very small scale of production or assembly. In *light engineering*, too, there was a sharp decline in the profit margin which was attributed to the increased cost of inputs and high inventory-carrying charges.

Table 14.9 gives the return (before interest and tax) on investment (total assets) for 1974-5. For BIM operating units as a whole, the return on investment (ROI) defined in this way comes to 7.4 per cent whereas if profits after interest had been used the ratio would have been 4.2 per cent. ROI (before interest) was 6.3 per cent in 1974-5 and 5.9 per cent in 1975-6. This performance was unsatisfactory compared to the cost of borrowing. Private enterprise, however, did not fare much better: ROI (after interest but before tax), for a sample of 242 companies quoted on the Karachi Stock Exchange, was 5.3 per cent in 1972-3 and 4.1 per cent in 1973-4 compared to BIM's ROI (similarly defined) of 3.3 per cent in 1974-5 and 4.2 per cent in 1975-6. Both the public and private sectors did not perform well as they were subjected to the same general set of economywide disturbances.

Assets are stated at book value which inflates the ROI because the value of the fixed assets bears little relationship to replacement costs. The figures also show the heavy burden of interest payments: they came to 75 per cent of net profits before tax (but after interest), for the BIM group as a whole in 1974-5, compared to 91 per cent in 1973-4 and 117 per cent in 1975-6. In 1974-5, relatively heavy interest payment burdens were incurred by automotives (88 per cent of profits), chemicals (204 per cent), heavy engineering (net loss), and petroleum (255 per cent), due largely to unsold inventories.

In terms of 1974-5 ROI, (before interest and tax) the best performer was the cement sector (11.1 per cent). Next came the automotive sector (10.4 per cent) followed by petroleum (8.1 per cent) and light engineering (8.1 per cent). Fertilizers show a ROI of only 3.8 per cent despite its high profit margin.

Conclusion

What conclusion can one draw from the performance of public sector enterprises during the years in which the People's Party was in power? On balance it can be said that the performance was a mixed one. The point which went least in its favour was the alarmingly high increase in employment which

Table 14.9: Return on Investment of BIM Units, 1974-5
(Rs million)

Sector	Net profit before tax	Total interest	Profit before interest	Year-end total assets	Return on investment[1]
Automotive	91.8	81.2	173.0	1,656.9	10.4
Cement	96.5	11.4	107.9	975.0	11.1
Chemicals	15.4	31.4	46.8	732.7	6.4
Engineering–light	57.4	8.3	65.7	814.8	8.1
Engineering–heavy	(40.5)	16.4	(24.1)	756.4	–
Fertilizers	12.9	2.6	15.5	404.7	3.8
Oil and petroleum	12.5	31.9	44.4	545.7	8.1
Textile–others (PIDC)	16.5	12.6	29.1	306.2	9.5
Total	262.5	195.8	458.3	6,192.4	7.4

1. Profit before interest and tax as a percentage of total assets in the balance sheet.
Source: IBRD, *Pakistan Development Issues Policies, Vol. 1*, Washington, 1978, p. 115.

could certainly not be justified in terms of increases in output and which had a very adverse affect on productivity. Its financial performance especially when compared to the private sector was fair. Therefore it can be said that although the public sector did not do all that well neither in the circumstances did it perform all that badly.

14.3.2 The Performance of Public Sector Enterprises: 1977-8 to 1981-2

To what extent did the performance of public sector enterprises improve as a result of some of the administrative and economic reforms introduced by the military government of General Zia?

Soon after taking over in July 1977, the military government initiated a review of the public manufacturing sector which culminated in two major reports. The first was the 'State Enterprises Review Commission Final Report' (referred to as the *Uqaili Report* after its Chairman) and the second was the 'Implementation Committee on Reorganization of State Industrial Enterprises' (known as the *Beg Report* after the Commission Chairman). The latter conducted no primary research but built on the *Uqaili* data base to make specific policy recommendations.

The *Beg Report* saw the solution to the administrative and management problems confronting the public sector enterprises in a major reform of the formal organizational structure including

a. the abolition of the Ministry of Production;
b. the abolition of the BIM
c. the abolition of the sector corporations;
d. the reduction of the number of operating enterprises from sixty-nine to twenty-four by closure or divestiture (sixteen cases) and merger (the remainder);
e. the creation of Boards of Directors at the enterprise level and the delegation of most control functions to them; and
f. the creation of a supra-ministerial state enterprise Board which would act as a government shareholder but would not be under any individual Ministry.

In short the *Beg Report* viewed the problem as one of increasing autonomy for the enterprises and recommended the abolition of the existing structure in addition to setting up a Board of Directors responsible to a supra-ministerial shareholding Board to achieve accountability.

The *Uqaili Report* was on balance similar to the *Beg Report* in its evaluation of the problems but rather different in the solutions it proposed. In common with the *Beg Report* it advocated a reduction in the number of operating units and a major role for the Boards of Directors at the company level. However, it explicitly considered the abolition of each of the supra-enterprise tiers and rejected each alternative. It concluded that the present organizational structure be retained but with the following modifications:

a. the number of sector corporations be reduced by re-grouping;
b. the functions of the different tiers be clearly spelled out;
c. mechanisms be introduced which enable performance to be evaluated at unit levels for proper remedial measures at appropriate management levels.

The actual response of the government was intermediate between the recommendations of *Beg* and *Uqaili*. The BIM was abolished, there was increased reliance on the Board of Directors, and a modest consolidation effort was made (the merger of the Heavy and Light Engineering Corporation, the sale of two units, and a few shut downs).

The more important question is regarding the performance of the public sector enterprises after 1977 in terms of both productivity and financial profitability, the extent to which there has been an improvement, the extent to which this improvement can be explained in terms of the coming into production of new units started by the previous government and the extent to which it can be seen as a result of measures introduced by the present government.

The results presented below rely heavily on the *Jones Report*[12] prepared for the Pakistan

Ministry of Production, Planning Division, and the World Bank, and covers the period till 1979-80.

In Table 14.10, an index of real labour productivity and total pre-tax profits are given. As compared to the earlier years they show a remarkable improvement in pre-tax profits as well as in real labour productivity. It is, however, well known that increases in pre-tax profits in current prices cannot be taken as indicators of efficiency as they can be produced in a variety of ways including·

i) raising output prices relative to input prices,
ii) accounting adjustments and increases in hidden subsidies
iii) changes in the set of firms (new profitable projects coming into production or old losing plants being shut down)
iv) increases in the quantity of outputs relative to the quantity of inputs.

Only the fourth case would represent a genuine increase in operational efficiency.

Although it was not possible for these various causes to be disentangled, the *Jones Report's* major conclusions were that the increase in profits was not due to either (i) or (ii). In the case of (iii) the closure of Special (People's) Steel eliminated losses of Rs 58 million and accounted for a 10 per cent increase in profits between 1978-9 and 1979-80. However, a major increase in profits was due to new capacity especially the addition of Pak-Arab to the National Fertilizer Corporation and increases in profits shown by the Petroleum Refinery Corporation.

In the case of labour productivity, there is an improvement after 1976-7 when General Zia's martial law government took over from the People's Party. Prior to that year, the annual rate of increase in labour productivity was 4.4 per cent whereas since then it has been 20.6 per cent. Since 1976-7, the work force has declined by 7.5 per cent while production has risen by 62.2 per cent.

Again, it is necessary to see how much of the improved performance is due to being rid of unproductive firms while adding new capital-intensive ones and how much is due to the improvement of existing firms. Part of the improvement is explained by the spectacular growth in the National Fertilizer Corporation and the Petroleum Corporation. However, data, for continuing firms only, also shows an improvement in real productivity and, even excluding Pak-Arabs, the National Fertilizer Corporation shows a 20 per cent increase in real productivity between 1977-8 and 1979-80.

We can therefore conclude that a significant increase in profits and productivity has taken place in the public sector enterprises since 1977. To a great extent, this can be explained by the coming into production of new units begun earlier. However, some significant improvement is also due to the administrative and other financial reforms introduced by the present government especially as regards real labour productivity where they have been able to cut down on surplus employment in public sector enterprises.

Table 14.10: Real Labour Productivity—Ministry of Production Units

Year	Production index	Employment index	Index of real output per worker	Total pre-tax profits (Rs million)
1972-3	100	100	100	—
1973-4	132	111	119	—
1974-5	160	na	na	290.2
1975-6	167	132	126	204.0
1976-7	162	133	122	152.0
1977-8	190	130	147	209.3
1978-9	203	129	158	155.8
1979-80	262	123	213	642.9

Source: L.P. Jones, *Efficiency of Public Manufacturing Enterprises in Pakistan*, Draft Report, 1981, Table II-2 and Table II-4.

14.4 Industrial Relations, Trade Unions and the Level of Real Wages[13]

The rapid growth of the large-scale manufacturing sector in Pakistan led to the existence of a substantial labour force employed in this sector. One of the criticisms levied against Pakistan's development strategy during the fifties and sixties has been that the gains of industrial growth have not been shared with the workers and, as evidence of this, the failure of any real increase in wages is often cited.

The level of wages in a surplus labour economy (which Pakistan definitely was especially in the fifties and sixties) would not necessarily be high given the limited demand and 'unlimited' supplies. However, if the labour force could organize itself into a strong bargaining force then wages would no longer be determined just by market forces. Whether labour is in a position to do this or is allowed to do so will depend very much on the existing labour laws (especially those relating to the right to strike) and the strength of the trade union movement. Also, the government may in certain cases introduce minimum wages so as to protect the interest of the workers. To see the interaction of these three forces, we can divide the overall period into three distinct sub-periods.

14.4.1 The Initial Years (1947-58)

After Independence, the Industrial Disputes Act 1947, along with the Trade Unions Act 1926 and other laws, was adopted by the government of Pakistan. The Trade Unions Act 1926 provided for the representation of workers by their trade unions and also accorded certain rights and obligations on the trade unions. The Industrial Disputes Act 1947 had been enacted by the British government after the end of the Second World War and *inter alia* provided for the constitution of Works Committees and the reference of a dispute by the government to a one man tribunal for adjudication of that particular dispute. The Industrial Disputes Act 1947 was amended in 1956 to provide speedy remedy to the workers and officers of trade unions for the redress of grievances out of dismissal and other punishment awarded during the pendency of industrial disputes. Another amendment was made in this Act in 1957 which placed restrictions on the right to strike and lock-out during the course of conciliation and adjudication proceedings.

As regards trade union activity, in August 1947, there were no more than seventy-five registered trade unions in the whole of Pakistan (including the East wing) compared to 1,057 in undivided India. These existing trade unions found themselves faced with two major problems. Firstly, in most cases they were branches of the All-India organizations and had no independent existence of their own. Secondly, most of them had been run by trade union leaders who left Pakistan in 1947 which deprived the movement of leadership and active members who had previously been provided by the central organization. The only segment of workers who were to some extent organized in West Pakistan were the railway workers, the employees in the Karachi Port Trust, and the Lyallpur Cotton Mills.

Table 14.11: Number of Registered Trade Unions and Membership—1951 to 1958

Month	Year	Number of registered trade unions	Membership
December	1951	309	393,137
December	1952	352	394,923
December	1953	394	424,563
December	1954	382	410,755
December	1955	474	325,610
December	1956	542	316,642
December	1957	611	366,317
January	1958	559	357,033
June	1958	635	376,029

Note: There were also a large number of unregistered trade unions. Their numbers however are impossible to estimate.

Source: Ministry of Labour, Government of Pakistan, *The Pakistan Labour Gazette*, Karachi, April-June 1958, p. 273.

Between 1951-8, although there was a large increase in the number of registered trade unions in the country, there seems to have been little increase in its membership as can be seen from Table 14.11.

The increase in the number of trade unions in this period was not a reflection of the strength of the movement but more of its dissensions and internal weaknesses. A number of these unions existed on paper only. In many cases, there were a large number of unions in the same factory whose major role was to fight amongst themselves rather than for the rights of the workers.

By the end of 1958, the first stage of Pakistan's industrial growth was beginning to come to an end. The opportunities for simple import-substitution-led industrial growth were being exhausted because of the failure of the domestic market to grow mainly as a result of agricultural stagnation. Similarly, the economy faced a foreign exchange constraint as the foreign exchange surplus earned during the Korean boom had run out and exports had failed to compensate for it. These factors led to a considerable slowing down in the industrial sector.

These years had also seen the initial growth of a trade union movement in the country. The increase in the industrial labour force which resulted from industrialization acted as an impetus for the growth of trade unions but this period failed to see the emergence of a strong and independent trade union movement. This was the result of the growing opportunism, factionalism, and alienation of the workers from the top leadership of the government patronized unions. All these factors played a significant part in keeping the level of real wages of workers at a standstill during these years (Table 14.13).

Table 14.12: Number of Strikes and Man Days Lost

Year	Number of strikes	Number of workers involved	Man-days lost
1948	57	36,231	135,580
1949	72	44,582	101,723
1950	32	16,836	83,164
1951	64	22,810	77,471
1952	95	28,035	126,173
1953	86	35,776	89,058
1954	107	69,831	283,944
1955	75	42,103	121,312
1956	150	111,831	374,915
1957	150	188,001	530,573
1958	93	89,954	–

Source: Ministry of Labour, Government of Pakistan, *The Pakistan Labour Gazette*, (Quarterly), Karachi, various issues.

Table 14.13: Index of Real Wages in Large-Scale Manufacturing
1959-60 = 100

Year	Index
1954	103.53
1955	97.30
1957	97.12
1958	99.64

Source: N. Hamid, 'The Burden of Capitalist Growth—A Study of Real Wages and Consumption in Pakistan', *Pakistan Economic and Social Review*, Vol. VII, No. 1, 1974.

14.4.2 Suppression and Stagnation (1958-68)

The military government, which took over in October 1958, repealed the Industrial Disputes Act 1947 and replaced it with another piece of legislation known as the Industrial Disputes Ordinance, 1959. The main aim of this legislation was to prohibit the workers the right to strike.

The main features of the new labour policy introduced by the military government soon after it came into power were:

i) Nearly all the major industries were declared 'essential industries' in which strikes were banned. These included the railways, post, telegraph, telephone, water electricity, ports, and defence related organizations. Also, a long list of industries was announced which were declared 'essential industries' for the time being and included cement, electrical equipment, vegetable oils, ceramics, iron and steel, mines, paper, petroleum, machinery, sugar, leather and leather goods, pharmaceuticals, cotton textiles, and jute manufactures.

Besides this, the central and provincial governments were given the powers to declare road, air and water transport, and food and beverage related industries as 'essential' during a period of emergency.

ii) In the case of industrial disputes, the government would appoint officials who were to act as arbitrators to investigate the causes of the dispute and to try to bring about an agreement between the two parties through negotiations. Only if such arbitration was to fail, and the government official was to give a certificate to both sides to this effect, could they go to a labour court.

iii) Permanent labour courts consisting of three members were established. The Chairman was a retired judge of the High Court or District Court. The other two members were representatives of labour and management but they only had advisory power.

iv) Before the workers could go on strike a number of preconditions were imposed and if these were not met the strike was declared illegal. These conditions were as follows:

  a. Before going on strike the administration was to be given fourteen days notice.
  b. During the period of negotiations there could be no strike action.
  c. If negotiations failed and one of the two parties obtained a certificate to go to a labour court then again there could be no strike action.

For all practical purposes, the right to strike was denied to the workers and the outlines of the industrial and labour policy made it quite clear that industrial growth in Pakistan in the early sixties was to be accompanied by considerable curtailment of trade union activity and the rights of the workers.

Despite the best efforts of the state to suppress the workers, the number of strikes, which had fallen drastically in the early years of martial law, more than doubled during 1963 and 1964 as can be seen from Table 14.14. One important reason for this was the removal of martial law and hence a gradual weakening of the authority of the military government which led to a decline in the 'fear' created by the authorities. Also, since no strike activity had taken place in the earlier years, there was an accumulation of discontent amongst the workers.

The ten years of Ayub's government saw the workers' rights being eroded but despite all the unfavourable conditions the number of trade unions and its membership showed a significant increase (Table 14.15). However,

Table 14.14: Number of Strikes during 1958-67

Year	Number of strikes	Number of workers involved
1958	93	89,954
1959	29	32,493
1960	42	25,749
1961	54	26,303
1962	121	69,482
1963	215	218,601
1964	228	243,943
1965	152	105,608
1966	170	177,309
1967	203	344,679

Source: Ministry of Labour, Government of Pakistan, *The Pakistan Labour Gazette*, (Quarterly), Karachi, various issues.

Table 14.15: Number of Trade Unions and Membership—1959-68

Year	Number	Membership
1959	618	347,522
1960	708	350,604
1961	723	398,723
1962	789	417,248
1963	831	448,735
1964	898	402,322
1965	965	512,225
1966	1,010	522,161
1967	1,039	521,181
1968	1,041	512,912

Source: Ministry of Labour, Government of Pakistan, *The Pakistan Labour Gazette*, (Quarterly), Karachi, various issues.

Table 14.16: Index of Real Wages of Large-Scale Manufacturing Sector

Year	Index
1959-60	100.0
1962-3	91.21
1963-4	92.94
1964-5	105.42
1965-6	109.30
1966-7	104.85
1967-8	105.73
1968-9	116.17

Source: N. Hamid, 'The Burden of Capitalist Growth—A Study of Real Wages and Consumption in Pakistan', *Pakistan Economic and Social Review*, Vol. VII, No. 1, 1974.

as in the earlier period, the increase in trade union membership was not necessarily an indication of its strength but far more a result of opportunistic leadership and in-fighting amongst different factions.

The weakness of the trade unions and the unfavourable labour legislation in which they operated meant that there was little increase in real wages during the sixties (Table 14.16).

14.4.3 Industrial Relations Ordinance, 1969

With the imposition of martial law in the country, in March 1969, labour became a central issue. The new military government announced its labour policy in July 1969 and then passed the new Industrial Relations Ordinance in November 1969. An important element of the Ordinance was that it consolidated the entire law relating to trade unions and industrial disputes. The salient features of the new Ordinance were as follows:

i) Unfettered right of association to workers and employers.
ii) Implementation of ILO Convention No. 87 and 98 relating to the freedom of association and protection of the right to organize and bargain collectively.
iii) Restoration of the right to strike and lock-out after failure of bilateral negotiations and conciliation efforts.
iv) Introduction of a system of voluntary arbitration.
v) Unions to be elected as collective bargaining agents having exclusive right to (a) raise demands; (b) undertake bilateral collective bargaining; (c) call for strikes; (d) nominate workers' representatives on work councils. There was no precondition of registration of unions for this purpose.
vi) Introduction of a check off system to trade unions certified as collective bargaining agents.
vii) Protection of office bearers of trade unions against victimization during the period of registration and pendency of disputes.
viii) Creation of three distinct and separate services for the registration of trade unions, mediation and conciliation, inspection and enforcement of labour laws, and strengthening of the labour administration.
ix) Workers participation in management at various levels and forums.
x) Introduction of a minimum wage.

The basic change brought about by this Ordinance was that it restored the right to strike to the workers. The government retained the right to prohibit strikes in only eight public utility services (ports, hospitals, fire-fighting services, watch and ward and security services, railways and airways, postal and telephone services, any system of public conservancy or sanitation, and the manufacture, generation or supply of electricity, gas, or water to the public).

14.4.4 New Labour Policy (1972)

In April 1972, the People's Party government announced the Labour Laws (Amendment) Ordinance, 1972 which amended almost all the existing Labour Laws including the West Pakistan Employees Social Security Ordinance, 1965, West Pakistan Industrial and Commercial Employment (Standing Orders) Ordinance, 1968, Companies' Profits (Workers Participation) Act, 1968, Industrial Relations Ordinance, 1969, and the Workers Welfare Fund Ordinance, 1971. The following were the main features of the new labour policy:

1. Workers' participation in the management of industry to be 20 per cent at the factory level.
2. In specified industrial units workers will have the authority to appoint an auditor to be paid by the management to inspect accounts, records, stores, etc.
3. Workers' share in annual profits under the Companies' Profits (Workers Participation) Act to be increased from 2.5 per cent to 4 per cent. On increasing the productivity, an additional 10 per cent of increased profits to go to the workers.
4. Each shop or Department of a factory to have a Shop Steward to be elected by secret ballot.
5. Labour Courts to give their decisions in twenty days for individual cases and thirty days for collective issues (and not sixty days as at present).
6. Works Councils to deal with all matters that can go before Labour Courts.
7. Either party, the workers or employers, may take the matter to the Labour Court.
8. Three days' strike notice to be sufficient provided it is so decided in a secret ballot by the general body of workers.
9. Lower supervisory levels in banks to be included

in the definition of 'workman' to obtain the benefit of collective bargaining.

10. Every order of retrenchment and termination to state reasons explicitly in writing.
11. Payment of bonus to be compulsory and to be linked to profits.
12. Labour under contractors to get the benefit of the application to them of Payment of Wages Act, 1936, and Industrial and Commercial Employment (Standing Orders) Ordinance, 1968.
13. Workers welfare fund for the housing of workers under the Workers Welfare Fund Ordinance, 1971, to be activated. Committees to be set up to examine the payment by employers of higher contribution than the legal minimum.
14. Free education up to matriculation for one child of each worker to be the responsibility of the employer.
15. Workers' contribution of 2 per cent under the Social Security Scheme not to be levied. Instead the employers' contribution of 4 per cent to be raised to 6 per cent.
16. Provision for old age pension to be made for all workers.
17. Compulsory group insurance for workers against death and injury while off duty to be introduced.
18. Social Security Scheme to be gradually extended to domestic servants.
19. Laws relating to safety measure and workmen compensation against death and injury to be revised.
20. Increased rates of compensation under the Workmen's Compensation Act, 1923, to be provided.
21. Group benefit schemes to be introduced as incentives to workers in increasing productivity.
22. Equitable distribution of employers' contribution to be ensured between workers in capital-intensive and labour-intensive undertakings.
23. Infringement of certain provisions of labour laws to be cognizable though bailable.
24. Measures to promote the growth of workers' movement on progressive lines to be undertaken.
25. A quasi-judicial body to be set up to promote genuine trade unionism at the trade level, to ensure representative character of unions, to help in the formation of a federation of unions industry-wise and at national level, and to deal with cases of victimization and unfair labour practices.
26. In due course, wages to be pegged to prices but immediate increase in cash wages not made.

Amongst the reforms introduced in the 1972 Labour Policy, the most important was that the concept of *termination simplicitor* or simple termination was abolished and it was made obligatory on the employer to give, at the time of termination, dismissal, discharge, etc., an order in writing explicitly stating the reason for the action taken irrespective of the nature of the employment of the worker, i.e., be he permanent, temporary, apprentice, or probationer.

Another important change was that the Workers Compensation Act, 1923, was amended to increase compensation and coverage. This compensation was further enhanced through the Labour Laws (Amendment) Ordinance, 1972, to Rs 12,000 in the case of death, to Rs 17,000 in the case of permanent disablement, and the maximum to Rs 21,000.

The introduction of a minimum wage in 1969 had increased money wages by almost 26 per cent between 1967-8 and 1969-70. The February 1972 reforms as discussed earlier had extended workers participation in management, made compulsory the payment of annual bonuses at stipulated rates, and set minimum standards for education, life insurance, and medical benefits. The workers' share in profits had doubled from 2.5 to 5 per cent. These fringe benefits, coupled with the residual effects of the 1969 minimum wage legislation, added more than 22 per cent to the earnings of workers in 1972-3.

In August 1973 the government adopted the Employees Cost of Living (Relief) Ordinance requiring employers in both the private and public sectors to award cost of living adjustments at a rate fixed by the government. There were three such adjustments under the 1973 Ordinance: Rs 35 monthly in August 1973; Rs 50 in June 1974; and Rs 25 in April 1975. Thus, a worker in an industrial area outside Karachi, earning the statutory minimum wage of Rs 125 in June 1973, was earning Rs 235 by June 1975—an increase of 88 per cent in two years. Since consumer prices rose by approximately 65 per cent, real wages of the least paid worker increased substantially during this period. The wage of the average worker rose by a smaller percentage than the increase in the minimum wage but it too, in real terms, showed an increase as can be seen in column 5 of Table 14.17. Even if we were to have some doubts about the reliability of the data on real wages (Table 14.17), especially since it is restricted to workers of the cotton textile industry, there is little doubt that at least real wages did not decline during this period. This in itself was a significant improvement over the situation in the sixties.

14.5 Government and Small-Scale Industries in Pakistan[14]

This section is divided into three parts. Part I analyses the role of the small-scale sector in the overall industrial strategy. Part II looks at the direct role of the government in developing small-scale industries, especially the contribution of the Small-Scale Industries Corporation, and the setting up of industrial estates. Part III looks at changes in economic conditions in the seventies and their impact on the rapid growth of the small-scale sector during this period.

Table 14.17: Real and Money Wages of Production Workers in Large-Scale Manufacturing
(Rupees per worker per year)

Year	Money Rupees	Wages 1959-60=100	Real Rupees	Wages 1959-60=100
1969-70	1,931	177	1,351	124
1970-1	2,094	192	1,384	127
1971-2	2,389	219	1,504	138
1972-3	2,914	267	1,679	143
1973-4	4,012	368	1,775	168
1974-5	4,953	454	1,730	159

Note: 1970-1 and 1971-2 : Government of Pakistan, Ministry of Industries. For all workers, no indication whether cash and non-cash benefits included.

1972-3 and 1974-5: Production and non-production workers in cotton textiles.

Source: S. Guisinger, *Wages, Capital Rental Values and Relative Factor Prices in Pakistan*, World Bank Staff Working Paper No. 287, 1978.

Table 14.18: Number of Strikes and Man Days Lost

Year	Number of strikes	Number of workers involved	Man days lost
1969	285	184,892	1,220,337
1970	304	193,807	2,747,959
1971	141	107,962	815,211
1972	779	361,149	2,018,308
1973	536	353,568	803,583
1974	370	301,753	1,433,553

Source: Ministry of Labour, Health, Social Welfare, and Population Planning, Government of Pakistan, *The Pakistan Labour Gazette*, (Quarterly), Karachi, various issues.

14.5.1 Role of the Small-Scale Sector in Overall Industrial Strategy

As a starting off point, we have to look at the overall development strategy pursued so far and, within this overall strategy, the relative importance of large and small-scale industries. We have already seen in earlier chapters that government economic policy had a pro-industry bias, especially in the fifties and sixties, when, through a combination of fiscal, monetary, and commercial policy measures, the industrial sector was given concessions which led to high profitability and high levels of investments achieved mainly at the expense of the agricultural sector. In the seventies some of these concessions were removed, especially the overvalued exchange rate which adversely affected profitability, and this together with unsettled political conditions led to a sharp decline in private industrial investment. However, the government launched a major investment programme in heavy and intermediate industries which compensated for the decline in private industrial investment. The industrial strategy has, however, been mainly implemented through the large and medium-scale units.

The arguments for industrialization through large and medium-scale industry are well-known and need not be repeated in any detail. The cost economics of large-scale production, the size of modern technology for manufacture of new products, and the generation of a larger investible surplus are amongst the main arguments given in their favour. Also, the fact that a country relies mainly on imported machinery for its industrialization process (and this is what Pakistan has done in the last thirty-five years with emphasis on consumer goods in the earlier phase of its industrialization) means that you have little choice as regards size of plants which are manufactured in and cater for the resource endowments of the advance industrialized countries.

The question of dependence on imported technology with its inherent bias for large and medium-scale industry has also been attributed by many economists to the government's economic policy which, at least in the fifties and sixties, through an overvalued exchange rate, underpriced import of capital machinery by at least two to two and a half times its true scarcity price. The link between the financing of industrial investment mainly through tied foreign aid and dependence on imported technology has not received the same degree of attention. During the sixties, almost all imported industrial machinery was financed through foreign aid disbursed by financial institutions and tied with import of machinery from the aid-giving countries themselves.

A commitment towards industrialization which was considered synonomous with modern technology, pricing policies which favoured import of capital intensive technology, and reliance on tied foreign aid loans has meant that industrial investment has been mainly chanellized towards large and medium-scale industry.

The results have been controversial. True, high growth rates of industrial production have been generated and an industrial base of heavy, intermediate, and consumer goods industry has been built (or is in the process of being completed). Dependence on imported industrial raw material and capital goods is, however, still significantly high even if that of consumer goods has been substantially reduced. The 'efficiency' of the industrial structure which has emerged in terms of 'world prices' has been seriously questioned.[15] The concentration of industrial economic power,[16] which was mainly a result of the industrial strategy followed, led to serious political repercussions. Inter-regional disparities were accentuated because of concentration of industry in certain cities and regions of West Pakistan and contributed to the dismemberment of the country.[17]

Some of these criticisms can well be disputed and considered peculiar to the economic and political setting of Pakistan. What cannot be denied, however, is that the employment-generation effect of industrialization has been most disappointing in the context of Pakistan's labour surplus economy and this had been the major case made out for promotion and development of small-scale industry in Pakistan.

14.5.2 Government Policies

One measure of the government's support and interest in small-scale industry can be had from the various Five Year Plan documents. In the First Five Year Plan (1955-60) it was stated that:

> 'Small industry has specific contributions to make to economic development. In the first place, it can contribute to the output of needed goods without requiring the organization of large new enterprises or the use of much foreign exchange to finance the import of new equipment. Secondly, it can provide opportunities for employment beyond the narrow boundaries of urban centres. Finally, as history shows, it can perform an important function in promoting growth, providing a training ground for management and labour, and spreading industrial knowledge over wide areas.'[18]

The Plan recommended the setting up of a Small Industries Corporation which would provide loans (upto Rs 10,000), give technical assistance, and help in marketing of products. It proposed the setting up of research institutes for the development of improved processes and designs for production for, according to the planners, 'if small industry is to survive and prosper in the face of increasing competition from large industry, it stands in need of technical guidance'.[19] It also recommended the creation of small industrial estates where the government could provide land, roads, water, power, and similar facilities.

The Second Plan (1960-5) noted that the implementation of the First Plan had fallen far short of its objectives and the major problems of small industries remained unsolved because of a lack of concerted effort to tackle them. It set out the following principles for the development of small industries

i. to adopt small industries to changing technological, economic, and social conditions;
ii. to stimulate production of implements and equipment required for agriculture;
iii. to encourage the processing of indigenous raw materials;
iv. to create additional employment opportunities;
v. to modernize such existing units as have sound economic prospects;
vi. to promote modernization by encouraging growth of small industries in rural areas in general and wherever resources and markets are available in particular;
vii. to bring about a closer relationship between the small and large industries through, for example, the production of spares and accessories or components for large-scale industry or through providing facilities for the maintenance and repair of equipment in use either by large-scale industries or in other sectors of the economy; and
viii. to preserve and promote traditional arts and crafts.

The Plan emphasized that the development of small industry within each province was to be the concern of a Provincial Small Industries Corporation with emphasis, as in the First Plan, on industrial estates, design centres, sales and display centres, and development-cum-training and training-cum-production centres for certain selected industries like carpets, woolen, pottery, leather tanning, and wood working. The central government was mainly to help establish technical training and technical and advisory centres.

In the Third Five Year Plan (1965-70) and Fourth Five Year Plan (1970-5) the principles for development of small industries stated in the Second Plan were repeated verbatim and the basic approach was to be identical with emphasis on Small Industries Corporations.

In the Fifth Five Year Plan (1978-83), it was stated that

> 'the small industries sector has considerable potential for growth but it suffers from a number of problems relating to organization, financing, technology, and marketing. To facilitate the development of this sector, there is need to have a closer look at the constraints under which this sector operates and to remove the hurdles which inhibit its healthy growth. There is also need to provide some special incentives and assistance to small entrepreneurs who have the resources or skill that can be profitably exploited. Fiscal and commercial policies will give due recognition to these factors during the Plan period.'[20]

The Plan documents clearly show the limited importance which small-scale industries had in Pakistan's overall development strategy. The major task of the development of these industries was to be carried out through the Small-Scale Industries Corporations and it is their performance to which we now turn.

a. *Small Industries Corporations*

On the recommendation of the First Five Year Plan, a Small Industries Corporation was set up for the Federal Area of Karachi in 1955 and another in East Pakistan in 1957. It was on the eve of the Second Five Year Plan, in 1960, that the first West Pakistan Small Industries Corporation was established and allowed to function in areas excluding Karachi and the Tribal Areas. In 1962, however, the two Small Industries Corporations operating in West Pakistan were merged with West Pakistan Industrial Development Corporation (WPIDC) to form its Small Industries Division (WPIDC/SID).

The government reconsidered its decision in 1965 and decided to establish a separate Small Industries Corporation for West Pakistan. Consequently, the WPSIC was established in September 1965. But in 1972, with the bifurcation of One Unit, this organization was also dissolved and separate corporations for each province were created.

Within the framework of its activities, the Small Industries Corporation had to carry out the following works:

1. Preparing and submitting to government schemes for the development of cottage and small industries.
2. Preparing schemes to establish service centres and common facilities centres to promote the development of cottage and small industries.
3. Establishing small industrial estates, artisans' colonies, design centres, handicrafts development institutions, and such other institutions which are needed for promotion and development of handicrafts and small industries.
4. Giving loans for the purpose of setting up small and cottage industries.
5. Furnishing guarantees to the commercial banks for the repayment of loans to borrowers for the development of industries and sharing losses on account of bad debts in accordance with the agreements between the Corporation and the bank.
6. Undertaking census and surveys to collect basic statistics for preparing programmes to support cottage and small industries.
7. Revising schemes for the improvement and reorganization of training institutions and other projects taken from WPIDC/SID.
8. Maintaining and running depots for the supply of raw materials and for the purchase and sale of finished goods from cottage and small industries.
9. Formulating and implementing schemes for training of artisans and small industrialists.
10. Importing raw materials and maintaining stocks of these materials for supply to non-licenced industrial units.
11. Introducing better means of production and new designs including prototypes.
12. Sanctioning funds for balancing and modernizing cottage and small industrial units established or likely to be established in and outside small industrial estates in West Pakistan.
13. Establishing in special cases, and with the prior approval of the Government, small and cottage industries in less developed areas.

At the time of its dissolution, the WPSIC had developed 87 projects in the public sector at a cost of Rs 40 million. A brief description of some of WPSIC's major projects is given below to indicate the nature of the production facilities and technical services offered by the Corporation.

i) *Small Industries Estates*

The Corporation established nine industrial estates at Peshawar, Gujrat, Sialkot, Gujranwala, Lahore, Bahawalpur, Sukkur, Larkana, and Quetta, which provided 2,276 fully developed factory sites. The prime object of this project was to ensure a planned development of small industries in these estates.

The amenities and facilities provided in these estates include:

a. Roads, sewerage, water, power, telephone, post and telegraph office;
b. Banks;
c. Raw material godowns, marketing depots, and centres to provide technical assistance and common facilities as are needed;
d. Worker's canteen, Co-operative stores, and recreation clubs;
e. Fire-fighting stations.

In 1969, there were 257 factories located in these estates with a value added of Rs 328 million and employing 7,048 workers. Industrywise breakdowns of projects set up are available for five estates in the Punjab up to June 1973 and show that the bulk of the projects are in textiles, light engineering, surgical goods, and rubber and plastics. (Table 14.19).

ii) *Small Industries Institute*

This Institute was designed to provide consultancy services in architecture, chemicals, engineering, economics, management, cost accountancy, and other related fields.

iii) *Service Centres*

The West Pakistan Small Industries Corporation had established fourteen centres to provide technical know-how, training, and production assistance to the specialized industries in different parts of West Pakistan. These centres were located at Lahore, Gujranwala, Karachi, Multan, Hyderabad, Sialkot, and Gujrat, and specialized in light engineering, textiles, leather, footwear, metals, cutlery, sports goods, ceramics, pottery, surgical instruments, rubber, and plastics. The services offered by these centres are mostly free and they have also trained a large number of apprentices through their regular training programmes.

iv) *Handicrafts Development Centres*

WPSIC developed fourteen handicrafts development centres with a total capital cost of about Rs 2 million. The main purpose of developing these centres was:

a. To train and produce craftsmen and artisans particularly in backward areas.
b. To provide new and improved designs and prototypes to craftsmen and artisans.
c. To organize production of handicrafts.

Keeping in view the traditional crafts of the areas, two crafts were assigned to each centre for development.

v) *Handicrafts Design Centre, Lahore*

This centre is engaged in producing new and improved designs and prototypes to be distributed amongst artisans and craftsmen for adaption and commercial production. The activities of the centre are limited to five broad categories of handicrafts, viz, carpets, pottery, textile, woodcrafts, and metal crafts.

vi) *Rural Institutions*

The following three institutions were set up to develop rural areas around Peshawar:

a. Metal and Wood Workshop at Pishoongri;
b. Textile Training Centre, Urmer;
c. Ceramics Training Centre, Pubbi.

vii) *Small Industries Information Centre, Lahore*

This centre aimed at providing information to small entrepreneurs willing to establish their own factories.

viii) *Industrial Fairs and Exhibitions*

This scheme aimed at the participation of WPSIC in the various exhibitions and fairs which were held in the former East Pakistan.

b. *Provincial Small Industries Corporations*

After the break up of One Unit, the WPSIC was broken up into four provincial corporations which have worked on the same lines as the WPSIC. Their achievements during 1972-8 are given below:

i) *Punjab Small-Scale Industries Corporation*

This Corporation's major achievements during 1972-8 have been the establishment of two small industrial estates located at Jhelum and Faisalabad and the establishment of seventy-seven carpet development-cum-training centres equipped to train over two thousand carpet weavers per year. A carpet training institute has also been established to

Table 14.19: Industrial Classification of Projects on Five Industrial Estates.
(on 30 June 1973)

Industrial classification	Number of Projects					
	Gujranwala	Sialkot	Gujrat	Lahore	Bahawalpur	Total
Textile and hoisery	51	11	1	12	7	82
Light engineering	48	9	1	1	2	61
Rubber and plastic	13	6	—	—	1	20
Food processing	4	—	—	—	2	6
Wood work	3	—	—	—	—	3
Surgical	—	25	—	—	—	25
Leather goods	—	2	2	—	—	4
Cutlery	—	5	—	—	—	5
Sports goods	—	13	—	—	—	13
Glass and ceramics	—	—	4	—	—	4
Fans	—	—	7	—	—	7
Miscellaneous	47	16	1	3	3	70
Total	166	87	16	16	15	300

Source: A. Singhera, *Development of Small Industries in Pakistan, (1960-70)*, Economics Department, Punjab University, Lahore (M.A. Thesis).

train supervisory staff for the carpet industry. A loan of Rs 2,500 on personal guarantee to each carpet trainee desirous of setting up his own carpet unit is also arranged. To improve the skills of the rural labour force, the Corporation has also established ten *Dehimazdoor* Workshops at the IRDP *Markaz* where training is imparted in the fields of welding, woodwork, and tractor repairs. The Corporation has also set up seven handicrafts development centres where training is imparted to local artisans. Nine service centres in the fields of ceramics, leather, metallurgy, light engineering, cutlery, sports goods, and rubber and plastics are also being run to render technical advice, common facilities, and technical training to the private entrepreneurs. To induce private investment, the Corporation also provides pre-investment counselling and guidance to the prospective entrepreneurs through the Small Industries Advisory Service.

ii) *Sind Small Industries Corporation*

Amongst its achievements has been the establishment of industrial estates at Sukkar and Larkana. By 1977-8, twenty-one new units had started production in the Sukkar estate and eight were under construction. Thirteen units of the Larkana industrial estate were in operation and three were under installation. These units were mainly in textiles, garments, cotton waste, and flour milling. It has also established two new carpet centres at Jacobabad and Badin.

iii) *NWFP Small Industrial Development Board*

The Board is presently engaged in the setting up of eight industrial estates at Peshawar, Mardan, Khalabat, Dera Ismail Khan, Mardan, Abbotabad, Swat, Kohat, and Bannu. By the end of 1979, 259 plots had been allotted and 55 industrial units had started operation in the industrial estate at Peshawar. Four cotton textile sizing units have been established at the industrial estates at Peshawar, Mardan, Khalabat, and Dera Ismail Khan. There are thirteen carpet development-cum-training centres run by the Board (imparting training to two hundred and sixty boys) and five textile, *patti,* blanket and drugget weaving centres (training a hundred and fifty boys).

iv) *Baluchistan Small Industries Directorate*

The department has set up a large number of industrial centres in different districts to impart training. By the end of 1976 there were ninety-four such centres. The directorate has also started a scheme to take carpet weaving to the threshold of carpet weavers and to provide incentives to them. In 1978-9, a hundred and fifty looms along with raw materials were distributed among selected weavers.

c. *Financing of Small Industries*

The institutions financing small-scale industry are the commercial banks, the Provincial Small Industries Corporations, the Industrial Development Bank of Pakistan (IDBP), the Equity Participation Fund (EPF), and the People's Finance Corporation which was set up in 1972 and which is the only specialized financial institution serving the small-scale sector.

It is extremely difficult to quantify the amount of financing which actually goes to small enterprises both because of a lack of records regarding borrowers as well as problems with definitions of small-scale enterprises. According to World Bank estimates[21] (which are based on weak data and are only indicative), during the twenty-one months between July 1972 and March 1974, out of an estimated investment of Rs 700 million by Household and Artisan Workshops (employing less than twenty workers) and Rs 200 million estimated investment in small factories (employing between twenty to ninety-nine workers), the total lending by these different institutions was Rs 131 million (or only about 14 per cent) and the rest came from private owners/sponsors and the curb market (Table 14.20). The evidence therefore indicates that small industries are not being adequately financed by 'institutional' sources and this applies particularly to the household and artisan workshops employing less than twenty workers since almost all the schemes for small-scale industry tend to concentrate on the small factor sector employing between twenty to ninety-nine workers.

14.5.3 Growth of the Small-Scale Sector in the Seventies[22]

During the sixties, although the government did initiate steps for the growth of the small-scale sector, the overall industrial policy framework with liberal tax incentives and overvalued exchange rate for the import of industrial machinery meant that most of the investment went into the large-scale industrial sector. However, during the seventies a number of important changes took place both in government policy and in economic conditions which had a favourable impact on the growth of small-scale industries. Let us look briefly at some of these important factors.

Table 14.20: Estimated Lending to Small-Scale Industry
1 July 1972 to 30 March 1974 (Rs million)

	Number	Amount
Commercial Banks' own loans[1]	na	292
(of which for fixed investments)	na	73
Commercial Banks/SIC's		
Punjab[2]	88	13.6
NWFP[3]	55	10.3
Sind[2]	20	1.5
Sub total	163	25.4
IDBP/SIC's (only in Punjab)[2]	8	4.6
IDBP own loans[4]	73	23.7
People's Finance Corporation[5]	626	6.6
Equity Participation Fund[6]	3	0.3
Total	na	130.8
Estimated investment in household and artisan workshop industry[7]		700.0
Estimated investment in small factories		220.0
Total		920.0

1. Fixed assets excluding land and buildings of Rs 1 million and below; fixed investments have been assumed to be 25 per cent of lending.
2. Fixed assets excluding land of Rs 2 million and below.
3. Fixed assets including land of Rs 3 million and below.
4. Total assets of Rs 2 million and below.
5. Net assets of Rs 50,000 or less.
6. Total assets of Rs 2 million and below.
7. Annual Plan estimate fixed investment in companies with less than twenty workers, i.e., household and artisan workshop enterprises.
8. Estimated share of small factories (twenty to ninety-nine workers) in total investment by registered manufacturing enterprises based upon their share of fixed assets in the 1969-70 Census of Manufacturing Industry.

Source: IBRD, 'The Role of Small-Scale Industry in Pakistan's Development: Opportunities and Constraints', Report No. 887, 1976, p. 25.

a. *Devaluation*

In the sixties, for all practical purposes, Pakistan had operated on a multiple exchange rate system under which import of machinery and equipment had been allowed at the official overvalued exchange rate. Since the price of capital was kept artificially low and credit was easily available, investment in large-scale industry was extremely capital-intensive. Under the circumstances, small-scale industry, which in effect paid the market (scarcity) price of foreign exchange for its imports of machinery and raw materials, found it difficult to compete with either the large-scale industry in the production of consumer goods or with imported machinery and other engineering goods. Devaluation changed this in several ways. (i) The cost advantage enjoyed by large-scale industry, because of cheaper raw materials and machinery, was reduced. (ii) The increase in the price of finished goods, such as machinery and equipment, was much greater than that in the price of raw material required for their manufacture. Thus the competitiveness of small-scale industry, *vis-a-vis* imports was also increased. (iii) The export-oriented small-scale industry such as carpets, garments and made up textiles, surgical instruments, sports goods, etc., also received a considerable boost. Thus as a result of devaluation, small-scale industry began to expand rapidly in all sectors, especially the consumer goods sector, machinery and fabricated goods in the engineering sector and the export-oriented sector.

b. *Remittances*

An important development which took place in the seventies was the rapid expansion in the domestic market for consumer goods as a result of the inflow of workers' remittances from the Middle East on a large-scale. By the end of the decade there were about 2 million Pakistanis working abroad and the earnings remitted by them accounted for almost 10 per cent of the GNP. Thus, on a conservative estimate, there are about 1 million families in Pakistan who are receiving remittances from abroad. In other words, in a period of ten years, 1 million families have been added to the middle class families who, prior to this development, did not own the basic consumer durables associated with that income level. This has resulted in a rapid expansion in the market for consumer goods a large proportion of which are produced by small-scale industry. Many new industries have come up and a very diverse range of consumer products are now produced by the small-scale sector. For example, the plastic industry produces tableware, utensils, water coolers, containers, toys; the engineering industry produces appliances such as desert coolers, washing machines, gas cookers, and ovens in addition to the traditional items like fans, sewing machines, and bicycles. The residential construction boom has given rise to related industries such as electric cables and fittings, sanitary-ware, wooden and metal fixtures. The list could be expanded much further but it is sufficient to give an idea of the diversity and the broad-based nature of the growth that has taken place in the last ten years. However, it should not be thought that this growth has been restricted to consumer goods only because most of the machines used to manufacture these commodities are produced by the local small-scale engineering industry.

c. *Nationalization and Labour Legislation*

On assuming power the PPP government nationalized a number of industries. As a result, private investment in large-scale industry declined sharply. A part of this capital was diverted to small-scale industry since the threat of nationalization did not apply there. The small-scale textile sector was the largest beneficiary as this was also a period (1972-3 and 1973-4) of a boom in textile exports. It is interesting to note that because of the devaluation power looms produced by the small-scale sector had become much cheaper than imported ones. Consequently, for a few years, there was rapid growth in the engineering industry producing power looms. When the demand for power looms declined, many of the producers switched to the manufacture of agricultural machinery and implements, an industry which was by then expanding fairly rapidly.

The growing trade union movement and the progressive labour legislation in this period also provided an incentive to industrialists to move towards smaller units. In the engineering industry, in some cases, this took the form of splitting up an integrated unit into smaller firms each performing a distinct operation. For example, 'casting' would be done in one place, 'machining' in another, assembly or fabrication in still another, and so on. The resulting specialization had an important indirect benefit—it reduced the cost of entry into the engineering industry. New entrants could concentrate on one operation: either buying the castings and other components from other small producers or selling their product to those undertaking the final finishing and assembling. Consequently, today there are so many specialized small engineering firms that it is possible for those fabricating large plants or manufacturing complicated products, such as tractors, to have most of the components manufactured on a subcontracting basis.

d. *Import Liberalization*

One of the most important problems faced by small-scale industry is the availability of imported raw materials. In the last few years, the government has followed a policy of import liberalization and simplified licencing procedures. As a result, small manufacturers now have much better access to imported raw materials and this has provided an additional boost to the small-scale industry.

e. *Other Factors*

Labour shortages in agriculture during the peak demand period and government policy of promoting mechanization in agriculture has led to a rapid growth of tractors in the country. This in turn has resulted in the rapid growth of the agricultural engineering industry which produces tractor-drawn implements, threshers, and other agricultural equipment. Since this is a potentially huge market, it is likely that the agricultural engineering industry will become increasingly important.

To what extent did these factors stimulate the growth of the small-scale sector in the seventies? Again, data problems are severe and, as we have pointed out, till 1969-70 the government made no attempt to estimate the growth rate of this important sector which was taken to be equal to the growth rate of population. However, the results of a recent study by Hamid, covering the period from 1966-7 to 1976-7, are revealing (Table 14.21). They show that as compared to an output growth rate of 7.2 per cent in the second half of the sixties, the growth rate during the seventies almost doubled to 13.5 per cent. More remarkable are the employment growth rates of this sector. Even if the figures for the sixties are underestimates, they do show the very high growth rate of 13.7 per cent for the seventies.

To conclude, the small-scale sector can play a dynamic role especially in employment generation in the manufacturing sector. The evidence for the seventies, even discounting for data limitations, clearly brings this out. What is therefore needed is active government support for the continuation of the favourable economic conditions which stimulated the growth of this sector during this period.

Table 14.21: Employment, Value Added, and Growth in Unregistered Small Manufacturing Establishments
All Pakistan

	Number of Firms (000s)	Employment (000s)	Value added (Rs million) Current prices	1969-70 prices
1966-7	26.8	112	275	316
1969-70	32.2	120	389	389
1976-7	76.7	294	2,140	943
Growth rates (per cent per annum)				
1966-7 to 1969-70	6.3	2.3	–	7.2
1969-70 to 1976-7	13.2	13.7	–	13.5
1966-7 to 1976-7	11.1	10.1	–	11.5

Source: 1966-7: Bureau of Statistics, P and D Department, Government of Pakistan, SHMI Census (WPSIC) as reported in CMI (1966-7), preliminary release, April 1969, pp. vii and viii. 1969-70: Statistics Division, Government of Pakistan, SHMI Survey, Karachi.
1976-7 : Statistics Division, Government of Pakistan, SHMI Survey, Karachi.
From N. Hamid, *Growth and Development of Small-Scale Industries in Pakistan*, Report for ILO/ARTEP, Bangkok, 1982.

NOTES

1. Soligo and Stern in *Pakistan Development Review*, Summer 1965, Lewis and Guisinger in B. Belassa et. al., *The Structure of Protection in Developing Countries*, Baltimore, 1971, and G. Hufbauer in Falcon and Papanek, *Development Policy: The Pakistan Experience*, Cambridge, Mass., 1971.
2. Ibid.
3. L. White, *Industrial Concentration and Economic Power in Pakistan*, Princeton, 1974.
4. Ibid.
5. Ibid., p. 26.
6. R. Amjad, 'Impact of Concentration on Profitability in Pakistan', *Journal of Development Studies*, April 1977.
7. G.F. Papanek, *Pakistan's Development: Social Goals and Private Incentives*, Cambridge University Press, Harvard, 1967.
8. Ibid., p. 67.
9. *Dawn*, 25 April 1968.
10. White, op.cit. and R. Amjad, *Private Industrial Investment in Pakistan, 1960-70*, Cambridge, 1982.
11. IBRD, *Pakistan: Development Issue and Policies*, Vol. I, Report No. 1924—Pak., April 1978. Section 14.3.1 is based almost completely on this report.

12. L.P. Jones, *Efficiency of Public Manufacturing Enterprises in Pakistan*, (Draft Report), 1981.
13. This section relies heavily on R. Amjad, and K. Mahmood, *Development of Industrial Relations in Pakistan*, August 1979, Institute of Labour Studies, ILO, Geneva.
14. This section relies heavily on R. Amjad, *Small Scale Industries and Rural Industrialization in Pakistan—A Review of Major Policies and Programmes, 1947-80*, written for ILO, World Employment Programme, Geneva.
15. See Section 14.1.
16. See Section 14.2.2.
17. See Chapter 6 for details.
18. Government of Pakistan, *First Five Year Plan*, National Planning Board, 1957.
19. Ibid., p. 473
20. Government of Pakistan, *Fifth Five Year Plan*, Planning Commission, 1978, p. 96.
21. IBRD, *The Role of Small-Scale Industry in Pakistan*, Report No. 887, 1976, p. 25.
22. This section is based on N. Hamid, 'Growth and Development of Small-Scale Industries in Pakistan', Report for ILD/ARTEP, Bangkok, 1982.

15 Commercial Policy and Management of Foreign Trade

15.1 Introduction

Pakistan's Commercial Policy is an amalgamation of sub-policies administered by different government agencies. These include: (a) the Exchange Control Policy administered by the Foreign Exchange Committee of the Ministry of Finance and aimed at regulating the inflow and outflow of foreign exchange and its allocation between the public and the private sectors; (b) the Import Licencing Policy dealing with the disbursement of foreign exchange allocated to the private sector between various uses and users and which is under the charge of the Chief Controller of Imports and Exports; (c) the Export Promotion Policy framed by the Ministry of Commerce and concentrated on providing the incentives needed to maximize exports; and (d) the Tariff Policy enforced by the Ministry of Finance and used mainly as a revenue raising device but also supposed to reinforce the import licencing and exchange control policies.[1]

Pakistan's Commercial Policy can be divided into three distinct periods. The first period (1947-58) was mainly devoted to short-term crisis management dominated by the Korean War boom and the ensuing recession. Starting from a very liberal import policy, the trade crisis from 1953 onward forced the government to restrict imports which was instrumental in accelerating the industrialization process. The second period (1958-71) was mainly devoted to a vigorous export promotion policy, minimizing direct controls, and liberalizing imports. But events in the second half of the sixties forced certain changes in the Commercial Policy. 1972-80 started with a massive devaluation of the Pakistan rupee which was supposed to be a better substitute for the export bonus scheme on the one hand and the import control system on the other. However, rising oil prices and the recession in world trade in the mid-seventies nullified some of the assumptions implicit in the devaluation decision.

15.2 The Objectives and Tools of Commercial Policy

Foreign trade management has a special significance for policy-makers in developing countries since it provides opportunities to stimulate the growth process. Even if production relations are given, foreign trade offers the policy-makers choices between import and local production, and export and domestic consumption, leading to a more efficient allocation of resources. Foreign trade can also transform the existing production relations by providing opportunities to remove domestic shortages of scarce factors of production, to overcome the dis-economies of the small size of the domestic market, and to exchange goods with less growth potential (for example, raw materials) with goods having more growth potential (for example, technical know-how and equipment). Commercial policy is the art of managing the exchange of goods and services between countries.

In a typical developing country, particularly in the early stages of development, the bulk of exports consists of primary commodities and export earnings, due to the relative inelasticity of supply and uncertain production levels of primary goods, are not only unpredictable but also vulnerable to a number of factors. The developing country also depends upon the advanced industrial countries for most of its developmental needs (technology, capital, and producer goods) and consumption requirements. The developing countries, therefore, find their external environment difficult as their terms of trade deteriorate, their access to the markets of the advanced countries is limited by tariff and non-tariff barriers, and the trade and payments gaps widen with the passage of time.

The only short-term solution available to them is to seek extensive external assistance which, in due course, creates its own compliations.

Within the context of the compulsions of economic development, commercial policy in developing countries may pursue the following objectives:-

i) Maintaining equilibrium in the balance of payments and balance of trade, or at least limiting the extent of disequilibrium;
ii) Attaining favourable terms of trade so that, with the same quantity of exports, the country is able to import greater quantities of goods and services and thus achieve a net addition to real income;
iii) Promoting exports to derive the full benefits of comparative advantages and also to finance the country's import requirements;
iv) Import substitution to protect domestic production, accelerate the rate of capital formation, create employment opportunities, narrow trade and payments gaps, and seek a certain degree of national self-sufficiency;
v) Ensuring adequate availability of imported goods for both development and other purposes;
vi) Keeping the internal and external values of the national currency at desired levels.

Governments usually have a wide range of instruments of commercial policy to achieve policy goals. The most commonly used tool is the tariff structure consisting of import and export duties. Import duties can be used to influence the relative profitability of importing various commodity groups (for example, taxing development imports at lower rates than non-development imports), and to restrict the access of certain commodities to the domestic market in order to encourage savings and investment. Export duties may be used to limit the export of commodities in short supply at home and also sometimes to fill the gap between low domestic prices and high world prices.

Non-tariff measures may be divided into direct and indirect trade restrictions. Direct measures comprise embargoes on the import or export of certain commodities or quota restrictions which are often specific to certain commodities, destinations, or currencies. The imposition of exchange control and the licencing of imports and exports, common in developing countries, also constitute direct trade restrictions. Licences may be issued for the import of certain commodities without much formality and with no restrictions on quantity or source. In Pakistan this is known as the Open General Licence (OGL) system. But for most imports, a proper licencing system is introduced which may restrict the importer to make purchases from a specific country or currency area.

Indirect trade restrictions include various incentives and disincentives designed to influence the flow of foreign trade or its composition, such as, a) raising or lowering margin requirements for letters of credit to import certain commodities or categories, b) fiscal incentives for industries using domestic materials aimed at reducing the demand for imported substitutes, and c) subsidies and credit concessions or priorities for certain import-replacing goods or exportables. A special tool, often used by developing countries but regarded unfavourably by international monetary and lending institutions, is the multiple exchange rate system. This seeks to maintain a high external value of the national currency in order to export goods with greater competitive advantage in the world market while importing high-priority commodities, and to maintain a low external value to export goods with lesser advantage and to import low-priority commodities.

Pakistan's Commercial Policy and management of foreign trade will be discussed in the following sections.

15.3 1947-58: Early Stages—An Uncertain Link with Development Priorities

In the early years after Independence, Commercial Policy was mainly restricted to the management of short-term crises and reactions to various developments in the foreign trade sector, particularly because the country's economy was heavily dependent upon foreign trade. Pakistan exported the bulk of the raw material it produced and imported a large part of its development and non-development requirements. The immediate concern of the policy-makers was to maintain adequate supplies of consumer goods in the country so that price levels could be stabilized. Initially, therefore, the government opted for a liberal import policy. Export earnings were quite stable and the country had a surplus balance of trade in 1948-9 (Table 15.1).

15.3.1 The Non-Devaluation Decision

The first crisis in foreign trade came in September 1949 when the Pound Sterling, with which the Pakistan currency was linked, was devalued by 31 per cent. Other members of the Sterling area also followed suit but Pakistan decided not to devalue its currency. This decision brought a crisis in Pakistan's trade relations with its major trade partners, India and the UK, who received 66.7 per cent of Pakistan's total exports in 1948-9 and from whom Pakistan received 67.8 per cent of its total imports.[2] India in particular was resentful and refused to recognize the new exchange rate of its currency in terms of the Pakistani Rupee. Trade between India and Pakistan was therefore paralysed the immediate reaction of which was a decline in Pakistan's export earnings. Pakistan was, therefore, forced to abandon its liberal import policy in September 1949.

Whatever the merits and demerits of the non-devaluation decision, the crisis created by it was short-lived. In June 1950, the Korean War broke out and with it, as the fear of a third World War spread all over, the demand for raw materials for stock piling purposes rose sharply along with their prices. This enabled Pakistan to boost its export earnings, and also to diversify its trade relations which until then were confined to India, the UK, and other Sterling area members.

Imports were again liberalized in mid-1950 and more and more commodities were placed on OGL. By June 1951, 85 per cent of the total imports were on OGL, i.e., virtually without licence.[3]

India recognized the new exchange rate and trade with India was resumed in February 1951 but on a much reduced scale.

Table 15.1: Balance of Trade 1948-58
(Rs million)

Year	Imports	Exports	Balance
1948-9	1,487	1,871	+ 384
1949-50	1,284	1,218	− 66
1950-1	1,620	2,554	+ 934
1951-2	2,237	2,009	− 228
1952-3	1,384	1,510	+ 126
1953-4	1,118	1,286	+ 168
1954-5	1,103	1,223	+ 120
1955-6	1,325	1,784	+ 459
1956-7	2,335	1,608	− 727
1957-8	2,050	1,422	− 628

Source: CSO, *Twenty-five Years of Pakistan in Statistics, 1947-72*, Karachi, 1972, p. 383.

15.3.2 The Post-Korean Recession

The Korean boom lasted almost the whole year but in mid-1951, as peace negotiations between the Super Powers started, world prices of raw materials began to decline and Pakistan's export earnings also decreased. The market was clearly heading towards a recession but Pakistan reacted too slowly to the changing situation. Liberal imports continued up to the middle of 1952 when only certain margin requirements for letters of credit were raised in an attempt to restrict the flow of credit to the import sector. This step was too weak to cause any reduction in the import level and, in fact, it only stimulated imports under OGL since importers went on to build up inventories before the anticipated import cuts were applied. The OGL was finally suspended in November 1952 but by this time exchange reserves had fallen to dangerous levels. Pakistan was exposed to instability emanating from its external markets and was forced to seek external assistance to meet its food shortage and to sustain imports at the barest subsistence level.[4] The importers who had built up large stocks, particularly of consumer goods, were able to earn excessive profits.

The government's reluctance to restrict imports and its pursuit of a liberal import policy till the very last moment was defended on the grounds that:

a. it was an effective anti-inflationary device;
b. it helped to increase exports to 'treaty' countries; and
c. it provided vital financial support to the country by sustaining customs revenues at high levels.[5]

The arguments emphasized essentially short-term considerations and took no account of such other choices as building exchange reserves, restricting imports as far as possible to development goods, and utilizing the Korean boom earnings for industrial and overall economic development.

The Korean recession forced drastic changes in Pakistan's approach to foreign trade management. Export earnings declined during 1951-5 (Table 15.1) and the terms of trade worsened (Table 15.2). Pakistan was forced to follow a highly restrictive import policy. More than 70 per cent of the exchange available for commercial imports was reserved for industrial requirements. Furthermore, the import trade was preserved for 'category holders' and licences were for the most part restricted to well established importers. The average value of imports for one licencing period was designated as the trader's category and, depending upon the exchange position, the licences were issued automatically, the basis for licensing being expressed as a percentage of the 'category'. Profit margins in the import sector remained very high since the landed cost of imports bore no relation to the scarcity prices prevailing in the market. This restrictive policy was able to protect the home market from outside competition and to bring about remarkable industrial growth.

Table 15.2: Terms of Trade (1948-9 = 100)

		Indices of Unit Value of	
Year	Terms of trade	Exports	Imports
1949-50	111.3	87.9	79.4
1952-3	84.7	65.8	77.7
1955-6	67.8	81.4	120.8
1958-9	53.3	82.5	154.9

Source: Government of Pakistan, *Pakistan Economic Survey, 1962-3*, 1962, p. 56, Statistical Annexure.

15.3.3 Export Promotion Policy

Up to this time, export promotion had received only limited attention and the earliest attempt to promote export was bilateral trade agreements with a number of countries. These agreements incorporated target quantities for import from and export to the treaty countries but made no guarantees that the same would in fact be actually transacted. Quite often there was a wide margin between the targets prescribed and the actual trading performance.[6] In 1954, the Export Incentives Scheme was introduced to promote a number of minor export items but this was not enough to stimulate exports. The Pakistan Rupee was therefore devalued in July 1955 and this brought about 45.8 per cent increase in exports in 1955-6 over the previous year. However, after this initial spurt, exports declined again. In 1956, a more elaborate Export Promotion Scheme, covering sixty-seven primary commodities and fifty-eight manufactured goods, was introduced which entitled exporters to be granted import licences for certain specific items to the extent of 25 per cent and 40 per cent on various categories of manufactured goods and 15 per cent on the export of raw materials.[7] The balance of trade showed a deficit from 1956 onwards as, while exports declined, imports increased sharply due to the growing development needs and the import of wheat and rice.

15.3.4 The Direction and Composition of Foreign Trade

The direction of foreign trade showed significant changes during this period. Between 1948-9 and 1958-9, India's share in exports declined from 55.8 to 4.1 per cent and in imports from 31.8 to 7.7 per cent. Exports to the UK increased from 10.9 to 24.3 per cent while imports declined slightly from 28 to 27.2 per cent during the same period. The USA and Western Europe emerged as major suppliers of import requirements, their share increasing from 8.1 to 35.7 per cent in the case of the USA and from 6.4 to 31.2 per cent in the case of Western Europe (France, West Germany, Belgium and Italy). Their share in exports also increased from 8.9 to 13.8 per cent in the case of the USA and from 10.4 to 25.6 per cent in the case of Western Europe in the same period. Japan also increased its share in exports from 2.4 to 13.9 per cent and in imports from 1.5 to 7.8 per cent between 1948-9 and 1958-9.[8]

The composition of foreign trade underwent significant changes. The share of five major primary commodities, i.e., raw jute, raw cotton, raw wool, hides and skins, and tea was about 99 per cent of total export earnings in 1948-9 and 93 per cent in 1951-2.[9] By 1958-9, their share declined to about 75 per cent while over 17 per cent of the total exports consisted of manufactured goods.[10]

The share of capital goods and industrial raw materials was negligible in imports in the early years and the bulk of imports consisted of consumer goods, cotton textiles, and cotton yarn which accounted for over 30 per cent of the total imports in 1948-9.[11] By 1958-9 the share of capital goods and industrial raw materials in total imports was over 42 per cent while consumer goods accounted for over 57 per cent.

15.3.5 The Import Licence System

The system of import licences as it developed during the fifties needs special mention since it still exists though in a somewhat modified form. It is generally agreed that import licences have been a more effective instrument of import control than the tariff policy and the pattern of imports, according to Thomas, was by and large dictated by the decisions and actions of the sanctioning authority.[12] All foreign exchange expenditure was regulated by a high level Foreign Exchange Committee which prepared the foreign exchange budget and allocated exchange to the government and the public and private sectors. Once these allocations were made the actual detailed import decisions were effected by three distinct systems:

a. *Government Imports*

Various ministries, departments, and government agencies submitted their import requests to the Foreign Exchange Committee which determined the amount of exchange to be allocated. On this basis, government account licences were issued by the CCI&E (Chief Controller of Imports and Exports).

b. *Capital Imports for Industry*

The policy for the import of capital goods was determined as part of the overall exchange policy reflected in the industrial investment schedule which laid down priorities between various industries. Investment was regulated by a number of government agencies like CIPCOC (Central Investment Promotion and Co-ordination Committee) and the Investment Promotion Bureau. The CCI&E issued licences for the import of capital goods upon the authorization of one of these agencies.

c. *Consumer Goods, Industrial Raw Materials, and Spare Parts*

The CCI&E issued licences for this category of goods which were the most important components of import. After the OGL was suspended, the licence system for this category was set up in 1952 in order to reduce imports. Although there were a variety of alternative methods to restrict imports, a system of rigid and detailed import licences was introduced with the government determining for every six-month shipping period the total value of licences to be issued and their allocation determined according to the commodity and the importer. The system proved effective during the post-Korean recession (1952-5) but, as is common with all control mechanisms, it not only failed to keep pace with the basic economic changes, it also became a source of corruption and bribery. It created a wide gap between the world prices and the internal prices of goods imported at the official exchange rate and it enabled importers to earn monopoly profits, particularly after the introduction of the category system. Another problem was the principle of 'essentiality' which governed the allocation of import licences giving least priority to consumer goods, particularly luxury items, and high priority to raw materials, spare parts, and machinery. This created a very protected and potentially profitable market for the domestic production of consumer goods when the highest protection was given to the least essential consumer goods industries. This protection was further enforced by the pattern of tariff duties.

The licence system also became a source of economic disparity between East and West Pakistan since West Pakistan's economy received about two-thirds of the public and private investments during the fifties and about the same ratio of total imports. The West Pakistani importers were also more numerous as well as larger and received more import licences.[13]

15.4 1958-71: Integration with the Growth Strategy

With the change in government in 1958 and a clearer policy of economic growth, the commercial policy was used as a tool to realize such objectives as changing the pattern of industrialization from consumer goods industries to intermediate and investment goods industries, and influencing the inter-sectoral terms of trade and flow of resources and income between various sectors and various regions principally through the use of an export bonus scheme. This period is also characterized by an increasing share of manufactured goods in exports and of capital goods and industrial raw materials in imports, larger imports of food grain, and a widening trade gap which led to a high proportion of imports being financed by foreign aid.

Throughout this period, exports expanded consistently except in the late sixties. Imports increased even faster but, in the second half of the sixties, their level fluctuated due to the after-effects of the 1965 War, a lesser availability of foreign aid, and growing exchange constraints. The trade gap remained high and exports as percentage of total imports declined from 84 per cent in 1958-9 to 44.8 per cent in 1964-5 but then rose to 62 per cent by 1970-1 (Table 15.3). The terms of trade remained mostly favourable (Table 15.4) although these figures may be misleading since the base year taken to calculate the terms of trade was 1954-5 when Pakistan's exports had still not recovered from the post-Korean recession.

15.4.1 Export Promotion

The commercial policy in this period was distinguished by a relentless effort to promote exports. The main instrument used for this purpose was the Export Bonus Scheme, introduced in 1959, which aimed at making exports more attractive by transferring part of the excess profits in imports to the export sector. Exporters of all commodities, except the traditional primary commodities, were entitled to bonus import licences worth a certain percentage of the exchange earned. Export items were divided into categories under this scheme and each category was entitled to a different percentage of bonus.[14] These licences, called bonus vouchers, could be used to import a large number of consumer goods, industrial raw materials, and capital goods. They could also be sold in the open market at a substantial premium ranging between 100 to 190 per cent of their face value.[15] The extent to which exports were actually stimulated depended upon the bonus voucher's prevailing price in the open market. Whenever the price fell to a level regarded as low, the government took care to raise it by adding more commodities to the bonus import list. The scheme was continuously modified with regard to its coverage, rates of bonus, and composition of items importable on the bonus vouchers. Major changes came in 1967 when a 'cash-cum-bonus' system was introduced whereby the regular licence system was used in conjunction with the Bonus Scheme for the import of a wide range of raw materials[16] and in 1970 when primary commodities were also entitled to a bonus.[17]

To what extent did the scheme serve to accelerate exports which was its primary purpose? There is no simple answer. The value of exports covered under the scheme did increase appreciably[18] but the data does not tell the whole story. The rise in exports of processed goods was at the expense of the raw materials that would otherwise have been exported. Also, to the extent that the diversion of certain goods from the home to the foreign market releases domestic purchasing power

Table 15.4: Terms of Trade (1954-5 = 100)

Year	Terms of trade	Indices of Unit Value of Exports	Indices of Unit Value of Imports
1959-60	80.81	126.52	157.79
1960-1	110.15	186.04	168.93
1962-3	85.47	144.32	168.85
1964-5	111.15	157.92	141.44
1965-6	94.60	158.52	167.57
1966-7	118.10	185.92	157.42
1967-8	101.60	162.14	159.59
1968-9	116.86	173.65	148.60

Source: Government of Pakistan, *Pakistan Economic Survey, 1969-70*, Islamabad, 1970, p. 137.

Table 15.3: Balance of Trade 1958-71—All Pakistan
(Rs million)

Year	Imports	Exports	Balance	Exports as percentage of imports
1958-9	1,578	1,325	– 253	84.0
1959-60	2,461	1,843	– 618	74.9
1960-1	3,188	1,799	–1,389	56.4
1961-2	3,109	1,843	–1,266	59.3
1962-3	3,819	2,247	–1,572	58.8
1963-4	4,430	2,299	–2,131	51.9
1964-5	5,774	2,408	–3,366	44.8
1965-6	4,208	2,718	–1,490	64.5
1966-7	5,192	2,913	–2,279	56.1
1967-8	4,655	3,348	–1,307	71.9
1968-9	4,897	3,305	–1,592	67.5
1969-70	5,098	3,337	–1,761	65.4
1970-1	5,178	3,362	–1,816	64.9

Source: CSO, *Twenty-five Years of Pakistan in Statistics, 1947-72*, Karachi, 1972, p. 383.

to procure goods which could otherwise be exported, there is a presumed loss of earnings. Moreover, allowing for a trend factor, some rise in exports may have taken place even if this scheme had not been introduced. Finally, many exporters sold their goods in the foreign market at lower prices, sometimes even below cost, since they calculated their return in Rupees in which terms the loss could be made up by the sale of bonus vouchers.[19]

The scheme was also criticized for introducing a complex system of multiple exchange rate which, along with the uncertainty of the bonus voucher system, weakened the protection of infant industries. The domestic producer found the protection he received substantially reduced whenever there was a fall in the bonus voucher premium or an annual increase in regularly licenced imports.[20] Griffin and Khan found that while the scheme gave protection to local industry, the rates of bonus and the resulting rates of protection were highly arbitrary and discriminatory.[21] However, the scheme succeeded in subsidizing and promoting exports as well as diversifying them away from traditional commodities and at the same time allowing a safety value on imports by making available to industry those scarce inputs which could not be imported on regular licences. All this was accomplished without damaging the basic structure of import controls.

There were many other steps taken to promote exports. In 1962, the Export Credit Guarantee Scheme was introduced to provide exporters with guarantees against certain financial risks which are not normally covered by insurance. Export Performance Licences for imports were also issued to exporters on the basis of the f.o.b. value of their exports. Recommendations as to the industries and firms entitled to export performance licences, and the percentage of the f.o.b. value of their exports which would be returned to them in the form of additional licences, were received from various government agencies particularly the Export Promotion Bureau. This was followed in 1966 by the Export Market Development Fund which financed a survey of foreign markets, for specified commodities and services, through grants. It also financed sales promotion efforts by establishing trade offices and display centres abroad. The government also decided to announce export policies on an annual basis from 1968-9.

15.4.2 Import Liberalization and Changes in the Licence System

The import policy underwent drastic changes in line with the general policy of emphasizing economic growth, relaxing economic controls, and greater reliance on the market forces. A restrictive import policy continued in the initial stages due to exchange constraints. But with the introduction of the Export Bonus Scheme, a 'marginal liberalization'[22] took place since imported commodities, which were in short supply in the domestic market, could now be imported on bonus vouchers and, with the breakdown of the monopoly of the category holders, the import trade became more competitive.

As export earnings rose, a new OGL system was introduced in 1961 which further eroded the monopoly of category holders by granting commercial licences to new-comers and providing for automatic repeat licences, i.e., additional licences of equal value could be automatically issued to old and new importers on proving the utilization of the original licences. Unlike in the early fifties, the OGL was this time a controlled system in the sense that there were restrictions relating to regional and sub-regional quotas, the country of origin, and the destination within Pakistan. By 1964 commodities importable under the OGL had risen to fifty-one as against eleven in 1961.[23]

In spite of these liberalizing measures, the import trade was still more or less controlled by the licence system which was strongly biased towards capital goods import. According to Naqvi, the share of consumer goods in industrial licences declined by 23.8 per cent between 1957 and 1963, the share of investment (capital) goods increased by 21.6 per cent but the share of intermediate goods (industrial raw materials) rose by only 2.2 per cent.[24] Even rising export earnings and larger exchange reserves during 1962-4 could not lead the authorities to increase the import of raw materials with the result that there was an acute shortage of industrial raw materials and a considerable under-utilization of industrial capacity.

A major step towards further liberalization was accordingly taken in 1964 when industrial raw materials and spare parts were placed on the Free List and could be imported without requiring a government licence. Another large group including tractors, vehicles, tyres, and office equipment were put on the OGL and automatic repeat licences. Many other industries were given more liberal licences for goods not covered by the Free List or the OGL.[25]

But the period of relatively free imports did not last long due to the 1965 War with India and substantial cutbacks in foreign economic assistance. There was a further setback in 1966 due to the unexpected diversion of a substantial amount of foreign exchange for food imports since the availability of food grains under the PL 480 Programme had been delayed and domestic agricultural production was low. The total volume of imports, therefore, had to be curtailed. The number of commodities on the OGL, fifty-one in 1964, was reduced to only eleven in 1966. Items on the Free List declined from sixty-six in 1964 to fourteen in 1968[26] and the same number in 1971.[27] The licencible List was cut down from a hundred and one in 1966 to thirty-one in 1968[28] and thirty-eight in 1970.[29]

These sharp cuts in imports on cash licences forced the government to rely more on bonus and cash-cum-bonus imports. The bonus list was expanded from 215 items in 1966-7 to 260 in 1968[30] and 277 in 1970.[31] The items covered by the Free, Licencible, and Cash-cum-Bonus Lists were also made importable under bonus.

It is worthwhile to point out that, during this period, the private sector imported goods under four types of import licences: (a) the Free List which allowed imports at an official exchange rate to entitlement holders on a first-come-first-served basis with a cut-off point when funds were exhausted. This was financed exclusively from foreign credits or arranged under barter agreements. (However, the Free List contained a number of restrictions in the form of minimum and maximum limits on individual orders of goods of each type, country/currency, area of origin, destination in Pakistan, and restrictions on some items to be imported by industrial users only. Thus the Free List, particularly after 1965, did not function so freely although it remained part of the import control system); (b) the Licencible List which was financed by Pakistan's own resources. These licences could be issued only to certain industrialists and commercial importers. Ceilings were fixed for each item and thus their import was strictly controlled. Mainly consumer goods and industrial raw materials were placed on this list; (c) the Cash-cum-Bonus Licence: the importers were allowed to use 50 per cent of cash licenses and 50 per cent of bonus vouchers mainly for the import of raw materials but a few consumer goods were also allowed. This was financed by the country's own resources; and (d) the Bonus List: licences on this list were issued automatically on surrender of a bonus voucher. There were no quantitative restrictions and items importable on the Bonus List included consumer goods, industrial raw materials, and capital goods.

15.4.3 Changes in the Composition and Direction of Foreign Trade

This period saw significant changes in the direction of foreign trade. Pakistan was able to diversify its export relations more successfully as compared to 1958-9 when over 63 per cent of its total exports went to four major buyers, i.e., UK, USA, Western Europe, and Japan. By 1970-1 their share had declined to 40 per cent as export markets in the Middle East were explored. In imports there was little change in the position of these major trading partners although there was a shift in favour of Western Europe and Japan at the cost of the UK and the USA (Table 15.5).

The Composition of imports also underwent major changes. There was a drastic reduction in the share of consumer goods in total imports and a corresponding improvement in the share of capital goods. There was, however, only a modest increase in the share of industrial raw materials (Table 15.6).

As regards the composition of exports, the share of manufactured goods increased substantially during this period from 17 per cent of the total exports to over 55 per cent. There was a corresponding decline in the export of industrial raw materials (Table 15.7).

Table 15.5: Direction of Foreign Trade 1958-71—All Pakistan
(Percentage of total exports and imports)

	Exports		Imports	
Countries	1958-9	1970-1	1958-9	1970-1
UK	18.3	9.7	17.2	10.5
USA	10.4	11.8	22.6	17.8
Western Europe	24.4	11.7	24.5	29.5
Japan	10.5	6.9	4.9	10.4

Source: (i) Government of Pakistan, *Economy of Pakistan, 1948-68*, Karachi, 1968, p. 106 for 1958-9 (compilation). (ii) Government of Pakistan, *Pakistan Economic Survey, 1972-3*, Islamabad, 1973, pp. 86-9 for 1970-1.

Table 15.6: Composition of Imports 1958-70—All Pakistan
(Percentage of total imports)

Year	Capital goods	Industrial raw materials	Consumer goods
1958-9	16.63	26.12	27.25
1964-5	50.04	27.85	22.11
1969-70	47.51	36.19	16.30

Source: (i) Government of Pakistan, *Economy of Pakistan, 1948-68*, Karachi, 1968, p. 105 for 1958-9. (ii) Government of Pakistan, *Pakistan Economic Survey, 1972-3*, Islamabad, 1973, p. 91, Statistical Annexure, for 1964-5 and 1969-70.

15.5 1972-80: New Disequilibria and New Adjustments

Once again, as in 1958, with the change in regime, there was a drastic change in the pattern of foreign trade management due mainly to the changed circumstances. The delinking of East Pakistan created structural changes in Pakistan's foreign trade as part of the country's internal trade was 'externalized'. West Pakistan's exports to East Pakistan amounted to Rs 1,652 million in 1969-70 which is about 50 per cent of Pakistan's total exports in that year. There was considerably less dislocation in imports. Imports from East to West Pakistan amounted to Rs 916 million in 1969-70 which was only 18 per cent of Pakistan's total imports for that year. Thus Pakistan had to find markets for substantial portions of a number of commodities previously sold to the Eastern Wing. These included primary commodities like oilseeds, raw cotton, tobacco, and food grain; and manufactured goods like cotton fabrics, yarn and thread, machinery, drugs and medicines,

Table 15.7: Composition of Exports 1958-70—All Pakistan
(Percentage of total exports)

Year	Industrial raw materials	Food, drinks, and tobacco	Manufactured goods
1958-9	75.7	6.3	17.3
1964-5	56.8	11.1	32.1
1969-70	36.5	7.8	55.7

Note: Percentages of 1958-9 do not add up to a hundred since classification at that time showed 'miscellaneous exports' separately.

Source: (i) Government of Pakistan, *Economy of Pakistan, 1948-68*, Karachi, 1968, p. 105 for 1958-9. (ii) Government of Pakistan, *Pakistan Economic Survey, 1970-1*, Islamabad, 1971, p. 92 for 1964-5 and 1969-70.

tobacco manufactures, and cement. Similarly, it had to find alternative sources of supply of many items like jute goods, tea, paper, and matches which previously came from East Pakistan.

In May 1972, the new government abolished the multiple exchange rate system and the controversial Export Bonus Scheme, and the Pakistan Rupee was devalued by about 58 per cent from the US dollar parity of Rs 4.76 to Rs 11.00. (Later, in February 1973, when the US devalued the dollar by 10 per cent, the parity of the Rupee in terms of gold was maintained and the new exchange rate was fixed at Rs 9.90 per dollar).

The decision to devalue, and the extent of devaluation, provoked much debate and controversy. The government put forward a number of arguments in support of its decision such as:

a) the export bonus scheme had distorted the allocations of scarce exchange resources in favour of the industrial and the corporate sectors;
b) the common man suffered as the domestic cost and price structure was affected by the high premium on bonus vouchers;
c) devaluation was essential to improve the agricultural terms of trade in relation to other sectors;
d) Pakistan's exports needed a major boost because of the loss of East Pakistan's market;
e) the genuine entrepreneur who had a sound and economically viable project must pay a realistic price of foreign exchange.[32]

But the devaluation decision was criticized on the following grounds:

a) devaluation on such a high scale could have been justified if domestic production of exportable goods could also be increased rapidly which was doubtful at that particular time due to the unsettled environment created by the loss of East Pakistan;
b) devaluation increased the cost of investment [involving foreign exchange] by about 131 per cent (which was the increase in the value of the dollar in terms of the Pakistan Rupee);
c) the internal price structure was adversely affected since devaluation raised the overall cost structure and thus accelerated the inflationary pressures on the economy.

Between 1972-3 and 1979-80 export earnings increased by 173 per cent (Table 15.8). This, together with the rapidly increasing invisible receipts of remittances by Pakistanis working abroad (from about US$ 124 million in 1972-3 to US$ 1,743 million in 1979-80 an increase of over 1,300 per cent),[33] could lead to substantial improvements in the overall payments position. But Pakistan's terms of trade took an unfavourable turn (Table 15.9) as the rise in world oil prices (which shot up the petroleum and oil products import bill from Rs 649 million in 1972-3 to Rs 3,744 million in 1975-6 and Rs 10,684 million in 1979-80)[34] and the worldwide inflationary trends caused the import prices index to rise much faster than export prices. The increase in imports between 1972-3 and 1979-80 was about 459 per cent.

Table 15.8: Balance of Trade 1972-80
(Rs million)

Year	Imports	Exports	Balance	Exports as percentage of imports
1972-3	8,398	8,551	(+) 153	101.8
1973-4	13,479	10,161	(–) 3,318	75.3
1974-5	20,925	10,286	(–) 10,639	49.1
1975-6	20,465	11,253	(–) 9,212	54.9
1976-7	23,012	11,294	(–) 11,718	49.0
1977-8	27,815	12,980	(–) 14,835	46.6
1978-9	36,388	16,925	(–) 19,463	46.5
1979-80	46,929	23,410	(–) 23,519	49.8

Source: Government of Pakistan, *Pakistan Economic Survey, 1980-1*, Islamabad, 1981, p. 97, Statistical Annexure.

Table 15.9: Terms of Trade (1969-70 = 100)

Year	Terms of trade	Indices of Unit value of Exports	Imports
1972-3	95.6	272.6	285.2
1973-4	106.4	439.0	412.6
1974-5	66.7	409.7	614.5
1975-6	70.5	410.8	582.6
1976-7	83.4	488.5	585.4
1977-8	81.0	508.5	628.1
1978-9	87.5	573.8	656.0
1979-80	83.9	673.4	802.8

Source: Government of Pakistan, *Pakistan Economic Survey, 1980-1*, Islamabad, 1981, p. 98, Statistical Annexure.

15.5.1 Export Promotion

The abolition of the Export Bonus Scheme and the devaluation of the Rupee were expected to boost the country's exports. The sharp reduction in the external value of the Rupee was presumably meant to be a substitute for export subsidies and concessions in export duties and other taxes to the export sector. But a number of factors debilitated the impact of devaluation and the consequent competitive edge of Pakistan's exports. Floods in 1973 and pest attacks in 1976 and 1978 caused extensive damage to the cotton crop adversely affecting raw cotton exports. The cotton textiles industry found itself needing concessions in export duties in spite of the price advantage due to devaluation. The export duty on all cotton manufactures had to be reduced and, on certain cotton products, abolished in 1974. In 1976, the export duty on some varieties of raw cotton was also abolished and reduced on other varieties. Among primary goods, rice became a major exchange earner. In due course, a number of manufactured goods lost the competitive edge gained by devaluation as the cost of balancing, modernization, and replacement began to increase and adversely affected their cost structure. The government was therefore compelled to build up a rebate on the export of textiles ranging between 7.5 to 12.5 per cent in order to compensate the industry for the increased prices of raw cotton, capital equipment, and imported inputs in 1978. Later, some other manufactured goods were also granted such compensatory rebates.

Rebates have also been given on excise and custom duties on a number of exportable goods. The Export Finance Scheme charges a concessional interest rate to finance the export of manufactured goods. Exporters also enjoy certain concessions in income tax.

Export Processing Zones are also being set up in Karachi and Lahore where Pakistani entrepreneurs can participate in joint ventures with foreign investors who will provide foreign exchange and technical know-how. These zones will be custom-free and will concentrate exclusively on developing export industries.

It now seems that, after stagnating in the mid-seventies, the export sector is again moving to higher growth rates (Table 15.10).

15.5.2 Changes in the Import Policy and Import Control System

Devaluation led to significant changes in the import policy in May 1972. The import of all luxury items was banned while import for development needs was liberalized. The import licence system was changed. All categories and entitlements in imports were abolished and regrouped into only two categories: (i) The Free List containing 327 items importable on cash as well as loans, credits, and barter from worldwide sources. The Free List was further sub-divided into three parts: (a) licences for all registered importers, (b) licences for industrial consumers only, and (c) licences for the public sector. (ii) The Tied List covering twenty-five items which could be imported only from tied sources. Except for a few items reserved for

Table 15.10: Growth of Exports—1972-80
(Percentage growth over previous year in terms of US dollars)

Year	Percentage
1972-3	38.4
1973-4	24.7
1974-5	1.2
1975-6	9.4
1976-7	0.4
1977-8	14.9
1978-9	30.4
1979-80	38.3

Source: (i) Government of Pakistan, *Pakistan Economic Survey, 1975-6*, Islamabad, 1976, p. 136 for 1972-3 and 1973-4. (ii) Government of Pakistan, *Pakistan Economic Survey, 1976-7*, Islamabad, 1977, p. 124 for 1974-5 and 1975-6. (iii) Government of Pakistan, *Pakistan Economic Survey, 1977-8*, Islamabad, 1978, p. 109 for 1976-7. (iv) Government of Pakistan, *Pakistan Economic Survey, 1979-80*, Islamabad, 1980, p. 133 for 1977-8 and 1978-9. (v) Government of Pakistan, *Pakistan Economic Survey, 1980-1*, Islamabad, 1981 p. 139 for 1979-80.

industrial users, all registered importers could obtain licences for any number of importable items. The import trade was thus thrown wide open and imports were again liberalized after having gone through a restrictive phase. This was done in order to increase the availability of all types of goods so that industries could improve their capacity utilization and increase production in anticipation of a higher demand for exportable goods as a result of devaluation. The liberalization trend continued during the seventies and the Free List was extended to 407 items in 1976[36] and 438 in 1978-9.[37]

This was done in spite of stagnating exports in the mid-seventies and rapidly rising prices of a number of major import items like petroleum and oil products, wheat, edible oils, fertilizers, chemicals, metals, and machinery. The government also allowed a number of consumer durables to be imported under the gift scheme to help Pakistanis working abroad remit their earnings home in kind particularly from those countries which had imposed monetary ceilings on cash remittances.[38]

But a continuous deterioration in the balance of payments position necessitated some modifications in the import policy. In late 1979, margin requirements for import letters of credit were raised substantially to curb speculative imports. The import licence procedure was tightened and the Free List was reduced to 435. The government also attempted to restrict the mushroom growth of importers by imposing a registration fee and an import licence fee of 2 per cent of the value of the licence. However, the growth rate of imports has ranged between 20 and 30 per cent (Table 15.11) in spite of the high Rupee cost of foreign exchange, import duties, and inflation abroad which underlines the price inelasticity of demand for almost all kinds of imported goods.

Table 15.11: Growth of Imports 1972-80
(Percentage increase over previous year in terms of US dollars)

Year	Percentage
1972-3	24.9
1973-4	71.9
1974-5	55.2
1975-6	(-) 4.4
1976-7	12.4
1977-8	20.9
1978-9	30.8
1979-80	29.0

Source: (i) Government of Pakistan, *Pakistan Economic Survey, 1975-6*, Islamabad, 1976, p. 141 for 1972-3 and 1973-4. (ii) Government of Pakistan, *Pakistan Economic Survey, 1976-7*, Islamabad, 1977, p. 128 for 1974-5 and 1975-6. (iii) Government of Pakistan, *Pakistan Economic Survey, 1980-1*, Islamabad, 1981, p. 146 for the rest.

15.5.3 The Composition and Direction of Foreign Trade

The country was able to diversify its trade relations and find new markets for exports after the loss of East Pakistan. The most significant change was the emergence of the Middle East as a market for export. Similarly, countries in East Asia have also emerged as

Table 15.12: Direction of Exports 1972-80
(Percentage of total exports)

Countries	1972-3	1974-5	1976-7	1979-80
USA	4.0	3.7	5.2	5.1
Western Europe	24.9	23.6	28.3	24.9
ECM	21.1	18.9	22.8	20.5
Eastern Europe	7.4	7.4	4.5	4.4
Middle East	9.2	29.2	31.6	26.0
RCD	0.7	5.8	8.4	4.1
Asia (excluding Middle East)	47.5	30.2	25.0	32.1
Japan	18.2	6.8	8.1	7.7
Hong Kong	11.2	7.7	6.3	7.8

Source: (i) Government of Pakistan, *Pakistan Economic Survey, 1974-5*, Islamabad, 1975, pp. 88-91, Statistical Annexure, for 1972-3 (compilation). (ii) Government of Pakistan, *Pakistan Economic Survey, 1977-8*, Islamabad, 1978, p.113 for 1974-5 and 1976-7. (iii) Government of Pakistan, *Pakistan Economic Survey, 1980-1*, Islamabad, 1981, pp.108-123, Statistical Annexure, for 1979-80 (compilation).

buyers of Pakistani goods whereas the position of the USA and Western Europe remains by and large unchanged (Table 15.12).

Over this period, the Middle East has replaced the USA and Western Europe as a major source of imports, mainly oil. Japan is also becoming an important supplier of capital goods and industrial raw material. The decline in the USA's share in our imports corresponds to the decline of the percentage share of that country in foreign aid (apart from the fact that goods from the Far East are cheaper as compared to American goods. Table 15.13).

Table 15.13: Direction of Imports 1972-80
(Percentage of total imports)

Countries	1972-3	1974-5	1976-7	1979-80
USA	24.9	14.8	14.7	11.1
Western Europe	28.0	25.6	26.9	23.9
ECM	25.0	22.6	23.5	21.3
Eastern Europe	6.6	5.3	4.5	4.0
Middle East	9.1	16.8	18.3	30.8
RCD	1.8	0.6	0.2	0.1
Asia (excluding Middle East)	23.0	27.2	29.2	23.8
Japan	8.6	12.6	14.3	11.5
Hong Kong	0.3	0.5	0.7	0.5

Source: (i) Government of Pakistan, *Pakistan Economic Survey, 1974-5*, Islamabad, 1975, pp. 88-91, Statistical Annexure for 1972-3 (compilation). (ii) Government of Pakistan, *Pakistan Economic Survey, 1977-8*, Islamabad, 1978, p.116 for 1974-5 and 1976-7. (iii) Government of Pakistan, *Pakistan Economic Survey, 1980-1*, Islamabad, 1981, p.148 for 1979-80 except the USA, Japan, and Hong Kong which were compiled from pp. 108-123, Statistical Annexure.

Table 15.14: Composition of Imports 1972-80
(Percentage of total imports)

Year	Capital goods	Industrial raw materials for Capital goods	Consumer goods	Industrial raw materials for Consumer goods
1972-3	29.8	9.9	30.8	29.5
1973-4	29.5	6.7	40.0	23.8
1974-5	29.4	8.6	39.5	22.5
1975-6	35.0	6.1	37.7	21.2
1976-7	38,0	6.4	39.7	15.9
1977-8	33.5	6.9	39.6	20.0
1978-9	30.1	5.9	42.4	21.6
1979-80	35.5	6.2	42.3	16.0

Source: Government of Pakistan, *Pakistan Economic Survey, 1980-1*, Islamabad, 1981, p. 107, Statistical Annexure.

Table 15.15: Composition of Exports 1972-80
(Percentage of total exports)

Year	Primary commodities	Semi manufactures	Manufactured goods
1972-3	39.4	30.2	30.4
1973-4	39.4	22.6	38.0
1974-5	48.0	12.7	39.3
1975-6	43.7	18.4	37.9
1976-7	40.9	16.7	42.4
1977-8	35.7	14.7	49.6
1978-9	32.3	20.6	47.1
1979-80	42.0	15.0	43.0

Source: Government of Pakistan, *Pakistan Economic Survey, 1980-1*, Islamabad, 1981, p. 103, Statistical Annexure.

The composition of imports has undergone one significant change, i.e., the share of industrial raw materials has increased considerably, mainly at the cost of consumer goods. The share of capital goods in total imports has risen but the share of industrial raw materials for capital goods, quite low in 1972-3, has since then declined further. This shows the country's increasing dependence upon the import of machinery and other capital goods (Table 15.14).

In exports, there has been an appreciable increase in the share of manufactured goods and an almost equivalent decline in the share of semi-manufactured goods (Table 15.15).

NOTES

1. S.N.H. Naqvi, 'Allocative Biases of Pakistan's Commercial Policy', in Nurul Islam (ed.) *Studies on Commercial Policy and Economic Growth*, PIDE, Karachi, 1970, pp. 51-2.
2. Government of Pakistan, *Economy of Pakistan, 1948-68*, Karachi, 1968, p. 101.
3. Andrus and Mohammad, *Trade, Finance and Development in Pakistan*, Oxford University Press, 1966, p. 25.
4. Ibid., p. 48.
5. Ibid., p. 47.
6. Ibid., p. 35.
7. Government of Pakistan, *Economy of Pakistan, 1948-68*, Karachi, 1968, p. 103.
8. Ibid., p. 101 for figures relating to 1948-9 and p. 106 for 1958-9.

9. Ibid., p. 99.
10. Ibid., p. 105.
11. Ibid., p. 100.
12. Thomas, 'Import Licensing and Import Liberalization in Pakistan' in Nurul Islam, (ed.), *Studies in Commercial Policy and Economic Growth*, PIDE, Karachi, 1970, p. 6.
13. Ibid., pp. 6-14. Also see Mahbubul Haq, *The Strategy of Economic Planning*, Oxford University Press, Karachi 1973, pp. 100-1.
14. Andrus and Mohammad, *Trade, Finance and Development in Pakistan*, Oxford University Press, 1966, p. 37.
15. Ibid., p. 37.
16. S.R. Lewis, *Pakistan Industrialization and Trade Policies*, Oxford University Press, 1970, p.30.
17. Government of Pakistan, *Pakistan Economic Survey, 1970-1*, Islamabad, p. 107.
18. Government of Pakistan, *Economy of Pakistan, 1948-68*, Karachi, 1968, p. 107.
19. Andrus and Mohammad, *Trade, Finance and Development in Pakistan*, Oxford University Press, 1966, p. 39.
20. Papanek, *Pakistan's Development—Social Goals and Private Incentives*, Harvard University Press, 1967, pp. 30-131.
21. Griffin and Khan (eds.), *Growth and Inequality in Pakistan*, MacMillan, 1972, p. 128.
22. Thomas, 'Import Licensing and Import Liberalization in Pakistan', in Nurul Islam (ed.), *Studies in Commercial Policy and Economic Growth*, PIDE, Karachi, 1970, p. 15.
23. Government of Pakistan, *Economy of Pakistan, 1948-68*, Karachi, 1968, p. 112.
24. S.N.H. Naqvi, 'The Allocative Biases of Pakistan's Commercial Policy, 1953-63', in Nurul Islam (ed.), *Studies on Commercial Policy and Economic Growth*, PIDE, Karachi, 1970, p. 64.
25. Papanek, *Pakistan's Development—Social Goals and Private Incentives*, Harvard University Press, 1967, p.131.
26. Government of Pakistan, *Economy of Pakistan, 1948-68*, Karachi, 1968, p. 113.
27. Government of Pakistan, *Pakistan Economic Survey, 1970-1*, Islamabad, p. 113.
28. Government of Pakistan, *Economy of Pakistan*, Karachi, 1968, p. 113.
29. Government of Pakistan, *Pakistan Economic Survey, 1970-1*, Islamabad, p. 115.
30. Government of Pakistan, *Economy of Pakistan*, Karachi, 1968, p. 114.
31. Government of Pakistan, *Pakistan Economic Survey, 1970-1*, Islamabad, p. 117.
32. Government of Pakistan, *Pakistan Economic Survey, 1972-3*, Islamabad, pp. 17-18 and 88-9.
33. Government of Pakistan, *Pakistan Economic Survey, 1980-1*, Islamabad, p. 9.
34. Ibid., p. 104-5, Statistical Annexure.
35. State Bank of Pakistan, *Annual Report, 1978-9*, p. 88.
36. Government of Pakistan, *Pakistan Economic Survey, 1976-7*, Islamabad, p. 127.
37. State Bank of Pakistan, *Annual Report, 1978-9*, p. 89.
38. Ibid., p. 89.

PART V

FINANCING OF ECONOMIC DEVELOPMENT

16 Fiscal Management

Fiscal policy consists of a set of policies relating to public budgeting. It includes policies governing the manner in which a government raises revenue both to meet its current requirements and to finance economic development. The revenue may be raised through taxation, non-tax measures, and internal and external borrowing besides borrowing from the banking system. Fiscal policy also refers to policies relating to the expenditure pattern of the government for various development and non-development purposes.

16.1 The Objectives of Fiscal Policy

In addition to the original objective of fiscal policy which was limited to raising revenues to meet the cost of running the government, a number of other objectives have assumed over-riding significance. These objectives are as follows:

a. Resource mobilization;
b. Resource allocation;
c. Maintenance of economic stability;
d. Redistribution of personal, sectoral, and regional incomes.

Resource mobilization for economic growth is the most compelling objective of fiscal policy in developing economies. While tax and non-tax sources and public borrowing mobilize financial resources to meet government development and non-development expenditures, the fiscal mechanism, through an edifice of incentives and disincentives, also attempts to create a climate conducive to savings and investments by influencing their relative profitability.

Allocations for different purposes and for different sectors and regions are made through the budgetary mechanism. Public resources are used to finance the government's activities. These would include the maintenance of law and order, defence, justice, and physical and social infrastructures. Now that governments in developing countries are more and more committed to economic development, the main allocative task consists of minimizing non-development expenditure and ensuring an optimal level and composition of investible resources.

Stabilizing general economic conditions is one of the most difficult objectives of fiscal policy. In a developing economy, price-stability and the maintenance of full employment are very important objectives though they are, at the same time, extremely difficult to achieve. Thus fiscal policy, in spite of declarations of intent to bring about stability through various means, is usually not very effective in this area.

Fiscal policy may also be used to correct imbalances resulting from the unequal distribution of the ownership of income-earning assets and the control of the access to new opportunities and resources. Even in those societies where growth as an objective receives precedence over distribution, the need to reduce extreme inequalities in income distribution still remains valid. This redistributive function can be performed by a judicious blending of various types of taxes in such a way that the rich are made to contribute more to the national exchequer in accordance with their ability to pay. A number of direct and indirect taxes can be levied to achieve this objective. Fiscal policy can also be used to correct imbalances between various regions or sectors. The development of backward regions can be promoted by a mixture of incentives and disincentives encouraging capital transfers from surplus regions to deficit regions. Similarly, fiscal policy may also be used to transfer excessive profit margins in one sector (for example, imports) to a low profit margin sector (for example, exports) through differential rates of taxation.

The management of the fiscal mechanism and its role in Pakistan's development will be discussed with reference to the objectives mentioned above. The analysis is based on data relating to consolidated revenue and capital receipts and expenditures of the federal and the provincial governments (Table 16.1). Using data relating only to federal government's fiscal operations will be inadequate for a meaningful appraisal primarily because of the greater role played by the provinces in the execution of development programmes but also because of a greater convergence between federal and provincial fiscal operations. This will be taken up later in this chapter.

16.2 Resource Mobilization

Resource mobilization in the fiscal sector takes place through two channels:

a. Revenue Receipts;
b. Capital Receipts.

Revenue receipts of the federal and the provincial governments consist of tax and non-tax sources of revenue. The main taxes imposed by the federal government are income and corporation tax, estate duty, gift tax, wealth tax, workers' welfare tax, federal sales tax, custom duties, federal excise duties, federal property taxes, and surcharges on natural gas, petroleum, and fertilizer. A part of some of these taxes is paid to the provinces. Taxes collected by the provinces include land revenue, property tax, motor vehicle tax, provincial excise, stamp duty, registration tax, and entertainment tax. Non-tax sources of revenue are state trading profits, earnings of commercial departments like the post office, telegraph and telephone, and interest charges on loans to provincial governments, local bodies, etc., for the federal government, and irrigation charges, forests, etc., for the provinces. Capital receipts include external borrowing and internal non-banking borrowing consisting of unfunded debt, public debt, treasury and deposit receipts besides the revenue account surplus and the surplus generated by the public sector,

Table 16.1: Consolidated (Federal plus Provincial) Government Finance
(Rs million)

	1949-50	1957-8	1960-1	1965-6	1966-7	1967-8	1972-3	1973-4	1974-5	1975-6	1976-7	1977-8	1978-9	1979-80
Revenue receipts	1,253	2,450	3,459	6,987	7,822	8,205	9,763	14,166	17,426	21,224	24,286	30,430	36,197	44,521
Tax revenue	947	1,670	2,440	4,350	5,310	5,350	7,353	10,347	12,812	18,079	20,547	21,534	24,618	32,151
Non-tax revenue	306	780	1,019	2,637	2,512	2,855	2,410	3,819	4,614	3,145	3,739	8,896	11,579	12,370
Revenue expenditure	1,253	2,413	3,031	8,116	7,527	8,002	10,619	15,164	21,183	24,213	25,698	31,752	40,844	46,364
Deficit/surplus on revenue accounts	–	37	–428	–1,129	295	203	–856	–998	–3,757	–2,989	–1,412	–1,323	–4,647	–1,842
Capital receipts	169	1,106	1,319	3,843	6,521	5,091	7,175	8,553	15,102	18,920	18,288	16,027	17,406	24,048
Capital expenditure	703	1,525	1,885	1,410	5,279	5,356	7,578	8,766	14,264	19,862	20,352	17,557	24,269	26,783
Overall deficit/ surplus	–534	–382	–140	1,304	1,537	–56	–1,259	–1,211	–2,919	–3,931	–3,476	–2,852	–11,510	–1,135

Note: (1) All data relating to the fifties and the sixties pertains to old Pakistan. (2) Increase/decrease in cash balances has been excluded from both capital receipts and capital expenditure in order to determine *net* receipts and expenditure.

Source: (i) Government of Pakistan, *Pakistan Budgets, 1969-70*, for Revenue and Capital Account Receipts (Table 43, pp. 97-8) and Revenue and Capital Expenditure (Table 46 pp. 100-1) for the fifties and the sixties except 1949-50 and 1957-8. (ii) Government of Pakistan, *Pakistan Budgets, 1968-9*, for data on Revenue and Capital Receipts for 1957-8 (Table 48, pp 101-2) and Revenue and Capital Expenditure for 1957-8 (Table 51, p. 105). (iii) Government of Pakistan, *Taxation Inquiry Committee Report, 1960*, for data relating to 1949-50 (p. 27). (iv) Government of Pakistan, *Pakistan Basic Facts, 1979-80*, Islamabad, for all the data for the seventies (Table 8.6 pp. 224-5).

etc. If, however, total receipts are not adequate to finance total expenditure, recourse is also made to deficit financing to meet both development and non-development expenditures. Provincial capital receipts are drawn from loans and grants from the federal government and permanent (long-term) and floating (short-term) debts.

Table 16.2 presents the consolidated revenue and capital receipts and their components in relation to the GNP. The data shows stagnating resource mobilization during the fifties especially in capital receipts. The government resorted to heavy deficit financing in order to finance development programmes during this period since tax mobilization also remained at a low level. During the sixties, the resource picture improved appreciably as revenue receipts increased from 9.9 to 14 per cent of the GNP and capital receipts from 4 to 7.7 per cent of the GNP between 1960-1 and 1965-6. This was the result of a rise in both tax and non-tax collections and an inflow of external resources. During the seventies, resource mobilization efforts again slowed down. Except for 1974-6, external resources remained almost static and as such the government had to rely on both inflationary and non-inflationary domestic resources. Tax and non-tax resources also showed signs of improvement. The quality of resource mobilization efforts in Pakistan can be judged in comparison to other developing countries. The ratio of tax revenues to the GNP for 1972-6, when tax collection in Pakistan did not exceed 14.5 per cent, was 16.0 per cent for seventeen middle income countries and an average of 16.3 per cent for twenty-four developing countries.[1]

Four crucial aspects of resource mobilization need to be discussed in detail. These are:

a. The structure of taxation;
b. The contribution of external resources to total government finance;
c. Deficit financing;
d. Fiscal relations between the federal and the provincial governments.

16.2.1 Pakistan's Tax Structure

Pakistan's tax structure has a narrow base in almost every sense. Indirect taxes contribute the predominant share to the total tax collection. Direct taxes (income and corporation tax, land revenue, workers' welfare tax, estate duty, wealth tax, gift tax) which contributed 25 per cent of the consolidated tax revenue in 1949-50 and 33 per cent in 1959-60, provided only 14 to 17 per cent during the seventies (Table 16.5). The total tax revenue is almost entirely dependent upon four major taxes, i.e., customs, federal excise duties, income and corporation tax, and sales tax.

Table 16.2: Resource Mobilization through Fiscal Mechanism

	1949-50	1957-8	1960-1	1965-6	1967-8	1972-3	1973-4	1974-5	1975-6	1976-7	1977-8	1978-9	1979-80
GNP (current factor cost) (Rs million)	19,893	28,400	34,786	49,685	60,737	61,253	81,058	105,787	124,415	141,166	168,701	191,584	227,617
As percentage of GNP (current)													
Revenue receipts	6.3	8.6	9.9	14.0	13.5	15.9	17.4	16.4	17.0	17.2	18.0	18.9	19.5
a. Tax revenue	4.7	5.8	7.0	8.7	8.8	12.0	12.7	12.1	14.5	14.5	12.7	12.8	14.1
b. Non-tax-revenue	1.6	2.8	2.9	5.3	4.7	3.9	4.7	4.3	2.5	2.7	5.3	6.1	5.4
Capital receipts	4.0	4.8	4.0	7.7	8.4	12.3	10.8	14.4	15.9	14.4	10.4	12.6	12.0
a. External resources	—	0.7	2.5	3.3	4.3	6.3	5.0	8.6	8.2	5.7	4.4	5.8	3.7
b. Deficit financing	3.1	2.7	0.6	2.6	0.7	NA	NA	NA	1.5	1.7	2.9	4.2	1.6
c. Non-inflationary domestic financing	0.9	1.4	0.9	1.8	3.6	NA	NA	NA	6.2	7.0	3.1	2.6	6.7

Note (1) Data for 1949-50 to 1967-8 relates to old Pakistan. (2) Non-inflationary domestic financing is equal to capital receipts minus (external resources plus deficit financing).

Source: (i) Government of Pakistan, *Pakistan Economic Survey, 1966-7*, p. 45 for GNP for 1949-50 to 1965-6. (ii) Government of Pakistan, *Twenty-five Years of Statistics in Pakistan*, 1972, pp. 296-7 for GNP in 1967-8. (iii) Government of Pakistan, *Pakistan Economic Survey, 1979-80*, Islamabad, p. 13 for GNP for the seventies. (iv) Ibid., Table 14.1 for tax revenue, and revenue and capital receipts for all years (compilation). (v) Government of Pakistan, *Public Finance Statistics*, 1979-80, pp. 7-9 for external resources in the seventies. (vi) Government of Pakistan, *Pakistan Budgets, 1969-70*, pp. 231-3 for external resources for 1949-50 to 1967-8. (vii) Ibid., Table No. 14 for deficit financing for all years.

Among indirect taxes, custom duties alone provide about half of the total yield of indirect taxes (Table 16.3). Taxes, like customs and federal excise duties, which normally should have a wide tax-base depend on a very small number of commodities for the bulk of their collection. Approximately 52 per cent of the custom duties are derived from four commodity groups: machinery, iron, steel and manufactures, vehicles, and textile. Nearly 84 per cent of the excise collection is raised from five commodity groups: sugar, POL, tobacco, vegetable products, and cement.[2]

How elastic is Pakistan's tax structure in relation to its tax-base? An elastic tax system should yield revenue that increases with the economy's growth without frequent rate adjustments. But since rate structures as well as the scope and the coverage of taxes undergo frequent readjustments, often for reasons other than raising revenue, it is difficult to calculate the yield of a tax after isolating it from all such changes. A simple method of measuring elasticity is by comparing the percentage change in tax yield with the percentage change in the relative tax base over a certain period which might be indicative of *arc* elasticity. It is true that the concept of *arc* elasticity has many limitations and that it expresses only the relative change that takes place between the years at the two ends of the period and that it takes no account of what happened between those two years. But it does serve to identify a certain trend in elasticity. Table 16.4 indicates the elasticity of certain major taxes in relation to their respective tax-bases.

Table 16.4 shows that taxes on imports and large-scale manufacturing sector have a high elasticity coefficient. The only exception is the sales tax on domestic goods whose tax-base has been eroded gradually by exemptions granted to a large number of goods classified as 'necessities', 'capital goods', 'raw materials for export industries' and 'cottage industry products'. Many other items classified as 'semi-necessities' are taxed at lower rates.[3]

Direct taxes on income and on agriculture have low elasticity coefficients insofar as the seventies are concerned. Income and corporation tax, fairly elastic in the earlier period, seems to lag behind the growth in its tax-base. Apart from its general limitations of a high exemption limit and the exclusion of agricultural incomes, the income tax-base has also been eroded by a number of allowances, concessions, and deductions which also reduced the effective rate of the tax.[4] Originally granted as incentives for investment and production, many of these allowances may have outlived their utility and need to be reviewed in the context of the changing needs of business and industry.[5] As many as eight deductions are allowed on income from property before it is taxed.[6] As regards taxes on agriculture, land revenue and irrigation charges are structurally inflexible and their rate structures bear no direct relation to price or income levels in agriculture. It is thus not surprising that these taxes have low elasticity.

The Planning Commission worked out elasticity coefficients for various taxes during 1952-3 to 1963-4. These are 1.3 for income and corporation tax, 1.0 for excise duty and

Table 16.3: Major Taxes–Pakistan
(Tax yield as percentage of consolidated tax revenue)

Tax	1960-1	1961-2	1962-3	1963-4	1964-5	1965-6	1966-7	1967-8	1973-4	1974-5	1975-6	1976-7	1977-8	1978-9	1979-80
Customs	25.4	28.3	27.8	23.1	27.6	24.6	24.3	32.4	39.9	39.0	33.7	35.1	38.9	39.9	39.1
Central excise	16.4	16.3	17.3	21.3	21.0	22.5	28.4	33.1	26.2	27.4	28.2	27.6	29.1	28.8	29.4
Income and corporation tax	15.5	17.8	16.9	17.4	16.6	16.5	15.0	13.0	11.8	11.2	14.1	15.2	13.0	13.0	15.5
Sales tax	19.3	19.0	18.6	19.5	17.9	18.2	16.6	10.7	6.6	8.4	7.8	7.8	7.3	7.3	7.2
Total	76.6	81.4	80.6	81.3	83.1	81.8	84.3	89.2	84.5	86.0	83.8	85.7	88.3	89.0	91.2

Note: Data from 1960-1 to 1967-8 relates to old Pakistan.
Source: (i) Government of Pakistan, *Pakistan Budgets, 1968-9*, p. 104 for 1960-1 to 1966-7. (ii) Government of Pakistan, *Pakistan Budgets, 1969-70*, p. 100 for 1967-8. (iii) Government of Pakistan, *Taxation Structure of Pakistan, 1980-1*, p. 3 for the seventies.

sales tax on domestic products, 0.7 for import duties, and 0.4 for sales tax on imported goods.[7]

It thus seems that, over the years, direct taxes have lost much of whatever degree of elasticity they possessed while some of the indirect taxes have higher elasticity coefficients. It also turns out that taxes on the import and the large-scale manufacturing sectors have out-paced the growth in these sectors but that the tax yield from the unorganized sector, trade and independent professions[8] (who are supposed to be covered by income tax), and agriculture has lagged behind.

Another feature of the tax structure is its heavy dependence upon indirect taxation. The share of direct taxes in the consolidated tax revenue has gradually declined as shown in Table 16.5.

Conventional wisdom regards the predominance of indirect taxes as a negative factor for any country's tax structure. While it may be desirable to make direct taxes contribute more towards the total tax effort, it should not be forgotten that indirect taxes are not as undesirable or indiscriminate in their incidence as is sometimes suggested. Indirect taxation, if used imaginatively, is a tool of differential government policy to encourage or discourage particular types of resource

Table 16.5: Direct Taxes as Percentage of Consolidated Tax Revenue

Year	Direct tax as percentage of consolidated tax revenue
1949-50	25[1]
1953-4	33[1]
1959-60	33[1]
1969-70	23[2]
1973-4	15[3]
1974-5	14[3]
1975-6	16[3]
1976-7	17[3]
1977-8	15[3]
1978-9	15[3]
1979-80	17[3]

1. Government of Pakistan, *Second Five Year Plan*, p.56.
2. Government of Pakistan, *Taxation Structure of Pakistan*, 1976, p.2.
3. Government of Pakistan, *Taxation Structure of Pakistan*, 1980-1, p.3.

Note: Data for 1949-50 to 1969-70 relates to old Pakistan.

Table 16.4: Elasticity of Major Taxes

Tax	Tax-base	1952-3 to 1963-4			1972-3 to 1979-80		
		Expansion in tax-base (percentage)	Increase in tax yield (percentage)	Elasticity*	Expansion in tax-base (percentage)	Increase in tax yield (percentage)	Elasticity*
Income and corporation tax	Value added in non-agricultural sectors	117	179	1.52	271	225	0.83
Import duties			NA	—	—	623	1.26
Sales tax on imported goods	Total imports	—	NA	—	494	619	1.25
Central excise	Value added in large-scale manufacturing sector	399	643	1.61	225	288	1.28
Sales tax on domestic goods			NA	—		104	0.46
Land revenue and irrigation charges	Value added in agriculture	67	54	0.80	202	66	0.32

Note: Data for 1952-3 to 1963-4 relates to old Pakistan.

Source: (i) Andrus and Mohammad, *Trade, Finance and Development in Pakistan*, Oxford University Press, 1966, p. 209 for data for income and corporation tax and central excise for 1952-3 and 1963-4. (ii) Government of Pakistan, *Twenty-five Years of Statistics in Pakistan, 1947-72*, 1972, pp. 296-7 for value added in agriculture, value added in large-scale manufacturing sector, and value added in non-agricultural sectors, and pp. 184-5 for land revenue and irrigation charges for 1952-3 and 1963-4. (iii) Government of Pakistan, *Pakistan Economic Survey, 1979-80*, Islamabad, pp. 12-13, for value added in agriculture, large-scale manufacturing sector and non-agricultural sectors for the seventies and pp. 203, 208, 212, 217 for irrigation charges for 1979-80. (iv) Government of Pakistan, *Pakistan Basic Facts, 1979-80*, Islamabad, p. 145 for total imports for 1972-3 and 1979-80, and page 205 for land revenue and irrigation charges for 1972-3. (v) World Bank, *Pakistan Economic Development and Prospects, 1980*, p. 111 for sales tax on imported goods, sales tax on domestic goods, and import duties for 1972-3 and 1979-80. (vi) Government of Pakistan, *Taxation Structure of Pakistan, 1980-1*, p. 3 for land revenue for 1979-80.

$$* \text{ Elasticity} = \frac{\text{Percentage change in tax yield}}{\text{Percentage change in tax base}}$$

utilization and to withdraw purchasing power from the private sector.[9] Being a tax on consumption rather than on income, it can be used to discourage consumption and thus indirectly encourage savings. It is also easy to administer. Direct taxes, on the other hand, have a highly restricted base in countries which have a low per capita income and a highly skewed income distribution.

16.2.2 External Resources

From revenue receipts we now turn to capital receipts and take up its two major components, i.e., external resources and deficit financing. External resources are made available to the federal government for both Plan and non-Plan expenditure. The federal government in turn makes part of these funds available to provincial governments. External resources for Plan expenditure consist of project loans for projects included in the Plan and also for projects under the Indus-Basin Programme. A small amount of non-project loans is also included. In addition, commodity aid under PL-480, which is paid for by the Pakistan Government in local currency, is also a part. Another element is grants for project and non-project purposes including Rupee grants out of the PL-480, counterpart funds. Table 16.6 shows external resources inflow and its contribution to total capital receipts. The Table indicates a high degree of reliance on external resources to finance developing programmes. This injects a corresponding amount of unpredictability, which is inevitably attached to external assistance, and rigidity since national priorities must coincide with the donors' preferences before funds are made available.

16.2.3 Deficit Financing

What is the contribution of deficit financing to financing development expenditure? This is a question of fundamental importance if one is to have a clear picture of domestic resource mobilization through fiscal mechanism. But unfortunately this matter is shrouded in a cloak of mystery. Very little information is available in published government documents on the extent of deficit financing or even the definition used to estimate its size. One is left to wander through the maze of public finance data and work out one's own estimates of this crucial variable on the basis of one's own definition. Mere mention of deficit financing, says the report of the panel of economists for the Second Plan, is often considered to be in bad taste. Perhaps it is the most abused as well as the least understood technique of mobilizing resources in under-developed countries.[10]

In countries suffering chronically from inflation, the governments, usually not very effective in controlling the price spiral, are embarrassed by the release of information regarding deficit financing or by open dis-

Table 16.6: External Resources Inflow and Consolidated Capital Receipts
(Rs million)

	1949-50	1957-8	1960-1	1965-6	1972-3	1974-5	1977-8	1979-80
Capital receipts	169	1,106	1,319	3,843	7,175	15,102	16,027	24,048
External resources	–	195	884	1,666	3,892	9,133	7,483	13,965
External resources/ capital receipts (percentage)	–	17.6	67	43.3	54.2	60.4	46.7	58

Note : Data for 1949-50 to 1965-6 relates to old Pakistan.

Source: (i) Government of Pakistan, *Pakistan Economic Survey, 1979-80*, Islamabad, Table 14.1 for capital receipts. (ii) Government of Pakistan, *Pakistan Budgets, 1969-70*, pp. 231-3 for external resources for 1949-50 to 1965-6. (iii) Government of Pakistan, *Pakistan Basic Facts, 1979-80*, Islamabad, p. 223 for external resources for the seventies.

cussions on the use of deficit financing which might throw light on how far the government policies have been responsible for expanding the money supply and the consequent price rise. But much of this embarrassment and the urge for secrecy about deficit financing is unnecessary.

It is true that governments are generally held responsible for causing inflationary pressures by resorting to deficit financing. But it should be remembered that inflation is not caused by the expansion in money supply alone. As Haq points out, in 1954-5, and also possibly in 1953-4, despite a rise of 7 to 8 per cent in the money supply, the price level fell. In 1958-9, prices rose by 10 per cent although the money supply increased by only 4 per cent.[11]

Deficit financing is a sound and necessary instrument of government finance[12] and its role, as also its desirability and limitations of its use in mobilizing revenues, must be properly analyzed in the context of its broad implications on the economy and compared to the adequacy of other techniques of resource mobilization. It should also be recognized that its incidence on the economy is somewhat indiscriminate and the ease with which it can be employed always carries the danger of its abuse in the hands of a hard pressed government.[13] But the absence of open discussion and the non-availability of authentic information on this issue only deprives the government, and the professional economists, of the opportunity to make a proper appraisal of the role of deficit financing which could enable policy-makers to see it as a potent policy instrument rather than a last resort for financing development and non-development expenditures.

Deficit financing, as Haq points out, is usually identified with budgetary deficits but the term 'budget deficit' could be taken to mean a deficit on the current account (as in Great Britain) or the excess of total budget expenditure on revenue and capital accounts both over total budget receipts (as in the USA). In a wider context, deficit financing can also be regarded as an aggregative concept indicating an overall imbalance between ex-ante national income and ex-ante national expenditure.[14] The definition used in the Third Plan (all official transactions in the public sector which have an expansionary influence on the money supply)[15] seems to be close to the aggregative concept. However, available data on national accounts does not allow empirical analysis on these lines.

However, in the context of Pakistan's fiscal and monetary situation, Haq has mentioned two concepts: (a) net borrowings by the government from the banking system which includes the State Bank of Pakistan and commercial banks but excludes non-banking institutions and individuals; (b) net borrowings by the government from the State Bank of Pakistan only.[16] The first definition seems to be used by the State Bank of Pakistan, the

Table 16.7: Deficit Financing/Borrowing from the Banking System
(Rs million)

Year	Deficit financing	Year	Deficit financing
1951-2	378	1965-6	1,318
1952-3	655	1966-7	−235
1953-4	247	1967-8	440
1954-5	208	1968-9 RE	426
1955-6	336	1969-70 BE	373
1956-7	418	1975-6	1,916
1957-8	769	1976-7	2,458
1958-9	162	1977-8	4,947
1959-60	−12	1978-9	8,191 (Provisional actual)
1960-5	1,135 ÷ 5=227 (Annual average)	1979-80	BE 3,808

Source: (i) Mahbubul Haq, *Deficit Financing in Pakistan, 1951-60*, PIDE, Karachi, 1961, p. 10 for data relating to 1951-60. (ii) Government of Pakistan, *Preliminary Evaluation of the Third Five Year Plan*, 1970, p. 16 for data relating to 1965-70. (iii) Government of Pakistan, *Fourth Five Year Plan*, Islamabad, p. 45 for data relating to 1960-5. (iv) State Bank of Pakistan, *Annual Report, 1979-80*, p. 96 for 1978-9 and 1979-80. (v) State Bank of Pakistan, *Annual Report, 1978-9*, p.91 for 1977-8. (vi) State Bank of Pakistan, *Annual Report, 1976-7*, p. 79 for 1976-7. (vii) State Bank of Pakistan, *Annual Report, 1975-6*, p.77 for 1975-6.

Planning Commission, and the Ministry of Finance. Table 16.7 shows deficit financing data (first definition) compiled from various sources.[17]

But the problems of definition do not end here. Public debt held by the banking system leads to the net creation of new spending power and therefore constitutes deficit financing *but* only if it does not effect the system's lending to non-government borrowers,[18] i.e., money is lent to the government out of the idle balances of the banks which would have been held if the government had not borrowed it. This makes a correct estimation of deficit financing extremely difficult particularly if one depends only upon published official data.

Very little information is available on the constituents of 'government borrowings from the banking system' or on the way it could be computed from public finance statistics. The Taxation Inquiry Committee (1960) defined deficit financing as the sum total of permanent debt (net), floating debt (net), *ad hoc* treasury bills, and use of cash balances.[19] A State Bank Annual Report defines deficit financing as the sum total of 'the drawal of cash balances and the *bulk* of the creation of treasury bills'.[20]

Most of the official data on deficit financing, it seems, relates to only that part of the net addition to the money supply which is spent on development purposes. Deficit financing for non-development purposes, for example, commodity operations, is not included in the data given in the Plans or the State Bank Annual Reports. To quote a concrete example, the estimate made in the Fourth Plan for deficit financing during the Third Plan period (1965-70) is given as Rs 2,635 million.[21] But a little later, in the same chapter, it points out that deficit financing during the Plan adds up to 'roughly Rs 4,000 million which includes government borrowing on account of wheat procurement, against sugar stocks, and for other state trading operations'.[22] Thus it seems that the data on government borrowings from the banking system may not indicate the full extent of expansionary financing. The annual reports of the State Bank of Pakistan present two different sets of data: (a) the government's contribution to changes in monetary assets which comprise budgetary support, commodity operations, and the effect of government deposits with commercial banks; (b) government borrowings from the banking system.[23] One can only guess that while the government's contribution to changes in monetary assets includes deficit financing for both development and non-development purposes, borrowing from the banking system refers to money creation used for development purposes only. The contribution made by deficit financing to domestic resource mobilization is brought out in Tables 16.8 and 16.9.

16.2.4 Fiscal Relations Between the Federal and Provincial Governments

The fiscal operations of the federal and the provincial governments are usually closely interlinked. In a federal set up, like Pakistan's, this inter-governmental fiscal relationship assumes special significance since each tier of governmental authority needs to be assigned those functions of resource mobilization which it can perform best. This relationship as it has evolved over the past decade in Pakistan takes two forms:

a. the distribution of sources of revenues between the federal government and the provinces;
b. federal loans and grants to the provinces.

The sources of revenue are divided into four categories:

i) Taxes levied and retained by the federal government, for example, customs, wealth tax, estate duty, and earnings of commercial departments.
ii) Taxes levied by the federal government but divided between the federal and the provincial governments, for example, income and corporation tax, and sales tax.
iii) Taxes levied by the federal government but distributed to the provinces, for example, stamp duty, terminal taxes, and gift tax.
iv) Taxes levied and retained by the provinces, for

example, land revenue, irrigation charges, provincial excise and sales duties, tolls, professional tax, entertainment tax.

It thus appears that the most productive sources of revenue are with the federal government and consequently the contribution of federal taxes to total tax revenue shows a continuous increase (Table 16.10). Between 1972-3 and 1979-80 the federal tax collection increased by 310 per cent while the

Table 16.8: Deficit Financing/Government Sector Contribution to Monetary Expansion
(Rs million)

	1972-3	1973-4	1974-5	1975-6	1976-7	1977-8	1978-9	1979-80
Deficit financing/government sector contribution to monetary expansion	1,564	1,364	3,056	5,240	6,621	4,855	8,816	5,597
Internal capital receipts	3,666	4,685	6,100	9,643	12,336	10,074	13,219	13,526
Total (capital plus revenue) receipts	17,321	22,932	32,659	41,086	44,638	47,987	60,466	72,012
GNP (current factor cost)	61,258	81,056	105,787	124,415	141,166	168,701	191,584	227,617
Deficit financing as percentage of internal capital receipts	42.6	29.1	50.1	54.3	53.6	48.1	66.6	41.3
Deficit financing as percentage of total receipts	9.0	5.9	9.3	12.7	14.8	10.1	14.5	7.7
Deficit financing as percentage of GNP (current)	2.5	1.6	2.8	4.2	4.6	2.8	4.6	2.4

Note: (1) Internal capital receipts is equal to total capital receipts minus external resources. (2) Total receipts is equal to revenue receipts plus capital receipts (consolidated).

Source: (i) State Bank of Pakistan, *Annual Report, 1979-80*, p. 29 for government sector contribution to monetary expansion. (ii) Government of Pakistan, *Pakistan Basic Facts, 1979-80*, Islamabad, Table 18.6, pp. 224-5 for internal capital receipts and total receipts, and Table 3.2, p. 20 for GNP.

Table 16.9: Deficit Financing/Borrowing from the Banking System in Relation to Total Receipts and the GNP
(Rs million)

	1975-6	1976-7	1977-8	1978-9 Provisional estimate	1979-80 RE
Deficit financing	1,916	2,458	4,947	8,191	3,808
Internal capital receipts	9,643	12,336	10,074	13,219	13,526
Total receipts	41,086	44,638	47,987	60,466	72,012
GNP (current)	124,415	141,166	168,701	191,584	227,617
Deficit financing/ Internal capital receipts	19.87	19.93	49.11	61.96	28.15
Deficit financing/ Total receipts	4.66	5.51	10.31	13.55	5.29
Deficit financing/GNP	1.54	1.74	2.93	4.28	1.67

Note: (1) Internal capital receipts is equal to total capital receipts minus external resources (consolidated). (2) Total receipts is equal to revenue receipts plus capital receipts (consolidated).

Source: (i) Government of Pakistan, *Pakistan Budgets, 1969-70*, Table 16.7 for deficit financing. (ii) Government of Pakistan, *Pakistan Basic Facts, 1979-80*, Islamabad, Table 18.6, pp. 224-5 for internal capital receipts and total receipts, and Table 3.2, p. 20 for GNP.

Table 16.10: Federal Taxes in Relation to Total Tax Revenue
(percentage)

Year	Federal tax as-percentage of total tax revenue
1960-1	83.9[1]
1964-5	87.8[1]
1969-70	85.4[2]
1973-4	90.4[3]
1974-5	90.6[3]
1975-6	90.7[3]
1976-7	90.9[3]
1977-8	92.9[3]
1978-9	91.9[3]
1979-80	94.3[3]

1. M. Akhlaqur Rahman, *The Structure of Taxation in Pakistan,* 1972, p. 17.
2. Government of Pakistan, *Taxation Structure of Pakistan, 1976,* p.2.
3. Government of Pakistan, *Taxation Structure of Pakistan, 1980-1,* p.3.

Note: Data for 1960-1 1964-5, and 1969-70 refer to old Pakistan.

provincial tax yield went up by only 147 per cent.[24]

The formula for the distribution of the sources of revenue is subject to a continuous review and re-appraisal. Originally laid down in 1937 under the *Niemeyar Award,* it was revised in 1951 through the *Raisman Award* and further reviewed by the National Finance Commissions in 1962, 1964, 1970, and 1974.[25]

At present 80 per cent of the net proceeds from the income and corporation tax and the federal sales tax is paid to the provinces. The share of each province is determined on a population basis.[26] The gift tax and surcharge on natural gas are collected by the centre but the entire net yield is paid to the provinces on a collection basis.

Financial assistance to the provinces is given for both development and non-development purposes and consists of loans and grants. Cash grants are given out of counterpart funds for various development projects. The federal government also finances provincial subsidies on fertilizer and tubewells, and population planning and road development. Non-development grants are meant for such purposes as flood and drought relief and they cover the provinces' revenue deficit. The federal government also pays a fixed subvention of Rs 100 million to NWFP and Rs 150 million to Baluchistan. It is also laid down that the provinces cannot raise any public loans without the federal government's consent. This has been necessitated by the fact that the federal government is responsible for the formulation of the country's overall fiscal and monetary policies and it must regulate the floatation of loans by provincial governments in order to properly discharge these responsibilities.[27]

Table 16.11 presents an overview of the inter-governmental fiscal relations. It brings out a number of significant facts. It shows that the provinces are becoming increasingly dependent upon the federal government. Federal tax assignments and loans and grants which contributed only 16.7 per cent of the consolidated provincial receipts in 1949-50 comprised 75 per cent in 1979-80. Federal loans and grants alone contribute 45 to 55 per cent of the provincial consolidated receipts.

There are many reasons for this trend towards greater centralization of fiscal effort at the federal level. Compulsions of economic development, which is the major national goal, and economic planning require greater central control over fiscal operations. The responsibilities of the federal government are larger and of a more varied nature and therefore its fiscal operations need greater flexibility and manoeuvrability. Aid-giving agencies also sometimes insist on forming national sector policies by the federal government before they agree to provide finances.[28]

Furthermore, certain tax rates need to have uniform structures throughout the country otherwise distortions may occur in the cost and production structure. In raising loans too it must be ensured that the federal and the provincial governments do not enter into competition for the limited loanable funds and that the financial requirements of each level of government do not clash with each other. However, care should be taken to ensure that the measures adopted are not such as will make provincial governments merely spending agencies while the entire tax mobilization is assigned to the federal government. As yet this situation has not arisen. But in practical terms all provinces now count on the federal government to pick up their deficits. Such situations usually encourage fiscal indiscipline. The provinces are assuming additional responsibilities which involve addi-

Table 16.11: Financial Assistance and Tax Assignments to Provinces by Federal Government (Excluding East Pakistan)
(Rs million)

	1949-50	1954-5	1959-60	1964-5	1969-70	1972-3	1974-5	1977-8	1979-80 (Budget)
I. Development assistance									
a. Grants	7	57	109	232	126	198.5	233.4	730.6	1,226.3
b. Loans	57	125	348	839	1,435	1,416.7	2,560.0	2,709.5	3,273.7
Total (a+b)	64	182	457	1,071	1,561	1,615.2	2,793.4	3,440.5	4,500.0
II. Non-development assistance									
a. Grants	–	–	14	95	18	349.6	628.8	1,676.3	2,133.8
b. Loans	–	19	5	5	—	97.8	10.7	–	–
Total (a + b)	–	19	19	100	18	447.4	639.5	1,676.3	2,133.8
Grand total (development and non-development)	64	201	476	1,171	1,579	2,062.6	3,432.9	5,116.8	6,633.8
III. a. Total revenue receipts of provinces	299	475	805	1,819	1,933	2,230	4,446	8,461	10,718
b. Total capital receipts of provinces	226	298	517	1,001	1,429	1,447	2,468	942	4,196
c. Consolidated receipts (a + b)	525	773	1,322	2,820	3,362	3,677	6,914	9,403	14,914
IV. Federal loans and grants as percentage of consolidated provincial receipts	12.2	26	36	38.4	47	56.0	49.6	54.4	44.4
V. Federal tax assignments	24	96	164	463	570	753	1,595	1,954	4,565
VI. a. Federal tax assignments as percentage of total revenue receipts of provinces (III a.)	8	20.2	20.3	25.4	29.5	33.7	35.8	23	42.5
b. Federal tax assignments as percentage of consolidated receipts of provinces (III c.)	4.5	12.4	12.4	16.4	16.9	20.4	23.0	20.7	30.6
VII. Federal loans and grants and federal tax assignments as percentage of provincial consolidated receipts (III c.)	16.7	38.4	48.4	54.8	63.0	76.4	72.6	75.1	75.0

Source: (i) Government of Pakistan, *Pakistan Basic Facts, 1979-80*, Islamabad, Table 18.5, p. 212-9 for financial assistance to provinces during 1949-50 to 1977-8, and Table 18.3, pp. 203-10 for revenue receipts of provinces during 1949-50 to 1979-80, and also for federal tax assignments for provinces during 1949-50 to 1969-70 (compilation). (ii) Government of Pakistan, *Public Finance Statistics, 1979-80*, Table IX, p. 30 for financial assistance during 1979-80 and Table VII, p. 20 for federal tax assignments for the seventies. (iii) Government of Pakistan, *Twenty-five Years of Statistics in Pakistan, 1947-72*, Table 11.11, p. 188-9 for capital receipts of provinces during 1949-50 to 1969-70. (iv) Government of Pakistan, *Pakistan Economic Survey, 1979-80*, Islamabad, pp. 205, 210, 214, and 219 for capital receipts of provinces for the seventies.

tional expenditure, particularly on social sectors such as education and health, and also heavy obligations on debts. But the revenue structure of the provincial governments hardly gives any scope for a significant expansion in mobilizing finances. The current situation, instead of strengthening the revenue effort of the provinces, encourages sluggishness since higher provincial revenues are likely to mean a smaller share in the future distribution of central taxes and other funds.

16.3 Resource Allocation

Resource allocation can be influenced by fiscal measures in two ways:

(a) fiscal incentives and disincentives, including subsidies, in order to encourage or discourage certain resource allocation patterns, consumption and production trends; (b) balance between development and non-development expenditure. The absorption of goods and services in an economy is made up of domestic production *plus* imports *minus* exports. The manner in which these three categories are taxed determines the composition of domestic consumption and the distribution of national output between exports and the home market. For example, considerations of balance of payments require maximum encouragement to exports and a corresponding reduction in supplies to the domestic market. Excise duties are therefore levied on local products consumed in the home market while rebates are allowed on excisable goods which are exported.[29] Balance of payments considerations have resulted in a rapid increase in the total collection of import duties, from Rs 1,544 million in 1972-3 to Rs 11,250 million in 1979-80, while export duty yields have declined from Rs 1,060 million to only Rs 200 million during the same period.[30] High import duties relative to excise on locally produced import substitutes encourage local industries and divert domestic resources to production.

The export duty on raw cotton in the past has also served to increase its local availability at prices lower than what would have prevailed otherwise. It thus became a subsidy to the domestic cotton textile industry which is financed by the foreign buyer if it can be passed on through higher export prices, otherwise its incidence is on the cotton growers.

The other aspect of the fiscal policy's allocative function is to maintain a balance between development and non-development expenditure so that while maximum resources are channelized into productive uses, non-development expenditure is minimized.

Development expenditure is defined as the expenditure designed to keep intact, to enlarge, and to improve the physical resources of the country; to develop the knowledge, skills, and productivity of the people and to encourage efficient resource utilization. Accordingly, development expenditure includes all those items in industry, agriculture, transport, communication, irrigation, power, banking, and insurance which replace or expand the existing capacity or create new capacity, non-recurring expenditure in education, health, social welfare and manpower development, and gross investments in buildings and roads including non-recurring expenditure on housing and settlement projects, and ancillary services like water supply and sewerage. However, maintenance expenditure for roads, buildings, canals, and other installations is regarded as non-developmental outlay.[31]

This concept of development expenditure creates a number of loopholes. The construction of buildings and roads, for example, may not always be related to development purposes. On the other hand, the level and efficiency of the maintenance of development works has a strong impact on the pace of development and on the benefits to be acquired from those works.

The ratio between consolidated development and non-development expenditure (Table 16.12) has remained more or less constant during the seventies being 1:2.2 in 1972-3 and 1:2 in 1979-80.

Non-development expenditure is generally regarded as being excessive and, therefore, subjected to persistent public criticism. Nevertheless its overall size seems to be quite inelastic and it has not been possible to improve the ratio of development to non-development expenditure. Major items under non-development expenditure are defence, civil administration, subsidies, and debt servicing which claimed 40 per cent, 19.4 per cent, 7.4 per cent, and 25.4 per cent respectively of the non-development expenditure in the revenue account of the federal government budget for 1979-80.[32] Social services which include education, health, social security, etc., (included under civil administration) claimed 2.9 per cent.

While there is no dispute with the need to minimize non-development expenditure, it should be remembered that too much preoccupation with this task may starve development projects and facilities of essential funds for maintenance and other purposes. The tendency to associate development with only capital spending and to neglect maintenance, staffing, and operation of these facilities is not very rational. Quite often the result is ill-equipped and under-staffed hospitals, dispensaries, and educational institutions, and arrears in the maintenance of roads, irrigation, electricity, and forest projects; and a lack of operating funds for many essential services like agricultural extension.

16.4 The Maintenance of Economic Stability

Fiscal policy can play a limited role in maintaining economic stability in the country. One of the means to achieve this purpose is taxation. For example, export duties can be raised in order to insulate the economy from effects of high inflationary pressures originating abroad. The export duty on cotton was raised during the Korean War boom (1950-1) and, in the early seventies during the 'cotton boom' in the world market, export duty was imposed on cotton yarn and other products.[33] Inflation at home can be contained by a rise in excise duty, sales tax, and import duties on items with a high income elasticity of demand so that some part of the increase in domestic spending is syphoned off for the public exchequer. The policy of taxing non-essential luxury goods at higher rates[34] is a good example of this policy. On the other hand, if the international market suffers from a recession, export duties are reduced or abolished in order to stimulate foreign demand and to maintain the incomes of the the domestic producers and their spending on domestic products. The abolition of export duties on raw cotton during 1967-72 and on *desi* cotton since 1978 were primarily the result of low prices in the world market. In general, manufactured goods are exempted from export duties. Instead, compensatory rebates have been allowed on the export of

Table 16.12: Consolidated (Federal Plus Provincial) Government Expenditure

	1972-3	1973-4	1974-5	1975-6	1976-7	1977-8	1978-9 (Revised)	1979-80 (Revised)
Development expenditure								
Revenue account	1,142	1,527	2,438	3,155	3,399	3,682	6,007	6,902
Capital account	4,494	6,494	10,734	13,213	16,111	15,723	16,737	16,891
Total	5,636	8,021	13,172	16,368	19,510	19,405	22,744	23,793
Non-development expenditure								
Revenue account	9,477	13,637	18,475	21,058	22,299	28,070	34,837	39,462
Capital account	2,996	2,127	2,927	5,742	3,786	1,357	6,926	9,892
Total	12,473	15,764	21,402	26,800	26,085	29,427	41,763	49,354

Note: Capital disbursement to private sector and increase/decrease in cash balances have been ignored.
Source: Government of Pakistan, *Pakistan Basic Facts, 1979-80*, Islamabad, Table 18.6, pp. 224-5.

cotton textile products since September 1978.[35]

16.5 The Redistribution of Income

Fiscal policy in under-developed countries is also expected to contain a certain social bias in favour of the low income groups. Both the tax system and the pattern of public expenditure are expected to be structured in such a way that the existing income inequalities are reduced. Fiscal policy must ensure that those sections of society which are capable of bearing heavier financial burdens are actually made to contribute more towards national development. Even if such objectives are regarded as too idealistic in some societies, a fiscal system should not at least accentuate the existing disparities.

Direct taxes on income and property are generally regarded as more effective insofar as equity considerations are concerned. Compared to indirect taxes, it is easier to incorporate the virtue of equity and elasticity in a system of direct taxation.[36] Higher income earners can be taxed at higher rates through a progressive scale of taxation, while people below a certain income level can be exempted altogether.

But this apparently effective instrument of equity has been rendered ineffective largely because of the familiar dilemma between the social desirability of a highly progressive rate structure and the need to provide incentives to the private sector to save and invest. The concern for saving and investment is legitimate subject to certain conditions. As Meir and Baldwin point out, income tax is no disincentive if high income recipients engage in luxury consumption, hoarding, capital flight, or unproductive speculative investment.[37]

The dilemma has been resolved in Pakistan by first imposing highly progressive rates of income tax and then diffusing its impact by permitting a number of exemptions and allowances which not only blunt the tax edge but also introduce an element of complexity.[38] The exemption limit is also fairly high, Rs 18,000 at present, which is more than six times the per capita income at current factor cost for 1979-80 (Rs 2,837).[39]

The equity effect of the income tax is also reduced by a widespread tendency to evade tax. To the extent that taxes are evaded, the progressivity in taxation is obviously of no help in reducing inequalities.[40] Indeed, since tax evasion is mainly an option for the top income brackets who can spend liberally on the fees of lawyers, accountants, and tax experts, tax evasion on a large scale may result in reducing the effective rate of tax on the richer tax payers. Tax evasion coupled with existing allowances and concessions reduce the effective marginal rate substantially and therefore the progressivity of the income tax.[41] The burden of income tax thus falls mainly on corporate profits and salary earners while the unorganized sector, traders and independent professionals who usually benefit by inflation, are able to evade taxation.

Taxes on property and wealth can also be used as instruments of equity. A tax on property counteracts the unequal distribution of wealth and incomes by preventing concentrated wealth from passing on from one generation to another.[42] Unfortunately, Pakistan has made a very limited and half-hearted use of these taxes which now serve as minor irritants rather than genuine sources of revenue. The federal government collects three property taxes, i.e., estate duty, wealth tax, and gift tax. Estate duty which earned Rs 7 million in 1978-9 was abolished in 1979. The yield of gift tax and wealth tax was Rs 9 million and Rs 367 million respectively in 1979-80.[43] Property tax imposed by the provincial governments brought in a total of Rs 45 million from the four provinces in 1979-80.[44]

The wealth tax originally regarded as a means to prevent undue concentration of wealth and offer incentives for the accumulation of capital in the form of assets which would yield the highest rate of return[45] is levied largely on urban property[46] and has a very small tax-base.

Indirect taxes are generally regarded as regressive or at least ineffective in influencing income distribution in a positive manner. But this view needs to be re-examined. Such taxes can be used for distributional purposes by taxing, at very high rates, goods and services mostly used by the rich.

Taking the tax system as a whole, it seems that it has proved of limited effectiveness in restraining the growth of inequalities in income and wealth. This was the conclusion reached by the Taxation Inquiry Committee in 1959[47] but more than two and a half decades later it still remains valid.

It should be noted that the manner in which public expenditure is distributed among various sectors and various purposes can have an equally strong impact on income distribution. The impact of even the most equity-oriented tax system can be nullified by an expenditure pattern mainly benefiting the affluent sections.

Fiscal policy can also be used to bring about a more equitable distribution of income between various sectors through a mixture of taxation and subsidies which influence the inter-sectoral terms of trade. This aspect has been dealt with in Chapter 9.

As for the development of the less developed regions and a reduction of the disparity between the more advanced and the less advanced areas, use has been made of a tax holiday for the less developed regions. This was in force during 1959-72. Exemptions from income tax up to a certain limit were granted to industries established in these areas for a certain number of years plus certain other tax concessions. The objectives of encouraging the dispersal of industries and bringing about greater regional balance, however, could not be fully achieved. A study made in the early seventies concluded that the tax holiday scheme, whose cost to the exchequer was estimated to be between Rs 864 million to Rs 1,293 million during 1959-72, led to an even greater concentration of economic power and encouraged the establishment of uneconomic units. Greatest benefits accrued to those industries which were already earning very high profit margins and in terms of a greater regional balance, the effect was minimal.[48]

The tax holiday scheme was reintroduced in 1978. The scheme includes a total tax holiday for a specified period in certain underdeveloped areas, the exemption of custom duties on the import of plants and machinery, a reduction in import duty on raw materials and components, and an increase in tax credits.[49] It remains to be seen whether this new scheme proves to be more effective than the earlier one or not.

NOTES

1. World Bank, *World Development Report, 1980*, p. 73.
2. Mahfooz Ali, 'The Structure of Taxation in Pakistan', in *UBL Economic Letter*, April 1980, p. 6.
3. Government of Pakistan, *Taxation Structure of Pakistan, 1980-1*, p. 26.
4. M. Akhlaqur Rahman, *The Structure of Taxation in Pakistan*, 1972, p. 10.
5. Mahfooz Ali, 'The Structure of Taxation in Pakistan', in *UBL Economic Letter*, April 1980, p. 6.
6. Government of Pakistan, *Taxation Structure of Pakistan, 1980-1*, p. 7.
7. Government of Pakistan, *Third Five Year Plan*, p. 68.
8. Mahfooz Ali, 'The Structure of Taxation in Pakistan', in *UBL Economic Letter*, April 1980, p. 8.
9. Lewis and Qureshi, 'The Structure of Revenue from Indirect Taxes in Pakistan', *Pakistan Development Review*, Autumn 1964, p. 491.
10. Government of Pakistan, *Report of the Panel of Economists for the Second Five Year Plan*, Karachi, 1959, p. 11.
11. Mahbubul Haq, *Deficit Financing in Pakistan, 1951-60*, PIDE, Karachi, 1960, p. 31.
12. Government of Pakistan, *First Five Year Plan*, p. 142.
13. Government of Pakistan, *Report of the Panel of Economists for the Second Five Year Plan*, Karachi, 1959, p. 11.
14. Mahbubul Haq and Khadija Khanum, *Deficit Financing in Pakistan, 1951-60*, PIDE, Karachi, 1960, p. 2.
15. Government of Pakistan, *Third Five Year Plan*, p. 72.

16. Mahbubul Haq, *Deficit Financing in Pakistan, 1951-60*, PIDE, Karachi, 1960, pp. 2-3.
17. (a) Ibid., p. 3.
    (b) Government of Pakistan, *First Five Year Plan*, p. 142.
    (c) Government of Pakistan, *Fifth Five Year Plan*, Part-I, Islamabad, p. 33.
    (d) State Bank of Pakistan, *Annual Report, 1979-80*, p. 96.
18. Andrus and Mohammad, *Trade, Finance and Development in Pakistan*, Oxford University Press, 1966, p. 223.
19. Government of Pakistan, *Taxation Enquiry Committee Report, 1960*, Vol. I, p. 27.
20. State Bank of Pakistan, *Annual Report, 1972-3*, p. 46.
21. Government of Pakistan, *Fourth Five Year Plan*, Islamabad, p. 45.
22. Ibid., p. 52.
23. The State Bank of Pakistan ascribes the difference between these two sets of figures to 'difference in coverage and timing'. See State Bank of Pakistan, *Annual Report, 1979-80*, p. 95.
24. World Bank, *Pakistan's Economic Development and Prospects*, 1980, pp. 112-3.
25. a. Government of Pakistan, *Pakistan Budgets, 1969-70*, pp. 1-7.
    b. Government of Pakistan, *Public Finance Statistics, 1979-80*, Table VII, p. 20.
    c. Government of Pakistan, *Report of the First National Finance Commission* appointed under Clause (I) of Article 160 of the Constitution, 1975, pp. 3-7.
26. Government of Pakistan, *Report of the First National Finance Commission*, 1975, p. 9.
27. Ibid., p. 8.
28. Bird, *Inter-Governmental Fiscal Relations in Developing Countries*, World Bank Staff Working Paper No. 304, 1978, p. 53.
29. Government of Pakistan, *Taxation Structure of Pakistan, 1980-1*, p. 25.
30. World Bank, *Pakistan Economic Development and Prospects*, 1980, p. 112.
31. Government of Pakistan, *Pakistan Budgets, 1969-70*, p. 11.
32. Government of Pakistan, *Pakistan Economic Survey, 1979-80*, Islamabad, p. 184, Statistical Annexure.
33. Government of Pakistan, *Taxation Structure of Pakistan, 1980-1*, pp. 47-9.
34. Ibid., p. 23.
35. Government of Pakistan, *Pakistan Economic Survey, 1979-80*, Islamabad, p. 44.
36. Government of Pakistan, Taxation Inquiry Committee, *Interim Report (Central Taxation)*, Karachi, 1959, p. 9.
37. Meir and Baldwin, *Economic Development*, John Wiley and Sons, New York, 1964, p. 286.
38. Mahfooz Ali, 'The Structure of Taxation in Pakistan', in *UBL Economic Letter*, April 1980, p. 6.
39. Government of Pakistan, *Pakistan Economic Survey, 1979-80*, Islamabad, p. 20.
40. Government of Pakistan, Taxation Inquiry Committee, *Interim Report (Central Taxation)*, Karachi, 1959, p. 10.
41. Meir and Baldwin, *Economic Development*, John Wiley and Sons, New York, 1964, p. 10.
42. Ibid., pp. 388-9.
43. World Bank, *Pakistan Economic Development and Prospects*, 1980, p. 112.
44. Ibid., p. 113.
45. Government of Pakistan, Taxation Inquiry Committee, *Interim Report (Central Taxation)*, Karachi, 1959, p. 72.
46. Government of Pakistan, *Taxation Structure of Pakistan, 1980-1*, pp. 20-1.
47. Ibid., p. 9.
48. B.A. Azhar, 'Tax Holiday for Industrial Development: An Evaluation', *Pakistan Economic Journal, 1973-4*, pp. 72-85.
49. Government of Pakistan, *Pakistan Economic Survey, 1979-80*, Islamabad, p. 44.

17 Trends in Monetary Management

17.1 Monetary Policy

17.1.1 The Role of Monetary Policy

Monetary policy comprises measures taken by the government and the central bank to regulate monetary flows. The policy covers not only the aggregate flows of cash and credit in the economy but also the cost, the regional, sectoral, and seasonal distribution of monetary and credit resources, and the dispersion of resources between public and private sectors. Thus, monetary policy is not only a regulatory mechanism, it also performs allocative functions in the economy. However, it must be remembered that monetary mechanism is a delicate instrument especially in a developing country. Its execution needs a cautious and balanced approach and in many cases the use of sophisticated indicators. Decisions regarding the flow of monetary resources and their allocation between competing demands have to be based on a realistic appraisal of the country's current situation along with projections of future economic trends.

Monetary policy is a difficult tool primarily because money expansion is comparatively easy, and consequently tempting, for the government. Unless caution and discretion are exercised, governments may be easily tempted into creating additional money supplies to tide over temporary resource constraints thereby escaping their political consequences. But miscalculations in such matters can be disastrous and can create complications both in the short as well as the long run and herein lies the difficulty of the central bank's job of restraining this tendency especially in capital-scarce economies.

While monetary policy needs constant revision, and seasonal and periodical adjustments in order to meet changing economic needs, the long-run implications of various policy measures must also be taken into consideration particularly the cost of investible funds, its relationship to industrial capacity utilization and general cost structure, and overall saving and investment behaviour. While over-expansion of credit may create an illusion of high resource-availability, it can in the long run discourage people's motivation to save and invest as a result of which scarce resources are diverted into non-essential, or even undesirable, uses.

17.1.2 The Objectives of Monetary Policy

Monetary policy is essentially an instrument for stabilizing the behaviour of such crucial variables as the external value of the currency, the balance of payments position, and the general price level and interest rates. These objectives can be attained if the monetary policy succeeds in balancing the money supply with the demand for money at any particular time. If the demand for money is even slightly overestimated or underestimated by the monetary authorities, the miscalculation can create a number of complications such as a distortion of saving and investment patterns and income distribution, and balance of payments problems. Central banks in developing countries, where money markets and institutions are not fully evolved and governments are politically weak, may face considerable difficulty in the task of influencing and controlling the supply and demand variables of money and credit.

In addition to these essentially short-term goals, monetary policy must also aim at achieving its prime objective: a) continuous economic expansion through the optimum utilization of resources; b) controlling inflation which is now becoming almost an integral part of the economic landscape in underdeveloped countries. While inflation cannot be completely eliminated under current circumstances, monetary policy must at least keep inflationary trends within certain restraints.

17.1.3 The Instruments of Monetary Control

Traditionally, the instruments of monetary control are divided into two categories: quantitative and qualitative: quantitative instruments include the bank rate policy, open market operations, credit rationing, and variable reserve ratio while qualitative instruments are moral suasion, publicity, consumer credit regulation, variable margin requirements for letters of credit and for advances against security of goods, and direct action. However, the following discussion relates mainly to instruments used in Pakistan since all the conventional control techniques are not applicable in developing countries like Pakistan.

Bank Rate

This is the rate at which the State Bank buys or discounts bills of exchange and other commercial papers. This is also the basic interest rate. All the other interest rates in the banking system, like the deposit rate paid by the banks to their depositers and the rates at which banks lend for short and long periods, are tied to it. With any change in the bank rate, similar changes take place in the entire interest rate structure of the banking system in particular and the economy in general. This technique is effective if the banks borrow heavily from the central bank and if both bank deposits and bank credit are interest-elastic so that if the bank rate is raised it encourages people to save and deposit more with the bank in order to earn higher interest and at the same time it discourages credit expansion due to the higher cost of borrowing. Thus a rise in the bank rate restricts the volume of credit whereas a reduction in the bank rate encourages credit expansion.

Cash Reserve Requirement

All scheduled banks are required to deposit a certain percentage of their total liquid assets with the central bank. Technically, the government can bring about a change in reserve requirement but normally the central bank exercises this authority on the government's behalf. A rise in the cash reserve requirement restricts the bank's lending operations while a fall can encourage them to advance more credit (this applies only if the banks do not have large idle cash balances). If the bank's liquidity position is comfortable, minor changes in cash reserve requirements may not influence the volume of bank credit. However, big changes in reserve requirements may induce the banks to reduce their long term advances or their financing of certain priority sectors since this instrument can control the size of the bank credit rather than its composition.

Selective Credit Control

The central banks usually have considerable authority to control the composition of bank credit. The State Bank of Pakistan can direct banks regarding the distribution of credit between different sectors and uses, between long-term and short-term loans, margin requirements for advances against certain types of assets, and the interest to be charged on different types of advances and from different borrowers. The main problem in monetary control lies in ensuring the maximum availability of funds for development needs and limiting the flow of credit to other uses so that while the total volume of credit is within control there is no shortage of funds for priority sectors. Developing countries resort most often to selective credit control although it has its own limitations. Its effectiveness is inversely related to the size of the excess liquidity in the banking sector and thus it works only in conjunction with effective quantitative controls.

Credit Ceiling

A credit ceiling for the banking system as a whole, or for each individual bank, can exercise some influence over the total volume of credit though not on its direction or use. However, this system, while keeping credit volume in check, may tempt the banks to provide more finances to low priority enterprises particularly if there is a differential interest rate schedule providing higher rates for advances to such undertakings.

Liquidity Ratio

This is the ratio between a bank's liquid resources and its total liabilities. While a low liquidity ratio may lower public confidence in the banking system and may also allow banks to liquidate their investments in government securities to finance credit expansion, a high liquidity ratio adversely affects the credit flow in the economy and the overall profitability of the bank. This ratio has a significant effect on the bank's capacity to expand credit but if used too frequently it can disrupt the smooth operation of the money market.

Open Markets Operations

This consists of the purchase and sale of securities by the central bank in the open market. The quantity of cash in the money market increases with the purchase of securities whereas their sale has contractionary effects. This instrument is used not so much to control credit as to iron out seasonal fluctuations in the money market. There is no large and specialized market for securities in Pakistan and therefore its effectiveness here is marginal.

Credit Quota

The central bank can also limit its own lending to banks by fixing a credit quota for each bank and borrowing over and above the limit may carry a higher interest rate.

In Pakistan, in addition to these instruments, the State Bank of Pakistan also offers informal advice, guidance, and persuasion to banks in various matters. Such informal control may have become fairly important particularly after the nationalization of banks and the consequent unification of their operational policies.

17.1.4 The Limitations of Monetary Policy

The success of monetary policy in achieving its objectives depends, on one hand, on recognizing its potentialities and impact on economic trends and, on the other, in identifying factors which limit its role and effectiveness in under-developed countries like Pakistan. In the first instance, there is a fairly large non-monetized sector of the economy which lies outside the scope of the monetary policy even though it may be indirectly influenced by what is happening in the monetized sector although a certain portion of the monetized sector itself is not subject to the control of the monetary policy (i.e., the unorganized money market consisting of non-institutional sources of credit). Even within the organized money and capital markets, the operation of monetary policy is subject to some limitations. Money and credit supply can increase only within certain limits as determined by the economy's overall productive capacity, general saving and investment levels, foreign exchange position, and the availability of physical complements to monetary investments. It should be understood that credit is not a substitute for savings and its expansion can increase investment only if real resources are released from consumption and diverted to capital formation. The investment level is determined by a large number of factors particularly patterns of social behaviour, business confidence, expected returns, foreign exchange, and the level of available technology.

The policies of foreign banks can also create

certain problems. The lending policy of foreign banks in Pakistan in the first two decades, particularly after the transfer of counterpart funds[1] to them in the early sixties, was instrumental in reducing the State Bank of Pakistan's ability to control the volume of bank credit.

The efficacy of various monetary instruments is also dependent upon changes in the attitudes of individuals and institutions concerning their preferences for liquidity, and the different economic variables which influence shifts in these preferences.

The international economic situation and the country's balance of payments position also limit the manoeuvrability and effectiveness of monetary tools. Furthermore, the degree of the central bank's prestige and influence over banks and other institutions in the money and capital markets also determines the extent of its success. Above all, monetary policy is less effective if too many economic and administrative controls are imposed and functions relatively more smoothly within a freer market mechanism.

It should also be remembered that monetary policy works best when used as a supplement to a fiscal and commercial policy which can strengthen the basic motivations behind savings, investment, production, and the availability of goods and services. Changes in the quantity of money provide critical additional support by maintaining the correct level of the availability of liquid assets.

17.1.5 Money Supply and Monetary Assets

Monetary policy is executed primarily by varying the total quantity of money circulating in the economy. In Pakistan, the concept of 'money supply' was originally used to denote the public's total purchasing power which constitutes the immediate demand on goods and services. Money supply consisting of liquid assets held by the public includes :

a. currency in circulation outside the banking system;
b. demand deposits, excluding inter-bank items; and
c. other deposits with the State Bank of Pakistan, after adjusting for counterpart funds, IBRD Indus Accounts, and IMF Account No. 1.[2]

The change in the definition of money supply to monetary assets was caused by the increasing use of 'near money' deposits in the sixties. The share of time deposits in total deposits increased appreciably from 32 per cent in 1960 to 52 per cent in 1967.[3] By the late sixties, there was a heavy rise in the demand for advances against time deposits which resulted in their increased monetization so that the frame of reference for the analysis of monetary conditions shifted from 'money supply' to 'monetary assets,' which, besides money supply, also included 'near-money' (time and saving deposits with scheduled banks plus post office saving accounts) because it was realized that the distinction between 'money' and 'near-money' is quite vague and also somewhat unrealistic in the light of certain developments (for example, banks were permitting depositors to withdraw time deposits of some categories and saving accounts, withdrawable by cheques, were being freely used for current transactions). Thus, for all practical purposes, time deposits, saving deposits, and postal saving accounts were influencing the current purchasing power and economic conditions.

Certain trends in the composition of the total monetary assets in Pakistan, indicating the growth of monetary forces, are also worth noting. Between 1965 and 1980, the share of currency in circulation in the total monetary assets had declined from 40 to 30 per cent while the share of time deposits increased from 25 to 32 per cent and that of demand deposits from 29 to 35 per cent.[4]

17.1.6 Causative Factors in Monetary Expansion

The changes in total monetary assets are attributable to the (a) private sector; (b) government sector; (c) foreign sector; and (d) miscellaneous.

The private sector, which also includes the public sector enterprises,[5] contributes to variations in monetary assets through net changes in the banks' advances to private and public sector enterprises, inland bills purchased and discounted by the banks, and the banks' investments in private securities. In addition, the State Bank's investments in private securities and its loans to non-scheduled banks and Co-operative institutions are also part of it. Any increase in the banking system's advances to the private sector or investment in private securities brings about an expansion in monetary assets, and vice-versa.

The government sector contribution to monetary assets is governed by net changes in the federal and provincial governments' borrowings from the banks, and investments by scheduled banks in government securities. The State Bank's holdings of government securities and treasury bills are also included. Funds drawn by the government from the banking sector are classified under budgetary support and commodity operations. The government sector's contribution to monetary assets must, however, be readjusted for changes in the government's cash balances with the State Bank. A decline in cash balances with the State Bank increases the aggregate money supply, and vice-versa. The counterpart funds which represent the sale proceeds of commodities received under aid arrangements also have an impact on the money supply. The commodities received as aid are sold in the country and the money so realized is credited in a special account in the State Bank from which the government finances development projects. A rise in counterpart funds held with the State Bank exercises a contractionary effect on the money supply.

The foreign sector is also a component of monetary assets. It affects monetary trends through changes in the State Bank's reserves of gold and foreign exchange. The foreign sector's impact on monetary assets is correlated with the country's overall balance of payments position. If the total foreign receipts exceed the total foreign payments and foreign exchange reserves increase, there is a net addition to money supply. Similarly, a deficit in the balance of payments has a contractionary effect on monetary assets.

The State Bank of Pakistan can contract the level of monetary assets by running down foreign exchange reserves and restricting the credit flow to the private sector and the government. Similarly monetary expansion can be attained by building up the foreign exchange reserves and expanding bank credit to the private sector and the government.

17.2 Phases in Pakistan's Monetary Policy

Pakistan's monetary policy can be broadly divided into four major phases. The early phase from 1947 to 1958 was marked by an increase in money supply mainly due to an expansion in the government's financial operations on which the State Bank had only limited control. The second major phase covers a period of industrial and financial boom from 1959 to 1965 ending with the Indo-Pak War and 1965-71 when monetary policy was mainly aimed at meeting the post-war difficulties. The third phase from 1972 to 1980 was marked by high levels of deficit financing, a rapid expansion in monetary assets, and a continous build-up of inflationery pressures. (It may be noted that the date used in this analysis relates to all Pakistan upto 1971 and to present Pakistan from 1972 onwards).

17.2.1 Trends During the Fifties

The monetary policy in the fifties was mainly limited to reacting to changes in the balance of payments position. This phase can be sub-divided into three sub-phases: 1947-52 which ended with the collapse of the Korean boom; 1952-5 covering the post-Korean recession; and 1955-8 which was marked by increased deficit financing by the government following the devaluation of the Pakistan currency.

The Early Fifties

At the time of independence, Pakistan was faced with an inflationary situation caused by the excess demand created during the Second World War and the acute shortage of consumer goods caused by the disruption of internal trade during the disturbances in 1947. The economic structure inherited by Pakistan was heavily dependent upon foreign trade for the export of raw materials and the import of almost everything except food. Understandably, the major aim of the monetary policy at the time was to protect the external value of the Rupee and the main instrument of monetary control was adjustments in margin requirements for letters of credit to import various commodities.

The State Bank of Pakistan was established in 1948 and took charge of the monetary situation. The Bank Rate was fixed at 3 per cent, cash reserve requirements for the scheduled banks was 5 per cent of current deposits and 2 per cent of time deposits, and the banks were required to maintain a liquidity ratio of 20 per cent. These rates were meant to encourage the expansion of credit supply so that trade and industry could rehabilitate itself and economic conditions could be normalized.

A policy of liberal imports was adopted in order to relieve the shortage of consumer goods, encourage the import of developmental needs, and curb inflation. This policy was justified by a fairly good export performance during 1947-9. However, the non-devaluation decision in September 1949 weakened Pakistan's export position and led to the hasty import of all kinds of goods in anticipation of import cuts. Forward booking of foreign exchange was, therefore, banned in August 1950 and a deposit requirement for opening letters of credit was fixed at 35 per cent (later 50 per cent) of the value of imported goods. The State Bank of Pakistan urged the banking system to restrict financial support to importers and to make more funds available for the export sector. For advances against government securities, the banks were required to pay interest rates according to a differential schedule.

These measures were gradually withdrawn as the Korean War boom prices in 1950-1 improved Pakistan's balance of payments situation. But full monetization of the export surplus and a rise in money supply was prevented by fiscal measures like higher export duties whose proceeds were funded,[6] i.e., not allowed to become part of the money supply. The government, preoccupied as it was with curbing inflation, resorted to further import liberalization to counter-balance the expansionary effects of higher export earnings. In spite of a sharp rise in bank advances in the winter of 1950, there was no significant addition to the money supply since the rise turned out to be primarily seasonal and there was a substantial recession of funds in the following slack season. No need was felt, therefore, to impose credit restrictions and in fact the State Bank provided the banking system with some additional funds through judicious open market operations.[7]

The Post-Korean Recession

The next sub-phase (1952-5) was dominated by the post-Korean recession. World prices and the demand for raw materials started declining in late 1951 but the government responded to the situation belatedly and ineffectively by raising the deposit requirement for opening letters of credit in mid-1952. This measure failed to discourage imports and in fact led to a rush for imports before the anticipated import cuts could be enforced (which did not happen until November 1952 when the open general licence, under which most of the import trade operated until then, was suspended). Consequently, Pakistan's foreign exchange reserves were reduced to dangerous levels and the country was forced to seek foreign assistance to sustain imports at the barest level of subsistence[8] and to meet food shortages which appeared in 1952-3. The government was heavily criticised for its failure to impose quantitative restrictions on imports in order to preserve its foreign exchange.

This phase was, therefore, characterized by a highly restrictive import policy, a shortage of imported goods, excessive profit margins for the small number of import category holders, and falling exports. The money supply increased rapidly mainly because the continuous government deficits were financed by the banking system. From 1953, government expenditure increased steadily but there was no corresponding rise in public revenues and non-inflationery borrowing.[9] Price, however, remained stable partly because the increase in money supply was neutralized by the contractionary effects of the post-Korean recession and the adverse movements of the terms of trade. The index of unit values (1948-9=100) fell to 85.4 in the case of imports and 64 in the case of exports while the terms of trade index fell to 75.4 in 1953-4.[10] This led to a decline in the internal purchasing power. The private sector's demand for credit was low due to a reduced level of both imports and exports. The banking system built up a considerable quantity of idle funds. The food grain supply position also improved and food prices fell as food production during 1953-5 was almost equal to the pre-1951 levels. In the case of cash crops, output reached record levels in 1953-4 and 1954-5 which depressed their prices even further.[11] Monetary assets increased from Rs 3,765 million in December 1952 to Rs 5,255 million in December 1955.[12]

Post-Devaluation Trends

During 1955-8, monetary assets rose rapidly (Table 17.1) but the State Bank adopted a relatively inactive role. This period was marked by balance of payments deficits (except in 1955-6).[13] Both industrial and agricultural production remained stagnant while government expenditures increased faster than revenues resulting in deficit financing which rose sharply from Rs 161 million in 1955-6 to Rs 679 million in 1957-8.[14]

This meant that the government was the prime source of expansion in monetary assets. In the private sector, money balances were disseminated which reinforced the inflationary pressures building up in the economy. The commercial banks confined their activities largely to financing the working capital needs of trade and industry in spite of their idle balances. As a result, the price level rose quite rapidly during this period. However, in the circumstances the State Bank of Pakistan had limited options. It was unable to restrain the government's financial operations since it did not have sufficiently effective means at its disposal. Variation in the bank rate, for example, was of no use since the level of rediscounting was low and interest-inelastic and variations in the cash reserve requirements of the banks could not produce the desired results since banks had excess liquidity. Secondary credit expansion could not be curtailed either due to the small magnitude of the credit multiplier,[15] high ratio of currency to money supply (66 per cent throughout the fifties), and the fear of possible adverse effects on industrial growth. Thus, the only positive action was the central bank's reaction in 1957 to evidence of bank finances being employed for speculative purposes. This action consisted of rather mild steps like restrictions on some types of advances and the reimposition of margin requirements on letters of credit aimed primarily at discouraging the commitment of funds for less essential, or undesirable, uses and influencing the composition, rather than the size, of bank credit.

Table 17.1: Annual Changes in Monetary Assets 1952-8
Change over previous year (June)

Year	Absolute change (Rs million)	Percentage change
1952	+ 113.4	3.0
1953	+ 138.3	3.6
1954	+ 418.6	10.5
1955	+ 365.3	8.3
1956	+ 756.0	15.8
1957	+ 507.3	9.2
1958	+ 523.6	8.7

Source: Government of Pakistan, *Pakistan Economic Survey, 1970-1*, Islamabad, p. 29, Statistical Annexure.

17.2.2 The Sixties

a. *The Industrial-Financial Boom (1959-65)*

When the Ayub regime assumed power in October 1958, some qualitative changes had taken place in the money and capital markets. A number of credit institutions specializing in sectoral financing were operating. The commercial banking sector had developed a wide network of branches thus expanding their operations. The money market was relatively better organized and could respond to monetary measures meant to influence the allocation of resources. With the retraction of economic and administrative controls, the return of food trade to private sector, import liberalization, export promotion efforts, and the increase in industrial and agricultural production, the private sector's demand for credit began to increase, slightly at first, but at an accelerated rate after 1962.

The Second Plan (1960-5) also signalled a change in government policies by underlining a greater reliance on the market mechanism and fiscal and monetary policies instead of on direct price, profit, and allocation controls.[16]

Monetary expansion in this period was rapid particularly after 1962 (Table 17.2). With the government now exercising much-needed financial restraint, the private sector found the changed economic environment conducive to an increased level of activity and it became the prime cause of monetary expansion. While the GDP between 1960-1 and 1964-5 increased by 17 per cent,[17] the money supply rose by 47.5 per cent[18] and 'monetary assets' (see Section 17.1.5) by 65 per cent.[19] The price situation was kept in check, except for a spurt in 1964-5, and the general index of wholesale prices rose by only 9.1 per cent.[20] The relative price stability in this period can be attributed partly to the improvements in the economic conditions outlined below although steps taken by the monetary authorities also played an important part.

Table 17.2: Annual Changes in Monetary Assets 1959-65

Change over previous year (June)

Year	Absolute change (Rs million)	Percentage change
1959	+ 238.8	3.6
1960	+ 500.4	7.3
1961	+ 303.0	4.1
1962	+ 517.2	6.8
1963	+ 1,354.6	16.7
1964	+ 1,515.4	16.0
1965	+ 1,580.0	14.4

Source: Government of Pakistan, *Pakistan Economic Survey, 1970-1*, Islamabad, p. 29.

Bank deposits in the early sixties increased quickly. Demand and time deposits increased by 128.6 per cent during 1960-5 as against only 64.7 per cent during 1950-5.[21] This trend was helped by a rise in industrial and agricultural production as well as brisk trading due to an increase in imports.[22] The legalization of declared wealth after martial law also added to the total deposits. But bank credit expanded even faster, by almost 295 per cent during 1960-5, as compared to only 83 per cent during 1955-60.[23] This was brought about by a rising demand for credit from trade and industry and the State Bank's readily available accommodation. The transfer of counterpart funds from the State Bank to foreign commercial banks also contributed to the situation. As cash balances with foreign banks who follow conservative lending policies increased, they were only too willing to lend to Pakistani banks who used this extra cash to expand their own credit operations.

In 1959, the State Bank raised the bank rate from the original level of 3 per cent to 4 per cent. But there is little evidence to show that it was meant to restrict the volume of credit. The State Bank's accommodation was still readily available and the volume of credit showed no signs of contraction. This step was taken presumably in order to bring the cost of credit up to a more realistic level. However, bank credit was still cheap and continued to expand.[24] Some selective credit controls were also introduced in 1960 and 1962 to discourage the use of credit for 'non-essential' purposes.

By 1963, the State Bank had a different view of the monetary situation. As monetary expansion accelerated, the cash reserve requirements, originally 5 per cent on current and 2 per cent on fixed deposits (assuming that fixed deposits represent a much lower degree of liquidity), were made uniform at 5 per cent for both. Since advances were being liberally made against fixed accounts, it was realized that these are only marginally less liquid than current deposits.

A credit quota was also introduced for the first time in 1963 when the quota for each bank was fixed at 50 per cent of the average level of its statutory reserves. Small loans (upto a limit) and counter-financing by commercial banks were exempted from calculations of the quota. The banks could borrow in excess of their quota but at higher interest rates.

b. *Post-War Trends*

Restraint was the keynote of Pakistan's monetary policy as the country launched the Third Plan. The rate of expansion in money supply ranged between 7 to 16 per cent (Table 17.3). Rising defence expenditure as a result of the 1965 War, deficit financing necessitated by a rise in non-development expenditure, and drastic cuts in aid inflows provided the major expansionary thrusts. The private sector also contributed particularly in the late sixties. The traders' anxiety to build up inventories and stocks of consumer goods was the main cause behind their high demand for bank credit and the consequent monetary expansion.

With the economy's increasing monetization and the money market's better organization and integration, the economy's responses to changes in monetary assets were becoming more direct and rapid. During 1965-71 monetary assets increased by over 82 per cent[25] a good part of which was absorbed by an increase in production (GDP at constant factor cost increased by over 38 per cent in this period).[26] The general index of wholesale prices rose by over 24 per cent.[27] The remaining gap between the increase in monetary assets on one hand and the increase in production and general price level on the other can be accounted for by the greater monetization of the subsistence sector and by the fact that while monetary assets influence both wholesale and retail prices, the changes in retail prices are generally faster and larger. This is not to say that all changes in prices can be attributed to monetary factors but only to underline an increasingly direct correlation between these three variables.

The State Bank on the whole followed a stringent policy except towards the end of the decade. In 1965 the quota system was abolished and the bank rate was raised from 4 to 5 per cent. The scheduled banks were asked to raise their deposit rates so as to pass on to their depositors some of the extra profit earned due to the abolition of the quota system.[28]

The statutory cash reserve requirements of the scheduled banks were raised and lowered quite frequently during this phase principally in order to curb the banking systems tendency to over-expand credit and to finance speculative activities and certain less essential purposes. The cash reserve requirement was raised from 5 to 7 per cent in 1965 and,

Table 17.3: Annual Changes in Monetary Assets 1965-71

Change over previous year (June)

Year	Absolute change (Rs million)	Percentage change
1965	+ 1,580.0	14.4
1966	+ 2,039.7	16.2
1967	+ 1,675.5	11.5
1968	+ 1,197.3	7.3
1969	+ 1,709.2	9.8
1970	+ 2,042.9	8.6
1971	+ 1,741.1	88.2

Source: (i) Government of Pakistan, *Pakistan Economic Survey, 1970-1,* Islamabad, p. 30 (ii) Government of Pakistan, *Pakistan Economic Survey, 1979-80,* Islamabad, p. 62.

after many changes, it was again reduced to 5 per cent in 1968. But the liquidity ratio for the scheduled banks was raised from 20 to 25 per cent and credit ceilings were imposed on all banks.[29] The State Bank, it seems, was testing various monetary instruments at its disposal in order to judge their relative effectiveness for different purposes. In order to impose greater discipline, annual credit budgeting was introduced from 1967-8 according to which both the size and the composition of bank credit was determined beforehand. The selective controls were relaxed in 1969-70 but in January 1971, when prices began to rise sharply, the credit quota was reintroduced and the banks could borrow beyond their allotted quota only at a higher rate. The margin requirements on advances against imported manufactured consumer goods were raised from 50 to 60 per cent. A margin requirement of 25 per cent was prescribed on advances for opening letters of credit covering all imports other than industrial machinery. The margin requirement of 40 per cent was imposed on advances against bank deposits, real estate, and purchase of bonus vouchers.[30]

17.2.3 Accelerated Monetary Expansion 1972-80

During the seventies, the trend towards monetary expansion was accelerated by a combination of internal and external factors. Monetary assets increased rapidly but, since growth in real output was slow, it was unable to absorb the additional purchasing power thus created. The general price level, therefore, bore the brunt and severe inflationery pressures were created in the economy. Monetary assets increased by about 280 per cent[31] between 1972 and 1980. But the GDP at constant factor cost increased by only 6 per cent[32] and the general wholesale price index by 191 per cent.[33]

The Indo-Pak war and the secession of East Pakistan had a profound influence on the economic situation especially in the early seventies as Pakistan struggled to cope with the trauma of the separation from the eastern wing and to adjust to the changed circumstances. The banking and monetary systems were disrupted. The banks faced an acute shortage of liquidity and the State Bank had to proyide them a liberal standby credit. Large scale demonetization was also undertaken in 1971 and 1972. The quota system was abolished in late 1971 but advances against food grain and some other essential items were prohibited in order to keep the availabilities position under control.

However, as the effects of the traumatic 1971 events and the change of regime began to fade, other problems arose causing heavy expansionary pressures on the money market. Prices in the world markets began to rise. Pakistan's import trade index rose from 155.9 in 1971-2 to 285.2 in 1972-3.[34] This trend was further fueled by an oil price rise in 1973. Pakistan, however, was also able to expand exports and had a trade surplus in 1972-3.[35] The Rupee was devalued in May 1972 and in June 1972 exchange reserves shot up by about 250 per cent as compared to March 1972.[36]

As a sequal to the devaluation of the Rupee, the bank rate was raised from 5 to 6 per cent in May 1972 (causing other interest rates to follow suit) and margin requirements were imposed against import of a number of commodities. In 1973-4, the liquidity ratio of the scheduled banks rose to 35 per cent and the bank rate to 8 per cent. The ceiling on advances rates was raised by 1 per cent, from 10 to 11 per cent in the case of bigger banks and 11 to 12 per cent in the case of smaller banks.[37] Credit ceilings were also imposed on individual banks in late 1973 but were withdrawn the next year in view of the impact of inflation and the oil price hike. In September 1974 the bank rate was further raised to 9 per cent.

This was strong medicine indeed which had the required effect and the rate of monetary expansion fell from over 24 per cent in 1973 to 11 per cent in 1974 and 8.7 per cent in 1975 (Table 17.4).

The seventies fully exposed the limitations of monetary policy at a time when overall economic trends were moving in the opposite direction. The government, eager to pursue its social programmes, tended to over-extend the resources at its disposal. It became a major causative factor in monetary expansion (Table 17.5) mainly through commodity financing operations during 1972-5 and 1978-80,[38] and budgetary support throughout this period. The State Bank found it difficult to control increasing government borrowings.

The private sector also contributed to the domestic credit expansion, the rate of increase in its borrowings ranging between 11.9 per

Table 17.4: Increase in Monetary Assets 1972-80
Change over previous year (June)

Year	Absolute change (Rs million)	Percentage change
1972	1,542.5	6.7
1973	5,997.8	24.5
1974	3,474.1	11.4
1975	2,976.0 @	8.7
1976	8,940.1	24.2
1977	10,632.0	23.2
1978	12,306.0	21.8
1979	13,205.3	19.2
1980 (March)	11,037.7	13.4

@ After adjusting for East Pakistani banks' portion of assets and liabilities.

Source: Government of Pakistan, *Pakistan Economic Survey, 1979-80,* Islamabad, p. 62.

Table 17.5: Causative Factors of Changes in Monetary Assets (IMF basis)
(Rs million)

	1972-3[1]	1973-4[1]	1974-5[2]	1975-6	1976-7	1977-8	1978-9	1979-80[3]
1. Government sector (net)	+ 1,564 (+12.1%)	+ 1,364 (+ 9.4%)	+ 3,056 (+20.9%)	+ 5,240 (+29.6%)	+ 6,621 (+ 29.0%)	+ 4,855 (+ 16.4%)	+ 8,816 (+25.6%)	+ 5,597 (+ 13.0%)
Budgetary support	+ 1,220 (+ 9.5%)	+ 792 (+ 5.6%)	+ 1,597 (+11.7%)	+ 4,296 (+28.2%)	+ 6,534 (+ 33.6%)	+ 5,095 (+ 19.5%)	+ 8,156 (+26.2%)	+ 4,408 (+ 11.2%)
(Commodity operations	+ 532 (+60.4%)	+ 856 (+60.6%)	+ 1,535 (+71.8%)	+ 1,110 (+30.2%)	+ 386 (+ 8.1%)	− 99 (− 1.9%)	+ 1,078 (+21.3%)	+ 1,043 (+ 17.0%)
Effective of government deposits with commercial banks	− 188 (−22.7%)	− 284 (−28.0%)	− 76 (− 6.6%)	− 166 (−13.5%)	− 299 (− 21.4%)	− 141 (− 8.3%)	− 418 (−22.8%)	+ 146 (+ 6.5%)
2. Public sector enterprises			+ 1,215 (+48.1%)	+ 1,368 (+36.6%)	+ 1,764 (+ 33.0%)	+ 2,081 (+29.3%)	+ 2,572 (+28.0%)	+ 1,914 (+16.3%)
	+ 1,827 (+13.3%)	+ 2,853 (+18.3%)						
3. Private sector			+ 2,938 (+22.5%)	+ 2,005 (+12.5%)	+ 5,273 (+ 29.7%)	+ 3,481 (+15.1%)	+ 4,397 (+16.6%)	+ 6,024 (+19.5%)
4. Counterpart funds	− 191 (−13.4%)	− 245 (−15.2%)	− 251 (−13.5%)	+ 7 (+ 0.3%)	− 71 (− 3.4%)	− 102 (− 4.7%)	− 254 (−11.2%)	+ 209 (+ 8.3%)
5. Other items (net)	+ 347 (+ 5.1%)	+ 1,089 (+16.9%)	− 876 (−24.8%)	− 110 (−2.5%)	− 754 (−16.7%)	− 1,494 (−28.4%)	− 803 (−11.9%)	− 1,055 (−13.9%)
6. Domestic credit expansion (net) (1+2+3+4+5)	+ 3,547 (+19.2%)	+ 5,061 ((+22.9%)	+ 6,082 (+24.5%)	+8,510 (+27.5%)	+12,833 (+32.6%)	+ 8,821 (+16.9%)	+14,728 (+24.1%)	+12,689 (+16.7%)
7. Foreign assets (net)	+ 1,462 (+41.4%)	− 1,438 (−28.8%)	− 1,008 (−31.7%)	+ 67 (+3.1%)	− 2,800 (−125.3%)	+ 3,069 (+542.2%)	−1,865 (−74.5%)	+ 2,026 (+317.6%)
8. Monetary assets (6+7)	+ 5,009 (+22.7%)	+3,623 (+13.4%)	+5,074 (+18.1%)	+8,577 (+25.9%)	+ 10,033 (+ 24.1%)	+ 11,890 (+ 23.0%)	+12,863 (+20.2%)	+ 14,715 (+ 19.3%)

1. Percentage changes worked out on the basis of outstanding position including data of former East Pakistan.
2. Covers the period 6 July 1974 to 27 June 1975.
3. Provisional.

N.B: Figures in parenthesis are percentage changes over the year.

Source: State Bank of Pakistan *Annual Report 1979-80*, p. 29.

cent in 1975-6 to 33 per cent in 1976-7.[39] Public enterprises also made an almost equivalent contribution as indicated by separate data on their borrowings which was available from 1974-5. As the public sector grew, its borrowings from the nationalized banks increased considerably. The foreign sector, except in 1972-3, 1977-8, and 1979-80, exercised some contractionary influence but this was too small to make an impact.

The bank rate was raised again in 1977 to 10 per cent, and minimum and maximum rates for advances by the banks were fixed at 11 per cent and 14 per cent, but the policy of providing concessionary finance to priority sectors continued.[40] Since 1977, the State Bank has relied mainly on variation in margin requirements for letters of credit for the import of different commodities and in minimum margin requirements for advances against certain stock.

17.3 The Safe Limit of Monetary Expansion

An important issue raised in the late sixties was that of fixing safe limits of monetary expansion. This issue arose mainly due to widespread feelings that monetary policy was instrumental in creating inflationary pressures on the economy which contributed to increasing income disparities. Deficit financing in particular came under heavy criticism. On the other hand, the private sector was highly critical of the State Bank's 'conservative and highly restrictive' policies.

The formula governing the safe limit of monetary expansion during the First and Second Plan periods laid down a monetary expansion equivalent to the target of real growth in GNP plus 2 percentage points to allow for the economy's progressive monetization at the appropriate level. Subsequently, when monetary analysis was related to 'monetary assets' instead of 'money supply' in 1968, an annual increase of 2.5 per cent above the GNP growth was considered as the safe limit.[41]

A special working group of experts refined this formula in the late sixties so that monetary expansion limits could be fixed directly in relation to the monetization of the subsistence sector. The Planning Commission worked out the safe level of monetary expansion by applying some of the changes in the marketable surplus of agricultural crops, the growth in other sectors of the economy, and the likely availability of foreign resources. The existing ratio of monetary assets to the flow of resources in the monetized sector so determined was used as the formula for the safe level of monetary expansion suggested in the Fourth Plan.[42]

NOTES

1. US commodity aid received under PL-480 was partly paid for in local currency. This money is kept in Pakistan and part of it is lent to Pakistan as 'Rupee aid'. See Section 17.1.6.
2. IBRD Indus Account refers to the money received from the Consortium for works under the Indus Basin Project. IMF Account No. 1 relates to amounts received by Pakistan for balance of payments support from the IMF.
3. Government of Pakistan, *Pakistan Economic Survey, 1972-3*, Islamabad, pp. 36-7.
4. Government of Pakistan, *Pakistan Economic Survey, 1979-80,* Islamabad, p. 62 Statistical Annexure.
5. Upto 1973-4, public sector contribution to monetary expansion was tabulated as part of the private sector presumably because it was small in size. As the public sector grew in size, its data was shown separately. See State Bank of Pakistan, *Annual Report, 1979-80*, p. 29.
6. S.A. Meenai, *Money and Banking in Pakistan,* Royal Book Co., Karachi, 1977, p. 142.
7. Ibid., p. 143
8. Andrus and Mohammad, *Trade, Finance and Development in Pakistan*, Oxford University Press, 1966, p. 48.
9. S.A. Meenai, *Money and Banking in Pakistan,* Royal Book Co., Karachi, 1977, p. 144.
10. S.M. Akhtar, *Economic Development of Pakistan, Vol. III*, Publishers United, 1979, Table 26.5.
11. Government of Pakistan, *Pakistan Economic Survey, 1979-80,* Islamabad, p. 25, Statistical Annexure.
12. Government of Pakistan, *Pakistan Economic Survey, 1970-1,* Islamabad, p. 29, Statistical Annexure.

13. Pakistan (West) had a continuous payments deficit since 1951-2. See Andrus and Mohammad, *Trade, Finance and Development in Pakistan*, Oxford University Press, 1966, p. 26.
14. Ibid., p. 192.
15. Ibid., p. 95. Credit multiplier indicates the number of times the money supply increases as a result of a given increase in credit.
16. Government of Pakistan, *Second Five Year Plan*, p. 8.
17. Government of Pakistan, *Pakistan Economic Survey, 1966-7*, p. 2, Statistical Annexure.
18. Ibid., p. 71.
19. Government of Pakistan, *Pakistan Economic Survey, 1970-1*, Islamabad, pp. 29-30, Statistical Annexure.
20. Ibid., p. 44.
21. Government of Pakistan, *Pakistan Basic Facts, 1979-80*, p. 173.
22. Government of Pakistan, *Pakistan Economic Survey, 1966-7*, p. 9 (agriculture), p. 17 (industry) and p. 31 (Imports).
23. Government of Pakistan, *Pakistan Basic Facts, 1979-80*, p. 173.
24. Government of Pakistan, *Pakistan Economic Survey, 1966-7*, p. 77.
25. Government of Pakistan, *Pakistan Economic Survey, 1970-1*, Islamabad, p. 29, Statistical Annexure.
26. Ibid., pp. 4-7.
27. Ibid., p. 44.
28. S.A. Meenai, *Money and Banking in Pakistan*, Royal Book Co., Karachi, 1977, p. 155.
29. Ibid., p. 136.
30. Ibid., p. 158.
31. Government of Pakistan, *Pakistan Economic Survey, 1979-80*, Islamabad, p. 62.
32. Ibid., p. 11.
33. Ibid., p. 87.
34. Ibid., p. 106 (1959-60: 100).
35. Ibid., p. 105.
36. State Bank of Pakistan, *Annual Report, 1978-9*, p. 126.
37. S.A. Meenai, *Money and Banking in Pakistan*, Royal Book Co., Karachi, 1977, p. 159.
38. State Bank of Pakistan, *Annual Report, 1978-9*, p. 33.
39. Ibid., p. 33.
40. Ibid., p. 41.
41. Government of Pakistan, *Fourth Five Year Plan*, Islamabad, p. 52
42. Ibid., p. 53.

18 Impact of Foreign Aid on Economic Development

This chapter is written by Omar Asghar Khan

The success or failure of foreign aid-supported development would depend upon two interrelated factors: (i) the terms and conditions under which aid is provided and, perhaps just as essentially, (ii) the commitment of the recipient country to make the best use of the aid. As a result of the combination of liberal aid from the USA under the Marshall Plan in the post-Second World War period, and efficient economic management, most of the war devastated economies of Western Europe were able to reach a stage of self-sustaining economic growth. Similarly, China presents a good example of the successful absorption of large doses of Soviet aid which financed a large part of China's industrial development effort during the fifties although since then Soviet aid has been almost negligible.

In contrast, Pakistan's experience of foreign aid over the past three and a half decades has not been at all satisfactory. Pakistan has still a long way to go before it can boast of having reached the stage of self-sustaining growth. The country has accumulated an enormously large foreign debt without having developed the socio-economic infrastructure necessary to sustain a growth process with a reduced quantum of foreign aid. Therefore, if, for some reason or other, foreign aid were suddenly to be cut-off the wheels of the economy would most probably grind to a halt. Deteriorating terms and conditions of foreign aid, accompanied by badly conceived capital-intensive import dependent projects, contributed towards a debt burden of almost US$ 9 billion[1] or Rs 90 million in 1979-80 which was equivalent to more than 30 per cent of the country's current GNP.[2]

The burden of excessive dependence on aid, contracted on stringent terms, is reflected not only in a phenomenally large outstanding external debt but also in the influence that aid-giving countries and agencies have come to exercise over Pakistan's economic policies. An analysis of the terms and conditions of different types of aid received by Pakistan from various sources reveals that Pakistan's relationship with the aid donors has not been based simply on the avowed objective of promoting economic development. Instead, it seems that aid has been used by donor countries and agencies to further their own strategic and economic interests to the detriment of the socio-economic interests of the recipient country. Thus, the role of foreign aid in Pakistan's economic development should be viewed both in qualitative as well as quantitative terms.

18.1 What is Foreign Aid?

Every thing about foreign aid is controversial: the purposes for which it is advanced, the terms and conditions under which it is transferred, its impact on the recipient country, and, above all, its very definition. Whether we can include international transfers advanced on non-concessional terms in the category of foreign aid, as is done in a large number of cases by economists and government officials, is open to discussion. It is important, therefore, to clear some of the conceptual ambiguity surrounding the definition of foreign aid by attempting to interpret the nature of foreign aid.

18.1.1 The 'Two-Gap' Approach

In an economy where the demand of investment cannot be met entirely by domestically generated savings nor through imports financed by the country's own export earnings, resources are transferred from abroad in the form of either loans, credits, grants remittances (private unrequited transfers), or direct private foreign investment. This is the traditional 'two-gap' or dual approach to the analysis of the role of foreign aid in economic development where foreign resources are assumed to fill both a savings-investment gap as well as a foreign exchange gap in the recipient country. According to the assumptions of the two-gap model, foreign aid, given a marginal propensity to save, raises the level of domestic savings by raising the level of income (and exports) with the result that, at some terminal date, foreign aid inflows are reduced to zero. The total amount of foreign resources transferred to the country (to cover both the savings-investment gap and the export-import gap) may be measured in terms of the current account deficit which in the familiar national income accounts identity is expressed as:

$$Y = C + I + G + (X - M)$$

where Y = National income or GNP
C = Consumption expenditure
I = Investment expenditure
G = Government expenditure
X = Exports of goods and services
M = Imports of goods and services

If imports of goods and services, M, exceeds exports of goods and services, X, foreign resources are transferred to the deficit country. When these foreign resources are in the form of loans or credits, as opposed to grants, they have to be repaid with interest and therefore entail a financial loss for the recipient country. Similarly, when foreign resources are in the form of direct foreign private investment, remittances of profits causes an out-flow of resources. This approach has come under heavy criticism for two reasons. Firstly, the two-gap model does not take account of the debt servicing charges and, secondly, it fails to incorporate the terms and conditions attached to the 'aid' which, in many cases, may prevent the recipient country from adopting policies that reduce its dependence on foreign aid.

18.1.2 Concessions and Foreign Aid

There is no consensus amongst economists as to whether all kinds of foreign resources transfers, i.e., loans, credits, grants, remittances, and direct investment are to be included in the category of foreign aid or only those which are made on concessional terms. One renowned Polish economist, Kalecki, has even gone so far as to assert that, in addition to the concessional element, foreign resources transferred to promote socio-economic development also qualify as foreign aid.[3]

The concessional element in foreign resource inflows may take any one or a combination of the following forms:

a. interest rates lower than those prevailing in the international money markets;
b. a longer period of repayment than in the case of commercial loans;
c. a grace period in the repayment of loans;
d. a grant which does not entail the repayment of either the principal or the interest.

Some economists contend that as the term 'aid' implies 'help', some form of concession may be considered a prerequisite for foreign resource inflows to qualify as foreign aid.[4] However, if we were to include only concessional foreign resource inflows in the category of foreign aid, a large proportion of what in official statistics and documents is termed as 'foreign aid' would have to be excluded because it has been transferred to Pakistan on commercial terms.[5]

As far as the conceptualization of foreign aid in terms of whether or not it promotes economic development is concerned, there is very little ground for agreement for the simple reason that there are no generally agreed upon criteria for evaluating the development process. It follows, therefore, that the twin criteria of concession and promotion of economic development cannot be considered a basis for an operational definition of foreign aid. This, however, should not be taken to mean that these two factors are of no consequence since the terms and conditions under which aid is given, and the type of development process it generates or supports, are of relevance to an analysis of the impact of foreign aid on Pakistan's pattern of development.

18.1.3 Towards a Definition of Foreign Aid

In order to examine the impact of foreign aid on Pakistan's economic development, our definition of foreign aid corresponds roughly to the nature of the official data available on foreign resource inflows. If we define foreign aid in terms of the official data, as compiled in the official sources, a number of foreign resource inflows will not be included. Official statistics on foreign aid (or foreign economic assistance) are compiled for only those foreign resources that are publically guaranteed and are made either on a government to government or a government-supported-financial-institution to government basis. Only economic aid is included in foreign aid statistics which means that military aid as well as the debt accumulated on loans for military purchases are excluded. Thus, besides military aid, direct private foreign investment and loans by private foreign banks and private financial institutions are excluded from the international transfers which we are treating as foreign aid for the purpose of this study.

The two main institutional sources of foreign aid are bilateral and multilateral. Examples of bilateral aid sources are governments of donor countries while examples of multilateral sources are the various international aid-giving agencies such as the World Bank-sponsored Aid-to-Pakistan Consortium where a number of countries pool in their resources to provide aid.

For a meaningful discussion on the definition of foreign aid, it is important to distinguish between pledges, commitments, disbursement, and utilization of aid. These terms are frequently used to describe the various stages through which foreign aid passes before being utilized in the recipient country. A *pledge* is a promise by the donor to advance a specified amount of foreign aid; *commitment* implies the allocation of foreign aid by the donor for specific projects or programmes; *disbursement* of aid means the transfer of resources from donor to the recipient; and *utilization* implies the actual implementation of foreign-aid-financed projects. In the case of Pakistan, as in most other developing countries, disbursements and utilization have often fallen short of aid pledged and committed by donors due either to Pakistan's inability to raise the domestic resource component or to a lack of absorptive capacity in certain sectors or to a change in the foreign aid policy of donor countries.

18.2 Pakistan's Dependence on Foreign Aid

To examine the extent of Pakistan's dependence on foreign aid, we should take a look at the amount of foreign aid the country has received so far as a proportion of the GNP. It is the ratio of foreign aid to the GNP, given the level of gross domestic investment, that tells us the extent to which a country depends upon foreign aid to finance its gross domestic investment. A country is said to depend on foreign aid when, on the one hand, gross domestic investment exceeds domestic savings and, on the other hand, imports exceed the country's total foreign exchange earnings. In such a situation, foreign aid, in the form of government to government medium and long-term loans or official transfers of grant-type assistance, contributes towards filling both a savings-investment gap and an export-import gap.

Pakistan's dependence on foreign aid increased both absolutely and as a proportion of the GNP during 1950-75. With gross foreign aid inflows almost negligible during the fifties, the first half of the sixties witnessed a rapid and substantial increase. From 1 per cent of the GNP in the fifties, gross foreign aid inflows increased only marginally to 2.75 per cent in 1961. But by 1964, foreign aid inflows were almost 9 per cent of the GNP. The expansion in foreign aid during the first half of the sixties was necessitated by the increase in the level of gross domestic investment which could not be financed entirely by domestic savings.

Towards the latter half of the sixties, foreign aid slowed down but increased again in the first half of the seventies growing from 3.61 per cent of the GNP in 1970 to 11.10 per cent in 1975. Since 1975, although gross foreign aid inflows remained almost static at around US$ 1 billion per annum,[6] foreign aid inflows as a proportion of the GNP fell to about 5 per cent of the GNP by 1980 (Table 18.1). As shown in the Table, foreign aid and domestic savings together financed only about 65 per cent of the gross investment in 1980 with the rest being financed largely by workers' remittances which compensated for the lower level of domestic savings and foreign aid inflows by raising both the country's foreign exchange earnings as well as the level of gross national savings.

While the country's foreign exchange earnings financed 46 per cent of the total imports[7] in 1964-5 (implying that 54 per cent of the imports were financed by foreign resource inflows) in 1979-80 about 87 per cent of the imports[8] were financed by the country's own foreign exchange reserves enlarged by increases in workers' remittances. The net factor income from abroad (almost wholly accounted for by workers' remittances) which stood at only Rs 3 million in 1970 had increased to Rs 18,187 million by 1980.[9] If we exclude workers' remittances from the country's foreign exchange earnings over the latter half of the seventies, both the foreign exchange gap (exports-import gaps) and the savings-investment gap would become larger. These workers' remittances, by increasing the country's foreign exchange earnings, reduced the deficit on the current account. To some extent this eased the total foreign aid requirements to finance a large import bill as well as an increased public sector expenditure programme.

To get some idea of the extent to which gross domestic investment has been dependent on foreign aid it may be observed that about 32 per cent of gross domestic fixed capital formation (investment) was financed by gross foreign aid in 1964[10] but only about 28 per cent in 1980.[11] Thus, between 1964 and 1980 the foreign aid component in the gross domestic investment was reduced by an increase in workers' remittances over the second half of the seventies.

Compared to other low-income developing

Table 18.1: Foreign Aid, Investment, and Savings in Pakistan*
(at current prices)

Percentage of GNP	1955	1961	1964	1970	1975	1980
Gross foreign aid	1.1	2.75	8.79	3.61	11.10	4.85
Gross investment	8.0	12.41	17.52	14.31	16.9	15.25
Domestic savings	6.9	7.88	8.57	11.10	5.85	6.16

* Up to 1970 data relates to united Pakistan and after 1970 to what is now Pakistan.

Note: Foreign aid plus domestic savings do not add up to gross domestic investment since private foreign resources inflows are not included.

Source: (i) Ministry of Finance, Government of Pakistan, *Pakistan Economic Survey*, Islamabad, various issues. (ii) Statistics Division, Government of Pakistan, *Twenty-five Years of Pakistan in Statistics*, 1965, p.8. (iii) Ministry of Finance, Government of Pakistan, *Pakistan Economic Survey, 1980-1*, Islamabad, pp. 12-13, Statistical Annexure.

countries, gross foreign resource inflows as a proportion of the GNP in the case of Pakistan have been quite high averaging 7 per cent and 11 per cent respectively in 1960 and 1978 (Table 18.2) while for all low-income developing countries it was 3 per cent in 1960 and 6 per cent in 1978. It is important to note, however, that foreign resource inflows (as opposed to foreign aid) include both public and private transfers of international resources which would be more than just foreign aid inflows in the case of Pakistan.

18.3 The Burden of Aid—Pakistan's Debt Servicing Problem

Our discussion regarding Pakistan's dependence on foreign aid has so far been in terms of gross foreign aid which does not take into account the annual debt repayment on loans received from foreign sources. By subtracting the annual debt servicing (repayment of principal and interest) from gross aid, we deduce the net foreign aid which is available to the recipient country for financing its imports and gross investment.

The annual debt servicing charges shown in official statistics are net of relief provided in the form of a moratorium. A moratorium on debt means the postponement of the annual debt servicing obligations till some later time which no doubt provides temporary relief to a foreign exchange crisis-ridden country. But since the debt has to eventually be repaid, a moratorium only delays the problem in the hope that the country, by increasing its foreign exchange earnings, would at some later stage be in a position to fulfil its debt servicing obligations.

Table 18.2: Foreign Resources as a percentage of the GNP for Pakistan and Selected Developing Countries

Low-income countries (per capita income of $ 360 or less)	1960	1978
India	3	4
Pakistan	7	11
Sri Lanka	4	5
Kenya	3	10
Niger	1	7
Average for all low-income countries	3	6

Note: Foreign resource Inflows as defined as $I_G - S_D = S_F$
Where I_G = Gross Domestic Investment
S_D = Gross Domestic Savings
S_F = Foreign Resource Inflows

Source: World Bank, *World Development Report, 1980*, 1980.

In the case of Pakistan, foreign debts assumed large and unmanageable dimensions after the break-up of the country in the early seventies. Since then, and until recently, a moratorium on the annual debt servicing has been granted to Pakistan so that the country may be able to tide over its foreign exchange problems. However, as shown in Table 18.4, relief in the form of a moratorium has gradually shrunk from 38 per cent of annual maturities in 1974-5 to 12 per cent in 1979-80. With most of the aid in the fifties and early sixties being either in the form of grants or soft loans accompanied by grace periods, net foreign aid inflows averaged about 85 per cent of gross aid during 1960-6 implying that debt servicing obligations averaged about 15 per cent of gross aid. However, as there was a general shift from grants to loans, the grace period on a number of loans began to expire, and net foreign aid inflows as a proportion of gross disbursements shrank from 84 per cent in 1966 to 46 per cent in 1973 (Table 18.3). Following the separation of East Pakistan in 1971, Pakistan was granted debt relief under a multilateral agreement by the Aid-to-Pakistan Consortium which provided debt relief amounting to approximately US$ 650 million over the period 1974-8.[12] Thus, the debt servicing figures in Table 18.4 are net of relief till 1978 after which period debt relief arrangements were not extended.

From Table 18.4, it may be observed that due to an increase in annual debt servicing charges, net transfers as a ratio of gross disbursements declined from 73 per cent in 1974-5 to 34 per cent in 1980-1 notwithstanding debt relief provided during 1974-8.

Thus, while 27 per cent of gross aid was returned to donor countries in 1974-5 in the form of debt servicing, it is estimated that 66 per cent of gross aid went back to donor countries as debt servicing charges in 1980. Out of the total gross aid disbursements of US$ 6,963 million from 1974-5 to 1980-1, US$ 4,102 million or almost 60 per cent was returned to donors as debt servicing (Table 18.4). Had debt relief in the form of a moratorium on annual maturities of the outstanding debt not been provided during this period, a higher proportion of gross aid would have had to be allocated for debt

Table 18.3: Net Transfers of Foreign Aid : 1961-74
($ million)

Year	Gross disbursements	Debt servicing	Net transfers	Net transfers as percentage of gross transfers
1961	106	17	89	84
1962	236	31	205	87
1963	307	47	260	85
1964	484	61	423	87
1965	376	62	314	84
1966	456	74	382	84
1967	498	96	402	81
1968	517	103	409	79
1969	561	154	407	73
1970	534	175	359	67
1971	612	182	403	66
1972	409	122	287	70
1973	355	193	162	46

Source: Government of Pakistan, *Pakistan Economic Survey*, various issues.

Table 18.4 : Net Foreign Aid received by Pakistan
($ millions)

Years	Gross aid	Total annual debt servicing during year	Relief provided during year	Debt servicing (net of relief)	Debt relief as percentage of annual debt servicing	Net aid	Net transfer as percentage of gross transfers
1974-5	976	419	160	259	38.0	717	73
1975-6	1,064	457	176	281	38.5	783	73
1976-7	961	531	167	364	31.4	597	62
1977-8	856	615	244	371	39.6	485	56
1978-9	948	645	151	496	23.4	454	48
1979-80	1,127	751	90	661	12.0	466	41
1980-1	1,031	648	NA	NA	NA	347	34

Note: In column 3 is shown the total annual debt servicing charges Pakistan should have incurred on the basis of the annual amortization of the debt and interest payments. However, because of an inability to pay the annual amortization and interest charges on loans disbursed, Pakistan has been provided debt relief by donor countries in the form of a moratorium on the outstanding debt shown in column 4. Subtracting column 4 from 3 gives us the actual annual debt servicing. Column 6 gives us the ratio of annual debt relief provided to outstanding annual debt servicing (column 5 divided by column 3). Column 7 shows the annual net availability of aid to Pakistan which is calculated by subtracting column 5 from column 2, i.e., subtracting actual annual debt servicing from gross aid. Column 8 shows the ratio of net transfers of aid as a proportion of gross aid.

Source: (i) Finance Division, Government of Pakistan, *Pakistan Economic Survey, 1979-80*, Islamabad, 1980, p. 153. (ii) Finance Division, Government of Pakistan, *Pakistan Economic Survey, 1980-1*, Islamabad, 1981, p. 156.

servicing thus reducing the net availability of foreign aid.

Thus, because of an increase in interest payments, and an amortization of the principal on outstanding loans in the seventies, a smaller proportion of net foreign aid has been made available to the country. While in 1971 the repayment of principal and interest took up roughly 61 and 39 per cent of debt servicing respectively, these ratios were 55 and 45 per cent in 1977[13] implying an increase in the share of interest payments in total debt servicing which points towards a hardening of the financial terms under which foreign aid has been provided to Pakistan.

The debt servicing ratio, defined in terms of the annual debt repayment divided by the country's foreign exchange earnings, averaged about 18 per cent during 1971-9[14] which, when compared to other low-income developing countries, is high. The debt servicing ratio, however, does not cover unguaranteed private debt or the debt incurred for purchases of military equipment although separate data is not available.

Amongst the South Asian countries, Pakistan had the second highest debt-servicing ratio in 1977 which was estimated at 13.6 per cent of foreign exchange earnings (Table 18.5).

In Table 18.5, debt servicing is taken as a ratio of *total foreign exchange earnings* which, in the case of Pakistan as well as other manpower exporting countries, includes workers' remittances from abroad. This is why Pakistan's debt servicing ratio in Table 18.5 seems low. However, in relation to export earnings, debt servicing is much higher since workers' remittances are not included in export earnings. In 1978-9, debt servicing as a ratio of export earnings stood at about 35 per cent.[15] Thus, the lower ratio of debt servicing to total foreign exchange earnings in the case of Pakistan is caused by large workers' remittances from abroad without which the debt servicing problem in the seventies would have assumed an acute dimension.

Table 18.5: Debt Servicing of South Asian Countries in 1977

Country	Debt servicing annual debt payment foreign exchange earnings
Bangladesh	11.7
Burma	13.2
India	10.5
Pakistan	13.6
Sri Lanka	14.6

Source: Third World Foundation, *The Third World Diary, 1981*, 1982, various pages.

The increase in Pakistan's accumulated debt as well as the annual debt servicing charges has been caused by, firstly, an increase in the volume of gross aid inflows and, secondly, by a shift in the composition of foreign aid from grant-type assistance to loans some of which have had to be repaid at almost commercial rates of interest.

The financial terms and conditions under which loans have been received by Pakistan from different sources have, on the whole, recorded a gradual stringency with the interest rate rising on the average from 2.5 per cent in the early fifties, repayable in forty years, to 3.9 per cent in 1969-70, repayable in twenty-two years. Again, in 1979-80, the interest on loans increased on the average to 5.16 per cent repayable in twenty-one years.[16] If we compare the financial terms and conditions of some of the foreign aid received by Pakistan with certain commercial loans advanced by private financial institutions, we can conclude that the concessional element is almost non-existent in some of the so-called 'foreign aid'.

Table 18.6 shows the decrease in concessional borrowing by Pakistan because of a shift in aid from concessional loans to hard loans. While in 1955-60, hard loans constituted 13 per cent of aid, in 1973-4 (the last year for which such data is available) hard loans were almost 40 per cent of all aid disbursements (hard loans are those loans that have to be repaid in foreign exchange as opposed to soft loans which may be repaid in goods or local currency). Although there has been an increase in East European credits, advanced on generally softer terms, the decrease in export credits and concessional loans has increased the proportion of hard loans in total borrowings from abroad.

While in the fifties the grant component in total foreign aid averaged about 59 per cent, in the seventies it had shrunk to about 13.4 per cent of the total external assistance (loans and grants)[17] the residual being accounted for by the loan component repayable to donors with interest.

Besides the change from grants, which do not involve repayment, to loans, foreign economic assistance has also shifted from soft loans, repayable in non-convertible Rupees, towards hard loans repayable in foreign exchange. While in the fifties the repayment of loans in non-convertible Rupees averaged about 16 per cent of the total assistance, during the seventies the entire amount of loans was repayable in foreign exchange[18] thus placing a burden on the country's meagre foreign exchange earnings as well as on the tax payer.

As a result of all these factors, Pakistan's outstanding debt (including Bangladesh) increased from US$ 0.2 billion in 1960 to US$ 3.6 billion in 1971.[19] During the seventies, debt accumulation was again very rapid with the accumulated debt (disbursed and outstanding) more than doubling to reach US$ 8.9 billion by the end of 1980 (this constituted about 32 per cent of Pakistan's GNP).[20] While the per capita accumulated debt burden of Pakistan was US$ 108[21] or Rs 1,060 in 1980, the per capita annual debt servicing burden in 1980 was US$ 7,[22] or Rs 70, implying that an average Pakistani whose per capita income in 1980 was Rs 2,875[23] was taxed, because of debt servicing obligations alone, to the tune of Rs 70. If Pakistan continues to accumulate debt at the present rate, the outstanding accumulated debt, most of which is advanced on non-concessional terms, would be US $20 billion by 1985 and US$ 122 billion by the year 2001. At this rate, the annual debt servicing payments in 1990 would be US$ 9 billion whilst the country's exports in 1980-1 were estimated at roughly one third this amount, i.e., US$ 2.9 billion.[24]

How does the debt burden affect the average Pakistani? In two ways. First, *directly* in the sense that as debt servicing obligations increase, a large proportion of personal income would be taken away by the government in the form of taxes to repay the out-

Table 18.6: Borrowing on Concessional and Hard Terms
($ million)

Period	Borrowing on concessional terms*	Hard term borrowings: Hard loans	Export credits	East European credits	Total borrowings
1950-1 to 1954-5	286 (77%)	—	—	—	372
1955-6 to 1959-60	768 (77%)	125 (13%)	100 (10%)	—	993
1960-1 to 1964-5	1,611 (68%)	504 (21%)	179 (8%)	71 (3%)	2,365
1965-6 to 1969-70	1,609 (60%)	541 (20%)	470 (17%)	81 (3%)	2,701
1970-1	427 (66%)	159 (24%)	54 (8%)	16 (2%)	656
1971-2	85 (91%)	—	8 (9%)	—	93
1972-3	410 (82%)	44 (9%)	14 (3%)	31 (6%)	499
1973-4	315 (53%)	231 (39%)	11 (2%)	34 (6%)	591

* Includes grant-type loans (repayable in non-convertible Rupees) $20 million in 1950-5, $172 million in 1955-60, $97 million in 1960-5, and outright grants.

Source: Government of Pakistan, *Pakistan Economic Survey, 1973-4*, Islamabad, 1974, p.134.

standing debt. Second, *indirectly* in that that the government, because of its inability to meet the rising debt servicing obligation in the face of inadequate foreign exchange earnings, would request donor countries for concessions which inevitably would involve Pakistan offering some *quid pro quo*. This would most probably require the Government of Pakistan adopting policies that are dictated by the donors but are not necessarily in the national interest.

18.4 Types of Foreign Aid

Foreign aid received by Pakistan may be broadly divided into tied and untied aid. Most aid has been tied to both source and utilization with the result that a variety of goods and services have been purchased on credit at uncompetitive prices (above average world market prices), with interest rates in most cases equivalent to commercial rates. It has been estimated by Dr. Mahbub-ul-Haq, Chief Economist to the Government of Pakistan in the sixties, that the prices of commodities supplied to Pakistan under a number of tied credit agreements have exceeded the lowest quoted price on the international market by up to 170 per cent.[25] Higher prices charged by creditor-suppliers inflates not only the principal that has to be repaid but also the interest payments. This imposes a heavy burden on the recipient of such aid and calls into question the idea of such credits being termed 'foreign aid'.

Out of the total foreign economic assistance contracted by Pakistan up to December 1980, 91 per cent was tied to specific projects or commodities and was also confined to purchases from donor countries.[26] The remaining 9 per cent was in the form of 'unrestricted' balance of payments support[27] out of which only certain country-to-country loans can be, strictly speaking, termed untied aid. The term 'unrestricted' balance of payments support for the remaining 9 per cent is therefore misleading since most of such balance of payments support is conditional on the recipient following policies dictated by the donors. IMF loans, the large bulk of balance of payments support, falls into the category of such 'unrestricted' balance of payments support. An example of untied aid to Pakistan is the balance of payments support provided in the form of cash foreign exchange loans by Iran and Saudi Arabia during the seventies.[28] This is the best form in which foreign aid may be provided after grant-type assistance (although grant-type aid may involve certain strings) and local currency loans. However, this is only so if the period of repayment is not too short and the interest rate not too high.

Besides balance of payments support, the major types of aid received by Pakistan may be classified as project, commodity, food, and technical assistance. Under these four types of economic assistance, various kinds of commodities for utilization in different projects and sectors of the economy have been supplied to Pakistan either on credit or under grant agreements. In general, all these four types of aid are of the tied nature as purchases have been tied to specific projects or commodities which in most cases have been supplied by the donor countries themselves.

From Table 18.7, we can see that, amongst the different types of aid, the share of project assistance has been the largest and has increased from 41 per cent during the First Plan period to about 73 per cent in 1979-80. The second largest share has been that of commodity assistance which, however, has declined from 34 per cent during the Second Plan period to about 23 per cent in 1979-80. The third largest share amongst the different types of aid has been that of commodity PL 480, Food Aid, which has also declined quite substantially from 21 per cent during the Second Plan period to about 4 per cent in 1979-80. As data on the share of technical assistance during the seventies is not available, we have shown the share of technical assistance for the Second and Third Plan periods only as 4 per cent and 2 per cent respectively (Table 18.7).

While examining the different types of aid received by Pakistan, it is important to assess their relative impact on the country's pattern of economic development. In doing so we should take account of the qualitative factors and examine the terms and conditions of different types of aid and their implications for the recipient country. Thus, the role of foreign aid in economic development cannot be judged purely in quantitative terms. This becomes obvious while discussing the various types of aid given to Pakistan since, besides affecting the country's socio-economic conditions through costs and prices, certain types of aid agreements have allowed certain powerful donor countries/agencies to influence decision-making in the country. Now we examine the impact of the different types of foreign aid on Pakistan's economic development.

18.4.1 Project Assistance

The large bulk of foreign aid received by Pakistan (Table 18.7) has been in the form of project assistance which is tied, in most cases, to both source and utilization. By *aid tied to source* is meant that once the recipient country has been given a loan, or grant, it has to make its purchases from suppliers in the donor countries. Similarly, when aid is *tied to utilization* the aid received in the form of loan, or grant, has to be disbursed on specific projects which in turn have to have the prior approval of the donor countries/ agencies.

Project assistance is aid allocated for particular developmental ventures like irrigation projects or large industrial and communication networks which require a substantial imported component. Except for loans to the Agricultural Development Bank, Small Industries Corporation, Pakistan Industrial Credit and Investment Corporation (PICIC), and the Industrial Development Bank of Pakistan (IDBP), (financial institutions which advance credit to the private sector) most loans/grants received from donor countries as project assistance are allocated to the public sector.

Besides the imported component, there is also a local finance component of a particular project which has to be covered by raising the necessary resources domestically. Once the domestic component of the project has been raised, the government has to open a special account for the project and withdrawals from this account are possible only after the approval of the Aid Mission of the donor countries/ agencies. Since major donor countries like the USA have traditionally preferred to finance a number of specific projects, rather than just one or two, they

Table 18.7: Types of Foreign Aid Received by Pakistan
(Rs million)

Type of aid	1960-5	%	1965-70	%	1972-3	%	1979-80	%
Project assistance	3,940	41.0	875	57.0	990	28.0	6,574	73.0
Technical assistance	430	4.0	350	2.0	NA	–	NA	–
Commodity aid (Non-food)	3,310	34.0	2,958	26.0	1,598	45.0	2,155	23.0
Food aid (PL 480)	1,970	21.0	2,325	15.0	942	27.0	317	4.0
Total :	9,650	100.0	15,384	100.0	3,530	100.0	9,046	100.0

Source: (i) Planning Commission, Government of Pakistan, *The Third Five Year Plan*, 1965, p. 91 for data on 1960-5. (ii) Planning Commission, Government of Pakistan, *The Fourth Five Year Plan*, 1970, p. 65 for 1965-70. (iii) Government of Pakistan, *Pakistan Economic Survey, 1972-3*, Islamabad, 1973, p. 73 for 1972-3. (iii) Government of Pakistan, *Pakistan Economic Survey, 1979-80*, Islamabad, 1980, p.155 for 1979-80.

may come to gain control over a large proportion of development expenditure. As has been pointed out in an earlier study on US aid to Pakistan,

> 'the proportion of the USA's contribution to the cost of the project is indicated by the fact that 18.6 per cent of the total development expenditure was financed by aid funds . . . . By providing less than a fifth of the expenditure, the US Aid Mission acquires control over Pakistan Government funds being expended on projects.'[29]

Not only does project assistance allow donor countries to increase their influence on the recipient country, by virtue of their control over the manner in which this aid is utilized, it also imposes a financial burden on the recipient country because of the monopoly position such aid confers on donors. Under the terms of such aid agreements, suppliers in donor countries can charge prices above the prevailing world market prices since a specific proportion of the goods and services have to be purchased from donor countries, (as pointed out earlier). These prices reduce the real value of the loan or grant by inflating the principal. The recipient, if it could purchase the same items from other suppliers at the world market rates, would receive more in terms of goods and services for the same amount of aid.

It is for the above reasons, and in particular the tying up of large amounts of resources in big long-gestation projects, that the Government of Pakistan has voiced its concern over the large bulk of foreign aid being tied up in project assistance. Towards the end of the Third Plan, the government approached the donor countries with the plea that:

> 'the most critical need will continue to be for more flexible resources in the form of programme or commodity assistance (Non-project assistance).[30]

As commodity assistance is not generally tied to long-gestation projects, the government, in view of the country's underutilized capacity, has on the whole preferred commodity over project assistance so that production can be increased in the short to medium term.

18.4.2 Commodity Assistance

Commodity assistance, the second largest component amongst the different types of aid received by Pakistan (Table 18.7), has allowed some degree of flexibility to the country by not being tied to utilization although in most cases it is tied to source. It is for this reason that Pakistan has preferred commodity over project assistance. However, commodity assistance, as a ratio of total aid, decreased from 34 per cent in 1960-5 to 23 per cent in 1979-80 (Table 18.7).

In commodity assistance, we do not include surplus agricultural commodities supplied by the USA under PL-480. Under commodity assistance, which is allocated between the public and the private sector, are included commodities ranging from industrial spare parts to various kinds of consumer goods.

18.4.3 PL-480 Commodity Assistance

The third largest component of aid received by Pakistan is commodity assistance under PL-480 provided by the USA through the sale of surplus agricultural commodities. These commodities, ranging from wheat to edible oil, have been purchased by the Pakistan Government from the United States Government and were paid for in Pakistani Rupees till 1967 and in Rupees and dollars after 1967. The funds generated by the sale of these surplus agricultural commodities are then deposited in a special 'counterpart' fund controlled by the US Government through its Aid Mission in Pakistan. The allocation of these funds, termed as 'aid', between different activities has been the prerogative of the US Government.

The total 'aid' generated by the sale of surplus US agricultural commodities may, if the statistics are taken at face value, seem quite substantial. But when account is taken of the fact that the USA, by virtue of its monopoly position, has charged above world-average-prices, the real value of the 'aid' is reduced in terms of the amount of commodities that could have been purchased from other sources if the aid were provided in the form of cash loans. According to the *New York Times* of 13 June 1953, shipping wheat aid to Pakistan in American ships cost \$ 26 per ton as against \$ 12 to \$ 14 per ton in a foreign ship.[31] Thus, the higher price and the condition that the wheat must be shipped in American carriers have imposed an undue burden on Pakistan. In Table 18.8, we present data on planned uses of counterpart funds under PL-480 up to 1958. This data is presented to give the reader a broad idea of the manner in which the counterpart funds were allocated amongst different activities.

We can see from Table 18.8 that the largest allocation of counterpart funds up to 1958 was as 'Loans to the Pakistan Government' which is essentially a financial transaction as it involves repayment with interest. Under *payment of US obligations* are covered those expenses of the US Government for which it would otherwise have had to remit dollars. Thus, through the generation of counterpart funds, the US has been able to pay for its obligations in surplus agricultural commodities instead of in dollars. Under *loans to business* the USA has traditionally advanced credits mainly to US controlled business rather than to local business. In *other uses* are covered costs of various cultural

Table 18.8: Planned Allocation of Counterpart Funds up to 1958
(\$ millions)

Development 'grants'	Loans to the Government of Pakistan	Payment of US obligations	Military procurement	Loans to business	Other uses	Total
12.3 (6)	89.1 (33)	50.0 (17)	79.4 (30)	28.7 (11)	8 (3)	268.5 (100)

Note: Figures in parenthesis are percentages.
Source: H. Alavi, and A. Khusro, 'Pakistan, the Burden of US Aid', in *Imperialism and Underdevelopment—A Reader*, edited by R.I. Rhodes, Monthly Review Press, New York, 1970, p.68.

Table 18.9: Allocation of Counterpart Funds in the Sixties (percentages) and 1970-1

	1964-5 to 1965-6	1966-7	1967-8 to 1968-9	1969-70	1970-1
1. US expenditures	11	25	8	11	20
2. Payment of US obligations	19	—	—	—	—
3. Grants to Government of Pakistan	50	75	22	50	50
4. Loans to Government of Pakistan	20	—	65	30	30
5. Loans to business (cooley loans)	—	—	5	9	—
Total	100	100	100	100	100

Source: (i) Ministry of Finance, Government of Pakistan, *Pakistan Economic Survey, 1964-5*, 1965, p.202 and *Pakistan Economic Survey, 1965-6*, 1966, p. 192 for 1964-5 to 1965-6. (ii) Government of Pakistan, *Pakistan Economic Survey, 1966-7*, 1967, p. 211 for 1966-7. (iii) Government of Pakistan, *Pakistan Economic Survey, 1967-8*, 1968, p. 170 and *Pakistan Economic Survey, 1968-9*, 1969, p. 187 for 1969-8 to 1968-9. (iv) Ministry of Finance, Government of Pakistan, *Pakistan Economic Survey, 1969-70*, 1970, p.192 for 1969-70. (v) Ministry of Finance, Government of Pakistan, *Pakistan Economic Survey, 1970-1*, 1971, p. 132 for 1970-1.

activities mainly of a propaganda nature.

From 1964-5 to 1970-1, the period for which official data was available, the allocation of Rupee counterpart funds between different activities were as given in Table 18.9.

We can see from the allocation of counterpart funds during 1964-9 that, while the proportion of US grants to the Pakistan Government declined from 50 to 22 per cent, the proportion of loans to the Pakistan Government as well as to US controlled local business increased from 20 to 60 per cent and from 0 to 5 per cent respectively. By the end of the sixties, and the beginning of the seventies, 80 per cent of the counterpart funds were being allocated for budgetary support.

Since a sizeable proportion of the US controlled counterpart funds have been allocated as grants and loans to the Pakistan Government (which has utilized them on developmental projects) the US Government (Pakistan's largest donor) has played an important role in influencing the country's development pattern through control over counterpart funds (see next section). During the seventies the generation of counterpart Rupee funds had almost ceased to exist since Pakistan's purchases of US agricultural surplus commodities were made mostly in the form of dollar credits. Whereas counterpart funds comprised 65 per cent of the total foreign economic assistance in 1961-2, in 1979-80 their share had fallen to only 4.1 per cent (Table 18.10).

18.4.4 Technical Assistance

Although technical assistance has comprised a small proportion of total foreign economic assistance, this type of foreign aid, because it covers the services of foreign 'experts' (as well as the training of Pakistani experts abroad), is of greater significance than suggested by a mere examination of the statistics in Table 18.7.

A large number of 'experts' have come to Pakistan under the guise of various aid programmes. We must, however, distinguish between those experts who are associated with specific projects at the operational level of design and actual implementation of projects and those experts who are concerned with overall planning and policy-making. It is the latter category of experts who, under the title of the 'Harvard Advisory Group', played an extremely important role in the formulation of Pakistan's Second Five Year Plan. To what extent the economic policies followed by us during the sixties, on the advice of the American 'experts', were in the 'national' interest is no doubt a question of fundamental importance but it lies beyond the scope of this discussion on foreign aid.

Foreign technical experts generally accompany particular projects which are a part of the project assistance provided to the recipient country. As these foreign experts are paid much higher salaries than what a local person of the same qualifications (some of whom may be foreign qualified and more experienced) can expect to receive, the real value of technical assistance is reduced with obvious resentment amongst local experts. Moreover, since the typical foreign 'expert' comes to Pakistan for a short duration (one or two years), by the time he has gained some experience of the local conditions, it is time for him to return with the result that he is unable to grasp the complexities of the social

Table 18.10: Counterpart Funds as percentage of Total Foreign Assistance
(All-Pakistan before 1971 and West Pakistan after 1971).

1961-2	1964-5	1967-8	1970-1	1973-4	1976-7	1979-80
65.0	21.0	6.5	6.8	–	4.2	4.1

Source: Government of Pakistan, *Pakistan Economic Survey, 1979-80*, Islamabad, 1980, p. 188-91, Statistical Annexure.

organization which have a direct bearing on the project's successful implementation.

18.5 Pakistan's Principal Sources of Foreign Aid

The relative importance of different countries/agencies as donors in different periods of time tells us something about the structure of a country's dependence on different sources of aid. Moreover, as most aid is tied to source (i.e., the recipient of such aid has to buy goods from the donor) the source structure of foreign aid also points towards the recipient's aid-determined-import-structure. The more diversified the sources of aid, the less the recipient country's dependence on any one source so that if there is any change in the foreign aid policy of any one important donor in terms of restrictions on aid flows the recipient can turn to other sources. Pakistan's sources of aid have been divided into four major groups:

1. Consortium
2. Non-Consortium
3. Islamic Countries
4. IMF Trust Fund

The *Aid-to-Pakistan Consortium* has provided aid to Pakistan through both bilateral (country to country) and multilateral (financial institutions to country) arrangements. The Consortium comprises most of the major West European countries, the USA, and Japan under the overall sponsorship of the World Bank. From Table 18.11, we can see that aid under Consortium arrangements (bilateral and multilateral) has comprised the largest share of total aid disbursed by the four major sources during 1950-80. (The official classification of Consortium aid, however, includes aid agreements between Consortium countries and Pakistan outside Consortium arrangements as well). However, the share of Consortium aid declined from 98 per cent in the First Plan period to about 69 per cent in 1978-9. Meanwhile, the share of Consortium multilateral institutions in total aid disbursed by the four major groups of countries/agencies increased from 18 per cent during the First Plan period to about 23 per cent in 1978-9. On the other hand, the share of bilateral Consortium aid in total aid declined from 80 per cent during the First Plan period to about 47 per cent in 1978-9. This increase in the share of Consortium multilateral aid in total aid, disbursed over the period under review, points towards a decline in the share of concessionary international resource transfers because Consortium multilateral financial institutions have historically transferred large amounts of resources to Pakistan in the form of loans whose financial terms and conditions in some cases have been equivalent to commercial loans (see Section 18.3).

Even though some of these multilateral

Table 18.11: Total Grants, Loans and Credits Contracted by Pakistan by Major Source
(Rs millions)

Lending Country/Agency	Pre-First Plan	First Plan (1955-60)	Second Plan (1960-5)	Third Plan (1965-70)	1973-4	1975-6	1978-9
Consortium (including outside Consortium)							
(a) Bilateral	266.925 (80)	944.98 (88)	1,890.8 (77)	2,012.38 (77)	483.37 (36)	473.98 (50)	690.15 (47)
(b) Multilateral	61.000 (18)	118.07 (11)	418.14 (17)	397.08 (15)	215.27 (16)	310.68 (33)	345.13 (23)
Total	327.925 (98)	1,063.05 (99)	2,308.94 (94)	2,409.46 (92)	698.64 (52)	784.66 (83)	1,035.28 (69)
Non-Consortium	7.72 (2)	11.24 (1)	135.69 (6)	206.00 (8)	17.49 (2)	11.55 (1)	219.60 (15)
Islamic Countries	–	–	–	–	610.00 (46)	148.00 (16)	145.33 (10)
IMF Fund	–	–	–	–	–	–	71.2 (5)
Total	335.64 (100)	1,074.29 (100)	2,444.63 (100)	2,615.46 (100)	1,326.13 (100)	944.21 (100)	1,471.4 (100)

Note: Figures in parenthesis are percentages. Until the Third Plan, the data relates to all-Pakistan after which, i.e., for 1973-4 onwards, the data relates to West Pakistan only.

Source: Finance Division, Government of Pakistan, *Pakistan Economic Survey, 1979-80*, Islamabad, 1980, pp. 159-63, Statistical Annexure.

financial institutions may lend on *apparently* concessional terms, a large number of these loans are in fact of a commercial nature. This has been true of a number of World Bank Loans lent through some of the World Bank affiliates. According to a study on the lending operations of the World Bank, a multilateral financial institution of the Consortium countries:

> 'knowing that the current interest rate charged by the World Bank is 9.25 per cent, and that commercial interest rates currently stand at 15 per cent, the observer would be led to believe that such funds are concessional. In fact they are not. The World Bank does not lend dollars to its borrowers but a basket of currencies of which the dollar is only a part. Many of these currencies carry market rates lower than the 9.25 per cent currently charged by the Bank. These currencies with a lower interest rate compensate the loss that the bank suffers by charging less than the market rate for the dollar portion of its loans.'[32]

Thus, given the terms and conditions imposed by certain groups of countries/ agencies lending to Pakistan, changes in the relative shares of the different sources also gives us an idea of the financial costs associated with receiving aid.

The decline in the overall share of Consortium aid in total aid during the seventies was caused by the emergence of the Islamic countries as an important source whose share was as high as 46 per cent in 1973-4 and about 10 per cent in 1978-9. Similarly, the share of Non-Consortium countries increased from about 8 per cent during the Third Plan period to about 15 per cent in 1978-9 (Table 18.11).

18.5.1 Pakistan's Major Donor Countries

The largest share in total aid up to 1969-70 was that of the USA (Table 18.12) although its share declined from 78 per cent during the Second Plan period (1960-5) to about 9 per cent in 1978-9 (Table 18.12). During the seventies USA's share in total aid was about 7 per cent. Total aid contracted during the seventies from all sources was US$ 8,270 million out of which US$ 1,445 million was from the USA. The share of US grant assistance in total US aid also declined from 63 per cent during the First Plan period to about 16 per cent during the Third Plan. After 1975-6, US grant assistance shrank drastically and was only 0.3 per cent of total US foreign economic aid in 1978-9. Thus, US aid after 1973-4 has almost entirely been in the form of loans repayable in foreign exchange.

The decline in USA's overall share in total aid contracted during the seventies was compensated for by the emergence of Iran as Pakistan's principal donor in 1973-4. It's share of US$ 150 million in total aid in 1973-4 was 12 per cent and about 9 per cent during the decade of the seventies. The entire aid from Iran was in the form of cash foreign exchange loans.[33] Amongst the Non-Consortium countries, the share of the Peoples

Table 18.12: US Aid to Pakistan
(US$ millions)

	Pre-First Plan	%	First Plan	%	Second Plan	%	Third Plan	%	1973-4	%	1978-9	%
U.S. Aid	216.206	(64)	752.280	(70)	1,404.63	(48)	1,207.815	(41)	149.157	(12)	127.423	(9.0)
Grant	181.206	(84)	472.883	(63)	504.093	(36)	197.376	(16)	24.056	(16)	0.423	(0.3)
Loan	35.000	(16)	279.397	(37)	899.970	(64)	1,010.439	(84)	125.101	(84)	127.000	(99.7)
Total foreign aid from all sources	336.821		1,074.752		2,910.285		2,937.013		1,268.614		1,497.468	

Source: Government of Pakistan, *Pakistan Economic Survey, 1980-1*, Table 10.9 for Grants and Table 10.10 for loans, Statistical Annexures.

Republic of China in total aid contracted from all sources during the Second Plan period was 2 per cent, which was the largest within the Non-Consortium countries group. Moreover, the entire amount of Chinese aid during this period was in the form of grant assistance.[34] During the Third Plan and the seventies, the Soviet Union replaced the People's Republic of China as the largest donor amongst the Non-Consortium countries and its share in total aid increased from 3 per cent during the Third Plan period to about 7 per cent during the seventies although the entire amount of this aid was in the form of loans.[35] However, notwithstanding the relative decline in the USA's position due to the emergence of Iran and the Soviet Union as major aid donors during the seventies, the USA, by virtue of its financial control over Consortium multilateral financial institutions and the IMF, still retains the top position in the hierarchy of Pakistan's major donor countries in terms of both bilateral as well as multilateral aid.[35]

18.5.2 IMF as a Source of Aid to Pakistan

The increase in the IMF Trust Fund Loans, from $47 million in 1977-8 to $71.2 million in 1978-9, signifies the increase in the IMF's importance as a source of aid (all of which has been in the form of loans with no grant element) to Pakistan. However, the IMF's importance as a source of foreign aid cannot be assessed merely by an examination of direct disbursements. By virtue of being a member of most Western aid Consortiums, the IMF occupies a pivotal position in the sphere of international financial transactions and can thus influence the aid-giving policies of a large number of Western countries/agencies. Moreover, since IMF credit is, in most cases, conditional on recipient countries adopting certain policies, the IMF can greatly influence the pace and pattern of their economic development.

With the loan agreement between the IMF and the Pakistan Government at the end of 1980, where the IMF is to provide Pakistan with nearly $2 million from its Extended Fund facility, it becomes important to assess the likely impact of the IMF's terms and conditions on the Pakistan economy. Loans from the Extended Fund Facility are granted only on very stringent terms. The disbursement of the $2 million IMF loan in three annual instalments is subject to the Pakistan Government accepting the IMF's demands of[36]:

a. lifting government subsidies on certain essential items, i.e., wheat, kerosine oil, and fertilizer;
b. increasing prices of utilities, particularly electricity;
c. liberalizing imports;
d. leasing further investment in public sector industries.

Whatever the merits and demerits of the IMF policy package (which in the short-run would most probably be expressed in rising prices, reduced profits for reinvestment for local manufacturers of goods which are also imported, and unemployment caused by reduced investment in public sector industries) the IMF has surely come to exercise significant control over domestic economic policies.

Thus, the source structure of foreign aid, besides telling us about how much aid has been received from where, points also towards the influence exercised by major donor countries/agencies over domestic economic policies at different times in the country's history.

Summary and Conclusion

To evaluate the impact of foreign aid on Pakistan's pattern of development, it is necessary to adopt both a quantitative as well as a qualitative approach. In the case of Pakistan, as we have seen, foreign aid has played an extremely important role in influencing the pace of economic development. Investment and imports have to a large extent depended upon the amount of foreign aid the country has received.

Without the inflow of foreign aid, investment and, therefore, income growth, both in the private as well as the public sector, would have fallen far short of that achieved by the country. However, this dependence on foreign aid has led, on the one hand, to the emergence of a rising debt burden and, on the other hand, to the development of an economic structure which is a far cry from the ideal state of 'self-sustaining growth'. The large doses of aid received by Pakistan in recent years demonstrate clearly that foreign aid has neither filled the savings-investment gap nor the export-import gap—the two gaps it avowedly was meant to fill.

The burden of excessive dependence on foreign aid has been caused largely by a combination of two factors. First, the shift in the composition of aid from grants to hard loans has, over time, taken up a relatively large share of the gross aid for debt servicing thereby reducing the amount of net aid available for financing imports and investment. Second, the terms and conditions attached to tied credits have imposed both economic as well as political costs on the country. The higher prices charged by suppliers in donor countries coupled with their control over economic policies have weakened the effectiveness of foreign aid as an agent of meaningful structural change in Pakistan.

As the terms and conditions of foreign aid transferred to Pakistan have become harder over the years, it becomes pertinent to wonder whether non-concessional foreign loans should be included in the category of foreign aid. If aid is supposed to 'help' the recipient rather than impose a burden, then there is every reason to exclude non-concessional transfers from the category of foreign aid.

Since foreign aid is now largely limited to tied loans and credits repayable at non-concessional terms, we must reduce our dependence on foreign aid. Otherwise, in the years to come, unless there is a fundamental change in the attitude of donor countries/agencies in terms of increasing the proportion of concessional aid, the debt burden is likely to assume very critical dimensions and it is quite likely that a stage will be reached when up to 100 per cent of gross aid would be paid back as debt servicing by Pakistan.

In order to reduce the debt burden as well as to develop a self reliant economy free of the whims and wishes of donors, the economy must be thoroughly restructured. This can only be achieved if a long-term development strategy orientated towards achieving self-reliance is initiated and the sacrifices and benefits of this are equitably distributed amongst the people and regions of the country.

NOTES

1. Finance Division, Government of Pakistan, *Pakistan Economic Survey, 1980-1*, Islamabad, 1981. p. 154.
2. Ibid., p. 154.
3. M. Kalecki, 'Forms of Foreign Aid: An Economic Analysis', in, *Essays on Developing Economies*, Harvester Press, 1979, pp. 64-5.
4. C.P. Kindleberger and B. Berrick, 'International Transfers', in *Economic Development*, McGraw Hill, 1977, pp. 299-301.
5. See Section 18.3 of this chapter.
6. Finance Division, Government of Pakistan, *Pakistan Economic Survey, 1980-1*, Islamabad, 1981, p. 156.
7. Statistics Division, Government of Pakistan, *Twenty-five Years of Pakistan in Statistics, 1947-1972*, 1972, p. 304.
8. Finance Division, Government of Pakistan, *Pakistan Economic Survey, 1980-1*, Islamabad, 1981, p. 14, Statistical Annexure.
9. Ibid., p. 14, Statistical Annexure.
10. Statistics Division, Government of Pakistan, *Twenty-five Years of Pakistan in Statistics, 1947-1972*, 1972, p. 304.
11. Finance Division, Government of Pakistan, *Pakistan Economic Survey, 1980-1*, Islamabad, 1981, pp. 14 and 156, Statistical Annexure.
12. Ibid., p. 160.
13. World Bank, *World Tables*, 1980, p.336.
14. Finance Division, Government of Pakistan, *Pakistan Economic Survey, 1979-80*, Islamabad, p. 154.
15. Ibid., p. 155.
16. Ibid. pp. 147-50, Statistical Annexures.
17. Ibid., p. 155.
18. Ibid., p. 152.
19. Ibid., p. 152.

20. Finance Division, Government of Pakistan, *Pakistan Economic Survey, 1980-1*, Islamabad, 1981.
21. Computed by simply dividing outstanding external debt of US$ 8.9 by total population of 83.3 million in 1980.
22. Computed by dividing the annual debt servicing in 1980 by total population in 1980.
23. Finance Division, Government of Pakistan, *Pakistan Economic Survey, 1980-1*, Islamabad, 1981, p. 13, Statistical Annexure.
24. Ibid., pp. 134-5.
25. N. Hamid, 'A Critical Appraisal of Foreign Aid Strategy', *Pakistan Economic and Social Review*, Vol. VIII, No. 2, December 1970, pp 149-51.
26. Finance Division, Government of Pakistan, *Pakistan Economic Survey, 1980-1*, Islamabad, 1981, p. 153.
27. Ibid., p. 153.
28. Ibid., p. 163.
29. H. Alavi and A. Khusro, 'Pakistan : The Burden of US Aid' in *Imperialism and Under-development –A Reader*, edited by R.I. Rhodes, Monthly Review Press, 1970, pp. 65-6.
30. Government of Pakistan, *Memorandum For the Pakistan Consortium, 1970-1*, Planning Commission, 1971.
31. H. Alavi and A. Khusro, 'Pakistan: The Burden of US Aid' in *Imperialism and Underdevelopment–A Reader*, edited by R.I. Rhodes, Monthly Review Press, 1970, p. 69.
32. *South*, June 1981, p. 12.
33. (i) Finance Division, Government of Pakistan, *Pakistan Economic Survey, 1979-80*, Islamabad, 1980, pp. 161-2, Statistical Annexure.
    (ii) Finance Division, Government of Pakistan, *Pakistan Economic Survey, 1980-1*, Islamabad, 1981, p. 163.
34. Finance Division, Government of Pakistan, *Pakistan Economic Survey, 1979-80*, Islamabad, 1980, pp. 159-60, Statistical Annexure.
35. Ibid. pp 161-3, Statistical Annexure.
36. *Far Eastern Economic Review*, 6-12 February 1981, p. 81.

Index

Sugarcane, 115, 144, 150; prices of, 150-1